physical education and sports

an introduction to alternative careers

**sheldon l. fordham
carol ann leaf**
university of illinois
at chicago circle

john wiley & sons
new york   santa barbara
chichester   brisbane   toronto

Copyright © 1978, by John Wiley & Sons, Inc.

All rights reserved. Published simultaneously in Canada.

Reproduction or translation of any part of this work beyond that permitted by Sections 107 or 108 of the 1976 United States Copyright Act without the permission of the copyright owner is unlawful. Requests for permission or further information should be addressed to the Permissions Department, John Wiley & Sons, Inc.

Library of Congress Cataloging in Publication Data:

Fordham, Sheldon L
  Physical education and sports.

  Includes bibliographies.
  1. Sports—Vocational guidance. 2. Physical education and training—Vocational guidance. I. Leaf, Carol Ann. II. Title.
GV733.F67   613.7'023   77-19115
ISBN 0-471-26622-1

Printed in the United States of America

10 9 8 7 6 5 4 3 2

preface

Physical Education and Sports: An Introduction to Alternative Careers is designed to inform the beginning student, who's interest lies in sports, about professional job opportunities other than teaching physical education. Six alternative careers can be explored from four aspects: the profession, curriculum, role of the professional, and preparatory learning experiences. The alternative careers include: physical education, competitive sports, coaching, sports administration, athletic training, corrective therapy, and health clubs.

The information provided in this text is of a general nature to provide a basic understanding of each alternative career. This affords the student with the necessary knowledge needed to decide which alternative career to choose. Once that decision is made, the curriculum providing the best preparation for that career can be selected.

It is believed that a physical education core of courses form the foundation needed to enter any of these alternative career curricula. The physical education core might include these courses: introduction to alternative careers in sports and physical education, human anatomy, physiology, kinesiology, lifetime sports, instructional techniques, and history of physical education and sports.

Those individuals choosing careers in teaching should be aware of and be prepared to cope with such problems in the schools as the lack of discipline, integration/segregation/busing, the use of drugs, the lack of proper facilities, inadequate financial support, and the pupil's lack of interest. Persons entering coaching should seek solutions to the hipocracy of some college and university athletic programs, the dilemma of juvenile sport, and the cost of programs that cater only to the elite.

A career in professional sports is perhaps the most glamorous of all the professions for young men and women. The lure of accolades from the public and high salaries must be tempered with the fact that only about 5 percent of those persons trying out for professional sports teams are successful. Sports administration represents a relatively new area of concentration but those persons who choose this field should be prepared to cope with the problem of obsession to win and the consequent lack of good sportsmanship. Athletic training specialists are likely to find themselves in situations where facilities are inadequate and there are too few qualified trainers to prevent and care for athletic injuries. The corrective therapist may require more than four years to graduate with a baccalaureate degree if he or she chooses to obtain an additional academic minor. The health club administrator faces a somewhat different task. In addition to possessing the necessary academic competencies, he or she also serves as the manager of a business performing the functions of sales and service.

Several chapters in the book are devoted to learning experiences. Institutions of higher learning, and in fact those at every level, must do a better job of educating people by creating meaningful and manageable learning environments. Students should be viewed as more than mere recipients of knowledge, and there should be involvement as active participants and contributors in the pursuit of knowledge. The material presented here provides for an expansion and enrichment of the student's total learning experience. Learning occurs when there is real participation in the activities which demand the assumption of responsibility.

Much has been written about humanistic education, particularly since the period of student unrest in the late 1960s and early 1970s, but the basic ingredients for any type of learning situation are those of sharing and caring between students and faculty. The relationship between the instructor and student is the most important component of university life. Whichever career is chosen these components remain the same.

Sheldon L. Fordham
Carol Ann Leaf

contents

section 1 physical education

1. teacher 5
2. educational level and program 29
3. community 51
4. learning experiences in physical education 63

section 2 competitive sports

5. facilities 83
6. recreational sports 97
7. interscholastic, intercollegiate, and professional sports 109
8. learning experiences in competitive sports 135

section 3 coaching and sports administration

9. the coach 151
10. sports administration 175
11. the program in sports administration 189
12. learning experiences in coaching and sports administration 197

section 4 athletic training

13 athletic training 205
14 care and prevention of sports injury 211
15 the athletic trainer 233
16 learning experiences in athletic training 249

section 5 corrective therapy

17 the profession 261
18 professional preparation in corrective therapy 271
19 role of the corrective therapist 289
20 learning experiences in corrective therapy 303

section 6 health clubs

21 health club industry and consumer 315
22 adult physical fitness 327
23 health club instructor 345
24 learning experiences for health club instructors 365

name index 377
subject index 381

section 1

physical education

Courtesy of the American Alliance for Health, Physical Education and Recreation, Washington, D.C.

**1
teacher
2
educational level and program
3
community
4
learning experiences in physical education**

chapter 1

teacher

Our work in physical education, our endeavors in education, and our expressions in life conduct are evidence of what we know well to practice and what we believe thoroughly enough to live and apply.[1]

Leona Holbrook

INTRODUCTION

Physical education is the leadership of individuals in activities occurring in an environment at some institution according to standards that will encourage development and adjustment. Further explanation of this definition is given on page 13. The scientific foundation of physical education consists of the historical, philosophical, biological, sociological, and psychological aspects of the individual and profession. Historically, physical education activities, from primitive through modern times, have been conducted for survival, health, religious, military, or educational reasons.

A more thorough and organized approach to understanding the individual and his or her relationship to activities is acquired by studying the philosophy of physical education. Usually this is divided into four main branches: metaphysics (the nature of reality), epistemology (the nature of knowledge), logic (the nature of relationships between ideas), and axiology (the nature

---

[1] Leona Holbrook, "AIAW-NCAA-Physical Education: An Unhappy Triangle?," *National College Physical Education Association for Men; Proceedings 78th Annual Meeting,* Leo L. Gedvilas (ed.), 148, University of Illinois at Chicago Circle, Chicago, 1975.

and sources of values). The biological aspect of physical education is concerned with the structure and function of the human being at all stages of life. Particular emphasis is given to the individual's movement and capabilities for a designated activity and environment.

Sociology of physical education depicts cultural differences as influenced by values, institutions, and social relationships. These differences exist among populations in various geographic areas as well as among groups within a particular society or community.

Psychology as related to physical education concentrates on analyzing human behavior in order to better understand how and why individuals function as they do. Knowledge about human behavior is needed for implementing instructional methods and techniques.

Do you remember your physical education teachers? Is there *one* teacher who immediately comes to mind? Do you know *why*? What was it that you liked about that teacher? Was there something different, unique, or special about him or her that inspired you to learn and gave you confidence to *try* new skills? Has your interest, enjoyment, and success as a participant in physical education and sports motivated you to teach physical education?

Knowing yourself as a participant, how do you perceive yourself as a teacher? One can have the ability to perform skills, but to teach skills one must be knowledgeable about more than human movement. This scientific body of knowledge is acquired through professional preparation or teacher education programs at many community colleges, colleges, and universities. The results of professional preparation can contribute to one's role as a physical educator and professional.

PROFESSIONAL PREPARATION

Throughout the country, the curriculum for professional preparation programs are many and varied. Even within the same institution there are differences in admissions, curriculum, and evaluation. In this era when there is an oversupply of educators and declining school enrollments, only the most qualified graduates will be hired.

This trend has already influenced the admission procedures for students entering professional preparation programs at some four-year institutions. At these institutions, through selective admissions, only a specified number of students are accepted into the professional preparation program. Selective admissions consists of interviewing and testing applicants in such areas as verbal communication, personality characteristics, physical and intellectual ability, health, and motivation for choosing physical education. The purpose of selective admissions is to acquire the most highly qualified students. For more insight about yourself refer to H. Donald Loucks' circlegram (p. 67) in Chapter 4," Learning Experiences in Physical Education."

Curriculum

The undergraduate curriculum for teacher certification and degree completion consists of general education, professional preparation and elective subjects in the general or professional curricula. General education contains basic courses in the sciences, humanities, and arts. Such subjects as physics, chemistry, biology, history, sociology, psychology, and philosophy fall into this category. Professional preparation in physical education consists of such courses as kinesiology, physiology, anatomy, history of physical education, and philosophy of physical education (see Figure 1.1).

Consider the relationship between general education and professional preparation in physical education as you visualize a person performing the forehand stroke in tennis. As the performer moves toward the ball to execute the forehand stroke, gravity, force, and body leverage affect the balance of the performer and direction of the ball. These movements illustrate the relationship between physics and kinesiology. And, as the performer moves, calories are expelled or there are changes in oxygen intake and carbon dioxide output, a relationship between chemistry and physiology.

The function and structure of the performer is evidenced by knowledge in biology and anatomy. The performer's reaction toward self and from others upon completing the forehand stroke emphasizes psychology, sociology, and motor learning. Other relationships between general education and physical education professional perparation include music to rhythms and dance, English composition and speech to written and oral communication, and psychology and sociology to understanding people as an individual and a group of individuals. These relationships reveal human movement as a study of the *total* person and as the primary concern of physical education. The terms human movement and physical education are used interchangeably as more professionals refer to the profession as the art and science of human movement.

Professional preparation programs in physical education or the arts and sciences of human movement often include two curricula. One is designed for the generalist, the other for the specialist. Both have a core curriculum; however, the generalist selects a minor area of study and the specialist pursues an area of physical education in depth. The curriculum for a generalist and specialist is approximated

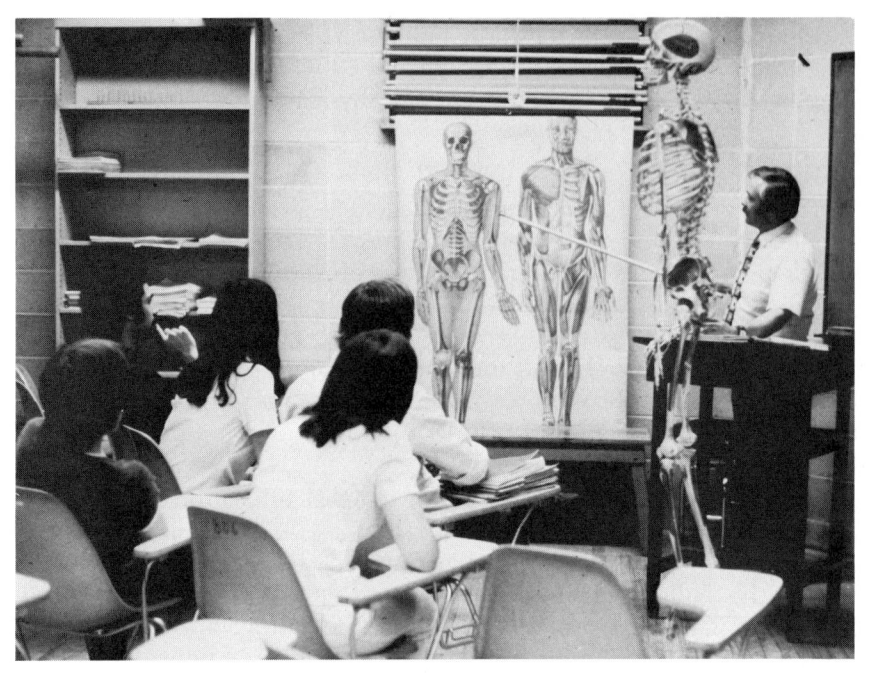

FIGURE 1.1 Anatomy classroom. Reprinted by permission of University of Illinois at Chicago Circle, Chicago.

for these five areas: general education (30%), physical education (35%), education (15%), minor or specialized area (17%), and elective subjects (3%) (see Figure 1.2).

The physical education core curriculum includes activity and theory courses. In the activity courses, emphasis is on skill performance in games, play, dance and individual, dual and team sports. As a participant and future physical educator, one must competently perform numerous skills because the demonstration of skills is inherent to teaching physical education. Furthermore, one must be knowledgeable about the history, objectives, rules, strategy, organization, equipment, teaching location, and safety factors of the activity. In physical education theory courses about activities, skills are emphasized according to teaching, analyzing, correcting, evaluating, and developing simple to complex progressions.

Courses in tests and measurements, teaching methods, and organization and curriculum are relevant to activities for elementary, middle, and secondary school students. Theory courses also provide knowledge in establishing performance objectives (skills or abilities that can be accomplished) for students. Planning a lesson and unit (predetermined number of lessons for a given activity) implements the traditional class

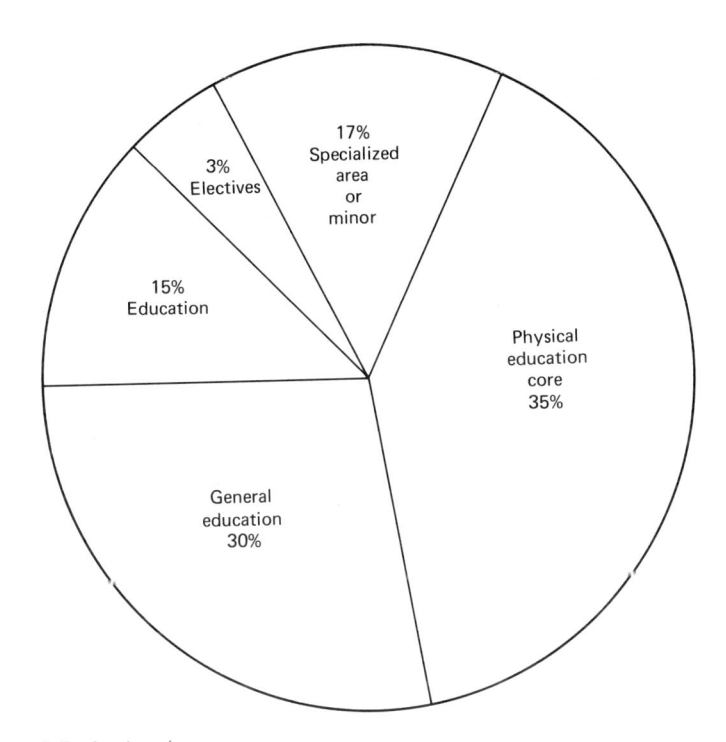

FIGURE 1.2 Professional preparation curriculum distribution for the generalist and specialist in physical education.

approach. The newer method of teaching is individualized instruction in which the number of lessons in the unit varies for each student. In professional preparation, both activity and theory courses concentrate on performing and teaching skills from the humanistic perspective of *how* and *why*. Some areas of specialization in physical education are elementary physical education, dance, gymnastics, aquatics, and adapted physical education.

In professional preparation programs both activity and theory courses are unified through such physical education experiences as observation, assisting, micro-teaching, and student teaching. These experiences vary among institutions but can begin in the sophomore year and continue through the senior year.

There are differences in the duration, credit hours, educational level, class size, supervisory procedures, and evaluation of these experiences. Observation or teaching experiences may be conducted on or off campus involving small or large groups of students. Supervision and evaluation of these experiences is made by college personnel (supervisor) or the full-time teacher (cooperating teacher) at the assigned school, or both. This can be accomplished by on site visitations or videotaped recordings. It is in these actual public school situations that one gains an understanding of students, practice in lesson planning and grading, and an opportunity to associate with administrators, guidance counselors, faculty, and staff. The breadth and depth of these experiences concern teaching behavior, responsibilities, duties and problems that facilitate the transition from student of physical education to teacher of physical education.

Evaluation of students in professional preparation may be based on a rating scale, the normal curve, performance or competencies. In performance-based teacher education (PBTE) evaluation is made of the individual from the observable performance of the teaching act. Competency-based teacher education (CBTE) is an evaluation of the individual's ability to accomplish designated competencies within the realm of the teacher's role and situation. This is assessed by an instructional module, which is a self-contained unit of one or a cluster of competencies. A demonstration of competency at one level allows the student to progress to the next one. The competencies derived from professional preparation depend on the individual's ability, desire, motivation, determination, and commitment to teach physical education.

Extracurricular Activities

Knowledge, skills, and experience in professional preparation can be enriched by participation in extracurricular activities related to the profession. Depending on time, interest, and ability of the student, countless activities are available both on and off campus.

On campus, one could decide to participate in intercollegiate athletics, intramurals, committees, student organizations, or professional organizations. Intercollegiate athletic participation may take the form of team member, manager, scorekeeper, timer, or statistician. In the intramural program, opportunities are available to participate, coach, officiate, time, or distribute and maintain equipment. On many college campuses students are taking advantage of unstructured or free-play opportunities for participation. Sports clubs are also becoming extremely popular throughout the country. See also Chapter 6 on sports clubs.

At many institutions students serve with faculty on departmental, college, or university committees. Student organizations for athletics, physical education, and the institution provide other avenues for involvement. Among these organizations are Physical Education Majors Clubs (PEM-Club), Organizations for Health, Physical Education and Recreation (OHPER), Delta Psi Kappa, (national physical education honorary fraternity for women), Phi Epsilon Kappa (national physical education honorary fraternity for men), and Sigma Delta Psi (national honorary athletic fraternity for men).

Professional organizations at the national and state levels invite students to join and participate in selected areas of interest. Through the American Alliance for Health, Physical Education, and Recreation (AAHPER), one may participate in activities on the state, district, and national levels by serving on the Student Action Council (SAC) as a member of the Association for Research, Administration, and Professional Councils and Societies (ARAPCS). Frequently, members of student physical education organizations also belong to the Student Action Council (SAC). Individuals who join the AAHPER may have membership in any two of the following associations.

National Association for Sport and Physical Education (NASPE)
National Association for Girls and Women in Sport (NAGWS)
National Dance Association (NDA)
American Association for Leisure and Recreation (AALR)
American School and Community Safety Association (ASCSA)
Association for the Advancement of Health Education (AAHE)
Association for Research, Administration, Professional Councils, and Societies (ARAPCS)

Benefits of membership include the selection of these periodicals: *Update, Journal of Physical Education and Recreation, Research Quarterly*, and *Health Education*. The AAHPER also publishes educational materials, produces films, directs placement services, provides low-cost group and liability insurance, and conducts workshops, conferences, and clinics. Applications for membership are available from:

American Alliance for Health, Physical Education and Recreation
1201 Sixteenth Street, N.W.
Washington, D.C. 20036

Student membership is offered at rates lower than for professionals.

Extracurricular activities off-campus are available through city and county park districts, community organizations, church-affiliated organizations, and private agencies and clubs. The opportunities to enhance one's professional preparation are vast and diversified; it remains the individual's choice.

Certification

Teacher certification requirements vary among the 50 states and are established by the State Department of Education, Chief State School

Officer, State Board of Education, or State Legislature. Criteria for teacher certification are determined within that state. These criteria are met in the form of courses included in the physical education professional preparation programs at each state institution and, in most instances, with the institution's program uniqueness maintained.

In each state certificates are issued according to subjects, educational levels, or both. Therefore, an individual could be certified in physical education for kindergarten through grade six (K-6), K-12, K-14, preschool to kindergarten, or adapted physical education.

Teacher certification consists of two types, emergency or standard. An emergency certificate allows the individual to teach on a year to year basis. The standard certificate, which is either permanent or provisional, contains the courses specified by a state agency. A permanent certificate allows one to teach in that state's public schools on a permanent basis. The provisional certificate also allows one to teach in the public schools provided that within a specified amount of time the individual attains permanent certification status from further course work, experience, or both.

Individuals with permanent certification in one state may be issued provisional certification when accepting a public school teaching position in another state. The exceptions to state certification are teaching positions in private schools or large cities such as Chicago, New York, Philadelphia, and St. Louis, which have their own certification board.

Placement

There are several ways of securing a teaching position. These include personal contact with a particular school or individual, placement services provided by colleges and universities, professional organizations, and private agencies. Most colleges and universities have a placement center or bureau that lists teaching positions for various subjects, educational levels, and geographical locations. These listings contain job descriptions, salaries, and information about the school and community. Frequently, interviews are scheduled and conducted within the placement center. These are services provided at no cost to future and postgraduates of that institution.

As previously mentioned, the American Alliance for Health, Physical Education and Recreation (AAHPER) provides placement services through the national headquarters office in Washington, D.C. Also, at the AAHPER national and district conventions there is a placement center where available teaching positions are listed, and interviews are scheduled and conducted. These placement services are available to all AAHPER members without cost.

The placement services of private agencies are conducted by correspondence and for a fee, a list of teaching positions in a specified subject area is forwarded. This list includes job descriptions and salaries for positions at different educational levels and various geographical locations. Any additional information about the teaching position and arrangements for interviews are made by the applicant who contacts directly the prospective employer. Private agencies can be identified for selection through advertisements featured in professional journals. The most effective method of obtaining a position is through one's own personal contacts. Those individuals already in teaching or administrative positions know when and where vacancies exist or are likely to occur, and the delay necessitated by a less direct method may mean the difference in finding a job.

ROLE

The role of a physical educator could be that of teacher, coach, advisor, sponsor, administrator, researcher, or scholar. However, as stated by Celeste Ulrich in "The Physical Educator as Teacher:"[2]

> Yet in all of these varied roles, he is always a teacher. He is a teacher because that is his essence, that is his commitment, that is his love.

A teacher is a leader, a guiding force, who has the function to educate and protect. In physical education, the teacher must know and understand people and activities as the *leader* of *individual (s)* involved in *activities* in an *environment*. This is the process of education. The product of education is for the individual to develop and adjust according to the standards. Education is both a process and product.

The leader needs to know and understand people and activities in order to control the environment and set the standards for quality development and adjustment that are necessary. This is based upon the formula for education, which is applicable to physical education:[3]

Organism + Activity + Leadership + Environment = Education

                    Process   Product

Teaching is a form of leadership. A teacher is a person with his or her own personality, values, beliefs, and attitudes. These are human ele-

---

[2] Celeste Ulrich, "The Physical Educator as Teacher, *Quest*, Monograph VII:61 (December 1966).

[3] N. P. Neilson and Alice Oakes Bronson, *Problems in Physical Education*, Prentice-Hall, Inc., Englewood Cliffs, NJ, 1965, p. 3.

ments of the teacher and, too, of students. It is through the verbal and nonverbal communication of these elements that teacher-student relationships develop. The teacher's self-awareness and sensitivity to students affects the kind of relationship that develops. This has been further substantiated in "We All Count—Or Do We?" where John F. Check claimed:[4]

> That the teacher is a dominant figure in the lives of students is an obvious supposition. The same teacher must realize that he has the most precious and pliable material in his hands and has the power to mold the lives of young people according to his designs . . . Teachers who consider the human elements of their students instead of merely their subject matter are the ones who epitomize humanistic teaching.

This teacher is *real* to students through expressions of sincere caring, trust, faith and respect.

Every person has self-worth and dignity, teacher and student alike, and each wants to be recognized by name. The humanistic teacher is one who cares about and tries to know every student's name. Then, whether in class or in the hall this teacher recognizes students by name, and with eye-contact and a friendly smile. This creates a comfortable, nonthreatening relationship. It is not a "buddy-buddy" relationship, but instead one of mutual understanding and respect, one human being to another. The humanistic teacher is cognizant that respect is earned, not demanded. This occurs by demonstrating competency, friendliness, and interest in students.

A genuine interest in students can only come from the "heart." But, before the two-way process of communication can begin in expressions of interest for the student, the teacher must acquire information about that student. This can be obtained from school records, conversations with counselors, faculty, parents and students, and by reading school bulletins and newspapers.

By listening and observing, the teacher is able to identify each student not only by name, but by characteristics, abilities, attitudes, interests, and needs. It is this information that facilitates communication. A genuine interest is evident when the teacher communicates to the student with "congratulations on winning a school election," a "pat on the back for performing a difficult skill," or just a "smile that shows—you tried." After all, to express enthusiasm, a sense of humor, compassion and empathy is *only* human.

[4]John F. Check, "We All Count—Or Do We?," *The Physical Educator*, 31:123 (October 1974).

A physical education teacher is also an ambassador for the profession by appearance, personality, and professional competencies as perceived by students, faculty, administrators, and parents. These are components of the physical education teacher's image. When a teacher portrays a positive, acceptable image it often results in student emulation, and administrative and parental support. Humanism in teaching is more than a role, it is a way of living.

The humanistic teacher relates similarly to all people—students, faculty, administrators, parents, and others. Unlike other faculty members, the physical educator wears a uniform and teaches in a gymnasium, not in a classroom. Because of these differences, it may be necessary for the physical educator to change clothes before and after school, or when going to the cafeteria or faculty lounge. Since the physical educator is either in the gymnasium, natatorium, locker room, or at an outside teaching station, contact with other faculty members is minimal. The humanistic physical educator reaches out. When not scheduled for class or conference, he or she tries to meet with other faculty members at the cafeteria or lounge.

Conversations with other faculty members affords a sharing of philosophies about education, information about certain students, or an exchange of ideas. This can result in mutual understanding and respect for one another and each other's profession. Call it human relations, professional relations, or public relations—it is all part of teaching.

There is a national communications network composed of physical educators who inform various segments of the public (parents, business leaders, and legislators) about the new approaches in teaching physical education. Movement education, perceptual-motor learning, and lifetime sports are examples of these new approaches. This communications network is known as Physical Education Public Information (PEPI), and it is sponsored by AAHPER's National Association for Sport and Physical Education (NASPE) (see also p. 181-185).

PEPI is implemented at the local community level by physical educators who inform these segments of the public about their physical education program. This information is disseminated at Parent Teachers Association (PTA) meetings, through newspaper articles, and radio interviews. Five PEPI concepts were developed and documented for the purpose of relating the values of physical education into language the public could understand. These five PEPI concepts are:[5]

[5]American Association for Health, Physical Education and Recreation, "The Physical Education Public Information Project," *Journal of Health, Physical Education and Recreation,* 42:54 (September 1971).

1. A physically educated person is one who has knowledge and skill concerning his body and how it works.
2. Physical education is health insurance.
3. Physical education can contribute to academic achievement.
4. A sound physical education program contributes to development of a positive self-concept.
5. A sound physical education program helps an individual attain social skills.

Instruction

One function of a leader is to educate. In physical education instruction is the vehicle. A physical educator needs to be knowledgeable about activities and students as part of the process of education. This knowledge is then utilized to plan instruction that incorporates performance objectives, teaching methods, and evaluation. The latter is the means for measuring education or the product.

A teacher may be scheduled for physical education activities that are compatible or incompatible with expertise and interest. Contingent to this are the facilities and equipment available for conducting the activities. (Facilities are discussed in Chapter 5.) The teacher's philosophy, competency, interest, and personality influence the kind of instruction planned and conducted.

Students, as well as activities, are an integral part of planning instruction. A teacher must have knowledge about the developmental aspects of students, since development results from engaging in some activity.

According to Neilson and Bronson there are four aspects of development: interpretive (thinking), impulsive (feeling), neuromuscular (skill and strength), and organic (endurance).[6] More commonly, these developmental aspects are identified as the cognitive (thinking), affective (feeling), and psychomotor (skill, strength, and endurance) domains. Consideration must be given to these aspects when formulating performance objectives for students. Although these objectives vary for each activity and age level, they can be stated according to observable behavior and criteria of acceptable performance by the student. Thus, performance objectives are meaningful in the subjective and objective evaluations of students.

[6]N. P. Neilson and Alice Oakes Bronson, *Problems in Physical Education*, Prentice-Hall, Inc., Englewood Cliffs, NJ, 1965, pp. 42-48.

Teaching methods or styles are selected in direct relation to the performance objectives established. One or several teaching methods can be employed. Among these are: command, task, reciprocal, small group, individual program, guided discovery, and problem-solving.[7]

Additionally, there is the humanistic method, as described by Donald R. Hellison:[8]

> *Humanistic methodology is based on the assumption that each student participant is a unique person with unique talents and capacities who is potentially better able than anyone else to discern what is most meaningful for him and how he best learns.*

Classes are conducted with the teacher *helping* students to experience success, correcting movement patterns with positive evaluation, and challenging students to their highest capabilities. The teacher is receptive to questions and comments about the activity and seeks ways for improvement. Through personal attention and accessibility before and after class, the teacher encourages the development of a positive self-concept. There is a time for praise and a time for blame, and the humanistic teacher knows when to give both. When discipline is necessary the teacher confers with the student privately, away from peers. Actual instruction may include the use of visual aids or audiovisual materials.

In student evaluation, the teacher is impartial and fair in subjective ratings of performance objectives concerning the affective domain. Through written and oral examinations, the established performance objectives serve to objectively evaluate the cognitive domain. This objectively is maintained by the established performance objectives concerning the psychomotor domain.

Constantly, the teacher evaluates his or her own performance in instructional methods, communication, responsiveness to students, and competency in that activity. This becomes more informative when accompanied by a student evaluation at the end of the unit. After reviewing both evaluations, the teacher is then able to make revisions to improve teaching effectiveness.

Organization is the "key" to planning, conducting, and evaluating instruction of self and students in the learning process. In Figure 1.3

---

[7]Muska Mosston, *Teaching Physical Educatin,* Charles E. Merrill Publishing Co., Columbus, OH, 1966, p. 227.

[8]Donald R. Hellison, *Humanistic Physical Education,* Prentice-Hall, Inc., Englewood Cliffs, NJ, 1973, p. 113.

Preactive Teaching Behavior—primarily performed prior to working with the students.	**Planning**—designing sequential and progressive movement experiences that challenge and encourage each student to work to his or her capacity
	Set Induction—ability of a teacher to provoke an interest in students (cognitive set), which is contiguous with the objectives of the teacher
	Movement Time—maximizing the percentage of time in which the students are involved in purposeful movement by minimizing the amount of teacher verbalization and organizational time
Active Teaching Behaviors—performed primarily while actually teaching students.	**Individual feedback**—providing students with accurate knowledge about their motor performance
	Stimulus Variation—variety of movement experiences and changes of pace employed by a teacher
	Closure—employed at the conclusion of a lesson to further enhance the learning experience of the student
Postactive Teaching Behavior—performed primarily after work with the students has concluded.	**Evaluation**—ability to judge: (a) the effectiveness of movement experiences provided and (b) personal teaching performance

FIGURE 1.3 Sample of seven teaching behaviors organized into a sequential progression. George M. Graham, "A Bridge Between 'What Is' and 'What Could Be,'" *The Physical Educator*, **32**:14 (March 1975).

appears "A Sample of Seven Teaching Behaviors Organized Into Sequential Progression," that was developed by George M. Graham. The preactive, active, and postactive teaching behaviors are illustrated in relation to planning, actual instruction, and evaluation of one lesson.[9] The physical educator's primary concern in instruction is to meet the interests, abilities, and needs of students. This must be considered in every lesson.

Supervision

This second function of a leader is to protect. In physical education this is accomplished by supervising students according to five aspects

[9]George M. Graham, "A Bridge Between 'What Is' and 'What Could Be'," *The Physical Educator*, **32**:14 (March 1975).

of protection: health, accident prevention, moral, asthetic, and interpretive.[10] Supervision is a continuous process requiring planning, observation investigation, and action by the physical educator.

In most public schools, policies have been established requiring students to have health examinations for admission, at designated education intervals, and for participation in physical education or athletics. Throughout their entire public school education, students should have had physical, dental, sight, and hearing examinations. A health record is maintained for each student indicating examinations, temporary or permanent structural and functional disorders, illness and accidents at school, and visits to the school health center.

These records provide vital information for the physical educator to use in determining the kinds of activities and amount of participation for students with health problems. By referring to these records, the physical educator can identify students with health problems and provide activities to meet their needs and abilities.

The physical educator can notice students with infections or growth defects by observation during class. When this occurs, the physical educator informs the school health supervisor for an appropriate course of action to be taken. The physical educator is responsible for protecting the students' health; however, diagnosis and treatment should be conducted by only the medical profession. The students' health protection is insured when the physical educator maintains sanitary facilities and equipment. There should be a close personal relationship between the physical education teacher, the school nurse, and the school physician. The primary concern of all three of these individuals is the students' health.

Accident prevention is the second aspect of protection. This consists of inspecting and supervising indoor and outdoor areas, keeping them free from hazards and debris. The equipment used for activity must be constantly inspected to insure safe participation. When faulty equipment is discovered, it should be repaired or removed.

The very nature of physical education activities increases the likelihood of accidents occurring. Therefore, the physical educator should establish and enforce safety procedures for the students to follow. This includes self-protection by students in using the equipment properly and safely and students' protection for one another when possible.

Students must be supervised before, during, and after activity as a standard procedure for accident prevention. Therefore, students must be told the policies used for roll call, excuses, showering, activity attire,

---

[10]N. P. Neilson and Alice Oakes Bronson, *Problems in Physical Education*, Prentice-Hall, Inc., Englewood Cliffs, NJ, 1965, pp. 100-101.

and distribution of equipment, towels, and supplies. The physical educator must establish and strictly enforce rules and regulations governing unsupervised participation, locker room behavior and moving to an outside area for activity. However, to prevent accidents and legal liability because of negligence, the physical educator should be present and watchful at the time class convenes and until dismissal. Unfortunately, in many schools, at every level, severe overcrowding exists in gymnasiums and play areas. This fact makes the physical educator's role in preventing accidents much more demanding. During activity, accidents can be prevented by not allowing students to go beyond what they sense to be their range of ability.

Since, indoors or outdoors, not *all* accidents can be prevented, the physical educator must be prepared to handle this situation. Therefore, one must be knowledgeable about the school's policy for administering first aid, and witnessing, reporting, and recording accidents.

The moral, aesthetic, and interpretive aspects of protection are dictated by society and the beliefs and values of each individual teacher.

Community Activities

Involvement in community activities is a teacher's choice. Those who are interested can participate in the community where they teach, live, or both. Community activities where one teaches may be selected because this is the place of employment. Often this is more indicative of a rural community than an urban area. Whether a rural, suburban, or urban community, each offers a variety of activities needing teacher input.

The professional expertise of a physical educator can be rapidly utilized in a community park and recreation program. The recreation program provides opportunities to supervise, plan, and conduct activities for youth, adults, and senior citizens on weekends, in the evening, or during the summer. Similar experiences are available in church-affiliated organizations, the Boy and Girl Scout associations, and senior citizen centers.

Professional Organizations

In elementary, middle, and secondary schools faculty members can participate in the Parent Teachers Association (PTA). In the PTA, a physical educator may want to serve the school and community by conducting physical education demonstrations, dance programs, or other school events. Affiliation with this association provides the physical educator opportunities to inform parents, faculty, and administrators about the physical education program.

At all levels of education, faculty members from different disciplines may choose to join the National Education Association (NEA) or the American Federation of Teachers (AFT). In most colleges and universities membership is available to the American Association of University Professors (AAUP) and the American Association of University Women (AAUW). In some institutions, there is a local chapter of the NEA, AFT, AAUP, AAUW, or other teacher associations. The cost of membership varies for each organization, and each provides unique benefits. Business is conducted at both the national and local levels. Usually members of the local chapter elect faculty to serve as officers and committee members. Local chapters of the NEA and AFT, in particular, have served as collective bargaining agents in teacher/school board negotiations.

A physical educator may choose from numerous professional organizations. The largest organization, with approximately 50,000 members, is the American Alliance for Health, Physical Education and Recreation (AAHPER). Membership in the AAHPER entitles the professional to select one or more special interest associations from the seven allied associations that were mentioned in professional preparation.

The AAHPER is composed of district and state Health, Physical Education and Recreation Associations. However, memberships for the AAHPER and a state health, physical education, and recreation association are separate. Physical educators who join state and national organizations have an opportunity to become informed about teaching methods, innovative equipment, recently completed research, and educational trends. This current information can then be implemented in the classroom.

Membership and participation in physical education professional organizations is a "giving-taking" proposition. Paying dues and contributing time and effort toward improving the profession is beneficial to the entire membership. The information and knowledge gained from this experience can certainly contribute to one's own teaching effectiveness. In a professional organization, people can learn from one another and together strive toward improving their profession.

The American Alliance for Health, Physical Education and Recreation has 23 national organization affiliates. The following is a selected list of national organization affiliates specific to physical education. These are:[11]

American Academy of Physical Education.
American College of Sports Medicine.

[11] John E. Nixon and Ann E. Jewett, *Physical Education*, Eighth Edition, W. B. Saunders Company, Philadelphia, 1974, pp. 25-26.

Canadian Association for Health, Physical Education, and Recreation.

Health and Physical Education Directors Association of YM—YWHA's and Jewish Community Center.

National Association for Physical Education of College Women.

National College Physical Education Association for Men.

Physical Education Society of the YMCA's of North America.

Society of State Directors of Health, Physical Education, and Recreation.

Young Women's Christian Association for the U.S.A.

The AAHPER also sponsors the International Council of Health, Physical Education and Recreations (ICHPER) and the National Foundation for Health, Physical Education and Recreation (NFHPER). The President's Council of Physical Fitness and Sports (PCPFS) is an agency of the federal government.

In each of these professional organizations, members can provide a valuable service in any number of ways. Conducting workshops and clinics, writing articles for publication, presenting research at conferences and conventions, serving or chairing a committee or task force, and accepting an appointed or elected office represent some of the possibilities.

Graduate Education

Professional or research programs of study are emphasized in graduate education for physical education. Beyond the bachelor's degree, graduate education sequentially consists of the masters, specialist, and doctorate degree. Five purposes of graduate education were identified in a report from the Conference on Graduate Education sponsored by the AAHPER. These include:[12] (see Figure 1.4)

1. To add to the store of human knowledge through basic research.
2. To extend the range of nonverbal expression (dance, games, sports, etc.) through encouragement of human invention and imagination.

---

[12]American Association for Health, Physical Education and Recreation, *Graduate Education in Health, Physical Education, Recreation Education, Safety Education, and Dance*, American Association for Health, Physical Education and Recreation, Washington, D.C., 1967, p. 21.

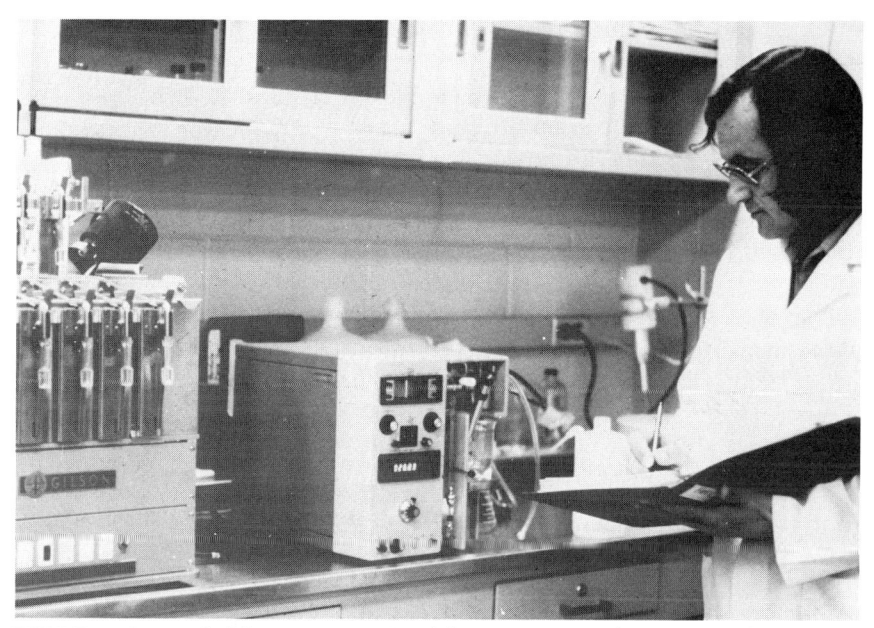

FIGURE 1.4 Research laboratory. Reprinted by permission of University of Illinois at Chicago Circle, Chicago.

3. To prepare scientific research workers and humanistic scholars.
4. To provide advanced preparation for practitioners (teachers, coaches, supervisors, activity specialists, and administrators) at various levels of competency.
5. To develop leaders who have the ability to think and to employ their national powers in gaining understanding, aesthetic sensitivity, and moral responsibility.

Admission to most graduate programs is based upon the undergraduate grade point average, scores earned on graduate examinations, or demonstrated motivation to pursue the degree. Graduate degree requirements can consist of one year of residency, completing a core curriculum (which may include one or two foreign languages), and designated specialization courses, written and oral comprehensive examinations, or a thesis or dissertation. Areas of specialization in graduate education include exercise physiology, motor-learning, biomechanics, history of physical education, sociology of sport, psychology of sport, curriculum and instruction, or administration.

One who enters graduate education, whether for further study or degree completion, develops personally and professionally. Through research, statistics, and facts, knowledge can be preserved, disseminated and discovered. From graduate study, a physical educator can transform this knowledge into understanding and wisdom in teaching physical education. Application of this knowledge may be a specialized area, such as biomechanics or at a particular educational level. The latter is discussed in detail in the next chapter.

SELECTED REFERENCES

American Alliance for Health, Physical Education and Recreation, "HPER Directory of Professional Preparation Institutions," *Journal of Health, Physical Education and Recreation,* **45**:37-48 (September 1974).

American Alliance for Health, Physical Education and Recreation, "HPER Directory of Professional Preparation Institutions Additions," *Journal of Physical Education and Recreation,* **46**:26 (January 1975).

American Alliance for Health, Physical Education and Recreation, "HPER Directory of Professional Preparation Institutions: Additions," *Journal of Physical Education and Recreation,* **46**:14 (May 1975).

American Association for Health, Physical Education and Recreation, "A Statement of Basic Beliefs About the School Programs in HPER," *Journal of Health, Physical Education and Recreation,* **44**:22-24 (June 1973).

Barrett, Robert J., "Teaching Experience—Early, Often, and Varied," *Journal of Health, Physical Education and Recreation,* **43**:70 (May 1972).

Berelson, Bernard, *Graduate Education in the United States,* McGraw-Hill Book Company, Inc., New York, 1960.

Berg, Kris, "Maintaining Enthusiasm In Teaching," *Journal of Physical Education and Recreation,* **46**:22 (April 1975).

Bing, Bonnie, "Nobody Looks At Me," *Journal of Physical Education and Recreation,* **46**:55-56 (February 1975).

Broer, Marion R., *Efficiency of Human Movement,* Third Edition, W. B. Saunders Company, Philadelphia, 1973.

Bucher, Charles A., *Foundations of Physical Education,* Seventh Edition, C. V. Mosby Company, St. Louis, MO 1975.

Caldwell, Stratton F., "Toward a Humanistic Physical Education," *Journal of Health, Physical Education and Recreation*, **43**:31-32 (May 1972).

Cassidy, Rosalind, and Stratton F. Caldwell, *Humanizing Physical Education: Methods for the Secondary School Movement Program*, Fifth Edition, W. C. Brown Company Publishers, Dubuque, IA 1974.

Chambless, Jim R. and Connie J. Mangin, "Legal Liability and the Physical Educator," *Journal of Health, Physical Education and Recreation*, **44**:42-43 (April 1973).

Clipson, William F., "Early Field Experiences as Teachers," *Journal of Health, Physical Education and Recreation*, **46**:35-36 (March 1975).

Cratty, Bryant J., *Career Potentials in Physical Activity*, Prentice-Hall, Inc., Englewood Cliffs, New Jersey, 1971.

Cratty, Bryant J., *Learning About Human Behavior: Through Active Games*, Prentice-Hall, Inc. Englewood Cliffs, NJ, 1975.

Dance Directory: Programs of Professional Preparation in American Colleges and Universities, American Association for Health, Physical Education and Recreation, Washington, D.C., 1974.

Davis, E. Craig, and Donna Mae Miller, *The Philosophic Process in Physical Education*, Second Edition, Lea & Febiger, Philadelphia, 1967.

De Armand, Murray, and Austin T. Parker, "Becoming Human," *Journal of Higher Education*, **39**:506-511 (December 1968).

Dougherty IV, Neil J., "An Experience Based Teacher Training Program," *Journal of Health, Physical Education and Recreation*, **44**:57-58 (February 1973).

Erickson, Audrey, "Assessment of Readiness for Teaching," *Journal of Physical Education and Recreation*, **46**:41-43 (March 1975).

"Excellence in Teaching: The Student's Point of View," *The Physical Educator*, **31**:51-60 (May 1974).

Finke, Charles W., "Use Evaluation Positively," *Journal of Health, Physical Education and Recreation*, **43**:16 and 88 (November-December 1972).

Fleming, A. William "A Workshop on the Development of Competency-Based Professional Preparation Programs in Physical Education," *National College Physical Association for Men: Pro-*

ceedings 77th Annual Meeting, Leo L. Gedvilas (ed.) 108-116, University of Illinois at Chicago Circle, Chicago, 1974.

Frost, Reuben B., Physical Educaiton: Foundations, Practices, Principles, Addison-Wesley Publishing Company, Reading, MA, 1975.

Gale, N. L., and Philip Wine, "Performance-Based Teacher Education," Teacher Education: The Seventy-fourth Yearbook of the National Society for the Study of Education, Part II, Kevin Ryan (ed.), 146-172, University of Chicago Press, Chicago, 1975.

Galloway, Charles M., "Teaching is More Than Words," Quest, Monograph XV:67-71 (January 1971).

Grebner, Flo, and Jo Mancuso, "A Product of Professional Involvement," Journal of Health, Physical Education and Recreation, 45: 73 (May 1974).

Green, Lance, "What is Competency-Based Education?," Journal of Health, Physical Education and Recreation, 44:87 (October 1973).

Grieve, Andrew, "Physical Education, Athletics, and the Law," Journal of Health, Physical Education and Recreation, 45:24-25 (October 1974).

Hanson, Margie R., "Professional Preparation of the Elementary School Physical Education Teacher," Quest, Monograph XVIII:98-106 (June 1972).

Hellison, Donald R., Humanistic Physical Education, Prentice-Hall Inc., Englewood Cliffs, NJ, 1973.

Henschen, Keith, P., "Needed Revisions in Professional Preparation Curriculumns," Journal of Health, Physical Education and Recreation, 43:69 and 72 (May 1972).

Herkowitz, Jacqueline, and Leigh F. Kieffer, "Structuring the Movement Environment for Preschool Children," Quest, Monograph XXIV:72-79 (Summer Issue, 1975).

Jackson, C. O., "Empathy," The Physical Educator, 31:115 (October 1974).

Kiesel, William B., "Student-Comments on State AAHPER Conventions," Journal of Physical Education and Recreation, 46:39-40 and 42 (April 1975).

Knowledge and Understanding in Physical Education, American Association for Health, Physical Education and Recreation, Washington, D.C., 1974.

Lawther, John D., Sport Psychology, Prentice-Hall, Inc., Englewood Cliffs, NJ, 1972.

Leonard, George, *The Ultimate Athlete*, The Viking Press, New York, 1974.

Ley, Katherine, "Teaching Understandings in Physical Education," *Journal of Health, Physical Education and Recreation*, **42**:21-22 (January 1971).

Lohse, Lola L., "What Makes a Good Teacher?," *The Physical Educator*, **31**:156 (October 1974).

Mathews, Donald K., *Measurement in Physical Education*, Fourth Edition, W. B. Saunders Company, Philadelphia, 1973.

Metzger, Paul A., "Our Other Job—Teaching Why," *Issues in Physical Education and Sports*, George H. McGlynn (ed.) 126-129, National Press Books, Palo Alto, CA, 1974.

Oberteuffer, Delbert, Celeste Ulrich, and Charles L. Mand, *Physical Education*, Fourth Edition, Harper & Row, New York, 1970.

Patterson, C. H., *Humanistic Education*, Prentice-Hall, Inc., Englewood Cliffs, NJ, 1973.

Pease, Dean A., "Competency-Based Teacher Education," *Journal of Physical Education and Recreation*, **46**:20-22 (May 1975).

Pelton, Barry, "Competency-Based Teacher Education in Physical Education Prospects and Problems," *National College Physical Education Association for Men: Proceedings 77th Annual Meeting*, Leo L. Gedvilas (ed.), 51-54, University of Illinois at Chicago Circle, Chicago, 1974.

Polidoro, J. Richard, "The Affective Domain: The Forgotten Behavioral Objective of Physical Education," *The Physical Educator*, **30**:136-138 (October 1973).

Professional Preparation in Dance, Physical Education, Recreation Education, Safety Education and School Health Education, American Association for Health, Physical Education and Recreation, Washington, D.C., 1974.

Rice, Emmett, A., John L. Hutchinson, and Mabel Lee, *A Brief History of Physical Education*, Fifth Edition, Ronald Press, New York, 1969.

Ross, Murray G., and Charles E. Hendry, *New Understanding of Leadership*, Association Press, New York, 1957.

Shockley, Jr., Joe M. "Needed: Behavioral Objectives in Physical Education," *Journal of Health, Physical Education and Recreation*, **44**:44-46 (April 1973).

Siedentop, Daryl, and Brent S. Rushall, *The Development and Control of Behavior in Sport and Physical Education*, Lea & Febiger, Philadelphia, 1972.

Singer, Robert N., "The Psychomotor Domain: Movement Behavior, Lea & Febiger, Philadelphia, 1972.

Society of State Directors of HPER, "A Statement of Basic Beliefs About the School Programs in Health, Physical Education and Recreation," Journal of Health, Physical Education and Recreation, 44:22-24 (June 1973).

State Requirements in Physical Education for Teachers and Students, American Association for Health, Physical Education and Recreation, Washington, D.C., 1974.

Stemmer, Vi, and Gerald Carlson, "Public Information—Ten Ideas for Student Clubs," Journal of Physical Education and Recreation, 46:45-46 (May 1975).

Ulrich, Celeste, "Implementing Agency: P.E.P.I.," The Academy Papers, M. Gladys Scott (ed.), 108, American Academy of Physical Education, Iowa City, IA, (September 1974).

Ulrich, Celeste, and Jesse Hawthorne, "Take the Current When It Serves—NASPE is Launched!," Journal of Health, Physical Education and Recreation, 45:19-20 (September 1974).

Ulrich, Celeste, and John E. Nixon, Tones of Theory, American Association for Health, Physical Education and Recreation, Washington, D.C., 1972.

Van Dalen, Deobold, and Bruce L. Bennett, A World History of Physical Education, Second Edition, Prentice-Hall, Inc., Englewood Cliffs, NJ, 1971.

Woods, John B., Thomas J. Mauries, and Bruce N. Dick, Student Teaching: The Entrance to Professional Physical Education, Academic Press, New York, 1973.

Wrenn, Jerry P., and Alice M. Love, "Wither Thou Goest, Physical Education," The Physical Educator, 30:139-141 (October 1973).

Yee, Albert H., "Becoming A Teacher in America," Quest, Monograph XVIII:67-75 (Spring 1972).

Zeigler, Earle F., Philosophical Foundations for Physical, Health, and Recreation Education, Prentice-Hall, Inc., Englewood Cliffs, NJ, 1964.

chapter 2

educational level and program

> At all institutional levels it is clear that curriculums must be more relevant to the needs of today's students, more creatively designed, more technologically efficient, and more adaptable to the individual participants.
>
> Ann E. Jewett

Physical education is part of the student's total education at elementary, middle, secondary, community college, and college and university levels. Ideally, the physical education programs in elementary through college and university progress sequentially. The repetition or redundancy of certain physical education activities, without new skills and knowledge, can cause students to lack interest in participating.

At each educational level, there is a particular organizational structure and physical education program designed to meet the needs of these students. Familiarity with these various educational levels may be derived from courses taken during professional preparation. Fundamental to developing and implementing quality physical education programs is the knowledge and experiences gained in preparing to teach physical education. This consists of formulating a philosophy of physical education; relating the physical,

[1] Ann Jewett, "Would You Believe Public Schools 1975," *Journal of Health, Physical Education and Recreation*, 42:41 (March 1971).

biological, and social sciences to the moving individual; and constantly evaluating and revising self, student(s), activity, and program.

ELEMENTARY

In most communities elementary, middle, and secondary schools are combined to form a school district. An example are the consolidated school districts of rural communities. In a school district, all educational levels are governed by the same board of education that is elected by the people and administered by one superintendent. The organizational structure for physical education at elementary, middle, and secondary levels is presented in Figure 2.1.

Notice the slight variation of this structure within each educational level. At the elementary level, physical education may be taught by an elementary classroom teacher or a specialist in the physical education department. The district consultant, physical education specialist, serves to periodically advise the elementary classroom teacher. A district consultant, however, may or may not be provided when there is a department of physical education.

Traditionally, the elementary level includes grades kindergarten through eight. But, a number of elementary schools are identified as kindergarten through grade six. At this level, many schools have recently changed from a traditional curriculum of self-contained classrooms to open or nongraded classes. Changes have also been made in the physical education curriculum from less emphasis on low-organized games, relays, and combative skills to more emphasis on rhythms and movement education.

Physical education classes at the elementary level are frequently scheduled for 30 minutes twice a week. A physical educator's schedule ranges from 8 to 10 classes daily. Boys and girls in grades one through six come to the gymnasium as a heterogeneous group. This coeducational group usually consists of 20 to 30 anxious and enthusiastic children. Grades seven and eight of an elementary school are often grouped heterogeneously with 20 to 30 students in one class. In most schools, students in grades one through six often participate in school attire and gym shoes, while grades seven and eight dress in activity clothes.

Students taught in elementary schools grow and develop at different rates; therefore, different physical education activities are needed, which biologically, socially, emotionally, and intellectually correspond. Beginning with grades one, two, and three, children should be offered a broad range of physical education activities that

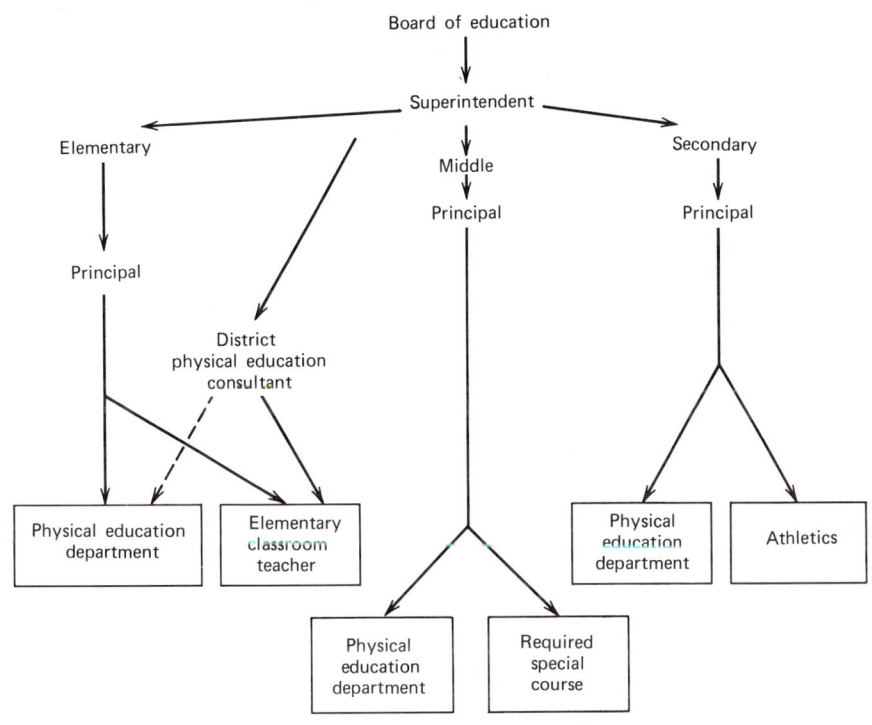

FIGURE 2.1 Organizational structure of elementary, middle, and secondary school physical education.

allow them to experience a variety of skills from simple to complex. Activities of this nature are often conducted through movement education, a term synonymous to physical education. Through problem-solving activities, the child learns body awareness or where to move in relation to space. Factors such as force, direction, tempo and distance then become meaningful as the student is challenged in self-directed physical education activities (see Figure 2.2).

In grades four, five, and six, students continue to experience a broad range of physical education activities with emphasis on perceptual motor learning. This is where the child develops eye (perceptual) and hand (motor) coordination. Now the student relates body awareness, force, direction, tempo, and distance to an object, for example, catching and throwing a bean bag or ball. At these grade levels, physical education activities should incorporate equipment such as hoops, ropes, scoops, balls, bean bags, and wands. And, students should be participating with one another in dual and team activities. It is during this interaction and especially during the selection of teams, that consideration must be given to the child's

FIGURE 2.2 The new physical education. Reprinted by permission of Martha Owens, Project Hope, Oscilla, Georgia, 1976.

social and emotional development. The physical education activities for grades seven and eight are discussed in the "middle school" section (see Figure 2.3).

There are many factors to consider in regard to teaching physical education in grades one through six. Foremost, is to know that children of this age are enthusiastic about learning and just "love to move." This requires the physical educator to be creative, expressive, and well prepared for each and every class.

A knowledge and understanding about the growth and development of each child is needed in order to provide appropriate physical education activities and humanistically relate to a class of *individuals*. Each child is unique and daily brings to class a different background of previous experiences, a particular attitude toward classmates and teacher, an identifiable behavior pattern, and a structural and functional capacity to learn and perform a skill. The physical educator must instruct, motivate and, most of all, humanistically interact with students.

FIGURE 2.3 The new physical education. Reprinted by permission of Martha Owens, Project Hope, Oscilla, Georgia, 1976.

Teaching physical education at the elementary level is not for everyone. It requires creativity, enthusiasm, patience, humor, and understanding. Elementary students are constantly having new experiences, experiences that are accepted or rejected and that ultimately compose the child's attitudes toward future experiences. Because these are the formative years, when learning is rapid, the kinds of physical education activities provided will become a part of that child's life and participation in activities as an adolescent and adult.

The importance of the elementary level of physical education cannot be overemphasized, and a number of colleges and universities offer this as an area of specialization with state certification for grades kindergarten through six. A newer trend included in college curricula concentrates on early childhood development or preschool education. This focuses on children between the ages of two to four. Preschool physical education may provide new teaching positions for those interested graduates unable to find elementary school jobs because of the oversupply of teachers and diminishing school enrollments. According to Stephen J. Knezevich in *Educational Futurism 1985*:

> By the middle of the next decade nursery education will be accepted as the starting point of formal preparation ... Programs

will place heavy emphasis on social, emotional, and physical health developments of the pupil as opposed to the traditional academic dimensions.[2]

The actuality of this prediction could be due to an inflationary economy necessitating both parents to work, the women's liberation movement, and another age level at which to value education.

MIDDLE

In the late 1950s a new educational level emerged, known as the middle school. This was designed to include grades 5, 6, and 7 or 6, 7, and 8. The concept of the middle school was to allow the student a smooth transition from elementary to secondary levels of education. There were approximately 500 middle schools established in 1965, and by 1972 this grew to nearly 2300.[3] During this time, intermediate schools (grades 7 and 8) and junior high schools (grades 7, 8, and 9) were maintained in many school districts. Traditionally, the intermediate and junior high schools have been "subject-centered" in their philosophy. However, the middle school has adapted a "student-centered" philosophy wherein modular scheduling, open laboratories, individualized instruction, team teaching, and other educational innovations are implemented.

The organizational structure of middle schools is illustrated in Figure 2.1 on page 31. Observe that physical education is either a separate department or grouped with other required special courses, such as art and music. Generally a physical educator in the middle school teaches six to eight class periods per day, and each period is from 45 to 50 minutes in length. Contact with each class ranges from two to three times per week with about 25 to 30 students in a class. Depending upon the physical education activities and implications of Title IX, (which by federal law stipulates non-discrimination on the basis of sex) students are grouped homogeneously and/or heterogeneously. This is accomplished by dividing the sexes, student election of activities or level of skill ability.

As at the elementary level, the middle-school physical educator must be knowledgeable about the growth and development of these

[2]Stephen J. Knezevich, "Perspectives on the Educational Program in 1985," *Educational Futurism 1985*, The 1985 Committee of the National Conference of Professors of Educational Administration, McCutchan Publishing Corporation, Berkeley, CA 1971, pp. 40-41.

[3]Elba Stafford and Herman Weinberg, "Confusion Concerning Middle Schools," *Journal of Health, Physical Education and Recreation*, **43**:61 (December 1972).

children. Categorically, students from 10 to 14 years old are often referred to as preadolescents. Frequently this stage of human development is called the transecence period, since it is that time span between the beginning of puberty and early adolescence.

Boys and girls in the transescence period grow and develop at extremely different rates. Girls often grow at a much faster rate than boys and consequently exhibit a higher level of skill ability in many physical education activities. During this period, both boys and girls are adjusting to social, emotional, intellectual, and organic changes occurring rapidly within themselves and their environment.

Typically, middle-school children appear energetic, silly, serious, awkward, and obnoxious. At times, students of this age display confidence, obstinance, and toughness but in reality are seeking peer support and adult guidance and understanding. An awareness of these characteristics or sensitivity to student's needs contributes to meeting these needs through planning and conducting physical education activities.

A physical education program for middle-school children usually includes individual and team sports, with the latter being more popular among students. In the more progressive middle schools, physical education activities may include yoga, modern dance, cycling, weight training, or snow skiing; in addition to team sports of volleyball, softball, and basketball.

Because students at this educational level are constantly seeking peer acceptance, participation in intramurals and interscholastics are extremely popular. These after-school activities are an integral part of the physical education program, which is the foundation for intramurals and interscholastics. Further discussion of this appears in Section II. In physical education, students develop basic skills and knowledge about an activity. When that same activity is included in intramurals or interscholastics, the student has an opportunity to participate according to his or her ability. In intramurals, students compete in activities within the school; and, in interscholastics, they compete with students from different schools. The interrelatedness of these three programs is illustrated in Figure 2.4. Notice that a student may enter intramurals or interscholastics directly from the physical education program or may enter interscholastics from intramurals and vice versa.

Supervision of intramurals or interscholastics may be included in the physical educator's teaching assignment. This usually consists of activities conducted one or two days per week. Whether teacher, supervisor, or coach, it is imperative that this person be knowledge-

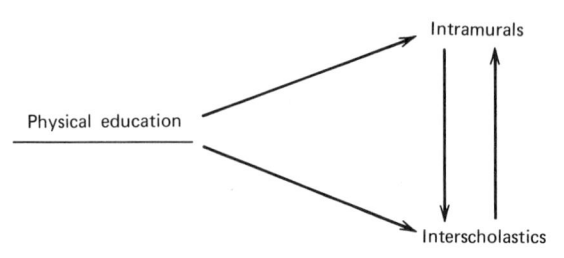

FIGURE 2.4 Interrelationship of physical education, intramurals, and interscholastics.

able and interested in transescent youth. When directing interscholastics, the coach should take appropriate action pertaining to competition because of the physical and psychological implications it could have for children of this age.

SECONDARY

The secondary educational level, commonly called the high school, incorporates grades 9 through 12. In the past, graduation from this level was regarded as the top of the educational ladder. Now, the completion of two years of college seems to be the accepted norm.

An overview of elementary through secondary educational levels yields different divisions of kindergarten through grade 12. For example, an elementary school composed of grades kindergarten through 4, a middle school containing grades 5 through 8, and grades 9 through 12 forming the secondary level together compose the 4-4-4 plan of education. Respectively, there are other educational divisions identified as the 8-4, 7-5, 6-6, 6-3-3, and 6-2-4 educational plans.

In a majority of states, formal education is compulsory through the tenth grade or until the child reaches 16 years of age. Therefore, decisions pertinent to terminating formal education are crucial in terms of the behavior, occupation, and status of these new adults entering society. It is during this educational experience that students decide to marry, drop out of school, pursue a career, enroll in a vocational school, or attend college. The decision made by each student may be inspired or fortified by peers, parents, teachers, or counselors. Sensitivity to students at this decision-making stage is essential in helping them select courses and attain future goals.

There are usually three courses of study available to high school students: general education, vocational-technical, and college preparatory. Another course of study and new educational concept is the "magnet school." This contains a limited number of specialized subject areas for the student to pursue in depth. Enrollment in the "magnet school" is open to all students within a school district who express interest and ability in a specialized area. However, this enrollment is limited because of the subject areas offered and student-qualifying examinations. There are two purposes underlying this new concept in education: (1) to provide subject area specialization, and (2) to place racial integration on a voluntary basis as opposed to forced busing.

The secondary school organizational structure for physical education as illustrated in Figure 2.1 on page 31 differs slightly from the elementary and middle schools because of additional administrators and an athletic and/or intramural director. Physical education at this level is either a separate or combined department. When there are separate departments for boys and girls each is chaired by a man or woman, respectively. Whereas one person serves in that capacity for a combined department. The size of a department varies from school to school and can number from 2 to 20 people.

In most high schools, physical education is a graduation requirement; however, sometimes health education, first aid, and driver education are included within this requirement. There are also schools in which athletic participation is substituted for physical education credit and where physical education is an elective subject for grades 11 and 12.

Generally, secondary school students are confronted with societal, parental, and peer pressure to mature into responsible adults. Each stage of emotional maturation, growth, and intellectual development is seen by the high school physical educator. It is during this period that the student leaves behind the childhood appearance and assumes the physical characteristics of an adult. However, the lack of knowledge and background of previous experiences causes the student constant frustration in adjusting to adulthood. An understanding of adolescent behavior is necessary to meet their needs in conducting and selecting physical education activities and developing positive student/teacher relationships.

Typically, ninth graders are eager to learn while tenth graders display disinterest. The more mature eleventh graders exhibit enjoyment and the twelfth graders are overzealous about graduation. These brief and general behavior characteristics serve to depict the various needs of students, which should be known and considered when planning and teaching physical education activities. The skills, knowledge, and social relationships developed at this age will influence the individual's participation as an adult. Therefore, students should be provided with individual and team activities that are appealing, challenging, and enjoyable.

The physical education department chairperson and faculty often jointly plan the yearly program of physical education activities. However, at the Secondary Center in Greensboro, North Carolina, students have planned, participated, and evaluated activities with faculty on an experimental basis. The results of this joint effort were to increase the number of individual and team activities offered and to graduate them into beginning, intermediate, and advanced levels.[4] This experiment and schools implementing modular scheduling, individualized instruction and competency-based programs could lend a flexibility that may contribute to student progress and interest.

Secondary school physical educators are generally scheduled for seven 50 to 55 minute periods per day. Five of these periods are designated for class, one for conference, and one for study hall supervision. Students report to class two, three, or five times a week. Depending on enrollment and faculty, the physical educator may teach health, first aid, or driver education in addition to physical education. Those teachers who supervise intramurals, coach athletics, or sponsor clubs often receive supplemental compensation.

COMMUNITY COLLEGE

In 1901, Joliet Junior College (Joilet, Illinois) became the first public community college established in the United States. During the past 20 years, the growth of community colleges has increased rapidly all across the country. These two-year institutions are either part of the local school district or a separate institution. Interchangeably, the community college is referred to as a junior, city, or technical college. This rapid construction of community colleges has been accompanied by soaring enrollments. Some of the reasons for these increased enrollments are: returning veterans, housewives seeking additional education, low-tuition, accessible location, and an "open admissions" policy.

In order to serve a large and diversified student body, most community colleges offer a dual curriculum: vocational-technical studies and university parallel programs. Frequently, students in the vocational-technical area are prepared in courses that coincide with local business and industrial employment opportunities. The university parallel programs focus on general education and introductory

[4]Robberta Mesenbrink, "Student Evaluation of Program Changes in the Secondary Center at Greensboro, North Carolina," *Journal of Health, Physical Education and Recreation*, 45:52 (May 1974).

courses for specialized areas. At the completion of an approved curriculum, totaling 60 to 65 semester hours, the student receives an associate degree. This is an Associate of Arts (A.A.) degree for the noneducational curriculum and an Associate of Science (A.S.) degree for the educational curriculum. Students transferring to a four-year institution with an associate degree must also submit a transcript of their course work for review and evaluation prior to acceptance.

The organizational structure of physical education in a community college consists of the State Board of Higher Education, State Community College Board, local community college board, president, deans and other administrators, and various departments. In Figure 2.5 the structure for physical education is similar to that in secondary schools whereby the department is either separate or combined. There may be one individual who is athletic director and department chairperson or these positions may be held by two people.

Students attending a community college represent a broad range of ages, experiences, previous education, interests, needs and goals. Physical education may be an elective or required subject within the college or for certain departments. If physical education is a requirement, there are sometimes conditions for exemption. This is usually for medical reasons, military service, age, or athletic participation. Whether required or elective, most physical education departments offer two programs. These are the general program and the professional preparation program.

The general program consists of physical education activities from which the student not majoring in physical education selects. In most instances students favor the individual or lifetime activities because it is a sport that is self-challenging and does not require a group of people for participation. Such activities may be for men, women or both and include: snow skiing, ice skating, archery, yoga, bowling, golf, tennis, weight training, and dance. However, to accomodate everyone's interest, team activites should also be provided. Often these are activities in volleyball, basketball, flag football, baseball, and softball (see Figure 2.6).

Students majoring or minoring in physical education are provided activity and theory courses within the professional preparation program. This university parallel program is designed for students who will transfer to a four-year college or university to complete a bachelor's degree and become certified to teach physical education. At the community college level, the professional preparation curriculum includes courses in general education, individual and

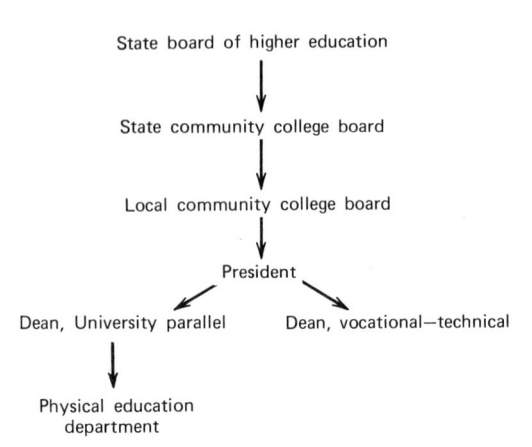

```
         State board of higher education
                      │
                      ▼
         State community college board
                      │
                      ▼
         Local community college board
                      │
                      ▼
                  President
                 ╱         ╲
    Dean, University parallel    Dean, vocational–technical
              │
              ▼
      Physical education
         department
```
FIGURE 2.5 Organizational structure of community college physical education.

FIGURE 2.6 College physical education classes. Reprinted by permission of University of Illinois at Chicago Circle, Chicago.

team activities, and theory of physical education. In the latter, emphasis is on orientation or history of the profession, human anatomy, body analysis, officiating and first aid.

Community college physical educators usually hold a master's degree and have taught at the secondary level. A typical class schedule consists of approximately 17 contact (clock) hours per week. This translates into about five activity classes and one theory class per week. Generally, each course meets twice a week for 50 to 55 minutes. Supervising intramurals, sponsoring a club, coaching an athletic team, or advising students are usually supplementary pay positions. Salaries in the community college are often equal to secondary schools and higher than many colleges and universities. In the community college, there is often more emphasis on teaching and less on service and research as compared to colleges and universities. And, unlike colleges and universities, there are fewer department and college committee responsibilities.

COLLEGE AND UNIVERSITY

The first four-year institution was Harvard University in 1636. Today, there are more than 2000 small and large, public and private colleges and universities in the United States. A college can differ from a university in title, organizational structure, size, and curriculum. A typical college or university organizational structure for physical education is given in Figure 2.7. This includes the State Board of Higher Education, board of regents (trustees or governors), president (chancellor), vice-presidents (vice-chancellors), administrators, deans, division heads, directors, and department heads. Private colleges and universities are self-supportive and governed by their own boards of trustees. However, final approval regarding curriculum and instruction rests with the State Board of Higher Education.

There are specific structural differences between a college and university. A college is usually organized into divisions, schools, and departments. For example, "X" College has the division of liberal arts and sciences that contains the school of education in which there is a department of physical education. A university includes colleges, divisions, schools, and departments. At "Y" University there is the college of health, physical education and recreation, which includes the division of athletics and department of physical education.

Some colleges and universities, usually in urban areas, are commuter campuses as are many of the community colleges. But, there are a number of four-year institutions with housing facilities. The advantages for students attending a commuter campus are often disadvantages to those at resident campuses and the reverse. For example, at a commuter campus, the cost of education is less, there are more job opportunities, and transportation is convenient. However, unlike the resident campus, there is a lack of camaraderie among students and faculty, fewer students seem to become involved in school activities, and time and distance limit the use of campus facilities. However, neither is true for all institutions.

```
                State board of higher education
                              ↓
                College or university board of regents
                              ↓
                           President
                              ↓
                        Vice—Presidents
                              ↓
                             Dean
          (College of health, physical education and recreation)
                              ↓
                         Division head
          (Division of health, physical education and recreation)
                              ↓
                           Director
           (School of health, physical education and recreation)
                              ↓
                        Department head
         (Department of health, physical education and recreation)
```

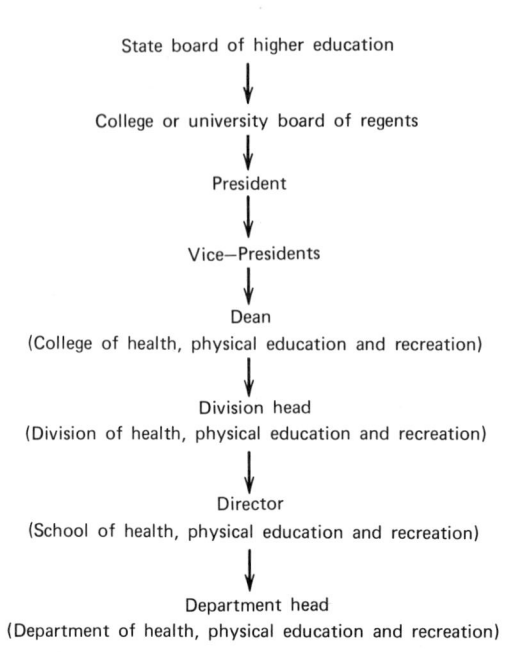

FIGURE 2.7 Organizational structure of college and university physical education.

College and university students are similar to community college students because of the varying backgrounds, experiences, interests, needs, and goals. At this educational level, students may obtain a bachelor's, master's, or doctorate degree. The kind of degree obtained depends on previous education and the curriculum followed.

In curricula requiring science courses, a bachelor of science (B.S.) degree is awarded. This is the degree received by students majoring in physical education. Those students in liberal arts receive a bachelor of arts (B.A.) degree.

At the masters level, a master of science (M.S.) degree requires science courses and written scientific research. A master of arts (M.A.) requires science courses plus an additional quarter or semester of work.

The curriculum for the doctorate degree is similar with a doctor of philosophy (Ph.D.) obtained at the completion of science courses, written scientific research, and frequently two foreign languages. A doctor of education (Ed.D.) requires science courses, written scientific research, and one foreign language and an additional quarter or semester of course work. There are a few institutions that offer degrees specific to physical education such as a masters in physical

42 PHYSICAL EDUCATION

education (M.P.E.) and a doctor of physical education (D.P.E.). Generally, the requirements for these degrees are synonymous to an M.S. and Ph.D.

At the college and university level, students pursuing a bachelors degree may enroll in physical education to meet a requirement or as an elective. Again, medical reasons, military service, age, or athletic participation may serve to exempt students from required physical education. Here, too, there are general and professional preparation programs. The general program consists of physical education activities for men, women or both, who are not majoring in physical education, and the professional preparation program includes activity and theory courses for students majoring or minoring in physical education.

In the general program students may elect individual, dual, or team activities for a limited number of credits and receive a letter grade (which may or may not be included in the cumulative grade point average) or receive credit on a pass/fail basis. However, in most colleges and universities, courses in professional preparation are based on a letter grade, which is part of the cumulative grade point average. In the professional preparation program students have activity courses in individual and team sports and theory courses in: history of physical education, introduction to physical education, first aid, athletic training, body analysis, officiating, coaching, anatomy, physiology, kinesiology, organization and administration, curriculum and instruction, physical education field experiences in observation, and student teaching. Student teaching is considered by many to be the culmination of the total university experience and, consequently, of extreme importance.

Teaching at this educational level requires a master's degree with elementary or secondary school experience. In many colleges and universities, students pursuing a masters or doctorate in physical education serve as graduate assistants and teach activity classes in the general program. Generally, teachers with a master's degree teach activity classes in the general and professional preparation program. Most often these are activities in which the teacher displays expertise. The theory courses within the professional preparation program are most often taught by those with a doctorate and expertise in a particular area. These teachers are also involved in the graduate program for masters and doctoral students.

Service, research, and teaching are the purpose of most colleges and universities. Therefore, faculty members are expected to serve their profession and university through involvement in professional organizations, conducting and reporting research, and teaching. A teacher's class schedule varies, but usually ranges between 10 to 15 contact (clock) hours per week. The class length and sessions vary for both activity and theory courses.

The reason for fewer contact hours, compared to the community college and other educational levels, is because of the time needed for service and research. Faculty members may also need to serve on department, college, or university committees to which they have been appointed, elected, or volunteered. Additional responsibilities are advisement and registration of students. The sponsorship of a club or organization is usually a voluntary responsibility; however, club sports sponsorship yields supplementary compensation, either monetarily or in reduced teaching load.

Teachers salaries in some colleges and universities are frequently the lowest of any educational level, but the base salary is near that of many secondary schools. The prestige and reputation of the institution is often the determining factor in the salary schedule. Accompanying salary is teaching rank. Progressively, from lowest to highest the ranks are: graduate assistant, instructor, assistant professor, associate professor, and professor. The rank of a visiting lecturer varies according to the person's rank from a previous institution. Contributions in the areas of teaching, public service, and research are criteria typically used in progressing up the professional ladder.

Supplemental income is often obtained by teaching evening or extension courses in the graduate program or conducting workshops or clinics. Supervision of intramurals or coaching intercollegiate athletics is either a full-time position or a joint appointment (50/50 or 60/40) with physical education.

SUMMARY

The levels of education are elementary, middle, secondary, community college, and college and university. At each level, there is variation in organizational structure, curriculum, salaries, and work load. Physical education programs at these levels differ in classification of students and activities, elective or required credits, and organization and supervision of intramurals, interscholastic and intercollegiate athletics. At each level, students differ in age, ability, interest, behavior, needs, and goals.

The professional preparation program and areas of specialization vary for physical educator between and within these levels. The interrelationship of organization and administration, students, physical education activities, and teacher preparation and responsibilities for each level should be thoroughly understood prior to job placement. On-site observation and teaching experiences in the professional preparation program acquaint the student with the school and community.

SELECTED REFERENCES

American Alliance for Health, Physical Education and Recreation, "Fresh Ideas for College Physical Education," *Journal of Physical Education and Recreation,* **46**:37-44 (February 1975).

American Alliance for Health, Physical Education and Recreation, "Standards for the General College Physical Education Program," *Journal of Physical Education and Recreation,* **46**:24-28 September 1975).

American Association for Health, Physical Education and Recreation, "Essentials of a Quality Elementary School Physical Education Program: A Position Paper," *Journal of Health, Physical Education and Recreation,* **42**:42-46 (April 1971).

American Association for Health, Physical Education and Recreation, "Guide to Excellence for Physical Education in Colleges and Universities: A Position Paper," *Journal of Health, Physical Education and Recreation,* **42**:51-53 (April 1971).

American Association for Health, Physical Education and Recreation, "Guidelines for Secondary School Physical Education: A Position Paper," *Journal of Health, Physical Education and Recreation,* **42**:47-50 (April 1971).

American Association for Health, Physical Education and Recreation, "It's What's Happening—the New Physical Education in Colleges and Universities," *Journal of Health, Physical Education and Recreation,* **43**:16-25 (October 1972).

American Association for Health, Physical Education and Recreation, "The New Physical Education," *Journal of Health, Physical Education and Recreation,* **42**:24-39 (September 1971).

American Association for Health, Physical Education and Recreation, "The New Physical Education," *Journal of Health, Physical Education and Recreation,* **44**:23-29 (September 1973).

American Association for Health, Physical Education and Recreation, "The Whole Thing," *Journal of Health, Physical Education and Recreation,* **44**:21-36 (May 1973).

Ashcraft, Rita, J., "Comparison of Employment Status of Men and

Women in Four-Year Public Institutions," *Journal of Health, Physical Education and Recreation*, **44**:60-62 (April 1973).

Belanger, Charles H., and Peter W. Everett, "Salaries of Physical Education Faculty in Selected Four-Year Institutions," *Journal of Health, Physical Education and Recreation*, **44**:58-60 (April 1973).

Bird, James, "Physical Education and the Middle School Student," *Journal of Health, Physical Education and Recreation*, **44**:25-26 (March 1973).

Blackmarr, Syd, "Every Child A Winner," *Journal of Health, Physical Education and Recreation*, **45**:14-16 (October 1974).

Blocker, Clyde E., Robert H. Plummer, and Richard C. Richardson, Jr., *The Two-Year College: A Social Synthesis*, Prentice-Hall, Inc., Englewood Cliffs, NJ, 1965.

Bucher, Charles A., "What's Happening In Education Today?" *Journal of Health, Physical Education and Recreation*, **45**:30-32 (September 1974).

Chapman, Sharon Lee, "Student Differences and Teacher Responses in Physical Education," *The Physical Educator*, **28**:29-31 (March 1971).

Cogan, Max., "Innovative Ideas in College Physical Education," *Journal of Health, Physical Education and Recreation*, **44**:28-33 (February 1973).

Conant, James B., *The Education of American Teachers*, McGraw-Hill Book Company, Inc., New York, 1963.

Cratty, Bryant J., *Social Dimensions of Physical Activity*, Prentice-Hall Inc., Englewood Cliffs, NJ, 1967.

Curriculum Improvement in Secondary School Physical Education, American Association for Health, Physical Education and Recreation, Washington, D.C., 1973.

De Maria, Carol R., "Movement Education: An Overview," *The Physical Educator*, **49**:73-76 (May 1972).

Douglas, J. William, "The Pollutants in Our Physical Education Environment," *The Physical Educator*, **30**:72-75 (May 1973).

Drost, Walter H., "ES '70's—The Educational Innovation of the 1970's?," *School and Society*, **99**:224-226 (April 1971).

Dykes, Archie R., "The Role of Physical Education in Higher Education," *National College Physical Education Association for Men: Proceedings 77th Annual Meeting*, Leo L. Gedvilas, (ed.), 15-18, Office of Publications Services, University of Illinois at Chicago Circle, Chicago, 1974.

Eddy, John, "Community College Enrollments in the 1970's," *Illinois Journal of Education,* **64**:29-30 (Third Quarter, 1973).

Fuchs, Ralph F., "A View from the Professional School," *AAUP Bulletin,* **50**:269-270 (September 1970).

Gleazer, Jr., Edmund J., "The Community College Issue of the 1970's," *Educational Record,* **50**:47-52 (Winter 1970).

Harrington, Wilma and Carol E. Gordon, "Some Implications of Title IX for Physical Education Programs," *Briefings 1, Title IX: Moving Toward Implementation,* 1-5, National Association for Physical Education of College Women and National College Physical Education Association for Men, Printed in the United States, 1975.

Heitmann, Helen (ed.), *College Physical Education: The General Program,* American Association for Health, Physical Education and Recreation, Washington, D.C., 1973.

Hellison, Donald R., "Physical Education and the Self-Attitude," *Quest,* Monograph XIII:41-44 (January 1970).

Hodges, Patrick B., "Status and Structure of Physical Education in Public Two-Year Colleges of the Midwest," *Journal of Health, Physical Education and Recreation,* **45**:13-15 (June 1974).

Howard, Alvin W., and George C. Stoumbis, *The Junior High and Middle School: Issues and Practices,* Intext Educational Publishers, Scranton, PA 1970.

Jewett, Ann E., "Who Knows What Tomorrow May Bring?" *Quest,* Monograph XXI:68-72 (January 1974).

Johnson, Perry G., "History, Status and Future," *College Physical Education, The General Program,* Helen Heitmann (ed.), 34-42 American Association for Health, Physical Education and Recreation, Washington, D.C., 1973.

Johnson, William P., and Richard P. Kelva, "The Community Dimension of College Physical Education," *Journal of Health, Physical Education and Recreation,* **44**:40-41 (April 1973).

Kehres, Larry, "Maslow's Hierarchy of Needs Applied to Physical Education and Athletics," *The Physical Educator,* **30**:24-25 (March 1973).

Kelley, Win, and Leslie Wilbur, *Teaching in the Community Junior College,* Appleton-Century-Crofts, New York, 1970.

Kindred, Leslie W. and Associates, *The Intermediate Schools,* Prentice-Hall, Inc., Englewood Cliffs, NJ, 1968.

Koos, Leonard V., *The Community College Student,* University of Florida Press, Gainesville, 1970.

Laughlin, Neil., "Physical Education—2000 A.D.," *The Physical Educator*, **29**:115-117 (October 1972).

Medsker, Leland L., and Dale Tillery, *Breaking the Access Barriers*, McGraw-Hill Book Company, St. Louis, 1971.

Miller, Donna Mae, "Personnel: Recruitment, Placement, Evaluation," *Briefing 1, Title IX: Moving Toward Implementation*, 35-44, National Association for Physical Education of College Women and National College Physical Education for Men, Printed in the United States, 1975.

Miller, Freeman, "Action Maps," *Movement Education Newsletter*, California Educators for Movement Education, Orange, CA, 7:4 (May 1975).

Munson, Corlee, and Elba Stafford, "Middle Schools: A Variety of Approaches to Physical Education," *Journal of Health, Physical Education and Recreation*, **45**:29-31 (February 1974).

O'Connell, Thomas E., *Community Colleges*, University of Illlinois Press, Chicago, 1968.

Overly, Donald E., Jon Rye Kinghorn, and Richard L. Preston, *The Middle School: Humanizing Education for Youth*, Charles A. Jones Publishing Company, Worthington, OH, 1972.

Oxendine, Joseph, "The Status of General Instruction Programs of Physical Education in Four-Year Colleges and Universities: 1971-1972," *College Physical Education: The General Program*, Helen Heitmann M. (ed.), 125-144, American Association for Health, Physical Education and Recreation, Washington, D.C., 1973.

Rarick, G. Lawrence (ed.), *Physical Activity: Human Growth and Development*, Academic Press, New York, 1973.

Razor, Jack E., and Florence D. Grebner, "Elective PE Programs: Expansion vs. Limitation," *Journal of Physical Education and Recreation*, **46**:23-24 (June 1975).

Resick, Matthew C., Beverly L. Seidel, and James G. Mason, *Modern Administrative Practices in Physical Education and Athletics*, Addison-Wesley Publishing Company, Reading, MA, 1970.

Seefeldt, Vern, "Middle Schools: Issues and Future Directions in Physical Education," *Journal of Health, Physical Education and Recreation*, **45**:32-34 (February 1974).

Singer, Robert N., "Pre-School Movement Experiences," *The Physical Educator*, **30**:194-196 (December 1973).

Stafford, Elba, "Middle Schools: Status of Physical Education Programs," *Journal of Health, Physical Education and Recreation*, **45**:25-28 (February 1974).

Tanner, Patricia, and Kate Barrett, "Movement Education: What Does It Mean?," *Journal of Physical Education and Recreation*, **46**:19-20 (April 1975).

This Is Physical Education, American Association for Health, Physical Education and Recreation, Washington, D.C. 1965.

Thomas, Jerry R., Doyice J. Cotten, H. Douglas Leavitt, and Judson Biasiotto, "Status of Physical Education in Junior Colleges," *Journal of Health, Physical Education and Recreation*, **44**:18-19 and 22 (February 1973).

Unruh, Glenys G., and William M. Alexander, *Innovations In Secondary Education*, Holt, Rinehart and Winston, Inc., Chicago, 1970.

Van Slooten, Philip H., "Four Theories of Development and Their Implications for the Physical Education of Adolescents," *The Physical Educator*, **31**:181-186 (December 1974).

Vannier, Maryhelen, Mildred Foster, and David Gallahue, *Teaching Physical Education in Elementary Schools*, Fifth Edition, W.B. Saunders Company, Philadelphia, 1973.

Weber, John D., "Motivational Wizard," *Journal of Health, Physical Education and Recreation*, **44**:50-54 (April 1973).

Weinberg, Herman, "Middle Schools: Selected Annotated Bibliography," *Journal of Health, Physical Education and Recreation*, **45**:35-37 (February 1974).

Weinstein, Gerald, and Mario D. Fantini, (ed.), *Toward Humanistic Education*, Praeger Publishers, Inc., New York, 1970.

Wilmore, Jack H., "Body Composition and Strength Development," *Journal of Physical Education and Recreation*, **46**:38-40 (January 1975).

chapter 3
community

The convergence of social, economic, political, and religious forces has for decades influenced and shaped urban, rural, and suburban communitities. It is important to depict the effects of these forces upon each community—effects in terms of community characteristics and cultures that have developed. Each community has similarities in political structure and governance, but differences exist in values, life-styles, home environment, and attitudes. Identification of these differences has implications for physical education programs and patterns of student behavior. Paterson and Hallberg have stated that:[1]

> The background and character of physical education are largely determined by the values, institutions and social relationships of the culture in which they exist . . . The prospective teacher must be able to direct the philosophy and programs of his field within a rapidly changing culture, all the while keeping in mind the future value of the activities and skills taught.

The following are general characteristics pertaining to the social and economic dimensions of an urban, rural, and suburban community.

[1] Ann Paterson and Edmond C. Hallberg, "Sociological Backgrounds," *Background Readings for Physical Education*, Holt, Rinehart and Winston, Chicago, 1965, pp. 457-458.

URBAN

Perhaps inner city, ghetto, or barrio are more familiar terms for an urban community. Essentially, the characteristics for each are the same. Differences occur within ethnic composition such as ghetto related to Blacks and barrio related to Chicanos, although poor Whites may also reside there.

Social

In the confines of any large city one finds substandard housing, overcrowded living conditions, transient populations, and highly noisy environments. Frequently, school buildings are over 100 years old, classes are overcrowded (more than 30 students per class), indoor and outdoor facilities are limited, and class periods are of minimal duration (45 minutes).

In the urban community there is a diversified population. There are professional, white-collar and blue-collar workers. Additionally, there are people who are high school drop outs, street-gang members, one-parent families, drug addicts, alcoholics, and prostitutes.

In terms of physical education, students coming from such environments may present disciplinary problems. This occurs because, inherently, students resent authority. From their point of view, the physical educator represents authority and is someone from a different socioeconomic class. Therefore, the philosophy is not to trust authority but instead to challenge it.

At home, these students are often subjected to crowdedness, noise, and interruptions. Unfortunately, these same things occur when they come to school. For example, in a physical education class, the student may be limited in space for participation, have to share equipment, or have only 25 minutes (twice a week) for actual activity. However, David Field has suggested that these conditions may be improving in some cities where urban schools are modernizing facilities and acquiring needed equipment and supplies.[2] The key factor in providing quality physical education programs in an urban

[2]David Field, "Inner City Physical Education," unpublished proceedings of Professional Education Section Meeting, Eastern District Association of the American Association for Health, Physical Education and Recreation, Philadelphia, pp. 3-4 (April 24, 1971).

community depends on the resourcefulness, creativeness, and leadership of the physical educator.

Economic

An urban community is faced with many economic dilemmas. Among these are unemployment, families on relief, and inadequate dietary and medical care. A noted authority on urban schools, Superintendent Paul W. Briggs reported:[3]

> Poverty in this country is concentrated in the ghetto. In Ohio our school district (Cleveland) has 7% of all the students in the state. We have one-third of all the relief children. These are the same kind of statistics you find in every city, every urban center. Today, one-fifth of all our children come from relief homes, and in some of the schools over 80% of the children in the building come from homes where the families are receiving public assistance. Looking at the relief pattern going back to 1950, we find in Cleveland there has been a 700% increase in the number of children coming from relief homes. This is happening in every urban center.

As a result of this conditon, those students report to physical education class usually without activity attire for participation. An outgrowth of this economic stress is the possibility of locker and equipment rooms being vandalized.

The urban board of education, which allocates funds for hundreds of elementary and secondary schools, may have received budgetary cutbacks. In some urban communities this has resulted in elimination of the physical education requirement. In others, monies are limited for equipment and supplies. However, a large portion of the budget is expended for teacher's salaries, which are usually higher than rural and often equal or above suburban communities. Two of the reasons advocated for teachers receiving higher salaries are: (1) to attract teachers to urban schools and (2) the fact that teacher unions are trying to receive annual salary increases.

Physical educators in urban schools are often plagued with a lack of funds to conduct their programs. In *Physical Education for Inner*

[3]Paul W. Briggs, "The Opportunity to be Relevant," *Journal of Health, Physical Education and Recreation,* **41**:42 (May 1970).

City Secondary Schools, authors Leonard M. Ridini and John E. Madden emphasize that program objectives and resources must be clearly identified in order to attain program goals.[4]

The provisions of sound physical education programs in urban communities necessitates qualified teachers who *genuinely* desire to serve these students and who are willing to tackle the social and economic problems posed. Only those future physical educators having a sincere interest in urban students and potential capability to resolve these problems should seek employment there. Firsthand observation and teaching experiences in an urban school as part of the early formal education helps one to decide.

RURAL

Rural and urban communities are no longer at extreme opposite ends of the continuum because of advances made in communication, industry, technology, and education. In the last 20 years, there have been rapid population shifts from rural to urban, urban to suburban, and now a trend of suburban to rural. Ten years ago, 15 million people lived on farms while fewer than 10 million were reported there in the 1970 census.[5] The ever-changing socioeconomic mobility of society serves as an indicator of population increases in particular communities.

Since the 1950s, rural communities have combined to form consolidated school districts. As a result, the era of the "little red school house" has practically vanished. These traditional one-room schools have been reported as less efficient and more expensive than consolidated schools.

In reference to supporters of consolidated school districts, Roger G. Barker and Paul V. Gump stated:[6]

> . . . that students benefit through better and more varied curriculums, better classifications, better facilities, especially in such subjects as science and music, contact with better teachers, opportunities to participate in better and more varied extracurricular activities, wider social opportunities and experiences, and

[4]Leonard M. Ridini and John E. Madden, *Physical Education for Inner City Secondary Schools*, Harper & Row, New York, 1975, p. 28.

[5]"Quiet Falls Across the Plains," *Life Magazine*, 22-31 (June 25, 1971).

[6]Roger G. Barker and Paul V. Gump, *Big School, Small School*, Stanford University Press, Stanford, 1964, p. 139.

more regular attendance as a result of being in some cases, transported from door to school ...

Frequently, in consolidated school districts, the high school is centrally located and serves as the hub for the surrounding communities. This location then affords the entire rural population of that community with the same educational, social, and recreational opportunities. Additionally, the centralized location reduces transportation costs.

Social

Populations in rural communities are relatively more stable than those in urban and suburban areas. An exception to this is the influx of migrant workers during harvest season. The year-round residents, however, are closely allied to family, church, school, and community. This life-style is congruent to the upsurge of consolidated school districts having modern school buildings and spacious outdoor facilities that serve as an educational and social center for the community.

Physical educators in rural schools, as in any other community, have a prime responsibility to their students. This is mentioned because community identification and alliance with the school is dual directional. Just as rural residents express close affiliation toward the school and faculty, they would like the faculty to express interest and involvement in the community. A relationship of this nature can be personally satisfying, but is dependent upon the activities selected and amount of involvement. It does afford community members and faculty an opportunity to know one another.

The relevance of the relationship between faculty and residents has been stressed by N. W. Kullman, Jr. and Julian E. Butterworth, who said:[7]

> It is necessary that the school leaders know the educational, political, economic, and religious backgrounds and interests of their people. What the patrons think and believe along those lines will largely determine their support of or opposition to the program of the schools. Their thoughts and beliefs will also determine the nature of the initial program of action the rural leader must undertake to secure support of his program.

[7]N. W. Kullman, Jr., and Julian E. Butterworth, "Pilot Programs in Rural Education," *Education in Rural Communities*, Nelson B. Henry (ed.), National Society for the Study of Education, University of Chicago Press, Chicago, Vol. 52, Pt. 2, 1952, p. 155.

Teaching physical education in a rural community commonly entails participation in community events, and perhaps provision and supervision of recreational activities for adults and children.

Economic

The source of income for families in rural communities is dependent upon agriculture, fishing, forestry, or mining. Some of the determining factors that may cause this economy to fluctuate are governmental regulation, extreme changes in the climate, and inflated commodities. Therefore, most rural communities remain economically conservative on matters such as the school budget.

Although outdoor facilities may be extensive, they can be in the form of the natural terrain. Perhaps funds were not available to level, pave, or maintain these fields. Indoor facilities usually contain one gymnasium to house all physical education classes and athletic teams during inclement weather. This presents difficulty in scheduling classes and selecting activities to offer.

In rural communities, teacher's salaries are often lower than in urban and suburban areas. And, there may be no or minimal pay for conducting extracurricular activities. Last, there may be a shortage of job opportunities for those physical educators seeking summer employment in a rural setting.

SUBURBAN

During the 1950s, there was a large exodus from the cities to the suburbs. This population shift has continued over the past 25 years, resulting in the construction of more schools, churches, and shopping centers. While it was the white middle-class city dwellers who originally fled from the cities, over the past five years, there has been a racial mixture of middle-class people. The primary reason for this exodus of the middle class to suburbia was a desire for better education. Thus minority groups and poor whites were left still living in the city. Governmental regulation of housing, busing the children to school, and industrial development have all contributed to the heterogeneity of suburbia.

Social

Characteristically, the suburban father is a professional person and usually commutes daily to his office in the city. The suburban mother may be employed on a part-time basis, unemployed, or active in community organizations. In terms of a college-oriented suburb, noted educator and author James B. Conant infers that families having above average professional positions, incomes, and real estate values contribute most to expensively operated schools, which provide the best education money can buy.[8]

The opportunity and emphasis for socioeconomic mobility has been instrumental in creating parental involvement on school issues and activities. Notably, education has been viewed as the vehicle toward increased socioeconomic status. Therefore, suburban secondary schools provide curricula that is college preparatory.

Student activism of the 1960s and subsequent curricula revisions and budgetary decreases in colleges and universities contributed to the elimination of required physical education at this level. Currently, a number of secondary schools, especially in the suburbs, are in the process of terminating required physical education. Consequently, several alternatives have evolved regarding physical education. These include: eliminating the requirement for juniors and seniors; evaluating physical education on a pass/fail basis; or excluding the physical education grade from the accumulative grade point average.

The implications derived from actions against physical education serve to stabilize school budgets by not hiring additional faculty and purchasing more equipment and to insure higher grade point averages for those students who excel in all areas except physical education. For these reasons, numerous suburban physical education programs provide activities from which students may decide to participate.

Economic

The high cost of living, increased taxes, and rising inflation have even affected the economy in the suburbs. An example of this has been a continual defeat of bond issues and school referenda by local taxpayers. In many secondary schools throughout the U.S., the defeat of proposals for additional tax revenue has resulted in the elimination of all extracurricular activites. As population growth approaches zero and school enrollments decline, school budgets shrink. In order for school boards to compensate for curtailed budgets, class size may be increased with faculty size remaining the same or decreasing.

Some schools are operating on a year-round basis under the "45-15" plan in order to limit expenditures. The "45-15" plan involves splitting the student enrollment into three segments. Each segment is on a different track with four sessions of 45 days. At the

[8]James B. Conant, Slums and Suburbs, The New American Library, New York 1961, p. 72.

end of each of these 180 day periods students have a 15 day vacation.

At one junior and two senior high schools in Miami, Florida, the extended school year plan known as the quinmester has been implemented. The selection and duration of physical education activities have been developed and explained by Hy Rothstein and Robert F. Adams, who described the quinmester program as:[9]

> ... five 9-week sessions, including the 180 instructional days which is the present state requirement, extended over a 12-month school year. Each 9-week term is called a quin. The student may elect to attend school any four of the five quins or during all five quinmesters. The calendar allows for the usual holidays, including Easter and Christmas vacations and teacher planning days when students are not in school.

Although this plan provides year-round employment for faculty, its educational soundness is highly debatable.

Whether the scheduling of students is conventional or contemporary, suburban teachers' salaries are higher than rural communities and comparable to urban areas. And the number and variety of extracurricular activites provides additional income. In most suburban schools, the buildings are modern and have outstanding indoor and outdoor facilties for physical education.

In preparation for a changing future, the AAHPER has provided a multidisciplinary model illustrating the adaptation to cultural change (see Figure 3.1). The outer circle represents areas of emphasis for health, physical education, recreation, dance, athletics, and safety. Circle 'C' classifies general education into physical, social, and cultural environments; human health and development; and symbolic organization and communication. Catagories effecting cultural change are identified in circle 'B', circle 'A' illustrates the individual's adaptation to cultural change.

The intensity of each area in categories D, C, and B vary within and among urban, rural, and suburban communities. It cannot be assumed that all urban areas, all rural communities, or all suburbs are the same culturally. Cognizance of these categories effecting cultural change may enhance one's ability to adjust to the community selected for a teaching position.

It is the people in each community who determine what is necessary for the education of their children. The physical educator's task is to know that community in order to develop a sound physical

[9] Hy Rothstein and Robert F. Adams, "Quinmester Extended School Year Plan," *Journal of Health, Physical Education and Recreation,* **42**:30 (September 1971).

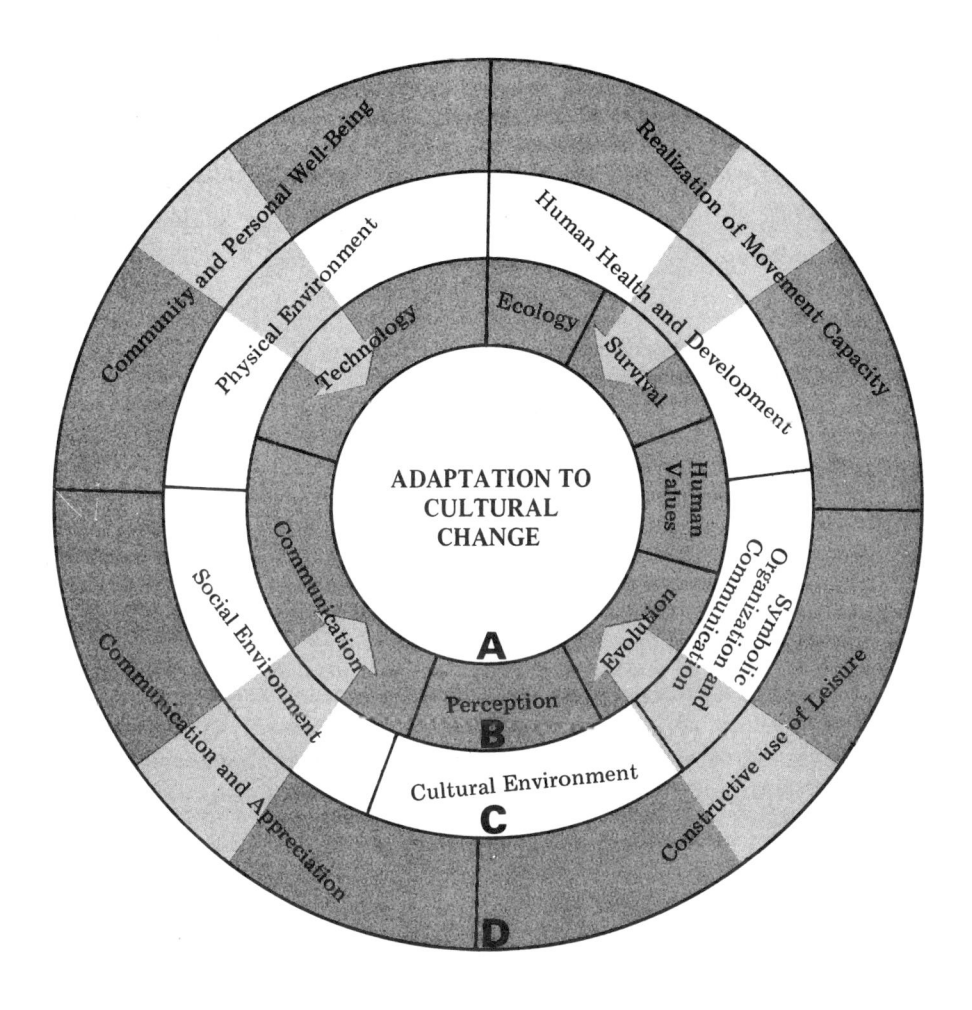

A = Central core of adaption to cultural change
B = Categories effecting cultural change
C = Categories of general education
D = Areas of emphasis for Association disciplines

FIGURE 3.1 Adaptation of cultural change chart. Reprinted by permission of the American Association for Health, Physical Education and Recreation, Washington, D.C., 1976.

COMMUNITY 59

education program within the established parameters. Once this has been accomplished it is important to inform the residents and school administrators about their quality physical education programs. When deciding a community preference, consider your personal goals; then arrange to visit a school in the community selected and meet with the physical educator. To gain more insight about yourself and physical education, explore the learning experiences that follow.

SELECTED REFERENCES

Cassidy, Rosalind, "Societal Determinants of Human Movement—The Next Thirty Years," *Quest*, Vol. XVI:49 (June 1971).

Educational Futurism 1985, The 1985 Committee of the National Conference of Professors of Educational Administration, McCutchan Publishing Corporation, Berkeley, CA, 1971.

Ezersky, Eugene, and P. Richard Theibert, "City Schools Without Gyms," *Journal of Health, Physical Education and Recreation*, 41:26-29 (April 1970).

Liberman, Myron, *The Future of Public Education*, University of Chicago Press, Chicago, 1960.

McHale, John, "The Sense in the Future," *Quest*, Monograph XXI:3-11 (January 1974).

McLendon, Jonathan C., and Laurence D. Haskew, *Views on American Schooling*, Scott, Foresman and Company, Chicago, 1964.

McMurrin, Sterling M. (ed.), *Resources for Urban Schools: Better Use and Balance*, Committee for Economic Development, New York, 1971.

Metcalfe, Ralph H., "The Education and Social Problems of the Modern Large City," *National College Physical Education Association for Men: Proceedings 73rd Annual Meeting*, C. E. Mueller (ed.), 15-18, University of Minnesota, Minneapolis, 1970.

"One-Room Schools," *New York Times Magazine*, 14-16 (May 30, 1971).

Reiss, Jr., Albert J. (ed.), *Schools in a Changing Society*, The Free Press, New York, 1965.

Sanborn, Marion Alice, and Betty G. Hartman, *Issues in Physical Education*, Prentice-Hall, Inc., Englewood Cliffs, NJ, 1969.

Selakovich, Daniel, *The Schools and American Society*, Blaisdell Publishing Company, Waltham, MA, 1967.

Smith, G. K. (ed.), *The Troubled Campus*, Jossey-Bass, Inc., San Francisco, 1970.

"Surprises from the Census," *Business Week*, 16-17 (August 8, 1970).

The Campus and the City, The Carnegie Commission on Higher Education, McGraw-Hill Book Company, New York, December, 1972.

Ulrich, Celeste, *The Social Matrix of Physical Education*, Prentice-Hall, Inc., Englewood Cliffs, NJ, 1968.

chapter 4

learning experiences in physical education

> We must provide opportunities for individual self-expression and individual self-fulfillment in physical education and sport.[1]
>
> Edward J. Sims

The profession of physical education has been presented from three aspects: teacher, educational level and program, and community. Concerning the breadth of each aspect, there are several questions posed to the student preparing to teach physical education. Will I teach in an urban, rural, or suburban community? Why? Will I teach physical education at the elementary, middle, secondary, community college, or college and university level? Why? What will be my role as a physical educator? Will I specialize in a selected area of physical education? Will I attend graduate school? Am I interested in conducting research?

By formulating answers to these questions in the freshman year, one can better prepare for the profession with identified goals, objectives for attaining those goals, and an evaluation of meeting those goals.

[1] Edward J. Sims, *Development of Human Values Through Sports*, Reuben B. Frost and Edward J. Sims (ed.), American Association for Health, Physical Education and Recreation, Washington, D.C., 1974.

These may not be possible for everyone as a large percentage of college students do not know in their freshman year, and even later, what they want to do in life, and those who make an early choice are often the exception rather than the rule. Planning, preparing, and performing learning experiences have been provided in this chapter to assist in knowing one's self—abilities, interests, and needs—in relation to physical education.

PLANNING

In the planning stage, one should identify his or her values and characteristics, establish a four year schedule of courses, and select extracurricular activities for participation. Although a number of methods exist for identifying one's values, a learning experience for this purpose has been selected and slightly modified.

This was originally developed by Marian Kneer as an exercise in the awareness of one's own values. Read carefully the following list and description of selected values:[2]

ADVENTURE (exploration, risks, danger, doing
   something new and/or untried)
BEAUTY (in the arts and in nature)
EMOTIONAL WELL BEING (ability to recognize
   and handle inner conflict)
ETHICAL LIFE (responsible living toward self
   and others, personal honor, integrity)
FAMILY HAPPINESS (mutual caring among family
   members)
FORGIVENESS (being willing to pardon others,
   bearing no grudges)
HONESTY (being frank and genuinely yourself with everyone)
LAW AND ORDER (respect for authority, property of others)
LOVE (warmth, caring and receiving of respect
   and affection)
MEANINGFUL WORK (sense of purpose, doing something
   that is relevant)
MONEY (plenty of money for things I want)
PERSONAL FREEDOM (independence, making own choices)
PERSONAL POWER (having influence and authority over
   others)

[2]Marian Kneer, "How Human Are You?," *Journal of Health, Physical Education and Recreation*, 45:33 (June 1974).

PHYSICAL APPEARANCE *(attractiveness—neat, clean, well-groomed)*
PLEASURE *(excitement, satisfaction, fun, joy)*
RECOGNITION *(being important, being well-liked, being accepted)*
RELIGION *(religious belief, relationship with God, meaning in life)*
SERVICE *(devotion to the interests of others)*
SKILL *(being good at doing something important to me/or to others)*
WISDOM *(mature understanding, insight, application of knowledge)*

In Figure 4.1 there appears a "Sample Profile of Charted Values." This contains the values described above and five levels of importance. Number one (1) represents the lowest level of importance and number five (5) the highest.

Values	\multicolumn{5}{c}{Levels of Importance}
	1	2	3	4	5
Adventure					
Beauty					
Emotional well being					
Ethical life					
Family Happiness					
Forgiveness					
Honesty					
Law and order					
Love					
Meaningful work					
Money					
Personal freedom					
Personal power					
Physical appearance					
Pleasure					
Recognition					
Religion					
Service					
Skill					
Wisdom					

FIGURE 4.1 Sample profile of charted values.

Duplicate this illustration and, by referring to the list of values, determine the level of importance for each at this time and place in life. In this self profile, notice the values having the highest and lowest levels of importance. What relationship can be drawn from this profile in:

1. Preparing to teach physical education?
2. Selecting the community in which to teach?
3. Determining the educational level at which to teach?
4. Perceiving one's self in the role of a physical educator?

Since values are often reflected through one's characteristics, H. Donald Loucks has selected 10 characteristics for the well-rounded physical education major. This is in the form of a circlegram containing 10 concentric circles as a one-to-ten rating scale (see Figure 4.2). The circumference of the smallest circle denotes number one (1) as the lowest rating. Number ten (10), the highest rating, forms the largest circle. This rating scale is consistent for all 10 characteristics.[3] Read carefully the following list and description of these 10 characteristics:[4]

APPEARANCE
    Has good posture
    Controls body movements
    Possesses good health
    Has no annoying mannerism
CULTURAL INTERESTS
    Appreciates the aesthetic
    Is diversified in his activities
EMOTIONAL STABILITY
    Is emotionally mature
    Seems well-adjusted
    Endures under pressure
    Has wholesome outlook on life
    Has no abnormal behavior patterns
LEADERSHIP
    Is forceful, dynamic
    Has ability to gain cooperation
    Seeks and accepts responsibility
    Is democratic in his leadership

[3]H. Donald Loucks, "An Educational Device for Developing the Well-Rounded Physical Education Major," The Physical Educator, 27:148 (December 1970).

[4]Ibid., p. 149.

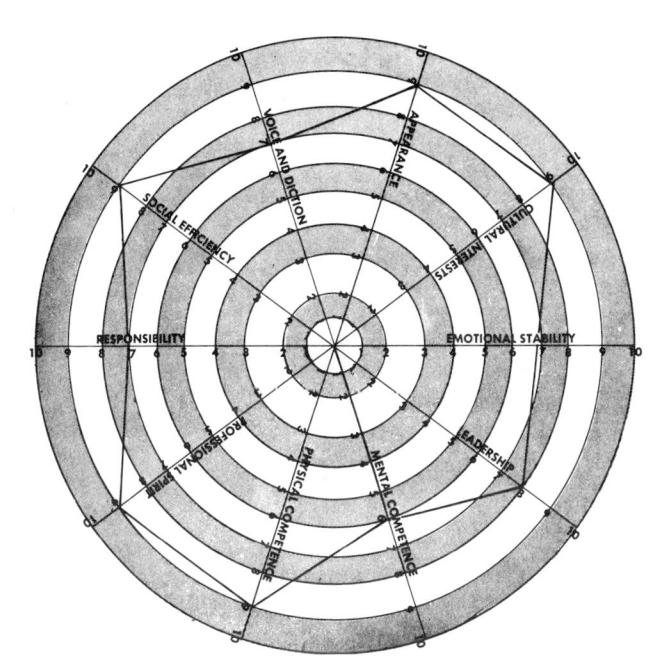

FIGURE 4.2 The well-rounded physical education major circlegram. Reprinted by permission of H. Donald Loucks, University of Nebraska, Lincoln, 1976.

Has administrative ability
Has the ability to communicate ideas
Shows initiative ability
MENTAL COMPETENCE
Is a clear thinker
Is logical in reasoning
Has a keen mind
Achieves well academically
Is resourceful in recalling ideas
Wants added intellectual maturity
PHYSICAL COMPETENCE
Has knowledge and mastery of sport skills
Is versatile in sports
Is active and energetic
Uses logic in game situations
Is alert to opportunities to broaden skills
PROFESSIONAL SPIRIT
Attends majors' club meeting
Belongs to professional organizations
Accepts professional ideals

LEARNING EXPERIENCES IN PHYSICAL EDUCATION

Has served actively in clubs
Is interested in advancing the profession
RESPONSIBILITY
Doesn't neglect duties and responsibilities
Is persistent in finishing tasks
Carries his share of the "load"
Is prompt in performing tasks
Actively seeks tasks involving responsibilities
Is industrious
SOCIAL EFFICIENCY
Works and plays well with others
Is cooperative
Practices good manners
Is patient, tolerant, tactful
Is friendly and good natured
Is well liked by peers
Is socially mature
VOICE AND DICTION
Has good voice quality
Enunciates properly
Uses good diction
Uses correct grammar
Has a good vocabulary
Pronounces words correctly

Duplicate the circlegram and plot a rating for each characteristic. Connect the dots and compare the results to the perfect circle. Another learning experience is to receive ratings from a family member or close friend. Compare these two ratings and discuss any distinct differences. What are the implications for these ratings to:

1. Professional preparation in physical education?
2. Membership in professional organizations?
3. Academic achievement?
4. Job placement?

A person's abilities, interests, and needs can be greatly influenced by values and characteristics. A case in point is the reasoning used in scheduling classes each term (quarter or semester). Indications of these influences may become evident in planning a four-year schedule of courses. Complete this learning experience by obtaining a sequenced program of study from the physical education department. In most programs, there is a designation of prerequisite courses, average credit load, and educational year (freshman, sophomore, junior, or senior) when these courses should be taken.

Develop a four-year schedule of courses that includes the term the course is offered and prerequisite courses. The community college student needs to first identify the four-year institution for transfer and obtain a program from that institution. Duplicate the "Four-Year Course Schedule" illustrated in Figure 4.3, adjust for quarters. Be certain to list all courses needed for graduation, including courses for specialization.

Accompany this four-year course schedule with a list of extracurricular activities identified for participation. Refer to the extracurricular activities mentioned in Chapter 1, pages 10 and 11. Select the school term for participating in these activities. By keeping a detailed record of participation (activity, dates and hours) in these activities, one has a valuable document of experiences that can be used for job placement.

PREPARING

In the preparing stage, learning experiences are provided for: (1) defining and determining the purpose of professional preparation courses, (2) recognizing professional leaders and organizations, (3) participation in research, and (4) developing communications skills.

The title and credit hours for professional preparation courses are usually listed on the program of study. One could also refer to the four-year course schedule completed as a learning experience. Included among this list of courses are: kinesiology, anatomy, physiology, biomechanics, motor learning, tests and measurements, history, philosophy, curriculum and instruction, or administration.

In preparing to teach physical education, one should know *why* these are required courses. Select three courses and investigate each to determine the definition and purpose of the course. This information should be obtained from the college catalogue, professional literature (books and periodicals), faculty who teach the course, and students who have completed the course.

In physical education, one should be knowledgeable about people who have served the profession in leadership roles. Among the various professional organizations, the largest is the American Alliance for Health, Physical Education and Recreation. This organization was started as the American Association for the Advancement of Physical Education in 1885. Since that time, it has changed names several times until it was recognized as the American Alliance for

	1977–1978	1978–1979	1979–1980	1980–1981
Fall	Course _____ Cr. hrs _____ Total cr. hrs _____	Course _____ Cr. hrs _____ Total cr. hrs _____	Course _____ Cr. hrs _____ Total cr. hrs _____	Course _____ Cr. hrs _____ Total cr. hrs _____
Spring	Course _____ Cr. hrs _____ Total cr. hrs _____	Course _____ Cr. hrs _____ Total cr. hrs _____	Course _____ Cr. hrs _____ Total cr. hrs _____	Course _____ Cr. hrs _____ Total cr. hrs _____

FIGURE 4.3 Four-Year Course Schedule

Health, Physical Education and Recreation in 1974.

During the past 90 years, hundreds of professionals in leadership roles have contributed to the function of this organization. However, for purposes of this learning experience, the national presidents have been selected as professional leaders. The name of the organization, national president (asterisks indicate deceased), and term of office include:[5]

American Association for the Advancement
of Physical Education
1885-1903

*Edward Hitchcock	1885-1887
*William Blaikie	1887-1890
*Dudley A. Sargent	1890-1891, 1892-1894, 1899-1901
*Edward M. Hartwell	1891-1892, 1895-1899
*Jay W. Seaver	1894-1895
*Watson L. Savage	1901-1903

American Physical Education Association
1903-1937

*Luther H. Gulick	1903-1907
*George L. Meylan	1907-1911
*R. Tait McKenzie	1912-1915
*Ernest H. Arnold	1916
*William H. Burdick	1917-1919
*Dudley B. Reed	1920-1922
*Carl L. Schrader	1923-1925
*Charles W. Savage	1926-1928
*Frederick W. Maroney	1929-1930
Mabel Lee	1931-1932
*Jesse F. Williams	1932-1933
*Mary C. Coleman	1933-1934
Strong Hinman	1934-1935
*Agnes R. Wayman	1935-1936
*William G. Moorhead	1936-1937

[5] American Alliance for Health, Physical Education and Recreation, *AAHPER Convention Program: March 14-18, 1975*, American Alliance for Health, Physical Education and Recreation, Washington, D.C., 1975.

American Association for Health and Physical Education
1937-1938

*Charles H. McCloy 1937-1938

American Association for Health, Physical Education, and Recreation
1938-1974

Neils P. Neilson 1938
*Frederick W. Cozens 1938-1939
*Margaret Bell 1939-1940
*Hiram A. Jones 1940-1941
*Ann Schley Duggan 1941-1942
*Jay B. Nash 1942-1943
*August H. Pritzlaff 1943-1944
*William L. Hughes 1944-1946
Helen Manley 1946-1947
*Vaughn S. Blanchard 1947-1948
Ruth Evans 1948-1949
Carl L. Nordly 1949-1950
*Dorothy S. Ainsworth 1950-1951
*Frank S. Stafford 1951
Bernice R. Moss 1951-1952
Clifford L. Brownell 1952-1954
Ruth Abernathy 1954-1956
*Ray O. Duncan 1956-1958
*Pattric Ruth O'Keefe 1958-1959
*Arthur A. Esslinger 1959-1960
Minnie L. Lynn 1960-1961
*Arthur S. Daniels 1961-1962
Anita Aldrich 1962-1963
Ben W. Miller 1963-1964
Catherine L. Allen 1964-1965
Reuben B. Frost 1965-1966
Leona Holbrook 1966-1967
J. W. Kistler 1967-1968

Mabel Locke 1968-1969
John M. Cooper 1969-1970
Laura Mae Brown 1970-1971
Louis E. Alley 1971-1972
Barbara E. Forker 1972-1973
Willis J. Baughman 1973-1974

American Alliance for Health, Physical Education
and Recreation
1974-1977

Katherine Ley 1974-1975
Roger Wiley 1975-1976
Celeste Ulrich 1976-1977

Complete this learning experience by choosing two professional leaders from the list of national presidents. Then, review the professional literature for biographical information and professional contributions of each.

The American Alliance for Health, Physical Education and Recreation is one of many professional organizations. A student preparing to teach physical education should be knowledgeable about these organizations. In this learning experience, refer to the professional organizations mentioned in Chapter 1. Select one organization and, by reviewing the professional literature, determine the founding, purpose, philosophy, and membership of that organization.

In physical education, the results from scientific research can be used to substantiate the need for people to exercise, to provide better teaching methods, and to improve the efficiency of human movement. Many four-year institutions have a laboratory for conducting research in physical education. In these research projects there is often a need for people to serve as subjects for testing physiological differences in performing identified skills or physical education activities. As a learning experience, one might volunteer to participate as a subject in a research project. This is dependent upon the availability of a research laboratory and permission to serve as a subject.

Communication is a two-way process of sending and receiving information. This is important to the teacher of physical education, who must choose the proper words for communicating movement patterns to students. Communication from teacher-to-student and student-to-teacher is either verbal or nonverbal. Therefore, watching and listening are critical elements in communication.

LEARNING EXPERIENCES IN PHYSICAL EDUCATION   73

Think about the "sound" made when someone attempts to hit a golf ball and misses. Whiff! Or, in basketball, when the participant makes a basket without hitting the rim. Swish! This, too, is communication—listening. A physical educator needs to listen to students speaking and moving.

Two learning experiences are given for practicing communication. In Figure 4.4 are five geometrical figures (square, triangle, rectangle, circle, and parallelogram) and a design composed of three of these figures. Among these five geometrical figures, select three. Use these three figures to compose an original design. Draw this design and do not show it to anyone. Ask someone to assist in this learning experience by drawing the exact same design (without seeing it) from your verbal description. Compare both designs. Was there a problem communicating this design? Why? Think about describing movement patterns to students in physical education. Even a demonstration of movement patterns requires a verbal description.

When describing a movement pattern to a student, that person may be one of 35 students in class. One way to gain that student's attention is to recognize him or her by name. A physical educator may have five classes of 35 students in a class—that equals 175 students and 175 different names.

Learning every student's name, which conceivably could number in the hundreds, is not always possible. However, knowing the student's name does enable the teacher to learn more about the student as an individual. Learning students' names is not a difficult task but does take practice. In this learning experience, try to learn the names of all classmates in just one class. There are several methods for accomplishing this. Use what suits you best. However names are learned by listening.

Try this in one class, listen to everyone's name during roll call, write it phonetically, and include some distinquishing feature about each person. This could be wearing glasses, a beard, or frosted hair. "Guesstimate" how many days it will take to learn everyone's name in just that one class. This process is facilitated with practice and eventually one develops his or her own system for remembering names.

PERFORMING

In the performing stage, learning experiences are provided for selecting a community in which to teach and case studies relevant to students in professional preparation. The decision to teach physical

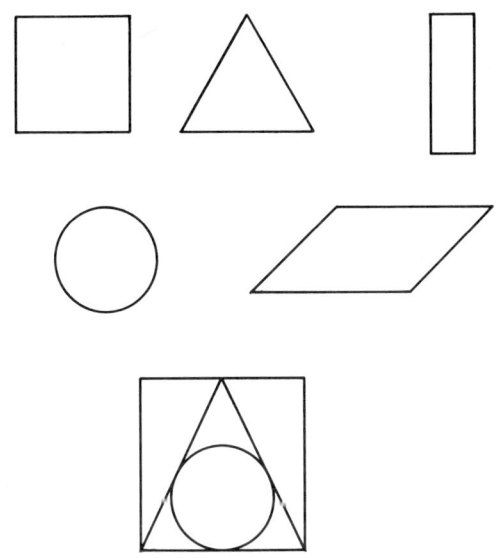

FIGURE 4.4 Communicating a geometrical design.

education in an urban, rural, or suburban community is a difficult task. Pertinent questions should be formulated concerning the community, school, and physical education department.

Information about a community may be obtained from a demographic study. This is an investigation and collection of data about a designated community. Select a community (town or city) and refer to governmental documents on vital statistics and census reports. Determine the population, tax base, and dwellings in the community. In these same documents, there is a record of the average age, family size, income, and occupation of community members. Additional information is acquired by visiting the community, provided that this is in accordance with the policies and procedures in the community college or four-year institution one is attending.

One can learn about a school or physical education department in urban, rural, and suburban communities by visitations. These visitations must be coordinated and conducted by faculty at the community college or four-year institution one is attending. This is necessary because of established policies and procedures regarding visitations and to insure positive relationships with faculty at various schools.

There are two types of visitations. One is a visitation to the institution by a physical educator from a selected school. The second visitation is by a professional preparation student or class to a

LEARNING EXPERIENCES IN PHYSICAL EDUCATION   75

selected school. During this visitation, one should inquire about the school location, facilities, enrollment, purpose, philosophy, organizational structure, faculty, and staff. Questions should also be formulated with regard to teaching salaries, schedules, and fringe benefits. In the physical education department, one can learn about the faculty, program, policies, class size, facilities, equipment, and supplies.

In these case studies, one problem is described. Read each case study, identify the problem, establish the facts and, by reasoning for and against the facts, determine the best solution.

1. Dorothy Star, an enthusiastic, vivacious freshman in physical education, enjoyed being away from home and particpating in college activites. She attended classes regularly, took notes, and studied. However, Dorothy was always late in completing assignments. It puzzled her as to how she could forget the due date for assignments.

Dorothy had one notebook that contained the course outline, assignment deadlines, and class notes for all her courses. One night, she discovered the English assignments were misplaced in the history section. She noticed she had missed two assignments in English. This notebook was so cumbersome that Dorothy really didn't know how to organize the assignment deadlines for all her courses. What are some suggestions?

2. At State University, Jerry Jones is a freshman majoring in physical education. His courses during this first semester are: English composition, basic mathematics, speech, nontackle football, soccer, introduction to physical education, and biology. Jerry became aware of the "cut-system" for classes at State and by midterm had reached the limit. This didn't bother Jerry because he was on the football team and would have no problem getting a 'C' average for the semester.

However, much to Jerry's surprise, he had an 'F' going in biology and introduction to physical education, and it was only one week before final exams. If Jerry doesn't pass these two courses, he will be ineligible for football next year. Could he complete the assignments missed? Should Jerry withdraw (drop) these courses? If Jerry told the football coach would this help? Should Jerry meet with the profs for biology and introduction to physical education? What is the best way to solve this problem?

3. Elbow Bend Community College is a commuter school for an

industrial town with a population of 100,000. Tom Wilson, a Viet Nam veteran and just recently married, was finishing his first year in physical education. However, because Tom works 30 hours a week he has had to schedule courses that were offered between 8:00 A.M. and 12:00 noon.

Tom was planning his schedule for next fall, but there were only two courses he could take; all the others conflicted in time. Three courses that Tom needs are offered in the afternoon when he works. If Tom doesn't schedule more than two courses for next fall, he will not receive funding from the Veteran's grant. This lighter load also means that Tom will need to remain at Elbow Bend at least another year and a half. Can Tom work, attend school, receive funding, and finish in one year? If so, how?

4. Darci Durango is a sophomore in physical education and plays forward on the women's basketball team at a small four-year college. One day, Darci would like to coach basketball and teach physical education at the secondary level.

During the first year, Darci had average grades with the exception of a 'D' in Biology. This semester Darci has anatomy and, at midterm, is getting an 'F'. Darci has always been weak in the science area and knows she will eventually take physiology and kinesiology. One of the most important goals for Darci is to teach physical education, but unless she does better in the sciences this may not be accomplished.

Darci has attended every class in anatomy, but continually receives 'F's on her assignments and examinations. She reads the text and takes notes, but somehow she gets the biceps, triceps, and the like confused! Since it is only midterm, Darci has time to improve her grade. How can Darci really learn about anatomy and raise her grade?

SELECTED REFERENCES

Clipson, William F., "Early Field Experiences as Teachers," *Journal of Physical Education and Recreation*, 46:35-36 (March 1975).

Henschen, Keith P., "A New Deal in Professional Preparation," *Journal of Health, Physical Education and Recreation*. 45:65-66 (May 1974).

Owen, R. C., "A Record of Physical Education Major's Participation in

Co-Curricular and Extra Curricular Activities," *The Physical Educator,* **23**:27-28 (March 1971).

Pape, Laurence A., and Louis E. Means, *A Professional Career in Physical Education,* Prentice-Hall, Inc., Englewood Cliffs, NJ, 1962.

section 2
competitive sports

Reprinted by permission of Athletic Department Bowling Green State University, Bowling Green, Ohio.

**5
facilities
6
recreational sports
7
interscholastic,
intercollegiate,
and professional sports
8
learning experiences
in competitive sports**

chapter 5

facilities

Don't be famous for building the last of the old; be famous for building the first of the new.[1]

Dick Theibert

The existence of adequate facilities is of vital importance in the conduct of physical education, recreational, and athletic programs at every educational level. Richard A. Cutting, a Cleveland, Ohio architect, states that facilities are not designed for use by college presidents, treasurers, athletic directors, or coaches. The ultimate judges of our competence and success are today's young men and women, young people who can accept making round trips to the moon, going to Paris for lunch and returning the same day, or even creating life in a test tube without so much as raising an eyebrow.[2]

Facilities management is one of the most important tasks faced by the physical educator or coach. Few schools, regardless of their location and educational level, have completely adequate facilities to conduct a broad program of instruction, recreation, and competitive sports, particularly those of an indoor nature. This lack of facilities, coupled with new federal legislation

[1] Dick Theibert, "New Developments in Facilities," *Proceedings of the Fifth National Convention of the National Association of Collegiate Directors of Athletics,* Michael J. Cleary (ed.), Michael J. Cleary Publishers, 4940 Viking Drive, Minneapolis, 1970, p. 18.

[2] Richard A. Cutting, "New Concepts in Modernizing Athletic Facilities," *Proceedings of the Third Annual Conference of the National Association of Collegiate Directors of Athletics,* Cleveland, June 24-26, 1968, p. 115.

(Title IX) requiring equal opportunities for participation for both men and women, and requests from outside agencies to use school buildings, has resulted in a completely different approach to the planning and construction of fields, gymnasiums, arenas, and the like. Some of the newer theories in the design of buildings, type of playing surfaces, and utilization are presented here. Research is continuing at many levels to improve the quality and utilization potential of activity areas, and many colleges and universities are now offering undergraduate courses to their physical education students in this subject. At the University of Illinois at Chicago Circle, members of the physical education faculty and students majoring in physical education serve regularly on juries with the College of Architecture faculty to review architectural drawings, blueprints, and models of new facilities prepared by architecture students.

PLANNING and CONSTRUCTION

Marvin Gans lists sequential steps essential in the planning and constructing of facilities.[3] They are: organizing to plan, the architect, conceiving the facility, specifying the facility, the project calendar and construction of the facility.

Although the architect is considered to be the key figure in planning, health, physical education, recreation, and athletic personnel should have an important role in terms of organizing to plan. Throughout the planning process, there should be student involvement, since they are to be the primary users of any type of facility. Many schools have included students in the group to visit other campus installations during the initial planning phase. Every planning group should realize the need for additional facility development and interpret their facility development needs to the institutional administration and the governing board. Many groups and individuals have roles to play in facility planning.

Those persons responsible for selecting the architect should establish the criteria for that selection and investigate his capabilities before the final decision is reached.

The conceptualization of any type of indoor facility in terms of space and facility requirements should include a projection of student enrollment, activities to be included in the physical education program, maximum number of students in each class section, number

---

[3]Marvin Gans, *Sequential Steps in Planning Facilities for Health, Physical Education, Recreation and Athletics,*, Unpublished doctoral dissertation, University of Utah, 1972, p. 7.

of class sections daily in each activity, specific sports to be included in the recreational and intercollegiate/interscholastic program, multiple use of facilties for both sexes, and a consideration of the special problems of planning facilities for nonsports events.

Gans' sequential steps with regard to specifying the facility are extremely important.[4] This check list should include:

1. The development of a comprehensive program statement.
2. A complete description of the educational program, which includes the policies and procedures relative to scheduling, operation, and use of the facility.
3. The development of educational specifications through:
   a. A writing of highly detailed qualitative and quantitative requirements for each area of the facility.
   b. Noting the interrelationships of specific areas within the facility.
   c. Including the type, kind, and size of fixed and movable equipment to be utilized.
   d. Official approval of the educational program and specifications.
   e. Interpretation of the educational program and specifications to the architect.

Gans' Facility Development Check List could be useful as a guide for those involved in planning or constructing facilities.[5]

Design

Both architects and users of athletic facilities agree that the most efficient layout for a building or complex of buildings has not yet been found. The same statement could be made in terms of finding the one most economical system of construction for wide-span structures or the one ideal playing surface. New ideas, new methods, and new materials are being developed every day. If facilities are to be designed for the future, the basic standards of measurement should encompass the metric system. Thus the design for a new track, or pool or field house should be in terms of meters as well as feet and inches.

[4]Ibid, p. 71.

[5]Ibid, pp. 114-130.

Daniel L. Dworsky, a Los Angeles architect, believes that we must prepare ourselves for a more complex environment of the future.[6] The major change that we are experiencing today is the acceleration of change itself. This applies to the problems related to the planning of freeways and transportation systems as well as increased participation in recreational and athletic activities by both men and women. He lists three sets of guidelines that should be followed in the design of new facilities: (1) we should attempt to project the rate of expanding needs and then incorporate within the design, the capability of expansion, as well as flexibility for conversion to other uses, (2) we should correlate the specific project under consideration with other structures in the immediate area so that facilities can be mutually shared rather than producing wasteful duplication, and (3) we cannot afford to build self-serving architectural monuments. Our buildings must be monuments to function and flexibility. They must serve the present needs while anticipating their own obsolescence.[7]

The ideal master plan of an indoor facility should contain six principal units.[8] These units are the core, the gymnasium, the natatorium, the ice rink, the basketball arena, and the field house. The core should include the "back-up" facilities (i.e., lockers, wrestling rooms, squash and handball courts, fencing and dancing rooms, visual-education rooms, offices, library, clubrooms, TV and radio studios, alumni offices). Another unit—the infirmary—could also be included in this same core. Each of the seven units should be designed for possible future expansion at the most minimal expense, or the facilities should be designed at the beginning to accommodate maximum expected use. The main entrance should be through the core, and its size directly related to the population of the school. It should be arranged in such a way that the general public, students and faculty, and alumni may enter the central complex in a central location, obtain their tickets or equipment, and proceed to their activities without having to pass through any other activity space, whether they are contestants or spectators. Every activity should be visible from some part of the core.[9]

[6]Daniel L. Dworsky, "Planning and Construction of Athletic Facilities," *Proceedings of the Second Annual Convention of the National Association of Collegiate Directors of Athletics*, Minneapolis, June 20-22, 1967, p. 127.

[7]Ibid., pp. 129-130.

[8]Richard A. Cutting, *Proceedings of a Study in Planning for Gymnasium—Field House Construction*, NACDA, New York, May 18-19, 1967, p. 12.

[9]Ibid., p. 12.

Many physical education teachers or coaches may not be fortunate enough to have the type of facility referred to above. They may be teaching in an inner-city area that has limited facilities. Their ability to cope with this problem depends greatly on their ingenuity and ability to organize facilities for maximum use.[10] A facility could be divided into mini-teaching stations if classes are large. In this way, the larger groups could be divided into smaller, more manageable groups. It is particularly important to analyze facilities in terms of site location, design, cost, and future use. In almost every inner-city situation, multiple use of the facility is required in addition to physical education, athletics, and recreation, and for vocational and administrative needs. Consideration should also be given to the needs of nonschool youth, adults, and the elderly.

Sullivan and Weatherill pose several questions that should be answered by those responsible for gymnasium design and construction.[11] What activities will be conducted in the building? How large will the physical education classes be now, and in the future? Where will the heavy traffic areas be? How much money will be available? Where should the building be located?

Theibert has initiated much of the research done on building design. He contends that building design should be done in such a way that every dollar purchases maximum space for the total program. This demands flexibility, new products, and new concepts.[12]

Playing Surfaces

Considerable research has been conducted on indoor and outdoor playing surfaces. The Educational Facilities Laboratory in New York City, along with industry, has been instrumental in introducing artificial playing surfaces, which has increased usage at least tenfold. However, longitudinal studies have been conducted that might provide answers to such questions as safety, longevity, toughness, and maintenance. Research is also underway on plastic ice, artificial dirt, hydraulic seating, air structures, and artificial ski slopes. Within the next 10 years, many of these products will be in use in our athletic

---

[10] Leonard M. Ridini and John E. Madden, *Physical Education for Inner City Schools*, New York, Harper & Row, 1973, p. 174.

[11] James V. Sullivan and Robert A. Weatherill, "Gym Design and Construction," *Scholastic Coach*, 37:7 (January 1968).

[12] Dick Theibert, "The Possible Dreams," *Scholastic Coach*, 37:10-11, and 71-73 (January 1968).

plants throughout the world. It is conceivable that such surfaces as wood, grass, snow, dirt, and ice are approaching obsolescence.

Industry is currently working on a plastic ice—not refrigerated—on which one can skate or participate in any other recreational pursuit. In the case of refrigerated ice, a hydraulic floor may be used to cover the ice. This could conceivably be done in 15 to 20 minutes, which would allow you to go from ice to basketball and thus get two spectators for each chair. In this way the multiple-use concept could be achieved, which would permit use for spectator and recreational sports, teaching stations, convocations, commencements, and community meetings.

Much use has also been made of an air bubble to cover an outdoor area. This arrangement can serve many users (i.e., tennis courts, ice rinks, track and field, etc.). The University of Pennsylvania has used it to give it the country's first track and field bubble.

Synthetic (artificial) grass and smooth (ground) surfaces are used extensively in all parts of the United States and abroad. The former material is ordinarily used outdoors, and the latter may be used both outdoors and indoors.

Artificial grass is a form of turf with individual blades protruding from a resilient base. It has many significant advantages; it dries quickly, maintains its even texture, wears like iron, will take cleated shoes; spots showing wear can be patched without being discernable, can be cleaned (brushed, vacuumed, or washed); adverse weather does not affect the life of the product, and may be used both outdoors and indoors. Much research needs to be done, however, to solve the serious questions regarding the safety of this product. Some professionals, as well as amateur athletes, are raising serious questions after being exposed to both natural and artificial turf.

Some recent research done on artificial grass renews some concern about heat injury because it creates a warm playing environment.[13] A summary of these research findings indicates that:

1. Body heat stress on hot days is higher on artificial turf as compared to natural turf.

2. The additional heat is gained by the player on artificial turf in three ways:
   a. Radiation from the artificial turf.
   b. Increase in air temperature.
   c. Conduction through soles of the shoes.

[13]Ellsworth Buskirk, J. L. Loomis, and E. R. McLaughlin, NACDA, *Microclemente Over Artificial Turf*, Cleveland, Spring, 1971, pp. 22-24.

Guidelines for conditioning, practice, and competition on artificial turf in order to avoid heat injury should take into account the potential for added heat stress.

One of the newest materials being used for football fields is called Prescription Athletic Turf (PAT).[14] The PAT system utilizes natural grass but solves the drainage problem associated with natural grass fields. This is accomplished by the installation of drainage lines 16 to 18 inches below the surface of the field and suction pumps to remove the water off the field. The cost is about $2.00 per square foot—one half less than artificial turf. Installations have been made in Goshen, Indiana; Grand Rapids, Michigan; and Lafayette, Indiana.

Location

The locations of outdoor physical education, recreational, and athletic facilities in relation to the academic area is extremely important from the standpoint of utilization. They should be accessible to those who use them most frequently, away from industrial buildings, and arranged so that effective supervision is possible with a minimum of cost and effort. Fields of competition should be located to provide a minimum of interference with the instructional program. Both instructional and competitive fields should be located to make effective exclusion of authorized persons from all activity areas as certain as possible. Playing areas should also be located to allow for future expansion.

Minimum standards for the size of land space for play areas varies with the type of school. Elementary schools in an urban area require 10 acres or more (a regulation football field is approximately four-fifths of an acre). A single school in a rural area should have 5 acres. A consolidated school in a rural area requires 10 acres. A combination junior high school and community center needs 25 acres with 40 acres required for a senior high school and community center combination. The amount of space for playing fields at colleges and universities often depends on location—urban or rural. In some highly concentrated population areas rooftops have been used to double the usable space.

Utilization

Most athletic programs are conducted in a physical education facility grouped into administrative units, service units, and instructional and

[14]Melvin J. Rabey, PAT: "Real Grass for Athletic Field," *Journal of Physical Education and Recreation*, 46:27-28 (January 1975).

FACILITIES 89

recreational areas. In determining the anticipated use of facilities, they should be planned for:[15]

1. Joint use by both boys and girls, men and women. New federal guidelines imposed by the Department of Health, Education and Welfare make it mandatory that equal facilities be provided for men and women in all public institutions receiving federal money of any kind.
2. Multiple use within limits of the principal function of the facility. The increasing cost of facilities forces institutions to plan for their multiple use, if they are to have facilities at all. The term *multiple use* means intelligent and appropriate use.
3. Local geographical and climatic conditions, so that opportunities are available for participation in both indoor and outdoor activities throughout the year.
4. Possible future expansion as participants in the extracurricular and intramural programs increase.
5. Community use when it does not interfere with the intended uses by the school or college, when there are ample funds for maintenance, repair, and supervision, and when such community use is necessary. In the case of athletic fields, it should be noted that they cannot be used continuously and be maintained in suitable condition for the best player safety and performance.
6. Health service facilities in or near the gymnasium and athletic fields to provide emergency care and other prescribed services maintained by the institution.
7. Flexibility, so that modifications within the facilities can be made without changing the overall construction.
8. Ease of movement of users from one facility to another, where functions are related. Gymnasiums, swimming pools, and other activity areas should be within easy reach of the locker, shower and dressing rooms, toilet facilities, and other service areas. Indoor dressing facilities should be readily accessible from outdoor areas without necessitating student traffic through other portions of the building.

In most cases the physical education, recreational, and athletic programs use the same facilities. It is common for the athletic program to be conducted during the 4:00 to 6:00 P.M. period, which

[15] Glenn W. Howard and Edward Masonbrick, *Administration of Physical Education*, New York, Harper & Row, 1963, p. 279.

FIGURE 5.1 College physical education facility. Reprinted by permission of University of Illinois at Chicago Circle, Chicago.

may require the recreational activities to be scheduled over a greater number of hours during the day and in the evening. Programs for both men and women are mandatory because of recent federal legislation, which necessitates the equal sharing of all facilities. When two or more programs use the same facilities, one person should be assigned the responsibility for coordinating the scheduling of events (see Figure 5.1).

Facilities for physical education, recreation, and athletic programs represent about 15 percent of all money spent for school buildings. The magnitude of such investments reveals the values assigned to these programs by the American people.[16]

SELECTED REFERENCES

American Association for Health, Physical Education and Recreation, *Planning Facilities for Athletics, Physical Education and Recreation*, Washington, D.C., 1974.

American Council on Education, *College and University Facilities: Expectations of Space and Maintenance Needs for Fall, 1974*, Washington, D.C., 1974.

[16]Chalmer G. Hixson, *The Administration of Interscholastic Athletics*, New York, J. Lowell Pratt and Company, 1967, p. 90.

Appenzeller, Herb, *Athletics and The Law*, Charlottesville, VA, The Michie Company, 1975.

Bischoff, David C., "Designed For Participation," *Journal of Health, Physical Education and Recreation*, **37**:29-31 and 62 (March 1966).

Bronzan, Robert T., "Game Plans For Getting The Facilities You Need," *Proceedings of The Twenty-Third Annual Conference of The National Intramural Association*, Champaign, IL, April 14-17, 1972, p. 9-17.

Coates, Edward, "Modular Design For Activity Spaces in the Physical Education-Intramural Complex," *Journal of Health, and Physical Education*, **45**:30-32 (January 1975).

Coleman, A. Eugene, "New Texas Size Facilities," *Journal of Physical Education and Recreation*, **45**:28 (January 1975).

Cutting, Richard A., "New Concepts In Modernizing Athletic Facilities," *Proceedings of The Third Annual Conference of The National Association of Collegiate Directors of Athletics*, Cleveland, June 24-26, 1968, p. 115-125.

Droscher, Ken, "Implementation and Utilization of Intramural Facilities," *Proceedings of The Twenty-Third Annual Conference of the National Intramural Association*, United States, NIA, April 14-17, 1972, p. 17-19.

Dworsky, Daniel L., "Planning and Construction of Athletic Facilities," *Proceedings of the Second Annual Convention of The National Association of Collegiate Directors of Athletics*, Minneapolis, June 20-22, 1967, p. 127-132.

Flynn, Richard B., "Sequential Planning of Facilities On A Landlocked Campus," *Journal of Physical Education and Recreation*, **45**: 23-24 (January 1975).

Gabrielson, M. Alexander (ed.), *Swimming Pools: A Guide To Their Planning, Design and Operations*, Fort Lauderdale, Hoffman Productions, Inc., 1972.

Gallon, Arthur J., *Coaching: Ideas and Ideals*, Boston, Houghton, Mifflin Co., 1974.

Gans, Marvin, *Sequential Steps In Planning Facilities For Health, Physical Education, Recreation, and Athletics*, Unpublished doctoral dissertation, University of Utah, 1972, p. 150.

Gores, Harold B., "New Trends In Athletic Facilities," *Secondary School Administration*, Washington, D.C., American Association for Health, Physical Education, and Recreation, January 1969.

Gray, Richard L., "An Architect Plans An Intramural Physical Education," *Proceedings of The Nineteenth Annual Conference of The National Intramural Association,* Dubuque, IA, Wm. C. Brown Book Co., 1965, p. 101-108.

Hanson, Robert F., "Playgrounds Designed For Adventure," *Journal of Health, Physical Education and Recreation,* **44**:34-36 (May 1969).

Hixson, Chalmer G., *The Administration of Interscholastic Athletics,* New York, J. Lowell Pratt and Co., 1967.

Holmes, Patti, "Liability: Prevention Practices Concerning Facilities and Equipment," *Proceedings of the Twenty-Sixth Annual Conference of The National Intramural Recreational Association* United States, NIA, April 23-27, 1975, p. 82-84.

Howard, Glenn, W., and Eugene Masonbrick, *Administration of Physical Education,* New York, Harper & Row, 1963.

Jensen, Clayne, "An Activity Center For Both Athletic Events and Cultural Events," *Journal of Physical Education and Recreation,* **45**:28-29 (April 1975).

Karabetos, John, "Facilities For The Seventies," *The Physical Educator,* **27**:171-172 (December 1970).

Keller, Roy J., "Making The Most of Your Old Facilities," *Journal of Health, Physical Education and Recreation,* **42**:26-28 (June 1971).

Kelsey, F. Lamar, "Sports Facilities: The New Breed," *Phi Delta Kappan,* **26**:1 (January 1975).

Kleindienst, Viola and Arthur Weston, *Intramural and Recreation Programs For Schools and Colleges,* New York, Appleton-Century-Crofts, 1964.

McAvaddy, Jim, "Facility Considerations for Handicapped Intramural Participant," *Proceedings of The Twenty-Sixth Annual Conference of The National Intramural Association,* United States, NIA, March 24-27, 1973, p. 5-10.

Meyer, John T., "The Conception and Conducting of An Intramural Facilities Survey at Iowa State University," *Proceedings of The National Intramural Association,* United States, by NIA, April 5-8, 1974, p. 133-138.

Mittelstaedt, Jr., Arthur H., "Planning School Grounds," *Journal of Health, Physical Education and Recreation,* **42**:37-40 (January 1969).

Mueller, C. E., "Facilities and Equipment," *Proceedings of the Nineteenth Annual Conference of the National Intramural Asso-*

ciation, Dubuque, IA, Wm. C. Brown Company, 1968, p. 13-16.

Olson, Gareth, R., "Creative Guidelines For Using Multiple Sports Facilities," *Journal of Physical Education and Recreation,* **45**:33-34 (January 1975).

Peterson, James A., "Trends In The Process for Planning Financing Intramural-Physical Education Buildings," *Proceedings of the Seventy-Fifth Annual Conference of The National College Physical Education Association for Men,* C. E. Mueller (ed.), 134-139, University of Minnesota, Minneapolis, 1972.

Pollock, Bernard, "How Not To Build A New Physical Education/Recreation Complex," *Proceedings, of The Twenty-Fourth Annual Conference of the National Intramural Association,* University of South Florida, Tampa, March 24-27, 1973, p. 15-18.

Puckett, John, "Two Promising Innovations In Physical Education Facilities," *Journal of Health, Physical Education and Recreation,* **43**:40-41 (January 1975).

Robey, Melvin J., "PAT: Real Grass For Athletic Fields," *Journal of Physical Education and Recreation,* **45**:27-28 (January 1975).

Schaake, Larry D., "Forms Follow Function: An Overview of the Recreation Facilities Building at Southern Illinois University of Carbondale," *Proceedings of The Twenty-Fourth Annual Conference of the National Intramural Association,* United States, NIA, March 24-27, 1973, p. 10-15.

Sheriff, Al, "Training Student Leaders," *Proceedings of The Nineteenth Annual Conference of the National Intramural Association,* Dubuque, IA, Wm. C. Brown Publishing Company, 1965, p. 61-63.

Stevenson, Michael J., "The Effects of Artificial and Natural Turf On Injuries, Player Opinion, and Selected Game and Team Variables in College Intramural Touch Football," *Proceedings of the Twenty-Fourth Annual Conference of The National Intramural Association,* United States, NIA, March 24-27, 1963, p. 178-187.

Theibert, Richard, "Educational Facilities Laboratories Concepts," *Proceedings of The Seventy-First Annual Meeting of The National College Physical Education Association for Men,* C.E. Mueller (ed.), 153-158, University of Minnesota, Minneapolis, January 10-13, 1968.

Theibert, Richard, "Innovations in Athletic Facilities," *Proceedings of The Seventy-Third Annual Meeting of The National College Physical Education Association for Men,* C. E. Mueller (ed.), 188-191, University of Minnesota, Minneapolis, 1970.

Theibert, Richard, "New Concepts In Facilities," *Proceedings of The Twenty-Second Annual Conference of The National Intramural Association,* United States, NIA April 18-21, 1971, p. 10-17.

Twitchell, Albert W., (ed.), *Proceedings of A Study In Planning for Gymnasium-Field House Construction,* National Association of Collegiate Directors of Athletics, New York, 1967, p. 111.

Wasson, William N., "A New Recreation Building," *Proceedings of the Twentieth Annual Meeting of The National Recreation Association,* Dubuque, IA, Kendall Publishing Company, March 23-26, 1969, p. 160-162.

Williams, Henry C., "Innovations In Outdoor Field Lighting," *Proceedings of The Twenty-Fourth Annual Conference of The National Intramural Association,* University of Southern Florida, Tampa, March 24-27, 1973, p. 18-39.

chapter 6

recreational sports

RECREATIONAL SPORTS

"The growth of popular intramural and recreational sports in the United States has emerged like a river with its course adapting itself to the nature of the country through which it flows, the mainstream continually augmented by tributaries and the very river itself ever growing both deeper and broader."[1] The above statement made at the twenty-fourth annual conference of the National Intramural Association clearly illustrates the prevailing attitude in today's society toward sport participation and physical activity. The term recreational sports has been chosen to replace the more traditional term—intramural sports—for several reasons. The authors believe the latter term is limiting in scope, represents only structured competition, and is not representative of the basic philosophy, attitudes, and responsibilities of professionals in the field.

Recreation emcompasses the formal self-directed programs as well as those "nonsport," leisure-time pursuits. Sports includes all aspects of the traditional men and women's intramural programs, extramural programs, recreational interest and sports clubs, and play days. Proponents of this term argue that it represents all areas of programming, making them identifiable to those less informed in the school or in

[1] Janice L. White, "Women's Intramurals—Past, Present, Future," Proceedings of The Twenty-Fourth Annual Conference of the National Intramural Association. Tampa, Fla, March 24-27, 1973, p. 74.

other social settings. They also contend that it separates them from the past and present and gives them a good start into the future.

History

The historical development of intramural sports programs extends back to the years before World War I. Many intramural departments were formed on college campuses, and they took over the active management of the programs. The years immediately following World Wars I and II brought an increase of interest in recreational type activities because service men had been exposed to them while in military service. Urbanization, effects of industrial change, shortening of the work week, and a universal desire to enjoy recreational activities had much impact on physical education curriculum content. As a result, courses were included that represented these changes.

Programming

Matthews lists three major emphases that have evolved in intramural programming during the last 15 years: (1) scheduling and construction of facilities for informal, self directed activities, (2) development of programs of co-recreation sports activities, and (3) phenomenal interest in and activation of sports clubs.[2]

Individuals responsible for programming of recreational sports at the college level need to consider six basic areas: intramurals, free play or informal, self-directed programs, sports clubs, special events, and extramurals. A brief explanation of these areas is necessary to understand the scope of a comprehensive recreational sports program.

The term intramurals refers to a highly organized competitive sports program for coeducational or corecreational activities. It should be noted that intramural sports are no longer looked on as a man's domain. An overwhelming number of schools currently offer cointramural programming. Along with this has come a trend to consider the cointramural program on an equal basis when scheduling facilities for intramurals. Those persons surveying such programs found greater emphasis on enjoyment and sportsmanship

[2]David O. Matthews, "The New Look in University and College Intramurals," *Proceedings of The Seventy-Third Annual Meeting of the National College Physical Education Association for Men*, C. E. Mueller (ed.), 6, Univerisity of Minnesota, Minneapolis, 1970.

within cointramural programs rather than winning, league standings, or awards. When viewed in the larger perspective of their contribution to the participants, cointramural programs can provide opportunities for social interaction between men and women that is meaningful; they can produce situations for participation in orderly social pressures; and opportunities where men and women can learn to respect differences in interest and abilities. Cointramurals are sweeping away the stereotyped programs, of reliance on awards, and the imposition of programs on participants. They provide more flexible, personalized programs to make enjoyment available to more people in more meaningful ways.

As noted earlier in this chapter, the spirit of free play and the desire to participate are important to intramural programs. It is true, however, that these factors are not enough to insure participation. The intramural program needs something to offer those who are not highly skilled, who do not have the time to practice, or to those who just want to play for fun. Some type of program is needed where the emphasis can be placed on widespread participation and enjoyment, rather than on competition and all university titles. This need may be met by offering corecreational programs, which nationwide surveys reveal are growing faster than any other type of intramural activity. The magnitude of this trend is illustrated by the construction of intramural buildings at three major universities in the midwest within the last two decades. These institutions are Michigan State University, Purdue University, and the University of Illinois-Urbana Champaign. Purdue's building and program is dedicated primarily to corecreational participation and is named the Co-Recreational gymnasium. The University of Illinois at Urbana Champaign occupied an 11 million dollar facility in 1971 with 265,482 gross square feet of space. This building represents the largest corecreation complex of its kind in the world (see Figure 6.1).

A list of some common activities to be included in a corecreational program are: golf, volleyball, basketball, tennis, swimming, field hockey, racquetball, and softball. Teams are made up with an equal number of males and females.

Many recreational sports leaders consider the free play or informal, self-directed program to be *the* most important aspect of the campus recreational sports program. More and more students are taking advantage of opportunities to participate in activities of their own choice and not be bound by the traditional structure of games and tournaments. Facilities should be made available for students with such interests.

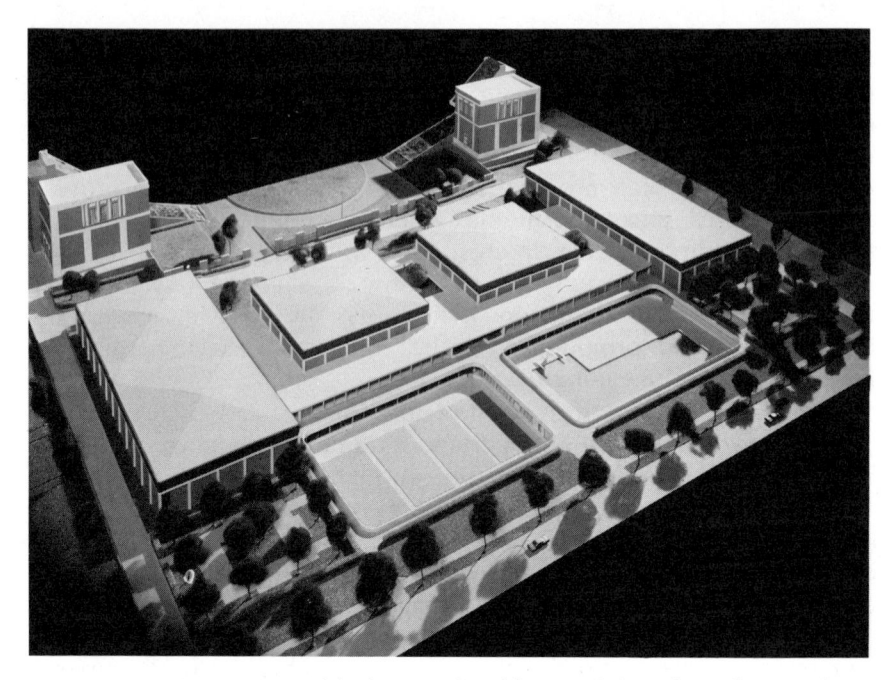

FIGURE 6.1 College intramural facility. Reprinted by permission of David O. Matthews, University of Illinois at Urbana-Champaign, 1976.

Sports clubs began forming on college campuses in the early 1960s and in the 1970s has become a major trend. A sports club may be defined as a group of individuals organized for the purpose of furthering their interest in common sport through participation in intraclub or interclub competition. Such a club may have a recreational-instructional emphasis or a more highly structured, interclub, competition oriented emphasis. Reasons cited for the growth and popularity of sports clubs are the desire for "outside" competition not offered by intramurals, desire of many students to "do their own thing" without being restricted by the sometimes rigid structure of existing intramural programs, students who choose not to participate in intercollegiate athletic programs, and younger people in graduate schools. Some of the characteristics of sports clubs are: (1) they are composed of an extremely captive audience; (2) participants possess an unequaled enthusiasm for their endeavors; (3) each individual is involved for a singular common interest—the particular activity that they are pursuing; (4) they are totally participant oriented; and (5) they are maintained and administered by the student. Sports clubs provide unlimited opportunities for social development. Members are placed in a nonacademic, social atmosphere in which they succeed or fail based on their personality and social attributes. This leads to some tremendous leadership opportunities, and it gives the students an opportunity to test their leadership ability in various situations. Each sport is a sort of mini-society with leadership roles in which everyone takes part in a majority of the decision-making processes. The magnitude of the sports clubs movement is illustrated by a 1969 survey (Jamerson), which revealed that there were 75 different sports with club status on U.S. college campuses.[3] Many of the larger colleges and universities may have as many as 20 different sports clubs, but in all instances there are adequate indoor and outdoor facilities available. Soccer and karate had the greatest popularity with sailing, skiing, judo, fencing, gymnastics, and rugby also on the most popular list. These clubs do pose some problems, however. Many intramural departments are reluctant to provide adequate funding because they are outside the regular structure and administered by students.

Special events comprise another facet of the recreational sports program. One's imagination is the limit, and activities include everything from dances to dog shows on one extreme and kite flying to arm wrestling on the other.

Extramural sports have general reference, in both high school and college, to those sports or programs that take place outside the confines or immediate surroundings of the school. The term extramurals, although sometimes used in its broadest connotation to mean all competition outside of the school, is usually reserved to describe intramural type activities and programs not primarily concerned with the highest level of skilled players and is planned to include competition between two or more schools.

The extramural program is usually an extension of the intramural program, with few or no eligibility requirements and minimal practice periods. The activities are planned as a day of competition between two or more schools without gate receipts and with emphasis on the social aspects as contrasted to a scheduled season of varsity games played before a large spectator audience. The satisfactions are derived from playing one's best with a group of equal ability.

Patterns of Organization and Administration

Although there is much variation in patterns of organization and administration for recreational sports programs in schools, the most

[3]Dick Jamerson, "Pros and Cons of Sports Clubs," *Proceedings of The Seventy-Second Conference of the National College Physical Education Association for Men*, C. E. Mueller (ed.), 48, University of Minnesota, Minneapolis, 1970.

successful have followed the administrative plan of assigning the program to a highly qualified director as his primary responsibility. This plan treats intramurals and recreation as one division of the complete field of health, physical education, and athletics. Figures 6.2 and 6.3 illustrate typical secondary school and university organizational charts.

Concepts and Competencies

The AAHPER published in 1974 a set of concepts and competencies required for professionals to be trained for positions in recreational sports. Curricula designed for personnel entering this area should reflect these standards.[4]

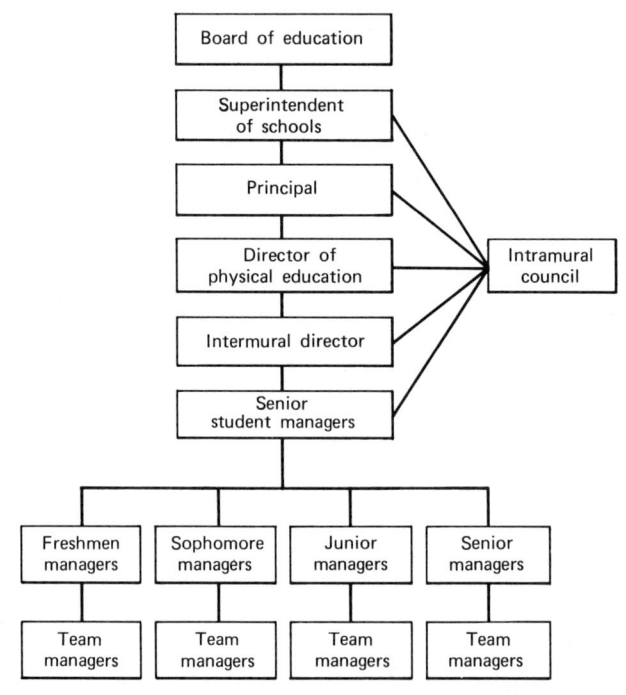

```
                    Board of education
                           |
                    Superintendent
                      of schools
                           |
                       Principal
                           |
                     Director of ───── Intramural
                  physical education      council
                           |
                   Intermural director
                           |
                       Senior
                   student managers
          ┌────────┬────────┬────────┐
      Freshmen  Sophomore  Junior  Senior
      managers  managers  managers managers
         |         |         |        |
       Team      Team      Team     Team
     managers  managers  managers managers
```

FIGURE 6.2 Diagram of the organization and administration of school intramural and recreational sports programs. Reprinted by permission of David O. Matthews, University of Illinois at Urbana Champaign, Champaign, 1976.

[4] American Association for Health, Physical Education, and Recreation, *Professional Preparation In Dance, Physical Education, Recreation, Safety Education and School Education, Health Education*, Washington, D.C., 1974, p. 47.

One of the pressing needs in the area of recreational sports is for trained women's intramural administrators, which will enable men and women to work together. They need to present their own needs and interests on an equal basis and through a trained eye to provide the stability, continuity, and consistency necessary to build a sound quality program, establish tradition, and meet the needs of all students—without emphasis toward physical education majors.

Some refer to the "golden age of intramural sports" being now at hand because of the rapid increase of participants in such programs. This is illustrated by a survey conducted by the National Collegiate Athletic Association in 1974.[5] Of the 663 member institutions surveyed, 1,953,162 men and women engaged in intramural competition in more than 50 different sports. It was shown in this report that participation in intramural activities increased 31.6 percent in the men's category and 67.3 percent in the women's grouping between 1967 and 1972. The 10 most popular intramural sports, in order, for men were: basketball, softball, touch football, volleyball, bowling, track and field, soccer, swimming, tennis, and handball. For the women, in order, they were: volleyball, softball, basketball, swimming, bowling, touch football, badminton, tennis, field hockey, and table tennis. In many schools men and women competed together in intramural activities.

Individual imagination and ingenuity are the only limitations to broad planning and operation of intramurals. A well-planned intramural program will allow students to be a part of the total decision-making process. In this way they can accept responsibility for their successes and failures and become involved in a useful learning experience. In no other area in the broad field of physical education is there more potential for growth and development. Equally important is that intramural programs are looked upon with favor in the eyes of the total community (school administrators, school boards, parents, citizens, and tax payers). It represents an area of great leadership opportunity.

SELECTED REFERENCES

Anderson, Don R., "Intramural Sports In A Changing Society," *Journal of Health, Physical Education and Recreation*, 42:67 (November-December 1971).

[5]The National Collegiate Athletic Association, *The Sports and Recreational Programs of the Nation's University and Colleges, Intramural Sports*, Shawnee Mission, Kans, 1974, pp. 15-17.

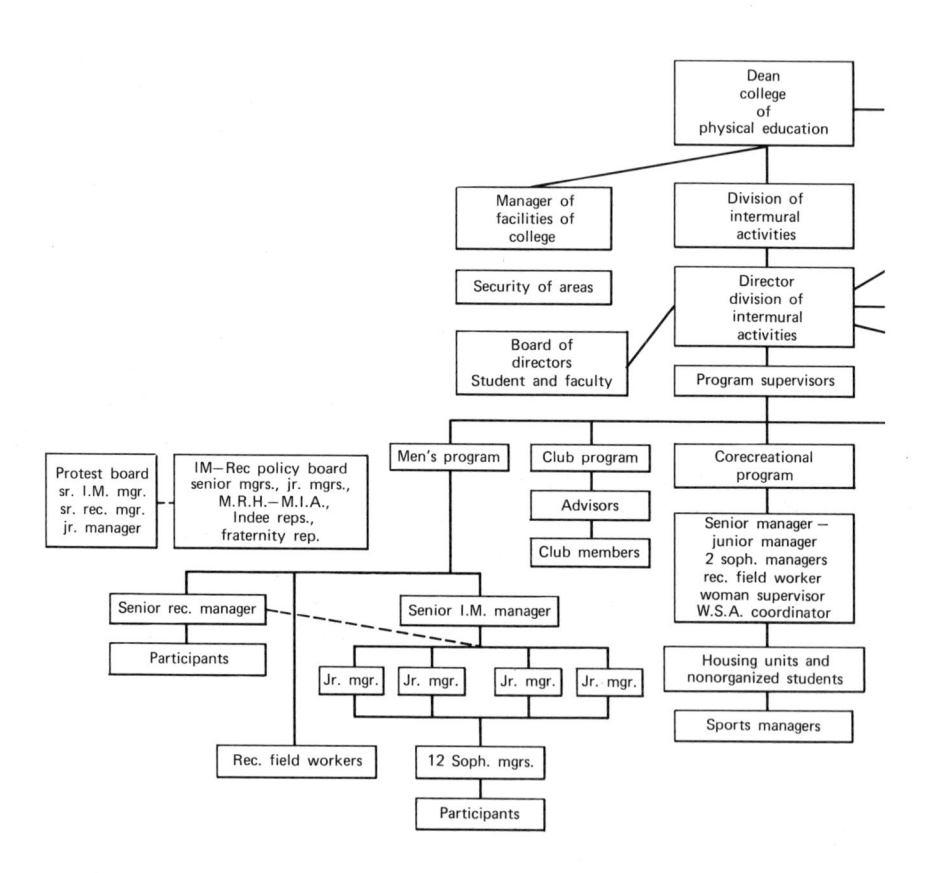

FIGURE 6.3 University of Illinois organizational chart for intramural sports programs. Reprinted by permission of Dr. David Matthews, Director of Intramural Sports, University of Illinois.

104 COMPETITIVE SPORTS

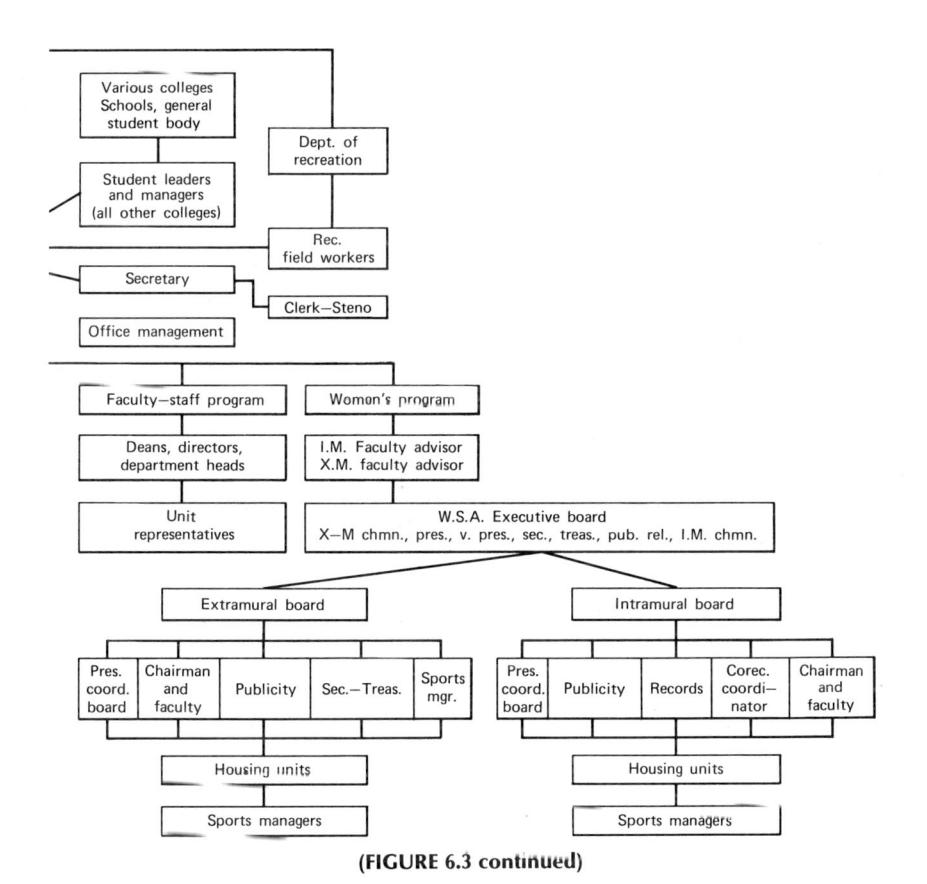

(FIGURE 6.3 continued)

RECREATIONAL SPORTS 105

Athletics In Education, American Association for Health, Physical Education and Recreation, Washington, D.C., 1963.

Barnes, Samuel E., "Sports Clubs," *Journal of Health, Physical Education and Recreation,* 42:23-24 (March 1971).

Berrafato, Peter R., "Community Recreation In The Commuter Institution," *Proceedings of the Twenty-Second Annual Conference of the National Intramural Association,* United States, NIA, April 18-21, Blacksburg, VA pp. 19-21, 1971.

Brumbach, Wayne, "Sports Clubs—Physical Education's New Partner," *Proceedings of the Seventy-Seventh Annual Conference of the National College Physical Education Association for Men,* C. E. Mueller (ed.), 81-87, University of Minnesota, Minneapolis, 1973.

Buck, Charles R., "Coeducational Intramurals," *Proceedings of the Twentieth Annual Conference of The National Intramural Association,* Los Angeles, 1969, pp. 52-56.

Clements, Anthony, "The Black Athlete In Intramurals," *Proceedings, of the Seventy-Seventh Annual Conference of The National College Physical Education Association for Men,* C. E. Mueller (ed.), 44-47, University of Minnesota, Minneapolis, 1973.

Fidler, Merrie A., "Women's Intramurals In Relation To Extramurals: An Historical Viewpoint," *Proceedings of The Twenty-Third Annual Conference of The National Intramural Association,* United States, NIA, 1972, pp. 180-194.

Ford, Judy, "Former Miss America Looks at Intramurals," *Proceedings of The Twenty-Third Annual Conference of The National Intramural Association,* United States, NIA, April 14-17, 1972, pp. 48-50.

George, Kathryn D., "Co-Intramural Sports," *Proceedings of The Twenty-Sixth Annual Conference of The National Intramural Recreational Sports Association,* United States, NIA, April 23-27, 1975, pp. 59-62.

Goehrs, Warren, J., "Recreational Aspects of The Intramural Program," *Proceedings of The Twentieth Annual Conference of The National Intramural Association,* Dubuque, IA, 1968, pp. 51-52.

Gunsten, Paul H., "The Impact of Title IX On Intramural and Extramural Programs," *Proceedings of the Twenty-Fifth Annual Conference of The National Intramural Association,* United States, NIA, April 5-8, 1974, pp. 142-143.

Harding, Carol, "A Women's View of Men's Intramural Sports," *Proceedings of The Twenty-Second Annual Conference of The*

National Intramural Association, United States, NIA, Blacksburg, VA, April 18-21, 1972, pp. 39-41.

Haniford, George W., "Intramural Sports at Purdue University," Proceedings of The Twenty-Third Annual Conference of The National Intramural Association, United States, NIA, April 14-17, 1972, pp. 64-67.

Hass, Walter, "Sports Clubs on Campus," Proceedings, of The Second Annual Conference of The National Association of Collegiate Directors of Athletics, Minneapolis, June 20-22, 1967, pp. 47-52.

Hewatt, Carolyn, "A Women's Viewpoint of Men's Intramurals," Proceedings of The Twenty-Second Annual Conference of The National Intramural Association, Blacksburg, VA, NIA, April 18-21, 1971, pp. 41-45.

Hewatt, Carolyn, "Women's Intramural Athletics," Proceedings of The Seventy-Seventh Annual Conference of The National College Physical Education Association for Men, C. F. Mueller (ed.), 56-58, University of Minnesota, Minneapolis, 1973.

Jamison, H. Toi, "The Organization of Women's Intramural Policy Board and Manager's Program," Proceedings of The Twenty-Fifth Annual Conference of the National Intramural Association, United States, NIA, April 5-8, 1974, pp. 35-37.

Keen, Paul V., "Contributions of Intramurals To the Education Program," Proceedings of The Twentieth Annual Conference of The National Intramural Association, Dubuque, IA, 1968, pp. 53-57.

Kurth, Bert, "Motivation for Participation In Intramurals At A Commuter University," Proceedings of the Twentieth Annual Conference of the National Intramural Association, Dubuque, IA, Kendall-Hunt Publishing Co., March 23-26, 1969, pp. 16-18.

McGuire, R. J., "Imaginative and Innovative Informal Recreation," Proceedings of the Twenty-Sixth Annual Conference of the National Intramural Recreational Sports Association, United States the NIA, April 23-27, 1975, pp. 52-53.

Nasiopulos, James, "A Positive Outlook for Commuting Minorities," Proceedings of the Twenty-Sixth Annual Conference of the National Intramural Recreational Sports Association, United States, NIA, April 23-27, 1975, pp. 87-89.

Oglivie, Bruce, "The Mental Ramblings of a Psychologist Researching in the Area of Sports Motivation," Proceedings of the Twentieth

Annual Conference of the National Intramural Association, Los Angeles, 1969, pp. 173-192.

Pollack, Bernard, "Student Involvement In The College Intramural Program," *Journal of Health, Physical Education and Recreation,* **40**:36-37 (March 1969).

Reznick, John W., "Junior College Intramural Recreational Programs: A Survey and Analysis," *Proceedings of the Twenty-Fourth Annual Conference of the National Intramural Association,* United States, NIA, March 24-27, 1973, pp. 164-170.

Rooker, A. A., "Historical Review of Women In The National Intramural Association," *Proceedings of the Twenty-Third Annual Conference of the National Intramural Association,* United States, NIA, April 14-17, 1972, pp. 82-83.

Sattler, Tom, and Larry Berres, "Important Issues For Commuter College Programs," *Proceedings of the Twenty-Fifth Annual Conference of the National Intramural Association,* United States, NIA, April 5-8, 1974, pp. 129-132.

Varnes, Paul R., Linda Hall, John D. Hester, and Gene Norman, "Innovative and Exemplary Practices for Intramurals," *Proceedings of the Twenty-Third Annual Conference of the National Intramural Association,* United States, NIA, April 14-17, 1972, pp. 83-91.

Weiner, M. Wayne, "High School Intramurals: The Need and Meeting It," *Proceedings of the Twentieth Annual Conference of the National Intramural Association,* Dubuque, IA, Kendall-Hunt Publishing Co., March 23-26, 1969, pp. 156-159.

Wittenauer, Jim, "Professional Preparation," *Proceedings of the Twenty-First Annual Conference of the National Intramural Association,* Macomb, IL, April, 25-28, 1970, pp. 65-68.

Zeigler, Earle F., "Intramurals: Profession, Discipline, or A Part Thereof," *Proceedings of the Seventy-Sixth Annual Conference of the National College Physical Education Association for Men,* C. E. Mueller (ed.), 85-89, University of Minnesota, Minneapolis, 1973.

chapter 7

interscholastic, intercollegiate, and professional sports

Under proper guidelines and leadership athletics can be a powerful force in the development of social and moral qualities as well as physical.[1]
Hally B. Poindexter
Carol Mushier

INTERSCHOLASTIC SPORTS

Middle School

The opportunity to participate in competitive sports extends in many institutions to the junior high school (middle school) level. Despite some differences of opinion among educators regarding the issue of whether athletics are suitable for the middle school student, there appears to be no philosophical debate as to the merits of competition. The debate is concerned with how soon, how much, and what kind. Singer cautions coaches to be aware of great differences in

---

[1] Hally D.W. Poindexter and C.W. Mushier, *Coaching Competitive Team Sports for Girls and Women*, W. B. Sanders Co., Philadelphia, 1973, p. 5.

maturational levels and to be sensitive to the needs, attitudes, and trainability of the participants.[2] Although much research is still needed about the benefits and harms that can result from athletic competition for junior high-school youngsters, it is generally agreed that they are more advanced maturationally, socially, psychologically, physiologically, anatomically, and emotionally than nonathletic counterparts of the same age. Regardless of the level of coaching, the key to a successful program is intelligent supervision based on sound educational principles.

The primary purpose of middle school athletics is to provide an opportunity for every youngster to participate in an activity. The practice of cutting the squad at this level should not be permitted because it is a period of time when the personality of the child is beginning to form. The negative effect of such action at this time, when the young athlete is trying to establish a sense of identity, may carry over into other areas.

Some young, ambitious coaches consider the competitive program in the middle school a tryout for the high school varsity and use the child as a device to enhance their status in the eyes of the head coach at the local high school. Because of the vast differences in maturational levels among adolescents, it is difficult to predict which youngsters will be the star athlete a few years hence in high school or college. The middle school years should be the time to teach skills, provide participatory activities, and create interest.

The major goal in coaching children at this age should be the development of the *person*. This is the time when the fundamentals of participation are in the process of being learned, which is the essential end product of athletic competition.

The anxiety expressed by the child during this period when he or she is on "display" for the first time may be quite pronounced. This anxiety may also be expressed by an overzealous coach or an ambitious parent, which could result in the activity becoming intolerable for the child.

Youngsters of this age need an athletic experience that is rewarding. If this occurs, it is likely that they will continue to participate.

Building a child's confidence is another goal for the coach of the preadolescent. Children at this age do not have a backlog of information about how the sport is to be played, nor previous experience upon which to base their conduct in the sport. The coach

---

[2]Robert N. Singer, *Coaching, Athletics and Psychology*, McGraw-Hill Book Company, New York, 1972, p. 62.

must give encouragement to the athlete until the child is able to build up his or her own confidence through actual participation and knowledge of the sports.

The young athlete who is placed in physical danger (i.e., ice hockey, football, baseball) needs careful supervision and understanding. The stress and anxiety resulting from such experiences must be understood by everyone who has a vital role in the competitive program (coach, parent, school, community).

The ability of the coach to deal with parents of participants in the athletic program at this level is of prime importance. Part of this process is the establishment of rapport with all parents—particularly with those who are overly protective or ambitious. The "pressure" exerted by parents who either want to relive their sport experiences or enhance their egos through their children represents a major challenge to the coach.

Tutko and Richards recommend a set of basic principles necessary for coaching the preadolescent.[3]

1. Be concerned with the person—not the performance.
2. Understand and attempt to meet the needs of the child.
3. Make athletic participation a positive experience.
4. Protect and support the child in situations he is not prepared to handle.
5. Focus on small but meaningful goals, reinforced by rewards.

Administrators and coaches responsible for junior high school athletics should never place program emphasis on competitive sports at the expense of a previously developed instructional and intramural program. When all the ingredients of a sound and diversified program have been provided, there is no reason why a sensible, modified, interschool program cannot be activated and maintained.

In recent years, there has been a rapid growth outside the schools of competitive sport programs organized outside the school by nonschool personnel and dominated by adults who are not trained as teachers. Two examples of such programs are Little League (baseball) and Pop Warner (football).

A large number of successful coaches and professional physical educators believe that many competitive programs that are often conducted are in reality adult recreation programs. Their reasoning behind this statement is that adults make the rules, choose the teams,

[3] Thomas A. Tutko and Jack W. Richards, *Psychology and Coaching*, Boston, Allyn and Bacon, Rockleigh, N.J. p. 62.

direct practice, choose who will play, get most excited over official's decisions, determine when and how long practices will be, get into fights (verbal and physical), choose All-Star teams and organize banquets.

The medical profession has expressed some concern, particularly among orthopedists. Many agree that preadolescent bone growth is more rapid than muscle development, so that temporarily the bones and joints lack the normal protection of covering muscles and supporting tendons. Consistently strong interschool programs will be much easier to attain and maintain if a broad and comprehensive program of class instruction and many intramural sports are provided as a basic and constant opportunity for all students. During this period, a youngster is particularly susceptible to dislocations of joints and bone injuries. Other medical doctors have been concerned over injury to the elbow associated with pitchers in Little League baseball. This usually occurs as a result of youngsters trying to throw hard curve balls. Some psychologists and sociologists have pointed to the emotional ramifications of participation at this level. They conclude that competition alone is not inherently antagonistic to human behavior but if winning becomes all-important to children, serious consequences may result.

A White House Conference on Children has made some statements regarding Little League Sports.

1. Adults should avoid exploiting youth by pressuring them into highly competitive organized activities toward which their minds and bodies are not adapted; they should recognize children as individuals rather than as projects in leisure-time pursuits.
2. Schools and communities should cooperate in designing out of school programs to provide constructive leisure time activities consistent with sound principles of child development, and counteract pressures for competitive athletics promoted by groups with good intentions, but limited knowledge of the physical and social needs of children.
3. Competitive sports for preadolescents should be supervised and trained by qualified leaders and further investigated as to their value for children.

The implications of Little League programs for the local junior and senior high school coach should result in an attempt to provide some sound leadership in order to keep the program and adults involved from exploiting the children who participate.

High School

It has been said that athletics has its greatest flowering at the high school level. In some schools over 60 percent of the boys and more than 30 percent of the girls participate on the athletic teams. The role of interscholastic athletics in education is clearly illustrated by a statement of educational purposes proposed in 1946 by the Educational Policies Commission of the National Education Association. This body listed four purposes as follows:[4]

1. Objectives of self realization or the development of the individual learner.
2. Objectives of human relationships involving the learner with his friends, neighbors, family, and fellow citizens.
3. Objectives of economic efficiency.
4. Objectives of civic responsibility.

The extent of the influence of the athletic program upon students in the high schools has been revealed by Coleman in his analysis of the adolescent society.[5]

Two groups, one at the state and the other at the national level, have been instrumental in improving the control and administration of high school athletics in recent years. They are the State High School Athletic Association and the National Federation of State High School Athletic Associations.

Adolescence is considered by many to be a testing period, and the athletic field can serve as a testing ground for adulthood. Consequently, the role of the coach is of extreme importance because of the need for the child to find a person with whom to identify. His behavior must be such that he can effectively handle those who come under his charge. Tutko and Richards list the following to represent a few of the essential elements of a coach's behavior.[6]

1. *The coach must be a model of what he/she says. There can be no double standard.*

[4] Educational Policies Commission, *Policies In Education In American Democracy*, National Education Association, Washington, D.C., 1946, pp. 193-252.

[5] James Coleman, *The Adolescent Society*, The Free Press, Glencoe, Il., 1961, p. 63.

[6] Thomas A. Tutko and Jack W. Richards, *Psychology and Coaching*, Boston, Allyn and Bacon, Rockleigh, NJ 1971, p. 62.

2. The coach must be willing to listen and consider seriously the needs of each athlete. The athlete is more inclined to respond in a positive manner if he/she realizes that the coach establishes a two-way street of communication.
3. The coach must never attempt to deceive or mislead the athlete. Solicitation of opinions from athletes when solutions to problems appear to be complex will assure them that the decisions can be shared.
4. The coach must be prepared for and willing to accept periods during which the athletes may attempt wild, off-beat, and sometimes blatantly exhibitionistic behavior.
5. The coach is in an excellent position to help the athlete establish a sense of identity with the team.
6. The coach must try to assume the role of a kind, considerate, emphatic father or mother figure rather than lord and master.

There are some distinguishing characteristics that separate the high school youngster from those in junior high school programs. They are easier to train, can concentrate and practice for longer periods of time, and in many cases possess the physical characteristics and motor skills necessary for high levels of athletic proficiency.

INTERCOLLEGIATE SPORTS

The increase in the number of junior or two-year community colleges in America has been significant over the past decade. Although California has been the historical leader in the development of this form of public education, most every state is now establishing these colleges—many in local areas according to population needs.

Facilities and programs in most of these schools are of a high quality, and many athletes go on to four-year colleges and universities to continue their athletic participation. Students who must stay at home because of limited funds are provided with opportunities to participate, which in the past were not available.

Job opportunities in these schools have increased with this expansion, and athletic achievements have risen markedly with national competition being held annually under the auspices of the National Junior College Athletic Association, NJCAA.

These institutions should be regarded as equal educational partners with the elementary schools, junior high schools, high schools, and four-year colleges in the athletic continunum.

College

College athletes find themselves in a much different arena when they arrive on campus because, in most cases, they are there as a result of their athletic ability. They find themselves under a new kind of pressure. One's celebrity status in high school may be replaced by a loss of identity. An early decision needs to be made as to whether they wish to be a potential professional athlete, particularly if they attend an institution that plays a major schedule. The role of the coach, as is the case at every level of competition, must be one of understanding of the pressures that are present. Other concerns may now tend to focus on the athlete's future profession, life goals, and marriage.[7]

Many activities have been added to college athletic programs, and it is not unusual to exceed 15 offerings for men and a similar number for women. The popularity of individual sports has increased dramatically to include such sports as cross-country, golf, swimming, track and field, and tennis. Along with the sports offerings has come higher admission requirements for college athletes. Research in some colleges has indicated that varsity letter award winners maintain a higher grade point average than all students and, furthermore, that the percentage of athletes who graduate is greater.

The task of providing overall guidance and control over college athletics is assumed by the National Collegiate Athletic Association, NCAA (over 650 larger schools) and the National Association of Intercollegiate Athletics, NAIA (more than 400 smaller schools). Some colleges are "independent" in athletics but the majority belong to athletic conferences that may also impose some regulations and control. Another body, the Amateur Athletic Union, AAU, exercises control over both men and women athletes who wish to compete within the United States, under affiliations not school connected, such as sports clubs, or when competing "unattached."

There has been much controversy in recent years between the NCAA and the AAU regarding the jurisdiction over amateur athletes and their selection and approval for international competition. Despite the appointment of an investigating committee at the national level to end this dispute, the controversy has not been settled. Flath has written about this problem in detail.[8] All persons

[7] Robert N. Singer, *Coaching, Athletics and Psychology*, McGraw-Hill Book Company, New York, 1972, p. 62.

[8] Arnold W. Flath, *A History of Relations Between The National Collegiate Athletic Association and The Amateur Union of The United States*, Unpublished doctoral dissertation, University of Illinois at Urbana Champaign, Champaign, Il., 1964, p. 54.

involved in any way with amateur athletics should be knowledgeable about the issues involved and possible solutions that protect the rights of the participant.

The President's Commission on Olympic Sports, appointed by President Ford in 1975, issued its first report in early 1976—a stinging critique of the United States' whole approach to amateur sports. This 22-member commission, which includes four U.S. senators, four congressmen, and 14 public members, noted that nothing less than a "thorough reorganization" of our amateur sports system is required to improve our declining performance in the Olympics, to protect the rights of college and other amateur athletes, and to increase public participation in a wider range of so-called "minor sports." They believe the poor performance of American athletes in comparison with the Soviet Union was not because their athletes were "professionals" but instead that our "minor" sports (other than basketball, football, and baseball) are badly supported. They cannot, without great sacrifice, find the coaching, money, and facilities to continue athletic careers after graduating from educational institutions.

There has been considerable controversy over who should assume control over the women's collegiate athletic program. The Association of Intercollegiate Athletics for Woman was formed in 1973, which functions in a similar manner to the National Collegiate Athletic Association and the National Association of Intercollegiate Athletics. It is readily apparent that coaches of women's teams are now facing many of the problems that men have experienced during their years of growth. These problems include eligibility rules, athletic scholarships, scheduling, and monetary costs. Solutions to some of these problems may be realized by educating administrators about competition for girls, proving quality leadership at all levels, and developing well-defined guidelines, principles, and control of the competitive sports program.

The popularity and growth of intercollegiate athletics for men is illustrated by figures developed by the NCAA in 1972.[9] Thirty-two different sports are offered by 663 NCAA member schools with a total of 172,447 participants. This represents an increase of 11.8 percent since 1966-1967 (see Figure 7.1).

[9]The National Collegiate Athletic Association, *The Sports and Recreational Programs of The Nation's Universities and Colleges*, Shawnee Mission, Kans., 1974, p. 5.

FIGURE 7.1 College ice hockey game. Reprinted by permission of University of Illinois at Chicago Circle, Chicago.

The number of participants in women's athletics doubled between 1966-1967 and 1971-1972 and has almost doubled again during the past four years.[10] (see Figure 7.2).

Individuals concerned in any way with sports or sports-related activities should be familiar with sports governing organizations and other major athletic groups. They are listed below.

1. Amateur Athletic Union of the U.S. Sports: athletics, track and field, basketball, bobsledding, boxing, judo, luge, swimming, water polo, weight lifting.
2. Amateur Bicycle League of America
   Sport: cycling.
3. Amateur Fencers League of America
   Sport: men's and women's fencing.
4. Amateur Hockey Association of the U.S.
   Sport: ice hockey.

[10]Ibid., p. 13.

INTERSCHOLASTIC, INTERCOLLEGIATE, AND PROFESSIONAL SPORTS   117

FIGURE 7.2 Women's softball game. Reprinted by permission of University of Illinois at Chicago Circle, Chicago.

5. Amateur Softabll Association
   Sport: softball.
6. American Canoe Association
   Sport: canoeing.
7. American Horse Shows Association
   Sport: equestrian sports.
8. Field Hockey Association
   Sport: field hockey.
9. National Archery Association
   Sport: archery.
10. National Association for Amateur Oarsmen
    Sport: rowing.
11. National Rifle Association of American
    Sport: rifle, pistol.
12. North American Yacht Racing Union
    Sport: yachting.

13. United States Figure Skating Association
    Sport: figure skating.
14. United States Gymnastic Federation
    Sport: men's and women's gymnastics.
15. United States International Skating Association
    Sport: speed skating.
16. United States Modern Pentathlon and Biathlon Association
    Sport: modern pentathlon and biathlon
        shooting, and cross-country skiing.
17. United States Ski Association
    Sport: alpine and Nordic skiing.
18. United States Soccer Football Association
    Sport: soccer.
19. United States Team Handball Federation
    Sport: team handball.
20. United States Volleyball Association
    sport: men's and women's volleyball.
21. National Association of Intercollegiate Athletics
    (college athletics—smaller schools).
22. National Collegiate Athletic Association
    (over 650 larger college institutions—men).
23. Association for Intercollegiate Athletics for Women
    (over 600 colleges and universities—women).
24. National Federation of State High School Associations.
25. National Junior College Athletic Association.

International organizations promoting sports and physical education are: (1) Council for Cultural Co-Operation of the Council of Europe, (2) International Council on Health, Physical Education and Recreation, (3) Olympic Games Organizations, International Olympic Committee, International Amateur Athletic Federation, United States Olympic Committee, and (4) The International University Sports Federation.[11]

PROFESSIONAL SPORTS

Professional sports has emerged as an integral part of American society over a period of about 50 years. The growth of such sports as

[11] Franklin Parker, "International Organizations Promoting Sports and Physical Education," The Physical Educator, 5:65-66 (May 1971).

basketball, baseball, football, and hockey partly has been due to their appeal to and the receptiveness of the American people. Shea and Wieman say that they are the natural product of a culture that has provided its people with increased leisure and income.[12] These sports, which exhibit an extremely high level of skill by the competitors, offer mass entertainment in exciting spectacles. The rapid expansion of men's professional sport programs has carried over into women's athletics. This was classically illustrated when a women's professional sport superstar competition was scheduled for the first time in 1973 matching the same event begun for men in 1969. Women professionals now compete in almost the same number of sports as men, with prize money in some cases being on an equal level. Federal legislation has made it mandatory for women's programs in physical education and athletics to be funded on a par with men's programs in the same areas. Under this legislation, women are entitled to a fair and equitable share of whatever opportunity a federally assisted educational institution offers. Therefore, no discrimination is allowed in admissions, scholarships, employment, rules and regulations, and physical education. Despite the fact that Title IX will be tested in the courts, its impact will be felt in women's professional sports because more women will be taking part at the interscholastic and intercollegiate levels.

The cultural and recreational life in the United States has been dominated by the commercial medium of television, which has accentuated professional sports in the minds of the American people.

Sport sociologists contend that professional sports have been both an evil and a blessing to society. They have encouraged participation and provided motivation to many youths, regardless of race, color, or national origin. On the negative side, they have made us a nation of spectators. Some maintain, however, that this is not a negative influence. Competition at various educational levels, particularly in college, has been given direction because of the influence of professional sports. Strict rules have been imposed on institutions and conferences, and all-out competition has been encouraged. This type of competition has removed the "fun" factor and is considered by some to be a negative influence. Professional sports provides therapeutic, physical, emotional, and psychological outlets for many people, but often it drains one's energy. Singer says that professional athletics affects the eating, television viewing, reading, and conversa-

---

[12]Edward Shea and Elton F. Wieman, *Administrative Policies For Intercollegiate Athletics*, Charles C. Thomas, Publisher, Springfield, Il., 1967, p. 254.

tional experiences of many people.[13] People at all socioeconomic levels consider it important to know about sports and identify with a team. It is understandable that people, especially those endowed with a high level of motor skills, aspire to be professional athletes because motivation is enhanced by the anticipation of fame and money. It is extremely important that the influences arising from professional sport be kept in proper perspective, especially by young athletes.

Economic Status of Athletes

It is understandable why a career in professional sports would be attractive to aspiring athletes because of the economic status of its participants. Many persons contend that athletes are overpaid.[14] (see Table 1).

Table 1.
Approximate 1975 Earnings of Athletes

SPORT	NO. OF PLAYERS	AVERAGE EARNINGS	TOP MAN	RANGE OF 2nd THROUGH 10th MAN
		($)	($)	($)
Baseball	600	46,000	500,000	250,000-160,000
National Football League	1200	42,000	450,000	300,000-150,000
National Basketball Association	200	107,000	500,000	450,000-350,000
National Hockey League	400	85,000	250,000	250,000-200,000
Golf*	300	76,000	300,000	300,000-130,000
Tennis*	150	40,000	600,000	300,000-160,000
Jockeys**	2600	10,000	450,000	400,000-250,000

*Men only, average for prize money available. Does not include World Team Tennis.
**Taken as 10 percent of total available. Jockeys also get set fees in addition to this share.

"Overpaid" in this context requires definition because it is a loaded word. It can be approached from three totally different directions. One is sociological value judgment: What are the services of the athlete—entertainer—"worth" as a contribution to society?

[13] Robert N. Singer, *Coaching, Athletics and Psychology*, McGraw-Hill Book Co., New York, 1972, p. 177.

[14] Leonard, Kappett, "Are Athletes Overpaid," *The Chicago Tribune*, Chicago, June 20, 1976, p. 3.

Another is strictly economic: How much money is generated by his efforts and what proportion of it is he entitled to retain? The third is comparative: accepting the athlete as an entertainer, how do his or her financial rewards compare with other entertainers? Until television became widespread after World War II, professional athletes were paid primarily from the sale of tickets to spectators, but by 1960 revenue from television networks reached millions of dollars, and athletes demanded a share of this money. Before 1940 the average professional athlete received less than $10,000 per year, and no sport except boxing approached baseball in its ability to generate money. This increased revenue resulted in athletes securing business agents to negotiate their salaries and fringe benefits.

Economic Status of Professional Sports

Despite the increased revenue from increased attendance and the virtual flood of television receipts, profits are lagging. Some experts believe that economic pressures have reached the crisis point, and the multimillion-dollar sports industry is in serious trouble. There are now 105 major league professional teams; baseball (24), football (26), hockey (28), and basketball (27).[15] See Table 2.

Table 2.
A Mixed Profits Picture In Sports

SPORT	NO. OF TEAMS	NO. MAKING MONEY OR BROKE EVEN	NO. LOSING MONEY	GROSS REVENUES	REVENUE FROM TELEVISION ONLY ($)
Baseball	24	12	12	180,000,000	46,000,000
Football	26	24	2	163,000,000	45,000,000
Hockey	28	18	10	90,000,000	11,000,000
Basketball	27	5	22	50,000,000	10,000,000

Table 3.
Professional Sports: Attendance

SPORTS	1968	1973	CHANGE (%)
Baseball	35,300,000	41,300,000	Up 17
Football	8,900,000	15,500,000	Up 74
Hockey	9,100,000	16,000,000	Up 76
Basketball	5,000,000	9,600,000	Up 92

[15]"Upheaval In Pro Sports," U.S. News and World Report, Washington, D. C., August 12, 1974, p. 51.

The interest shown in professional sports by the American people is illustrated below in Table 3.[16]

The player reservation system, which limits competition among teams for players, was placed in jeopardy in 1976 when the professional football players voted to strike against the owners. (Figure 7.3). As a result, the owners negotiated a modification of the reserve system in which a player could become a free agent after eight years in the big leagues. Agreement was reached between the owners and the players to continue negotiations and implement some machinery for controlling the movement of free agents and, in 1976, a merger of the National Basketball Association and the American Basketball Association did occur. This event brought both good and bad news to the players. Pro players, already paid an average of $109,000 per year, would get higher minimums, better insurance and pension benefits, and a cost of living clause. The news for the rookies, however, was bad. They would be deprived of their

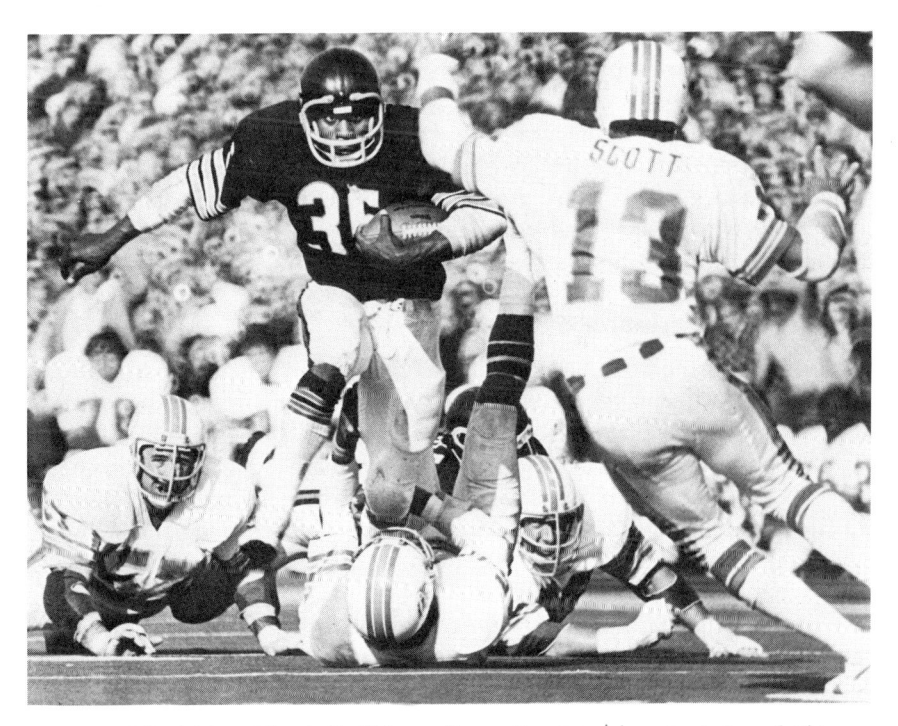

FIGURE 7.3 Professional football, Chicago Bears. Reprinted by permission of Chicago Bears Professional Football Team, Chicago.

[16] Ibid., p. 52.

bargaining power against the rival leagues, which meant that they would lose huge bonus packages.

The Brookings Institution, one of the nation's leading economic think tanks, published a report in 1976 entitled, "Government and the Sports Business," which enraged most professional sports owners.[17] The report contends that professional sports practically eliminates business competition among its members, operates as a cartel, depreciates employees as if they were physical assets, condones a system of indentured servitude, and remains outside much of the government's regulatory process and the Federal Antitrust laws. Brookings recommended that Congress end virtually all of pro sports' restrictive practices, including reserve clauses and exclusive territorial rights for franchises. These changes would (1) compel teams to share broadcast and gate receipts more equitably, thus equalizing the advantages gained by big-city teams over the smaller competitors, (2) delineate objective financial standards that, if met by prospective franchises, would automatically give them a franchise in the city of their choice, and (3) set a payroll limit in the newly competitive atmosphere to prevent one well-healed team from buying up all the best talent. Players would be allowed to bargain freely. The report further states that open contract bargaining between players and management—especially in baseball and basketball—probably would help superstars more than the athletes. The data suggests that the superstars with their six-figure salaries are actually underpaid in relation to the receipts their appearance generates in the box office.

The Player Reservation System

Persons contemplating a career in professional sports should be familiar with the player reservation system, which limits competition among teams for players. This system includes three different rules; (1) the governing of the signing of new players, (2) promotion of players from minor to major leagues—hockey and baseball, and (3) transfer of players from one major league roster to another. Those rules differ in detail from sport to sport, but their intention is everywhere the same—to limit, if not prevent, the competitive bidding among teams for the services of players. It is not the intent of the authors to debate the system but instead to point out its existence and encourage the prospective professional athlete to study it. The component of the players' reservation system that receives the most public attention is the so-called reserve clause—that is, a clause in

[17] Roger G. Noll, *Government and Sport Business*, The Brookings Institution, Washington, D.C., 1974, p. 3.

the contract of each player that assigns to a specific team the exclusive right to deal with him for his playing life. Baseball and hockey actually are the only sports with a reserve clause. Football and basketball have an option clause stating that a team has the exclusive right to retain players' services, without their consent, for one year after the term of the contract has expired. Under an option system the team has exclusive rights to deal with a player for only one year beyond the term of the contract, whereas under a reserve system the right is perpetual.

Professional Preparation

The so-called course of study or curricula for the aspiring professional athlete has yet to be developed. Logically and traditionally the skilled college athletes were delivered into professional sports on a carefully devised assembly line. The good ones were selected, and those that failed went on to other careers. This was true especially in football and basketball. Those who were drafted were gifted athletes, many of whom were "blessed" with good coaching during their secondary and collegiate years. Their ability to perform at the highest level was closely scrutinized by professional scouts, and the mechanics of the draft was put into operation. The college campus has always been the training ground for professional sports and provided an orderly transition for athletes. The rapid expansion of professional sports teams, particularly in football and basketball, has made the recruiting of athletes extremely important. Professional sports teams in the past were not allowed to draft players until their college eligibility had expired. However, the National Basketball Association decided in 1971 that its clubs could sign college players before their college eligibility expired if they could prove financial need and their inability to obtain employment in other fields. This was known as the "hardship" draft. The consequence of this action has resulted in many players signing contracts directly out of high school or sometime during their college years. Some players doubt the value of a four-year degree because they spend so many hours practicing, travelling, and playing that there was no time for the books. Colleges have been known to overlook the academic levels of star athletes in advancing them from one grade to another.

It should be clearly stated, however, that the authors support the premise that the student who plans a career in professional sports should complete his or her college education. John Fuzak, Director of the School for Advanced Study at Michigan State University, says that the goal of becoming a professional athlete is a socially acceptable goal. It should not be put ahead of completing one's college education because even success in professional athletics is usually short-lived and it is much better to be prepared.

Not all prospective professional athletes enroll in a physical education curricula, but there are advantages if the individual wishes to prepare for a career in coaching after completing the pro "tour." General liberal arts courses can be helpful for the prospective athlete in the same manner as for any other college student. Courses in law, business, and public speaking could also be valuable for one who wishes to become a professional athlete.

Of utmost importance is the selection of a college or university that will prepare the athlete best for the career that he or she chooses.

Pitfalls For The Prospective Pro

The effort involved in deciding on one's future is well spent, and each career presents both advantages and disadvantages. What should I know about a career in professional athletics?

1. Seldom is a high school performer good enough or mature enough to attract professional employers with the possible exception of baseball and tennis.
2. Despite the fact that big-time professional sports in synonomous with money, it is there for only a few.
3. The fame and status that comes to an outstanding professional athlete is not directly negotiable.
4. There are very few openings in the field and competition for them is intense (i.e., baseball, football, and basketball employ fewer than 2500 men annually).
5. Competitive athletic careers are very brief. Most athletes do not compete past their middle thirties even under the most ideal conditions.
6. Positions in coaching/administration/recreation are not assured only because one is a good competitor.
7. A second career is difficult because many have no training or experience in anything but competitive athletics.

The questions one faces while making career choices are much the same as those raised by the athlete as he or she selects a college.[18]

[18]William F. Stier, "Everything The Athlete Always Wanted to Know About a College," *Scholastic Coach*, **43**:80 (January 1974).

The same high-quality education, good interpersonal relationships, superior faculty, and excellent athletic programs are all applicable to the prospective pro athlete.

Careers In Professional Athletics

Note that most of the discussion has dealt with the professional athlete. Remember that physical education majors with an athletic background often can become involved with professional sports as a: business manager, publicity director, athletic trainer, equipment manager, official, ticket manager, and scout. The business manager, ticket sales manager, publicity director, or trainer need backgrounds similar to their college counterparts, but no special preparation is needed for other areas except an athletic background.

What The Pros Say

Interviews were conducted with several professional athletes and coaches. Their comments extended beyond the range of professional sports, but we have selected only those statements pertinent to this section of the book.

Professional Football Player[19]

Question: How did you become interested in athletics?
Answer: Father was a high school coach and teacher; was exposed to sports at an early age; good athlete in high school; went to the University of Kansas on a football scholarship.
Question: How did you get into professional athletics?
Answer: Drafted from college; individual has no choice regarding who drafts him; this rule may be challenged in the courts; always wanted to play pro ball; was an excellent baseball player as well as football but chose football.
General Information:
Most athletes who have played for a major college team feel they can make it on a pro team. Of the people who try out for professional football: only about 5 percent make it to the pros— 3 to 4 rookies each year of a beginning squad of 90 athletes make it; approximately 3 athletes are drafted each year from a major college team; believes it is very important to complete one's college education; more and more athletes beginning to

---

[19]Bobby Douglas, *Interview*, August 21, 1975.

realize the need for an education sooner or later; the average player is out of professional athletics between 25 and 30 years of age; much more uncomfortable if one is older; most athletes today have completed college; the student out of high school must be made more aware of the need for an education, especially if he or she wants to go into teaching and coaching; absolutely imperative that a student compete in athletics if student expects to coach; sports have become bigger in both college and the pros; professional athletics has not adversely affected college sports.

Question: Problems in negotiating a contract?

Answer: Every athlete should seek the advice of 3 or 4 people he trusts; it really amounts to an experience "thing"—many young men not mature enough to make decisions at 22 years old; National Football League Players Association or a good lawyer are suggestions for advice; The Players Association is located in Washington, D.C.; many times agents will take advantage of athletes, thus the need for sound advice from someone they can trust; it's ridiculous for a player to negotiate his contract.

Question: Who bears the cost of travel, food, and lodging?

Answer: All professional teams pay all costs for pro athletes.

Question: Human side of professional athletics?

Answer: Professional football is the greatest job in the world; it has given me more than I will ever receive; is doing something I like and getting paid for it; everyone has a need for a certain amount of ego; it decreases each year to a situation where what you think is more important; 90 percent of the players have worked hard but say it was worth it; better than average living; negative aspects of economic side is that if you begin working at 28 years old and someone else began at a place like Sears you may be behind; looks like a lot of glamour but most fans look at top 10 percent of pro players and forget about the other 90 percent; the fans tend to look at it differently than what it actually is.

Question: Importance of physical side of football?

Answer: Cannot say enough about the importance of the physical side; extremely tough game physically; playing with injuries is a part of the game; must realize that there will be injuries; the fact that you enjoy the physical part of the game is important.

Question: Training program in off season?

Answer: Most pro athletes have an off-season program; I play many different sports; take about one month off; run 2-3

days each week in good weather (two miles); lots of weight lifting to keep legs strong.
Question: Has coaching improved?
Answer: Yes, definitely; techniques have improved; film study of great help; better coaching in all sports; also better equipment.

Professional Basketball Player[20]

Question: What was your background in athletics prior to professional basketball?
Answer: Played in high school and college with good success at both levels. I majored in food and nutrition in college.
Question: How do you assess professional sports as a career?
Answer: Professional sports may look extremely glamorous but a total commitment and effort must be made; it's not really girls, Cadillac cars, diamond rings and mink coats. The average number of years for a professional basketball player is five years. Every athlete aspiring to go into professional sports should realize that only relatively few make it—consider alternate careers.
Question: How important is a college degree?
Answer: Extremely important; athletes should complete their college work before signing with the pros. Extension courses for college credit may be taken while still an active player and players may take courses during the "off" season.
Question: How important is the physical side of professional basketball?
Answer: The professional athlete should *never* get out of shape. The physical requirements for basketball are so great that conditioning must be maintained throughout the year. Care should be exercised in choosing the right food at all times.
Question: How important is the legal side when signing contracts?
Answer: Do not sign any contract unless you know exactly what you are signing. Seek legal advice if needed.
Question: How can one enter the pro ranks in basketball?
Answer: Strive for excellence in your academic work and in sports. Seek the advice of your coach when you believe it is needed. Specific information can be obtained from professional team publicity directors. Talk with your friends who are playing professional ball.

[20] Bob Love, *Interview,* August 3, 1975.

Professional Football Coach[21]

Biography: Born in western Pennsylvania; went to small high school; interested in sports at early age but was small; recruited by many colleges; chose Purdue University; entered physical education curricula as a freshman; as sophomore entered industrial economics curricula; football throughout college was center of his life; thought college was only a place to be while playing football; withdrew after injury in senior year but went back and graduated; recruited by Cleveland Browns; played 9 years with Cleveland and New Orleans; entered business world as manufacturer's representative but not happy; decided he wanted to enter professional football as a coach and signed with Tampa, Florida of the World Football League; receives a great psychological lift in pro-football coaching; came to Chicago Bears in 1976.

Question: What kind of information should we give to our students regarding pro athletics?

Answer: Once a person enters pro sports he tends to forget how he got there; during his high school and college career he was small and consequently had to make a strong commitment to excell; no dates, smoking, drinking etc.; when a man goes into professional athletics he must devote all of his energy to be the best at that position.

Question: What are some of the pitfalls facing a professional athlete?

Answer: Concentration absolutely required particularly for first year men; in some cases an athlete who is married has an advantage; it keeps him off the streets; "weirdos" and "kooks" are attracted to professional athletes and they must learn to say "no"; many give advice but athletes should seek out people they can trust; sometimes money can be athletes' own worst enemy.

Question: Do you think the Rozelle rule will be changed?

Answer: No—everyone can't play in Miami or Los Angeles.

Question: What are some of the problems faced by coaches?

Answer: There is a great psychological factor existing between an established athlete and a rookie; rookies are a threat to the pros and many times they are literally "run off"; used the illustration of a veteran place kicker and a rookie in which case the vet "psyched" out the rookie and rookie was traded; older vets have great psychological advantage.

[21] Ross Fichtner, *Interview*, August 21, 1975

General Information:
He believes that professional coaching is a great way to make a living, although it is a short tenure; an experience as a pro player is of good advantage to everyone; does a lot for a person; when pro team goes on a trip it is a business trip and not a "lark." Pro athletics is humbling because there is so much to know and it takes many years to know the game; average tenure of a pro football player is 5 years.

Collegiate Conference Administrator[22]

Question: What should a college athlete do to prepare for a professional sports career?
Answer: Excel in at least 1 sport in order to be recruited by the pros; choose a school that has both a high-quality athletic and academic program; make a total commitment to your goal.
Question: How important is a college degree?
Answer: Extremely important. It is always difficult to go back and complete the work if you have left college before graduating.
Question: What are the chances of success for women in professional sports?
Answer: Possibilities are excellent because of the rapid growth of professional sports for women. Great need for qualified women coaches. Know and understand the terminology used in pro sports.
Question: What are the best areas for employment after completing one's playing career?
Answer: Athletic administration, managers of tennis, ski, handball, clubs, and resorts. There is a need for a strong business background for club positions.

The authors are aware that the interviews conducted with these athletes, coaches, and administrators represents only their opinion and should be interpreted as such. There does appear, however, to be considerable consistency in answers to questions that were asked.

SELECTED REFERENCES
"Antitrusters Take on Professional Sports," *Business Week,* McGraw-Hill Co., New York, October 9, 1971, pp. 60-61;63.
Betts, John Richards, *America's Sporting Heritage,* Addison-Wesley Publishing Co., Reading, Ma., 1974.

[22]C.D. Henry, *Interview,* May 6, 1975.

Bryant, James E., "Some Possibilities For Employment in Physical Education's Allied Fields," *The Physical Educator,* **31**:193-195 (December 1974).

Clumpner, Ray A., "America's Unknown Leader of the Sixties: Lombardi," *Proceedings of the North American Society for Sport History,* University Park, PA, 1973, pp. 37-38.

"Conference on the Economics of Professional Sport," *Proceedings of the Conference on the Economics of Professional Sport,* National Football League Players Association, Washington, D.C., 1974, p. 72.

"Cossel Bored with Sports," *The Chicago Tribune,* Chicago, May 2, 1976, p. 3.

Edwards, Harry, *The Revolt of the Black Athlete,* The Free Press, New York, 1969.

"Former Pro Looks at Sport Industry," *The Chicago Tribune,* Chicago, March 28, 1976, p. 30.

Frost, Reuben B., and Edward J. Sims, (ed.), "Development of Human Values Through Sports," *Proceedings of a National Conference,* AAHPER, Washington, D.C., 1974, p. 96.

Fuzak, John, "Academics vs. Athletes: Two Views," *College and University Business,* **55**:66 (September 1973).

Gilbert, Bill, "What Counselors Need to Know About College and Pro Sports," *Phi Delta Kappan,* **56**:121-124 (October 1974).

"Great Escape In NFL," *The Chicago Tribune,* Chicago, May 4, 1975. p. 3.

Gregory, Paul M., *The Baseball Players:* An Economic Study, Public Affairs Press, Washington, D.C., 1956.

Harris, Dorothy V., *Involvement in Sport,* Lea & Febiger, Philadelphia, 1973.

Hart, M. Marie, *Sport in the Socio-Cultural Process,* William C. Brown Co., Dubuque, IA, 1972.

Herskowitz, Mickey, *The Golden Age of Pro Football—A Remembrance of Pro Football in the 1950's,* Macmillan Publishing Co., New York, 1974, p. 207.

Jauss, Bill, "Judge Suggests ABA, NBA Talk About a Merger" *The Chicago Tribune,* Chicago, April 13, 1976, p. 32.

Kniker, Charles R., "The Values of Athletics in Schools: A Continuing Debate," *Phi Delta Kappan,* **56**:116-120 (October 1974).

Koppett, Leonard, "Are Athletes Overpaid?" *The Chicago Tribune,* June 20, 1976, p. 1.

Leonard, George, *The Ultimate Athlete*, The Viking Press, New York, 1974.

Loy, John W. Jr., and Gerald S. Kenyon, *Sport, Culture and Society*, The Macmillan Co., New York, 1969.

Mathews, Basil, *The Spirit of the Game*, George H. Doran Co., New York, 1926.

"More Prep Cagers Eye Hardship Route," *The Chicago Tribune*, Chicago, May 13, 1975, p. 2.

Noll , Roger G., *Government and the Sports Business*, The Brookings Institution, Washington, D.C , 1974.

"Players 1, Owners 0," *Newsweek*, March 29, 1976, p. 71.

"Playing for Profit," *Newsweek*, July 29, 1974, pp. 62, 64.

"Pro Sports: A Business Boom in Trouble," *U.S. News and World Report*, July 5, 1971, pp. 56-58.

Roberts, Howard, *The Story of Pro Football*, Rand McNally and Co., New York, 1953.

Sack, Allen L., "Yale 29—Harvard 4: The Professionalization of College Football," *Quest*, Monograph XIX:23-24 (January 1973).

Schwank, Walter C., (ed.), "The Winning Edge," *Proceedings of the First National Sports Psychology Conference*, AAHPER, Buffalo, N.Y., 1974, p. 135.

Shea, Edward J., and Elton E. Wieman, *Administrative Policies for Intercollegiate Athletes*, Charles C. Thomas Publishers, Springfield, Il., 1967.

Singer, Robert N., *Coaching, Athletics and Psychology*, McGraw-Hill Book Co., New York, 1972.

Stier, William F., "Everything the Athlete Always Wanted to Know About Selecting A College," *Scholastic Coach*, 43:80-81, 94 (January 1974).

"The Sports and Recreational Programs of the Nation's Universities and Colleges," NCAA, Shawnee Mission, Kans., 1974, p. 47.

"Upheaval in Pro Sports," *U.S. News and World Report*, August 12, 1974, pp. 51-54.

Weiss, Paul, *Sport: A Philosophic Inquiry*, Southern Illinois University Press, Carbondale, Il., 1969.

Wind, Herbert Warren, *The Gilded Age of Sport*, Simon and Schuster, New York, 1961.

Wismer, Harry, *The Public Calls It Sport*, Prentice-Hall, Inc., Englewood, Cliffs, NJ., 1965.

Woodhouse, Edward, "Rockne and Lombardi: Models of Certainty in

Uncertain Times," *Proceedings of the North American Society for Sport History,* University Park, PA, 1973, pp. 35-36.

chapter 8

learning experiences in competitive sports

The only way an individual can acquire, or strengthen, or weaken controls of conduct, in other words, learn, is through his own activity.[1]

Seward C. Staley

One of the most important decisions for every young man and woman as they complete their high school education is the choice of a career. Many enter college with the idea that career choices may be made after they have had an opportunity to "sample" some of the courses being offered. In some instances this approach is satisfactory but many times it results in an extension of their formal education with the accompanying financial, social, and emotional problems associated with answering the question "What do I want to do with my life?"

The profession of physical education has an obligation to assist students in making correct career choices as early as possible and to prepare them to be qualified and competent teachers or coaches.

Most college curricula offer core courses during the first two years with specialization coming after these requirements are met. The primary responsibility,

[1] Seward C. Staley, *The Curriculum in Sports*, Stipes Publishing Company, Champaign, IL, 1940, p. 36.

however, rests with the student. The freshman year is not too early to decide what road to follow.

This chapter will deal with types of learning experiences for the beginning freshman as he or she prepares for a career in competitive sports. The authors have divided these experiences into planning, preparing, and performing stages and have also included some hypothetical case studies to provide a practical base for decision making.

PLANNING

Several learning experiences are provided for planning to coach sports or direct recreational programs.

Leona Holbrook identified a list of human values recognized by individuals as having been developed through their sports experience.[2] Using the sample chart appearing in (Figure 8.1), list your own rating of these values in terms of your sport experience. (1=high; 5=low)

Students who wish to enter the coaching profession should be aware of the advantages and disadvantages connected with it. Rank these items in your order of importance on the sample profile charts. (See Figure 8.2).

Beginning teachers or coaches are often at a disadvantage when they apply for their first position because of their lack of experience. This problem can be partially solved by participation in cocurricular and extracurricular activities while in college. R. C. Owens[3] has developed a point value and rating scale system for participation. The point values could be recorded on a form and included with the student's academic record. Using the sample point values and rating scale appearing in Table 4. Keep your own record of participation for one term, quarter, or semester.

Professional preparation programs are designed to develop competencies in every area of specialization. If you have plans to enter coaching give your own rank of importance to those items appearing on the sample profile chart: 1 = high; 2 = above average; 3 = average; 4 = low (Figure 8.3).

[2]Leona Holbrook, "Human Values in Sports Their Relationship To Social Ends," *Proceedings of a National Conference On Development of Human Values Through Sports*, Springfield, MA, 1973, pp. 25-32.

[3]R. C. Owens, "A Record of Physical Education Major Participation In Co-Curricular and Extra-Curricular Activities," *The Physical Educator*, 27-28 (March 1971).

	Values				
	1	2	3	4	5
Identify self as an individual					
Develop habits, ideas, and values that have led to happiness					
Develop understanding of a standard of performance of the group as well as attaining personal significance in a team structure					
Learned about freedom					
Learned value of competition					
Gained value of objectivity					
Worth of human values learned from the leader					

FIGURE 8.1 Profile of human values in sports. Reprinted by permission of Ralph J. Sabock, Pennsylvania State University, State College, 1976.

Bruce Ogilvie has written about personality characteristics of physical educators and coaches.[4] Using the sample profile chart in Figure 8.4, rank these items in terms of how you view them in order of importance (1=high; 5=low).

PREPARING AND PERFORMING

Learning experiences for the preparing and performing stages are almost unlimited. A partial list appears below:

1. Visit and observe new facilities and talk with authorities regarding good and bad features of the plant.
2. Select the sport (s) you plan to coach and prepare a model or diagram of the facility where the activity is to be conducted in-

[4]Bruce Ogilvie, "Personality Characteristics of Secondary School Athletic Directors and Coaches," Speech Given at Western States Conference on Secondary School Administration, Las Vegas, Nevada, December 11-14, 1970.

LEARNING EXPERIENCES IN COMPETITIVE SPORTS   137

Table 4.

	POINT VALUE	RATING SCALE	PER SEMESTER
Varsity sports	10	0 - 25	Poor
Intramural sports	5	26 - 50	Fair
Volunteer services	10	51 - 75	Good
Team manager, assistant coach	10	80 & Above	Excellent
Umpire, referee, scorer, timer, etc.	5		
Awards	10		
Organization officers	5		
Attendance at professional meetings, workshops, clinic, etc.	10		
Physical education meetings	5		
Other activities and services	5		
Possible points per term	75		
Total possible points	600		

cluding all appropriate markings, and the like.

3. Develop a library of official rules for sports.
4. Attend on a regular basis the athletic events and recreational sports activities at your school.
5. Develop a set of policies to be followed by the coach in the conduct of a nonschool athletic program. Include such items as length of practices, length of season, number of contests, and relationships with parents and other coaches.
6. Compile materials from the following national organizations dealing with cocurricular and extracurricular activities (NCAA, AAU, NAIA, AIAW, National High School Federation).
7. Participate as a subject in research studies (nutrition, physical fitness, etc.).
8. Become familiar with the common terms associated with sports and be able to define them in your own words.
9. Interview coaches, teachers, athletic directors, athletic trainers, and recreational directors regarding such matters as experience, background of participation, reasons for entering field, role in society, and job security.
10. Observe coaches and recreational directors in stressful situations and assess their ability to handle them.

	LOW	AVERAGE	ABOVE AVERAGE	HIGH
Security				
Tenure				
Family life				
Criticism				
Vacations				
Relationships with athletes				
Relationships with school administration				
Relationships with faculty				
Self concept				
Retirement				
Physical and emotional demands				
Respect in the community and school				
Financial security				
Legal aspects	LOW	AVERAGE	ABOVE AVERAGE	HIGH

FIGURE 8.2 Profile of the coaching profession.

11. Observe the behavior of athletes in both practice and game situations.
12. Attend lectures given by sociologists, physiologists, psychologists, and historians speaking on the topic of sports.
13. Prepare a demographic study of a community and use the information as a planning guide in the development of a community recreation center.

	1	2	3	4
Relationship of athletic program to total educational program				
First aid and safety				
Legal liability				
Biological, social, moral, emotional and spiritual values				
Growth and development				
Care and prevention of injuries				
Conditioning				
Public speaking				
Psychological principles				
Fundamental offenses, defenses, strategies and teaching methods				
Local, state and national rules of the sport				

FIGURE 8.3 Profile of coaching competencies.

14. Attend professional meetings and coaching clinics and workshops (local, regional, national).
15. Interview amateur and professional athletes regarding advantages and disadvantages of synthetic floor and field surfaces.
16. Talk to orthopedic surgeons regarding positive and negative effects of nonschool athletics (Little League baseball, Pop Warner football, ice hockey, etc.).
17. Assist coaches in scouting assignments.
18. Assist coaches in keeping shot charts for basketball; keep statistics for football, basketball, baseball, etc.
19. Serve as an intramural manager; official; intramural board member.

	1	2	3	4
A need for high achievement				
A need to exert leadership and an ability to get others to follow directions				
A fair amount of inflexibility				
Aggressiveness				
A solid sense of right and wrong				
Emotional stability				
Tough mindedness and an ability to face facts				
Great determination				
Organization				
A lack of anxiety				
A willingness to accept Blame and pay the physical and emotional price for success				
A willingness to listen to authorities and acknowledge leaders in the field				

FIGURE 8.4 Profile of personality characteristics of physical educators and coaches. Reprinted by permission of Bruce Ogilivie, University of California, 1976.

20. Compete in a varsity sport.
21. Participate in the recreational sports program.
22. Talk to coaches regarding how they handle criticism from athletes, public, school officials, Rotary Club, and the like.
23. Assess the personality charateristics of amateur and professional athletes that you see on television.

24. Talk with coaches and teachers regarding their views on discipline.
25. Assess the different philosophies of coaching expressed by your coaches in junior high school and high school, and to what extent do you agree and disagree? How does yours as a prospective coach coincide or differ?
26. Develop a bibliography of books and periodicals dealing with techniques of coaching.

Case Studies: Competitive Sports

Working Together In the School

Harper High School had enjoyed much success in its interscholastic athletic program. A variety of sports were offered for both men and women, and the facilities were more than adequate for a well-rounded program. The athletic and physical education staff worked well together, and there was a mutual sharing of ideas and problems. The relationship, however, between the academic teachers and the physical education teachers and coaches was less than satisfactory, and there appeared to be jealousy and ill feeling between the two groups. The principal was aware of this problem and informed the athletic director that steps should be taken to correct it. What should he do?

Choosing a College

Mary Nelson was an outstanding basketball player while in high school. Several college recruiters contacted her, relative to attending their institution, but because of financial constraints she decided to attend the college located in the city where she lived. This presented a problem because she wanted to coach, and the school had only a mediocre basketball program. She felt that playing on a championship or highly rated team would enhance her possibilities for a good coaching position when she graduated. What solution do you recommend and why?

Participation In The Athletic Program

Harold Wagner entered Maryville College as a beginning freshman majoring in physical education. He hoped to become a physical education teacher and basketball coach in a high school. During the first semester in school, he was told that all physical education students were required to either compete on a varsity team or participate in the intramural program while in college. This presented a serious problem because he held a part-time job to help defray his college expenses. Without this source of funds, he could not continue in school. What should he do?

Choosing a Career

Bill Evers had been a very successful athlete in Little League baseball. This sucess was continued in high school when he was named to the All-State team as a pitcher. During his senior year in high school, he became disenchanted with all competitive athletics and withdrew completely from all competition. He felt that the so-called athletic establishment had a dehumanizing influence on many of the players, and he did not want to be a part of it. Despite this attitude, he decided to go to the state university and enter the physical education profession. The first year of college was spent taking general education courses but he was still undecided regarding a special area of study. To whom should he go to seek a solution to this problem? Why?

Planning a New Facility

John Erickson was a physical education teacher and assistant basketball coach in his first year at Eisenhower High School. The school building was over 50 years old, and the facilities used for the program were inadequate. The athletic director was instructed to appoint a committee to begin planning for a new facility. John was asked to serve on this committee and to make recommendations concerning the building needs for a basketball program. How should John handle this assignment in order to be a contributing member of this committee?

Use of Facilities

Weber High School had only one gymnasium that was shared by both the girls and boys for the instructional and interscholastic program. The boys' program had utilized the gymnasium in the afternoon for the competitive program with little interference from any group. However, a significantly larger number of girls expressed a desire to expand their competitive program and asked for "equal" floor time. The intramural program was also experiencing rapid growth and the director of that program requested more afternoon time and space. The principal charged the athletic director with the responsibility of responding to these needs. Assume that you are the athletic director. How would you handle the matter?

Case Studies: Professional Sports

Individuals planning a career in professional sports are entering a most glamorous area of endeavor. Given our natural infatuation with sports and publicity, praise and money laid on athletes, it is a rare person who, if given the opportunity, would not opt for a game-playing job no matter what his or her other talents and prospects.[5] Some people believe that it is more important for these persons to seek dispassionate, objective information and advice than for anyone else seeking career decisions. We hope that the case studies proposed here will be of assistance to the student as he or she prepares for a career in professional sports.

1. Mandel has studied the psychological aspect of professional sports—especially football.[6] He asks the question, "Given roughly the same amount of athletic ability, why do some men fail and others succeed in pro football?" He hypothesizes that it is because the personality orientations of the latter better fit the tasks. He further states that in other fields as well, appropriateness of personality to one's role may be perhaps the most single determinant of success and happiness. Research this subject in the library and decide if this statement is correct based on what you have read.

2. There are several schools of thought regarding the effect of college athletics on pro sports. Some believe that most college athletic programs are training grounds for professional sports and that the true meaning of sport has been destroyed in the process. Ask your instructor in the introductory physical education course for permission to debate this issue in class with several students—both men and women.

3. Professional sports are reported on regularly in the media. Radio and television devote significant time slots to a wide

---

[5]Bill Gilbert, "What Counselors Need to Know About College and Pro Sports," *Phi Delta Kappan*, 21, 55. (October, 1974).

[6]Arnold J. Mandel, "A Psychiatrist Looks At Football," *Readers Digest*, pp. 89-92. (January, 1975).

variety of activities, but relatively few people are familiar with special newspapers devoted solely to pro sports. Compile a listing of these periodicals for the following sports: football, basketball, baseball, golf, tennis, swimming, bowling, and track and field, including the name of the newspaper, publisher, where published, and a short resume about each one.

4. Former President Ford has appointed a Commission On Olympic Sports because of the controversy regarding governance and funding of amateur sports. Hopefully, this commission will make recommendations that will eliminate many of the problems that confront America's amateurs in training and competition. Secure a copy of all the testimony presented to this commission since it was appointed on June 19, 1975. Summarize the pertinent information from these meetings and present it in the form of an oral report to your classmates. Write to members of this commission for specific information if needed.

5. The President's Council on Physical Fitness and Sports is the federal agency representing sports within the United States. This body wonders why two very popular professional sports, football and baseball, are not Olympic sports. Discuss this issue with amateur and professional sports experts to find out the reason and report your discussions to your teacher and classmates.

6. Choose two professional sports and conduct a study of the average number of years professional athletes and coaches spend in their sports. Report your findings at a seminar for students planning to enter professional sports.

7. Talk with three pro athletes, each from a different sport, and from these discussions compile a list of physical and mental qualifications considered important for success.

8. Talk with the following persons about job opportunities in professional sports:

   a. High school counselor.
   b. College counselor.
   c. Professional athlete.
   d. College coach.
   e. High school coach.
   f. Athletic trainer (college).

Prepare a resume of these discussions and present it orally at an undergraduate seminar. Rate these people from 1-5 in terms of the validity of their remarks. (1=high; 5=low).

9. Debate the following statement in one of your physical education classes: What evidence is there that good athletes have better or worse intellectual capacity or powers than nonathletes?

10. Talk with the team physician and athletic trainer regarding how one prepares himself/herself for entry into pro sports as a competitor.

SELECTED REFERENCES

Hewatt, Carolyn, "Women's Intramural Athletics—Issues and Directions," *Proceedings of the Seventy-Seventh Annual Meeting of the National College Physical Education Association for Men*, C. E. Mueller (ed.), 56-58, University of Minnesota, Minneapolis, 1973.

Jamerson, Dick, "Pros and Cons of Sports Clubs," *Proceedings of the Seventy-Second Annual Conference of the National College Physical Education Association for Men*, C. E. Mueller (ed.), 48-49, University of Minnesota, Minneapolis, 1969.

Marciani, Louis, "Competency-Based Learning Module Sequence for the Training of Sports Officials," *Proceedings of the Twenty-Fifth Annual Conference of the National Intramural Association*, Tempe, Ariz., 1974, pp. 116-121.

Marciani, Louis, "Independent/Mediated Training of Intramural Officials," *Proceedings of the Twenty-Fourth Annual Conference of the National Intramural Association*, Tampa, Fla., 1973, pp. 58-61.

McGuire, Raymond J., "Student Power in a Postive Direction—A Student Manager Program," *Proceedings of the Seventy-Third Annual Meeting of the National College Physical Education Association for Men*, C. E. Mueller (ed.), 21-22, University of Minnesota, Minneapolis, 1969.

Mitchman, Nels, "Problem Solutions in Intramurals," *Proceedings of the Twenty-Third Annual Conference of the National Intramural Association*, Champaign, IL, 1972, pp. 54-56.

Poling, Dow P., "The Extent and Effectiveness of Student Involvement in the Administration of the University Intramural Program," *Proceedings of the Twenty-Third Annual Conference of the National Intramural Association*, Champaign, IL, 1972, pp. 165-171.

Pollock, Bernard, "Student Involvement in the College Intramural Program," *Journal of Health, Physical Education and Recreation*, 36-37 (March, 1969).

Resick, Matthew C., *Modern Administrative Practices in Physical Education and Athletics,* Addison-Wesley Publishing Company, Reading, MA, 1970, p. 291.

Sheriff, Al, "Training Student Leaders," *Proceedings of the Nineteenth Annual Conference of the National Intramural Association,* William C. Brown Book Company, Dubuque, IA, 1968, pp. 61-62.

Simon, J. Malcolm, "Student Leadership in Intramurals," *Proceedings of the Twenty-Sixth Annual Conference of the National Intramural Association,* New Orleans, 1975, pp. 122-124.

Sisley, Becky, "Laboratory Experiences for Developing Coaching Competencies, the Preparation of Women for Coaching Responsibilities," *The Physical Educator,* Indianapolis, Ind., 30.182 184 (December 1973).

section 3

coachingandsports administration

Reprinted by permission of the College of Health Physical Education and Recreation, University of Illinois at Chicago Circle.

9
the coach
10
sports administration
11
the program in sports administration
12
learning experiences in coaching and sports administration

chapter 9

the coach

He who would kindle another must glow himself.[1]
                    David O. Matthews

An overwhelming majority of schools, both public and private, offer opportunities for interschool athletic competition beginning at the junior high school level and continuing through college. Many students who were skilled performers during college years choose to enter coaching, which represents one phase of the physical education profession. However, that exceptional ability as an athlete does not guarantee a successful career in coaching.

There is some difference of opinion regarding the relationship between teaching and coaching, but it is generally agreed that there is an overlapping of results and rewards. Some believe that because coaching involves many different facets, which are unique to the general overall pattern of teaching, it is teaching. Moore says that a good coach is a good teacher and a great coach is a good teacher and a good organizer.[2] Gallon writes that coaching in actuality is teaching not only because sports are a psychologically educational

---

[1] David O. Matthews, "The New Look in University and College Intramurals," *Proceedings of the Annual Meeting of the National College Physical Education Association for Men*, C. E. Mueller (ed.), University of Minnesota, Minneapolis, 1971, p. 6.

[2] J. W. Moore, *The Psychology of Athletic Coaching,* Burgess Publishing Company, Minneapolis, 1970, p. 1.

experience but also because players must be instructed in the proper use of skills.[3]

NATURE OF THE PROFESSION

"One of the aspects of coaching which sets it apart from other professions and occupations is that it is a life dealing with all kinds of people. These people could be adults, youngsters, fellow teachers, pleasant people, not-so-pleasant people, friendly people and antagonistic people—each with their own hopes, dreams and goals in life".[4]

Individuals considering coaching as a career should be aware that it has undergone extensive changes at every level since the middle 1960's when students began to question the relevance of educational and extracurricular programs in high schools and colleges. Coaching, like teaching, is much harder today. Men coaches, especially, are finding that athletes are not so willing to accept training or training rules as they have in the past, nor do they accept discipline as a part of athletics as they once did.

Coaching at any level, particularly in college or in the professional ranks, offers little security. Security in the coaching profession can be described simply as the odds against getting fired. Three broad areas should be considered to ensure the coach a reasonable amount of security in his job. They are: (1) ability to prepare athletes to play the game well, (2) faith in the players on the team and in the coaching staff, and (3) recognition of the necessity to cooperate with the administrators of the program. In the case of school programs, remember that athletics represents only a small part of the total school program.

The life of a coach can never be described as dull or boring, regardless of the level of competition. The opportunity to observe youngsters through their years of competition and to share with them the happenings and experiences of a sports season is a most satisfactory and rewarding experience.

Like any other profession, coaches may experience frustration. It may be caused by impatience in achieving goals set in advance or by an administration that fails to give the coach an opportunity to develop a program that is compatible with these goals. Frustration

---

[3] Arthur J. Gallon, *Coaching—Ideas and Ideals*, Houghton Mifflin Company, Boston, 1972, p. 12.

[4] Ralph T. Sabock, *The Coach*, W. B. Saunders Co., Philadelphia, 1973, p. 6.

should not be allowed to grow because of the possibility of its damaging or destroying the effectiveness of the coach's efforts.

Coaching is an extremely demanding occupation. The commitments in terms of time involved, energy, family life, and physical well-being dictates a relatively short span of time as an active coach (average about 15 years), particularly for those in head-coaching positions. A dedicated coach is completely involved mentally, physically, and emotionally. A majority of coaches quit coaching long before they retire from the teaching profession. It has been estimated that a coach will probably make up to six moves before finally reaching the desired position. These moves might not be voluntary. This is not the case for women coaches, however, because of the increased number of interscholastic and intercollegiate sports with the accompanying need for qualified personnel.

Emotional tension is a factor that must be seriously considered before one enters coaching. It is a very real thing for coaches who care about their team and how it performs. The coach's product appears before a discriminating audience on a regularly scheduled basis, and the way a team plays is a direct reflection on the coach and his or her ability to teach. The concern over winning and losing adds to the emotional stress every coach experiences. This occurs in direct proportion to the ambition of the coach, the popularity of the sport involved, and the interest of the community toward that sport.

Another task with which the coach must cope is to learn how to live with critics. It is impossible to completely satisfy all of the "experts." The following story illustrates the fallacy of attempting to satisfy critics.[5]

> There was an old man, a boy and a donkey. They were going to town and it was decided that the boy should ride. As they went along they passed some people who exclaimed that it was shameful for the boy to ride and the old man to walk. The man and boy decided that maybe the critics were right so they changed positions. Later they passed some more people who then exclaimed that it was a real shame for that man to make such a small boy walk. The two decided that maybe they both should walk. Soon they passed some more people who exclaimed that it was stupidity to walk when they had a donkey to ride. The man and the boy decided maybe the critics were right so they decided that they both should ride. They soon passed other people who exclaimed that it was a shame to put

[5] Ibid., p. 117.

such a load on a poor little animal. The old man and the boy decided that maybe the critics were right so they decided to carry the donkey. As they passed a bridge they lost their grip on the animal and it fell into the river and drowned. The moral of the story is that if you try to please everyone you will finally lose your ass.

Obviously this is a dramatization of what the coach faces in each competitive event. "In spite of the nature of the profession, which requires much more of a coach than merely teaching youngsters to play a game, and in spite of the fact that there can be unpleasant aspects in coaching, it is still a fascinating way to earn a living."[6]

Qualifications

Sports at every level should be conducted by professionally prepared personnel of integrity who are dedicated to the optimal mental, emotional, physical, and social development of those entrusted to their supervision.

In addition to a thorough knowledge of sports, a coach must be a certified teacher who has expertise in guiding students in the pursuit of excellence in competitive sports. An understanding of the place and purpose of sports in education and of the growth and development of children and youth is of primary importance.

It is generally agreed that those involved with athletics should have special competencies over and above those required for standard teacher certification. Professional preparation programs should provide the prospective coach with the following competencies:[7]

1. An understanding of the relationship of the interscholastic program and the particular sport they are coaching to the total education program.
2. A knowledge of first aid and the safety practices and techniques pertinent to the sport they are coaching.
3. An understanding of the possibilities of legal liability as well as sound practices and preventive measures.
4. A thorough knowledge and understanding of the biological, social, moral, emotional, and spiritual values that may accrue from the activity and the best methods of bringing about these desirable outcomes.

[6] Ibid., p. 119.

[7] AAHPER, *Professional Preparation in Dance, Physical Education, Recreation Education, Safety Education, and School Health Education*, Washington, D. C., 1974, p. 52.

5. A knowledge of the most acceptable principles of growth and development and their implications for the sport.
6. An understanding of the basic principles in the care and prevention of injuries together with an understanding of the proper relationship of the coach to the school or team physician.
7. An understanding of the best methods of developing and conditioning members of athletic squads.
8. The ability to speak in public to bring credit to the profession and the school and to more effectively inform the public of the educational possibilities of the sport.
9. An understanding of the basic psychological principles of motivation, stress, play, emotion, and group interaction.
10. A thorough knowledge of the fundamentals, offenses, defenses, strategies, and teaching methods involved in the particular sport. Included will be squad organization, coaching techniques, and sound motivational procedures.
11. A knowledge of and a sense of responsibility for local, state, and national rules.

In addition to educational and professional qualifications, coaching requires certain physical competencies that are not related to size, speed, and weight. These include good health, an acceptable standard of motor skill, and good personal appearance.

The mental and social demands of coaching at every level makes good health a necessary attribute and, though coaches are not necessarily expected to be All-American performers, they need above-average coordination and the ability to demonstrate effectively the physical skills required of their sport. The image presented by coaches in terms of their personal appearance will have a beneficial effect upon the athletes with whom they work. The specific role an athletic coach fulfills in the lives of impressionable youngsters and the fact that he or she does teach by personal example necessitates a life guided by high moral standards. A coach should take great care in avoiding the hypocracy in the eyes of his or her students—he or she should not teach a set of values verbally while practicing the opposite. Honesty is another moral qualification that must be understood and practiced by every coach. It must be taught and demonstrated by the coach in dealing with the players, their parents, officials, opposing coaches, in observance of the rules of the game and in the strategy of how to play the game.

One of the most serious mistakes made by students contemplating coaching careers is failure to participate as a member of the varsity team of the sport to be coached. Neither can optimum results be obtained by coaches whose only qualifications are that they were letter winners in high school or college.

Certification

The rapid expansion of athletic programs, particularly at the interscholastic level, has resulted in a major problem in the United State because approximately one-fourth of all head coaches of junior and senior high school teams have had no professional preparation for such responsibility. To combat this problem, the AAHPER Division of Men's Athletics appointed a Task Force on Certification of High School Coaches. This body proposed a program that every secondary school head coach should possess.[8] Sixteen semester hours of courses were proposed to include: medical aspects of athletic coaching, theory and techniques of coaching, kinesiological foundations of coaching, and physiological foundations of coaching.

Frost recognized several national trends in certification that have implications for persons who choose to coach:[9]

1. All coaches must be certified teachers. This is now a practically unanimous requirement.
2. The general trend toward reciprocity in certification is also affecting physical education.
3. Institutions are being given more autonomy and more responsibility. Programs of professional preparation rather than individuals are being approved and registered.
4. Institutions in order to be registered are being checked for regional accreditation to ascertain their quality as a general education institution and for NCATE accreditation to determine their competency in professional preparation.
5. Broader statements of certification requirements are being urged.
6. The above trends are indicative of the main one, that of raising standards and improving instruction.

[8] Matthew Maetzo (ed.), *Certification of High School Coaches*, AAHPER, Washington, D.C., 1971, p. 27.

[9] Reuben B. Frost, "Recent Trends in Certification of Men Physical Education Teachers and Coaches," *Journal of Health, Physical Education and Recreation*, **41**:36-37 (May 1970).

7. There is a trend toward requiring all teachers to teach in their major or minor field. Because there are so few physical education minors graduated, the effect will be to put more qualified physical education teachers in these positions.

Legal Aspects

Regardless of the level of coaching, every coach should understand certain legal aspects of athletics. In the past, school boards and teachers have claimed that they are agencies of government and thus have "governmental immunity." More recently some state courts have ruled that school boards can be held liable for their actions. All persons connected in any way with interscholastic or intercollegiate athletics should be familiar with the definition of terms used in a legal sense. All states have some variations in statutes, and coaches should be familiar with the statutes in the states where they are employed.[10]

Most cases brought against individual coaches or school boards have dealt with tort liability (negligence) or prudence. Gallon defines negligence as behavior that is not prudent and results in injury to another person. Prudence is defined as "wisdom shown in the exercise of reason, forethought, and self-control." In negligence cases each must be considered on its own merits because of the absence of specific statutes that define it. In conducting athletic activities, coaches should exercise prudence and make every attempt to avoid possible problems.

Proper supervision is considered by many to be the key factor in reducing the possibility of legal problems. Supervision must be provided at all times in all areas, and professional preparation programs must offer prospective coaches proper formal training to teach their sports. From a legal standpoint previous participation in an activity is considered inadequate preparation.

Safe equipment and athletic facilities are responsibilities of the school and the coach. No detail should be overlooked that might cause injury to the participant. Other items that need to be considered by coaches are providing safe transportation, conducting physical examinations, and administering first aid.

Recently, athletes have contested the coach's right to bar them from participation if they do not conform to training, grooming, or

---

[10]Andrew Grieve, The Legal Aspects of Athletics, A.S. Barnes and Company, New York, 1969, p. 72.

dress regulations. However, the courts have upheld the school's—and thus the coach's—right to make such rules as long as they are reasonable. Regulations should contribute to athletic excellence and apply equally to all players. Gallon lists a glossary of legal terms that the high school coach should understand.

It is possible that new laws and statutes will be passed in the near future thus altering existing regulations. Grieve lists the following future trends:[11]

- a. School districts throughout the nation will not retain their immunity from legal action for any length of time.
- b. There will be an increase in the member states providing "save harmless" protection for their teachers.
- c. It is possible that the number of legal actions against the school districts will increase within the next several years.
- d. There will likely be financial settlements because of a change in attitude regarding the ability of youngsters to think and act in a reasonable manner.
- e. There will be an increase in slander and libel cases involved with individuals connected with athletics.

Career Opportunities

A coaching career has been called by many "a business filled with laughter and tears."[12] Most coaches do not spend their entire professional lives actively engaged in coaching, but several factors should be considered before taking the first and subsequent positions. Moore lists the following as primary considerations:[13]

- a. Type of institution
- b. Philosophy of the institution
- c. Location
- d. Type of community
- e. Sports tradition
- f. Interest of other coaches
- g. Material on hand
- h. Other duties

[11] Ibid. p. 76.

[12] J. W. Moore, *The Psychology of Athletic Coaching*, Burgess Publishing Company, Minneapolis, 1970, p. 234.

[13] Ibid., p. 234.

i. Attitude of the faculty
j. Assistants
k. Chances for advancement
l. Housing available
m. Schools
n. Salary
o. Fringe benefits

There are usually opportunities throughout a coach's career that might be called "points of decision."[14] Some coaches may decide to coach all of their working years while others may have opportunities for related careers before retirement. Coaches should be aware of these possibilities, try to anticipate 5, 10, or 15 years ahead, determine priorities, and begin to prepare for them. Figure 9.1 presents three possible directions for the college graduate: (1) high school assistant, (2) graduate student, and (3) high school head coach[15] (see Fig. 9.1).

Having completed college, the new coach will need to decide whether to enter graduate school or seek a teaching position. An advanced degree means a higher salary in the public schools. If the decision is made to go to graduate school, three choices must be made: (1) obtain a coaching position in a college, (2) apply for a head coaching job in a high school, or (3) apply for an assistant coaching job in a high school. Many young coaches assume that the route to the college ranks is by going to graduate school, which is not necessarily true. The obtaining of an advanced degree also does not ensure a head coaching position in a high school. There is no prescribed format for making decisions on coaching positions. Each individual must weigh all the factors before deciding which route to follow. In every respect, it is an individual decision.

Career opportunities for women in coaching are excellent. The increase in women's interscholastic and intercollegiate athletic teams is national in scope. The implementation of federal regulations requiring equitable athletic budgets, facilities, and staff for men and women has resulted in a shortage of qualified women at most every level (see Fig. 9.2).

Some women coaches, as with men, seeking high school positions, probably will find that they would be responsible for only one sport;

[14] Ralph J. Sabock, *The Coach*, W. B. Saunders Company, Philadelphia, 1973, p. 84.

[15] Ibid., p. 86.

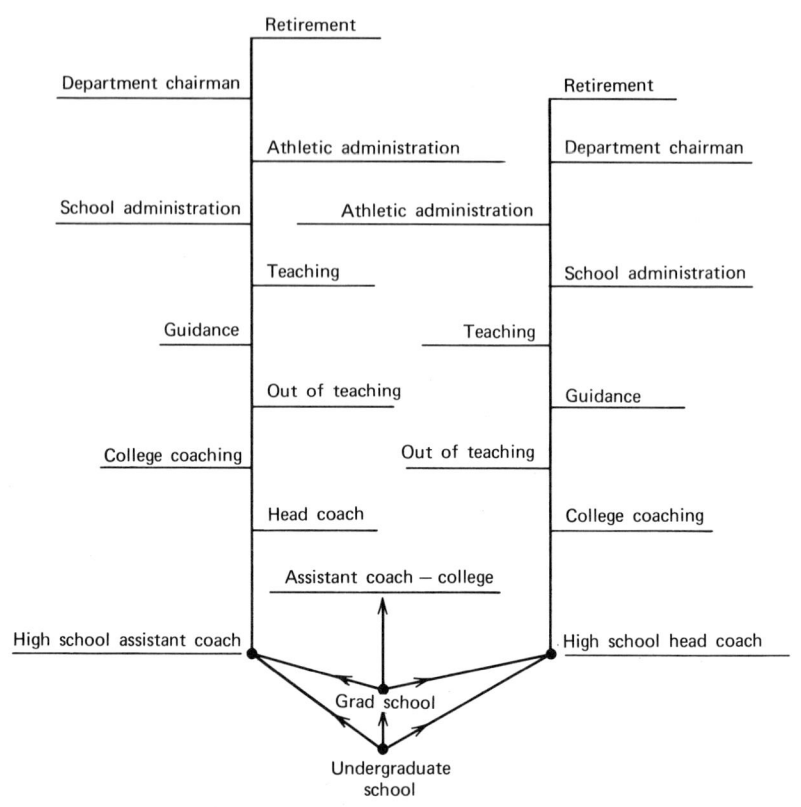

```
                              Retirement
   Department chairman           |                    Retirement
                                 |
                         Athletic administration    Department chairman
   School administration    Athletic administration
                                                    School administration
                              Teaching
       Guidance                              Teaching
                           Out of teaching
                                                       Guidance
       College coaching               Out of teaching
                            Head coach
                                                    College coaching
                       Assistant coach — college
                                  ↑
High school assistant coach •─────┼─────•  High school head coach
                             ←──┐ │ ┌──→
                              Grad school
                                ↑ │ ↑
                                │ │ │
                            Undergraduate
                               school
```

FIGURE 9.1 Three possible directions: (a). High school assistant. (b) Graduate student. (c) High school head coach. Reprinted by permission of Ralph J. Sabock, Pennsylvania State University, State College, 1976.

others, particularly in small schools, would be expected to coach two or three teams. At the college level, the situation is somewhat different. Since a variety of organizational patterns for intercollegiate athletics for women are evolving, women teachers of physical education are rather suddenly faced with an added or changed responsibility for coaching; on the other hand, sport specialists are being hired on a part-time basis to coach only in their sport.

Both men and women coaches are finding numerous positions with various kinds of sport clubs, health spas, sport camps, and recreation programs. These areas are discussed later.

ROLE OF THE COACH

Regardless of the level of coaching, every coach has an important role to play in American education. As far back as the early part of

FIGURE 9.2 Girl's athletics. Reprinted by permission of University of Illinois at Chicago Circle, Chicago.

the twentieth century, physical education leaders considered the athletic field as a laboratory where useful lessons could be learned. The coach is the teacher and facilitator for what occurs in that laboratory. Clark Hetherington, writing in the American Physical Education Review in 1910, stated that the fundamental character of education through the guidance of conduct in play is not completed in childhood. It continues through youth—long after formal education and intellectual inspiration has begun. The athletic field of the late adolescent years is as much a laboratory of conduct as is the playing field of the child. This is the last chance for intensive moral training by direct personal guidance and discipline. Fourteen to twenty is the critical period in which all the fundamental social traits and moral habits are formed, and they are formed in a large measure on the play side of life.[16]

Sherwood Woods considers the coach to be one of the most potent objects for identification of the young male.[17] He symbolizes

---

[16] Clark W. Hetherington, "Fundamental Education," *American Physical Education Review*, **15**:633 (December 1910).

[17] Sherwood M. Woods, "The Violent World of the Athlete," *Quest*, Monograph XVI: 55-60 (June 1971).

the strength, competitive competence, independence, and masculinity that the child and adolescent are so desperately struggling to attain. Furthermore, he is not a "parent" from whom one has the task of separating and therefore whose ideas must often be rejected out of hand. In the best of all possible worlds, where rationality prevailed, he would certainly be paid not by whether or not his teams won, but in terms of what kind of man he helped to build. As a model for identification, his actions, views, and values are highly potent forces for educational change. Baker sees the coach's role as that of a psychologist.[18] He is often responsible for instilling the motivation in an individual so that he can be successful. He understands the various needs. For some athletes, the coach becomes a central figure in their lives.

Lawther believes that the coach has a closer relationship and greater influence on youngsters than almost any other teacher. In his content area (athletics), in which physical, moral, and social behavior are of vital importance, the coach has a great influence on these youngsters. His influence is inescapable in spite of the fact that it thrusts upon him an almost fearful responsibility for directing character formation. The competitive world—in children's play, in athletics, in life—is neither gentle nor kind.[19] Bucher considers the coach in a favorable position to teach concepts more effectively than any other faculty member.[20]

It would be erroneous to believe that everyone shares the belief that coaches have a positive role in physical, moral, social, and emotional behavior of athletes under their charge. Others challenge the concept that a carry-over exists between competition in sports and competition in life. Competition in and of itself is neither good nor bad; it is good only when there is proper leadership and guidance toward sound goals.[21]

In 1972 Stern wrote of a culture crisis in American sports. In his attempt to understand this crisis, he emphasized the changing coach-

[18] Terry W. Baker, *Athletics in America*, Oregon State University Press, Corvallis, Ore., 1972, pp. 64-65.

[19] John W. Lawther, "The Role of the Coach in American Education," *Journal of Health Physical Education and Recreation*, **36**:65-66 (May 1965).

[20] Charles A. Bucher, *Foundations of Physical Education*, C. V. Mosby Company, St. Louis, MO, 1975, p. 393.

[21] Hally B. Poindexter and Carol L. Mushier, *Coaching Competitive Team Sports for Girls and Women*, W. B. Saunders Company, Philadelphia, 1973, p. 5.

athlete relationship in educational institutions as the dimension of the dilemma that most accurately reveals the new directions that school and university athletics must take if they are to maintain their prominent place in American youth culture. His analysis of the problem is that student athletes perceive a conflict between the sports culture in which they operate and the larger culture, which values (or at least pays lip service to) the principles of participatory democracy and achievement on the basis of merit. Students raise questions concerning the limit of the coach's power and authority in governing sports competition. As in other areas of students life, students are requesting—in fact, demanding—greater voice and vote in making decisions that directly affect their lives.[22]

There is much diversity among coaches on how best to deal with issues such as training rules and team loyalty. The issue of team loyalty can be resolved by the coach and players agreeing on the kinds of competing loyalties and commitments that do not detract from one's performance on the team. When these are decided upon, the coach should negotiate with the athletes. Training rules should be reasonable. After there is agreement on what the rules will be and the consequences of breaking them, athletes can be expected to abide by them. Most modern day coaches see a change in their role because many students resent the power that coaches have over the nonathletic aspects of their lives. Schultz proposes that coaches should become aware of the changing youth culture and its values and they should modify their own behavior and programs accordingly. A greater social equality between the athlete and the coach will help create a more honest and fruitful human relationship.[23]

Physical educators and coaches who are seriously interested in reemphasizing the educational value of athletics and who wish to quiet the legitimate criticisms leveled at their profession might consider these guidelines when making decisions affecting either people or programs in athletics. First, seek to broaden the educational experience rather than narrow it. Second, try to relate to rather than conflict with the major social concerns of today's student. Finally, resist the temptation to substitute absolute rules for those that are right and ethical in the immediate situation.

[22] Barry E. Stern, "The Cultural Crisis In American Sport," Journal of Health, Physical Education and Recreation, **43**:42-44 (April 1972).

[23] Frederick D. Schultz, "Broadening the Athletic Experience," Journal of Health, Physical Education and Recreation, **43**:45-47 (April 1972).

Philosophy

Every person contemplating entering the coaching profession needs to develop a personal philosophy of coaching and athletics. Most coaches need several years of experience in their role to develop a philosophy while others may imitate former coaches and immediately reflect that philosophy into their coaching.

Moore defines a person's philosophy as the way he views things, events, relationships, and the values he sets upon them.[24] A coach's philosophy is really the how and why of the program of activity for which he or she is responsible. Todays' coaches are challenged and questioned by many people and it is essential that they know what they believe in and why. Their philosophy must be dynamic and ever changing in order to move with the times. In the final analysis coaches must decide what is best for their players, team, and themselves. Most experts believe that the coach's philosophy of coaching must of necessity be related to their philosophy of life. It is important not only for coaches to know what they believe in and why but for their staff as well. The coach's philosophy provides the staff with a sense of direction but, regardless of the number of people on the staff, the program and the staff will reflect that philosophy.

Tutko and Richards state that to develop his philosophy, a coach must consider some of the more salient aspects of the sport and decide whether his approach toward these will have a positive or negative effect on the athletes.[25] These so-called salient aspects are the coach's attitude toward (1) competition and winning, (2) approaching the athlete, (3) motivating the athlete, and (4) losing. It is expected that the educational program leading toward certification to coach plus the college experience where one is a competitor in an athletic program would supply the necessary knowledge to provide answers to those items listed above.

Most coaches at every level of competition want to be liked by their players but consider it more important to be respected. The qualities possessed by coaches that contribute to this respect are numerous but those considered to be most important are: (1)

[24] J. W. Moore, *The Psychology of Athletic Coaching*, Burgess Publishing Company, Minneapolis, 1970, p. 1.

[25] Thomas A. Tutko and Jack W. Richards, *Psychology of Coaching*, Allyn and Bacon, Boston, 1971, p. 3.

knowledge of the sport, (2) individual concern for the athlete, (3) fairness, (4) the coach as the example, and (5) maturity.[26] A coach's actions should ensure the welfare of the athlete, the team, the school, the community, and the coach himself.

Relationship to Physical Education

A 1971 survey conducted by the American Association for Health, Physical Education and Recreation revealed a trend toward an administrative division between physical education and athletics. Despite this trend, however, a majority of schools and colleges include athletics as a part of the physical education department. Thus all coaches should be members of the physical education staff and should assume certain responsibilities toward that department. The most sane attitude toward athletics is that the coaches should consider the athletic program to be an educational program. The most widely accepted objectives of education are those that may be reached as readily through a physical education program, including athletics, as through a teaching program in any subject.

William Reed, formerly the Big Ten Athletic Conference Commissioner, stated that unless school or school-sponsored athletics are truly a part of the educational structure, faithful to the standards of educational dignity and purpose that our sponsoring institutions represent, we have no justification for their existence.[27]

Many members of the profession believe that athletics are not physical education. One aim of physical education is to develop within individuals all of which they are capable of becoming through physical, mental, social, and emotional elements. The medium for this transition is through appropriate and diversified activities selected according to needs, interests, and process capabilities. On the other hand, the program of athletics aims to nurture these unique and special talents that already exist so that victory in competition can become eminent. The students are different, the process is different and, in short, the reason for the program even existing is different.[28]

[26] Ibid., pp. 10-12.

[27] William R. Reed, "Big Time Athletics, Commitment To Education," *Journal of Health, Physical Education and Recreation*, **34**:29-30: 64-65 (September 1963).

[28] Douglas Wiseman, "Athletics Are Not Physical Education," National College Physical Education Association for Men, *Proceedings of the Seventy-Sixth Annual Conference*, C. E. Mueller (ed.), University of Minnesota, Minneapolis, 1973, p. 17.

Proponents of "academic" physical education place high priority on differentiation between exhibition and entertainment in athletics, and serious physical education. The credibility gap that exists between physical education and athletics is of serious concern, since physical educators ponder whether or not questionable values demonstrated in the operation of some athletic programs and widely publicized conduct of athletics will denigrate physical education.[29]

Physical educators willing to search their souls and be candid will readily admit that the purposes, methods, and objectives of physical education often have no relationship with those in intercollegiate athletics, particularly at schools that support high-powered sports programs.[30]

Few question the fact that the values of society are shifting. Physical educators cannot stop the shift; perhaps they should not try. But they must view it in contemporary perspective, and they must meet the exigencies of the times. Identified as dominant issues in open-end comments are inequities in budget, overemphasis in competition, athletics as a money-making business, and maintenance of a positive perspective.[31]

COACHING MALE AND FEMALE ATHLETES

The emergence of competitive sports experiences for women on the American scene is best illustrated by the fact that in 1967, Sports Illustrated magazine estimated that it had included more than 200 stories and articles on womens' athletics and had featured them on 44 covers. Athletic competition for high school, college, and adult women is now accepted as an important contemporary cultural phenomena in American society. Expansion of competitive sports competition for girls and women will continue to accelerate. The implementation of federal legislation in 1975 provided a legal mandate for equal athletic opportunity regardless of sex (Title IX). Institutions offering professional preparation programs in coaching must include information dealing with the differences between men and women in body type and body composition; physiological and

---

[29] Dorothy L. Fornia, "Signposts for the Seventies," *Journal of Health, Physical Education and Recreation*, **43**:33-36 (October 1972).

[30] Paul Governali, "The Physical Educator As Coach," *Quest*, Monograph VII: 30-33 (December 1966).

[31] Dorothy L. Fornia, "Signposts for the Seventies," *Journal of Health, Physical Education and Recreation*, **43**:33-36 (October 1972).

metabolical factors; and developmental and environmental factors. Neal summarizes these items as follows:[32]

1. Most physiological research indicates that sports competition for women is not detrimental to their health, normal function or well being.
2. There are differences between men and women morphologically. It is possible there are greater differences between the performances of different girls than there are between the performances of girls and boys.
3. There have been and still are, cultural and social influences that greatly handicap the performances of the woman athlete.
4. Because of the biological differences between the male and the female, most women are incapable of equalling the performances of most men in strength, power and endurance events.
5. Educators should be careful that they do not set up inflexible programs on the basis of the "average." Coaching the woman athlete should thus be done on an individual basis, taking into consideration the ability and potential of a person. At the same time, coaches should be selected on the basis of their qualifications not on the basis of their sex.
6. Physiologically, women react to training in the same way men do. Training programs for men and women may differ in degree and intensity, but not necessarily in technique.
7. Participation in sports does not have a harmful effect on the normal function of the reproduction system.
8. The belief that participation in sports tends to masculinize women is a myth.
9. Much research is needed in the area of sociological and psychological factors of competition.

If we can begin to evaluate and understand sport involvement in terms of it being a human experience rather than one that is sex-linked, then we will have made great strides toward understanding all dimensions of involvement. This comment made at a national research conference on women and sport illustrates the emergence of women sports programs upon the national scene. The expansion of competitive sports opportunities for girls and women will continue to accelerate.

[32] Patsy Neal, Coaching Methods for Women, Addison-Wesley Publishing Company, Reading, MA., 1969, pp. 29-30.

SELECTED REFERENCES

Adams, Samuel H., "A Practical Approach to Preparing Coaching," *Journal of Health, Physical Education and Recreation,* **45**:65, (May, 1974).

Alexander, Ruth, and Vern Alexander, *Teachers and Torts,* Maxwell Publishing Company, Middletown, KY, 1970.

Ashenfelter, John, "One Coach's Philosophy of Coaching," *Journal of Health, Physical Education and Recreation,* **36**:22-23 (February, 1965).

"Athletics as Academic Motivation for the Inner City Boy," *Journal of Health, Physical Education and Recreation,* **43**:40-41 (February, 1972).

Bowlus, Warren C., "How Well Do Our College Athletes Fare?" *Journal of Physical Education and Recreation,* **46**:25 (June, 1975).

Briggs, Paul W., "The Opportunity to be Relevant," *Journal of Health, Physical Education and Recreation,* **41**:41-45 (May, 1970).

Brundage, Avery, "Guest Editorial," *Quest,* Marvin H. Eyler (ed.), Monograph X:iv, v, NAPECW and NCPEAM, University of Maryland, College Park, (May, 1968).

Bula, Michael R., "Competition for Children," *Journal of Health, Physical Education and Recreation,* **42**:40 (September, 1971).

Burke, Thomas R., "Athletes, Athletic Performance, and Conditions In the Environment," *Quest,* Monograph VII:56-60, NAPECW and NCPEAM, Lawrence F. Locke (ed.), University of Massachusetts, Amherst, 1972.

Cheska, Alyce, "Current Developments in Competitive Sports for Girls and Women," *Journal of Health, Physical Education and Recreation,* **41**:86-91 (March, 1970).

"Coach," *Quest,* Monograph XVI: 71, NAPECW and NCPEAM, Margaret A. Mordy, (ed.), University of North Carolina, Greensboro, (June 1971).

Cratty; Bryant J., *Physchology in Contemporary Sport,* Prentice-Hall Inc., Englewood Cliffs, NJ, 1973.

Crase, Darrell, "Athletics In Trouble," *Journal of Health, Physical Education and Recreation,* **43**:39-41 (April, 1972).

Deach, Dorothy, F., "Preparation of Women Coaches," *Proceedings of the National College Physical Education Association for Men,* Leo L. Gedvials (ed.), 9-12, University of Illinois, Chicago Circle, Chicago, 1975.

DeBacy, Diane L., Ree Speath, and Roxanne Busch, "What Do Men Really Think About Athletic Competition for Women?", *Journal of Health, Physical Education and Recreation*, 41:28-29, 72 (May, 1970).

"Development of Human Values Through Sports," *Proceedings of a National Conference*, Springfield College, Springfield, MA, October 12-14, 1974.

Durrant, Sue M., "And Who May Compete,"? *Quest*, Betty Spears (ed.), Monograph XXII: 104-109, NAPECW and NCPEAM, University of Massachusetts, Amherst, (June, 1974).

Ewers, James R., "Move Over Men: The Women Are Coming," *Proceedings of the Seventy-Third Annual Conference of the National College Physical Education Association For Men*, C. E. Mueller (ed.), 175-180, University of Minnesota, Minneapolis, 1970.

Fahey, Thomas D., "Anabolic Steroids and Athletics," *The Physical Educator*, Indianapolis, Ind, 30:40 (March, 1973).

Felshin, Jan, "The Triple Option For Women In Sport," *Quest*, Betty Spears (ed.), Monograph XXI:36-40, NAPECW and NCPEAM, University of Massachusetts, Amherst, (January, 1974).

Flath, Arnold (ed.), *Athletics in America*, Oregon State University Press, Corvalis, Oreg. 1972.

Fornia, Dorothy L., "Sign Posts for the Seventies," *Journal of Health, Physical Education and Recreation*, 43:33-36 (October, 1972).

Gallon, Arthur J., *Coaching—Ideas and Ideals*, Houghton Mifflin Company, Boston, 1974.

Gerber, Ellen W., *Sport and the Body*, Lea & Febiger, Philadelphia, 1972.

Governali, Paul, "The Physical Educator as Coach," *Quest*, Pearl Berlin (ed.), Monograph VII:30-33, NAPECW and NCPEAM, Wayne State University, Detroit, (December, 1966).

Grieve, Andrew, *The Legal Aspects of Athletics*, A. S. Barnes and Company, New York, 1969.

Grosse, Susan J., "Bridging the Gap In Competitive Sports," *Journal of Health, Physical Education and Recreation*, 44:90-91 (January, 1973).

"Guidelines For Inter Scholastic Programs for Junior High School Girls," *Journal of Health, Physical Education and Recreation*, 37:36-37 (September, 1966).

Happ, William P., "Only When Competition Is Properly Guided Is It Beneficial to Children," *Journal of Health, Physical Education and Recreation,* **38**:29 (June, 1967).

Harper, William A., "Man Alone," *Quest,* Margaret Mordy (ed.), Monograph XIII:57-60, NAPECW and NCPEAM, Ohio State University, Columbus, Ohio, (May, 1960).

Harris, Dorothy V., *Women and Sport: A National Conference,* Pennsylvania State University, August 13-18, 1972.

Hillyer, James H., "Integration and Athletics," *Proceedings of the National Federation's Fifth Annual National Conference of High School Directors of Athletics,* Hershey, PA, December 8-11, 1974, pp. 7-11.

Hult, Joan, "Competitive Athletics For Girls," *Journal of Health, Physical Education and Recreation,* **45**:45-46 (June, 1974).

Jernigan, Sara Staff, "Mirror of Time: Some Causes For More American Women in Sport Competitions," *Quest,* Betty Spears (ed.), Monograph XVII:82-87, NAPECW and NCPEAM, University of Massachusetts, Amherst, (June, 1974).

Kesling, Karen, "Competitive Sports," Address given at National Convention of the American Alliance for Health, Physical Education and Recreation, Atlantic City, NJ, March 16, 1975.

Kleinman, Carol, "Making Room for the Women Athlete," *The Chicago Tribune,* September 15, 1975, Chicago, Illinois.

Lambert, Charlotte, "Pros and Cons of Intercollegiate Athletic Competition for Women," *Journal of Health, Physical Education and Recreation,* **40**:75-78 (May, 1969).

Leonard, George, *The Ultimate Athlete,* Viking Press, New York, 1974.

Loy, Jr., John W., "The Nature of Sport: A Definitional Effort," *Quest,* Marvin H. Eyler (ed.), Monograph X:1-15, NAPECW and NCPEAM, University of Maryland, College Park, (May, 1968).

Mabley, Jack, "What Do Kids Get From Sports Today?", *The Chicago Tribune,* August 20, 1975, Chicago.

Mabley, Jack, "Winning Should Not Be the Only Thing," *The Chicago Tribune,* January 27, 1976, Chicago.

McAfee, Floyd H., "A Balance of Pride," *Journal of Health, Physical Education and Recreation,* **41**:24-27 (September, 1970).

Malumphy, Theresa M., "The College Women Athlete," *Quest,* Margaret Mordy (ed.), Monograph XIV:18-27, NAPECW and NCPEAM, Ohio State University, Columbus, (May, 1970).

Meadows, Paul E., "Are We Really Coaching Fundamentals?", *Journal of Health, Physical Education and Recreation*, **34**:34 (March, 1963).

Metz, Paul R., "A Course To Build Player-Coach Rapport," *Journal of Health, Physical Education and Recreation*, **43**:50-51 (April, 1972).

Miller, Donna Mae, *Coaching the Female Athlete*, Lea & Febiger, Philadelphia, 1974.

Moore, J. W., *The Psychology of Athletic Coaching*, Burgess Publishing Company, Minneapolis, 1970.

Morgan, William P., (ed.), "Research Studies On The Female Athlete," *Journal of Health, Physical Education and Recreation*, **46**:32-46 (January, 1975).

Murphy, Elizabeth, and Marilyn Vincent, "Status of Funding of Women's Intercollegiate Athletics," *Journal of Health, Physical Education and Recreation*, **44**:11-15 (October, 1973).

Neal, Patsy, *Coaching Methods for Women*, Addison-Wesley Publishing Company, Reading, MA, 1969.

Neal, Patsey, "Heroes, Heroines, and Seagulls," *Proceedings of the National Federation of High School Directors of Athletics*, Hershey, PA, 3-6 (December 8-11, 1974).

Ogilvie, Bruce, "What Is An Athlete?" *Journal of Health, Physical Education and Recreation*, **38**:48 (June, 1967).

Olson, Edward, "Intercollegiate Athletics, Is There No Way To Live With it?", *Proceedings of the National College Physical Education Association for Men*, C. E. Mueller (ed.), 18-22, University of Minnesota, Minneapolis, 1973.

Ping, Charles J., "The Drama of College Athletics," *The Chronicle of Higher Education*, September 23, 1974 pp. 1-3.

Poindexter, Hally B., and Carol L. Mushier, *Coaching Competitive Team Sports for Girls and Women*, W. B. Saunders Company, Philadelphia, 1973.

"Policies On Women Athletics Change," *Journal of Health, Physical Education and Recreation*, **44**:31-32 (September, 1973).

"Professional Preparation in Dance, Physical Education, Recreation Education, Safety Education and School Health Education," Washington, D.C., 1974.

"Project On the Status and Education of Women, What Constitutes Equality For Women In Sports,"? *Association of American Colleges*, Washington, D.C., 1972, p. 17.

Ray, Robert F., "Trends In Intercollegiate Athletics," *Journal of*

Health, Physical Education and Recreation, **36**:21-22; 70 (January, 1965).

Reed, William R., "Big Time Athletics' Commitment To Education," Journal of Health, Physical Education and Recreation, **34**:29-30, 64-65 (September, 1963).

Russell, Kathryn, R.E., and Donna Mae Miller, Sport: A Contemporary View, Lea & Febiger, Philadelphia, 1971.

Sabock, Ralph J., The Coach, W.B. Saunders Company, Philadelphia, 1973.

Sadler, Jr., William A., "Competition Out of Bounds: Sport in American Life," Quest, Lawrence F. Locke (ed.), Monograph XX:123-132, NAPECW and NCPEAM, University of Massachusetts, Amherst, (January, 1973).

Sage, George H., "The Coach As Management," Quest, Lawrence F. Locke (ed.), Monograph XX:35-40, NAPECW and NCPEAM, University of Massachusetts, (January, 1973).

Schultz, Frederick, D., "Broadening the Athletic Experience," Journal of Health, Physical Education and Recreation, **43**:45-47 (April, 1972).

Schurr, Evelyn L., "Women Sports Officials," Journal of Health, Physical Education and Recreation **42**:71-72 (November-December, 1971).

Singer, Robert N., Coaching Athletics and Psychology, McGraw-Hill, Book Company, New York, 1972.

Smith, Gary, "Violence In Sport," Journal of Health, Physical Education and Recreation **42**:45-47 (March, 1971).

"Sports As Agents of Change," Journal of Health, Physical Education and Recreation, **40**:35-42 (April, 1969).

Stark, Barry, "To Work With the Young Athlete of the 70's," Journal of Health, Physical Education and Recreation, **42**:42; 57 (January, 1971).

Stern, Barry E., "The Cultural Crisis In American Sports," Journal of Health, Physical Education and Recreation, **43**:42-44 (April, 1972).

Thorp, Roland G., and Ronald Gallimore, "What A Coach Can Teach a Teacher," Psychology Today, **35**:37 (January, 1976).

Turner, Edward T., "Creativity and Coaching," The Physical Educator, Indianapolis, Ind., **30**:134-136, (October, 1973).

Tutko, Thomas A., and Jack W. Richards, Psychology of Coaching, Allyn and Bacon, Boston, 1971.

Ulrich, Celeste, "She Can Play As Good As Any Boy," *Phi Delta Kappan*, Bloomington, Ind. pp. 113-117, (October, 1973).

Vanderzwaag, Harold, "Sport, Existential or Essential," *Quest*, Marvin H. Eyler (ed.), Monograph XII:45-56, NAPECW and NCPEAM, University of Maryland, College Park, (May, 1969).

Vanderzwaag, Harold, "Sports Concepts," *Journal of Health, Physical Education and Recreation*, **41**:35-36 (March, 1970).

Walter, Don, "The Coach and Drugs," *The Physical Educator*, Indianapolis, Ind, **30**:154-156 (October, 1973).

Wiseman, Douglas, "Athletics Are Not Physical Education," *Proceedings of the National College Physical Education Association For Men*, C. E. Mueller (ed.), 17-18, University of Minnesota, Minneapolis, 1973.

chapter 10
sports administration

DEFINITION

Sports administration is a relatively new area of specialization for professionals in physical education/athletics. Many institutions of higher learning are instituting programs at both the undergraduate and graduate level. The University of Massachusetts has such a program and defines it as an academic curriculum designed to prepare individuals seeking managerial positions within sport oriented organizations, such as college/university athletic programs, intramurals, interscholastic programs, professional sports teams, civic centers, halls of fame, sporting-good manufacturing, and leisure sports enterprises. Sports administration programs accommodate but are not limited to athletic administration.[1]

Note that this section of the book is devoted to a different connotation of sports. Consequently, the term "sports" should be differentiated from "athletics." Sports can be defined as a kind of diversion that has for its direct and immediate end fun, pleasure, and delight and is dominated by a spirit of moderation and generosity. Athletics is essentially a competitive activity oriented toward victory in the contest, and it is

[1] Interview with Harold J. Vanderswaag, March 9, 1975, University of Massachusetts, Amherst, MA.

characterized by a spirit of dedication, sacrifice, and intensity.[2] Loy and Ingham define sports as a social institution with legitimations that justify its existence, rules that guide the interactions of individuals holding positions within its structure, and prescriptions for the ways in which individual's appearances are to be managed.[3]

NEED FOR SPORTS ADMINISTRATORS

Those persons who question the importance of sports in our society would be surprised by the amount of space devoted to it in American newspapers. One of the most respected newspapers in the United States, *The New York Times,* devotes more space to sports than it does to art, books, education, television, or the theater. It devotes more space to sports in its daily edition than to all of the above named subjects combined. The July 21, 1976 issue of this newspaper printed for the first time a picture of the Olympic champion gymnast on its front page. Sports participation figures have increased steadily in the past decade in a multitude of sports activities. Effective and competent administrators are needed to provide the necessary leadership for individuals who are participating in these activities. It is obvious to many, however, that American sports is not without problems. How do we solve such current problems as: (1) the obsession to win and consequent lack of good sportsmanship, (2) the failure to produce widespread physical fitness, and (3) the centralization of sports activities resulting from an increase in people watching sports on television?

STATUS OF THE PROFESSION

Some may question whether sports administration may be considered to be a profession. If we define profession as a group of people who are brought together by a common interest in a significant and identifiable area of human affairs and who attempt to serve mankind

[2] Robert G. Osterhoudt, "The Kantian Ethics as a Principle of Moral Conduct in Sports," *Quest,* Lawrence F. Locke (ed.), Monograph XIX:121, NAPECW and NCPEAM, University of Massachusetts, Amherst, (January, 1973).

[3] Alan Ingham and John W. Loy, "The Social System of Sport: A Humanistic Perspective," *Quest,* Lawrence F. Locke (ed.), Monograph XIX:3, NAPECW and NCPEAM, University of Massachusetts, Amherst, (January, 1973).

by activity relevant to this area of common interest, the answer is affirmative.[4]

Most physical educators tend to identify an athletic director as the primary example of a sports administrator. Administrative positions cut across many facets of the sports world and are not confined to educational enterprises. The many possibilities for employment will be discussed in Chapter 11.

WORKING RELATIONSHIPS

The success or failure of any enterprise (industrial, commercial, educational, etc.) depends largely upon the nature of working relationships. Research evidence from studies in industry consider the attitudes and practices of persons responsible for the implementation of policies to be of the highest importance. What kind of working relationships would a successful sports administrator establish with his or her employee? Those persons contemplating a sports administration career should be aware of the attributes listed by Melby.[5]

1. Respect for personality
    a. An administrator must have fundamental attitudes of respect and admiration for all.
2. Power of humility
    a. The most pronounced effect of the administrator's own attitude toward human beings is not upon others, but upon himself.
3. Leadership is more than staff selection
    a. Employees, no matter how good they actually have been, must continually grow if their capacities are to be developed to the fullest possible extent.
4. Employees must be viewed in totality
    a. More attention should be given to our capacity to help people achieve rather than to the mere factor of selection.

[4] Ernie McCoy, "Professional Status of Athletic Directors," Report of the Third National Conference of the National Association of Collegiate Directors of Athletics, Washington, D.C., AAHPER, 1965, p. 15.

[5] Ernest Melby, Administering Community Education, Prentice-Hall, Inc., Englewood Cliffs, NJ, 1955, pp. 262-280.

5. The administrator must not fear incompetence
   a. The moment one stops looking upon himself as an administrator, as one who dominates or controls, and sees himself as a servant of others, he will have a different attitude toward his associates and exert a surprising influence for the growth and development of people.
6. Listen sympathetically
   a. Every administrator should develop the capacity to listen patiently.
   b. Work schedules should be arranged to deal with employees in an unhurried fashion.
7. Be accessible
   a. Every effort should be made to make oneself accessible to people and to make conversation and communication easy.
8. The power of faith
   a. The creative administrator seeks always to get his associates on the team, and one of the best ways to enlist people is to trust them.
9. Allow for mistakes
   a. Set as little routine as possible for the positions of the people with whom you work.
   b. Learn to evaluate each person in the aggregate rather than in terms of details.
10. Help people to see their problems and their opportunities
    a. A skillful administrator works with one's associates in a way that reveals to them the nature of the problems they face, without producing a feeling of inferiority or guilt.
11. Try to understand your associates
    a. Be attentive to problems of your associates and make every effort to understand the nature of these problems.
12. Use your staff resources
    a. The creative administrator assembles groups that exercise an effective influence upon one another.
13. Recognize achievement
    a. The effective administrator will devote herself to the task of helping people find greater satisfaction in their work, irrespective of the status of the position.
14. Get acquainted with people
    a. Life is always enriched by stimulation through knowing people.

b. An effective administrator always keeps in touch with the activities of his staff; he knows what they are doing and is aware of their problems and their successes.
15. Help people to paint on a large canvas
   a. Creative administrators help their associates to broaden their horizons and to see the relationship between their own activities and those of other people.
16. Try to eliminate annoyances
   a. The removal of annoyances and obstacles should represent an ongoing task for the administrator.
17. Help people to sense resources in each other
   a. A competitive attitude on the part of staff members exists in most educational institutions. An effective administrator encourages excellence from all persons because it enhances the status, reputation, and productivity of the educational unit.
18. Be sure budgetary policies help and not hinder
   a. The policies of reward and promotion are extremely important in every enterprise. Encourage good teamworkers and the whole operation will prosper.
19. Stimulate group efforts
   a. A creative administrator can do much to help people gain satisfaction from group participation.
      1) Conduct group activities in a pleasant and stimulating manner.
      2) Express appreciation for the contributions of both individual members and group achievements.
20. One touchstone is integrity
   a. The difference between the smart and great administrator is likely to be found in the presence or absence of such qualities as unselfishness, humility, integrity and total dedication to human service.
21. The final touchstone is creativity
   a. One's creative power as a leader is increased by stimulating others.

The reader may feel that this exhaustive list of attributes is unattainable. Some reflection on persons whom you have known to serve in administrative positions, however, should provide insight on the importance of these competencies in the success of the enterprise.

MANAGEMENT AS A FUNCTION OF THE SPORTS ADMINISTRATOR

Curricular programs for training sports administrators will be dealt with in Chapter 11. A review of courses to be completed reveals courses in management and public relations. These are not so-called "typical" courses for physical education students but, because we consider them to be of great importance in the preparation of the sports administrator, we are devoting the rest of this chapter to these two topics.

A successful sports administrator operates under sound management concepts and principles regardless of the geographical location, the nature of the organization, or the size of the company. What are some of the valid concepts in management for the sports administrator to know and to understand?[6]

1. Management is working through others.
    (a) The manager should spend the bulk of his time performing management functions, which requires him to develop subordinates through proper assignment, motivation, and control.
2. Management is a basic process that consists of several specific functions on the part of the manager. These functions are:
    (a) To plan.
    (b) To organize.
    (c) To decide.
    (d) To communicate.
    (e) To activate.
    (f) To control.
    (g) To evaluate.
3. Management is a science and an art.
    (a) The science of management is the application of the scientific method (use and analysis of facts after the primary problem has been identified) of general management problem solving and decision making.
4. Management principles and concepts have universal application.
    (a) Any manager at any level in any kind of organization, whatever the objectives, located anywhere in the world will engage in the management processes referred to in item 2 above.

[6]Francis J. Bridges, "Synopsis: Application of Management Principles to Athletic Administration," *Proceedings of the National Federation's Fifth National Conference of High School Directors of Athletics,* Hershey, PA, Dec. 8-11, 1974, pp. 45-49.

5. Management is by objectives.
   (a) Objectives give direction to staff efforts and stand as a target for measuring performance. Each individual must work and be managed by objectives whether they be short-run, interim, or companywide.
6. Management is totally responsible.
   (a) Both the highest ranking executive and the lowest ranking manager is fully responsible—the former for the success or failure of the entire organization in achieving it's primary goals or objectives and the latter for the success or failure of his or her unit's reaching it's objectives.
7. Management is judged on results.
   (a) End results must be used to judge and evaluate managerial personnel.
8. Management is people oriented.
   (a) Managers attempt to understand and satisfy the basic job needs, wants, and desires of subordinate personnel to a satisfactory degree.
9. Managment is decision making.
   (a) Making decisions is a basic management function. A manager is one who makes things happen.
10. Management is the difference between organizations.
    (a) Management decisions regarding ideas, innovations, recruitment and selection of personnel, planning skill, utilization of resources, training, and employees, gradually separate the superior firm from the mediocre firm.

PUBLIC RELATIONS

It has been said that the lifeblood of organizations is accurate communication. This statement is particularly applicable to sports administrators. Communication is a two-way process that includes credibility, content, commitment, and consistency.[7] Credibility means that the public must be pleased. Content refers to the fact that the message must be important and relevant to the audience in clear, concise, and familiar language. Commitment is achieved by exemplifying the sincerity of what is being communicated. Consistency means that all messages should be coincided as they relate to the various facets of the public.

[7] Carol Ann Leaf, "Public Information Toteboard," Journal of Health, Physical Education and Recreation, Washington, D.C., 45:59 (January, 1974).

One important facet of the communications process is public relations, which is defined by Cutlip and Center as the planned effort to influence opinion through socially responsible performance based on mutually satisfactory two-way communication.[8]

Public relations is generally conceded to have four basic characteristics: first, it is a philosophy of management. Philosophy of management is best explained as an attitude of mind. This attitude of mind places the interests of *people* first in all matters pertaining to the conduct of any organization or association (i.e., industrial, social service, bank, utility, trade, and professional). Second, it is a function of management that evaluates public attitudes, identifies the policies and procedures of an individual or an organization with the public interest, and executes a program of action to earn public understanding and acceptance. Remember that there is a difference between public relations as an operating concept of management and public relations as a specialized staff function in management. The former is a general operating principle, which guides administrators to a greater or lesser degree and is the responsibility of every person identified with an enterprise. The latter is a dynamic, specialized function for which managers have skilled practitioners.[9] Third, it is a technique of communication through which the public learns about the aims and accomplishments of an organization. Every person instinctively wants to know what is going on that affects his or her interests. The same is true for every public affected in any way by an organization. There must be a willingness on the part of management to communicate its policies and activities to all the facets of the public that are affected. It is also important that communications be a two-way system for conveying information (i.e., from management to its public and vice versa). Methods of communication may be classified as: (1) word-of-mouth or personal communication media such as public speaking, public-address systems, radio and television broadcasts, recording, individual conferences, meetings, open houses, films, and educational courses; (2) printed or graphic media that include advertising, publicity, periodicals, books, letters, comic books, exhibits and displays, bulletin boards, bulletins, annual reports, handbooks and manuals, signs, pay envelope inserts, posters, direct-mail booklets and folders, and charts. Fourth, it involves good public

---

[8]Scott M. Cutlip and Allen H. Center, *Effective Public Relations*, Prentice-Hall, Inc., Englewood Cliffs, NJ, 1971, p. 2.

[9]Ibid., p. 4.

impressions made by the people associated with an enterprise. Everyone associated in any way with an organization or association creates an image of the unit that may be positive or negative. A business or social organization may express a pleasing personality in the same way as a person, and the same characteristics create confidence in both instances. It is essential for a sports administrator to assign persons of good personality to positions involving business relations with the public. A successful administrator will also organize and conduct an internal public relations program for *all* employees.

The public-relations process involves finding the facts, establishing a policy, planning a program and communicating the story to the internal and external publics.

Many educators are not aware of the many facets of the public of public relations. Each have their particular interests and problems. The business public includes: (1) the employee, (2) the owner or stockbroker, (3) the consumer, (4) the supplier, (5) the community, (6) the government, (7) the trade or competitor concerns in the same industry, and (8) the distributor and dealer. Social, religious, labor, educational, charitable, and nonprofit organizations have their particular public also.[10]

A cataloging of the different sectors of the public for a university might appear as follows:

Student relations.
Faculty relations.
Staff relations.
Community relations.
Alumni relations.
Donor relations.
Government relations.
Foundation relations.
Trustee relations.
Press relations.

The public referred to above may be reached through the following media:

[10] Bertrand R. Canfield, *Public Relations*, Richard D. Irwin, Inc., Homewood, IL, 1956, p. 25.

Formal public opinion polls.
Informal opinion surveys.
Questionnaires.
Personal contacts.
Correspondence.
Company newspapers, magazines.
News releases.
Radio and TV programs.
Exhibits, displays.
Special events.
Bulletin boards.
Employee awards.
Annual reports.
Motion and slide films.
Payroll inserts.
Employee letters.
Shareholder letters.
Shareholder magazines.
Speeches.
Art shows.
Booklets, brochures.
Open house, plant tours.
Materials for schools.
Essay contests.
Photographs.
Suggestion systems.
Visitors' parking.
Recreational programs.
Dividend inserts.
Advertising.

The mass media of today—radio, television, and the press—comprise part of modern civilization's environment and serve as a background for many of our activities. Sports administrators should have a basic understanding of the role and importance of the mass media as it relates to their organizations.[11] The persons who make the greatest contribution in providing the mass media with information for dissemination are the sports reporters. Because these persons occupy such an important position in the sports administration hierarchy, their professional training must be of the highest order. McIntosh suggests that they must have: (1) high linguistic ability and impeccable judgment on events, (2) a deep technical knowledge of the sports on which they have to comment, (3) continuous training in all the related media press, radio, and television, and (4) a full respect for the accepted ethical rules and code of practice.[12]

Professional physical educators have not distinguished themselves in the past in interpreting sports and particularly physical education to their public. The American Alliance for Health, Physical Education and Recreation addressed itself to this problem in 1971 and embarked on a national program called PEPI (Physical Education Public Information). This project was in effect a grand design of responsibili-

[11] Alan (Ed) Wells, *Mass Media and Society*, National Press Books, Palo Alto, CA, 1972, p. 3.

[12] Peter McIntosh, "Mass Media: Friends or Foes in Sport," *Quest*, Betty Spears (ed.), Monograph XXII:42, NAPECW and NCPEAM, University of Massachusetts, Amherst, (June, 1974).

ties for the profession. A national director was appointed, who, in addition to having outstanding educational competencies, possessed exceptional skill in public relations.[13]

Afterward, four regional workshops were conducted and local, state, and district coordinators were appointed to implement this new grand design. A group of leaders in physical education prepared a list of PEPI project concepts that appeared on page 16. These concepts were geared to provide information to the general public and were identified concepts that provided the direction for new experiences in physical education.

The history of the PEPI project has resulted in a significant gain in public acceptance and belief in the value of physical activity. Every administrator should be familiar with and join in this national effort to publicize physical education and sports. It is reasonable to assume that we are now becoming a nation of participants rather than spectators if newspaper coverage is one criteria to be considered. A July 22, 1976 issue of the Chicago, Illinois *Tribune* listed the following activities that were being conducted in the metropolitan area for the period of July 22 to 26: archery, backpacking, badminton, baseball, billiards, bowling, camping, canoeing, cricket, cycling, diving, equestrian, fencing, football, golf, hiking, hockey, ice skating, Irish games, karting, orienteering, rugby, running, soccer, softball, swimming, tennis, track and field, volleyball, water skiing, and wrestling.[14] In running alone, 10 different events were listed. Swimming had 5 events. Ice hockey showed 6 events, despite the fact that they were scheduled in July. Ninety-five of these events were for amateur contestants. Sports administrators take heart—you do have a profession.

SELECTED REFERENCES

AAHPER, "It's Up To You To Do Something About Physical Education," *Journal of Health, Physical Education and Recreation*, Washington, D.C., 39:39-49, (February, 1968).

Barnes, Samuel E., "Criteria for Evaluating the Administration of Intercollegiate Athletics," Unpublished doctoral dissertation, Bowling Green State University, 1971, 132 pages.

[13] Fay Biles, "The Physical Education Public Information Project," *Journal of Health, Physical Education and Recreation*, Washington, D.C., 42:53-55 (September, 1971).

[14] "The Chicago Tribune," *Recreation Directory*, Chicago, July 22, 1976, p. 4.

Biles, Fay, "The Physical Education Public Information Project," *Journal of Health, Physical Education and Recreation*, Washington, D.C., **42**:53-55 (September, 1971).

Bridges, Francis J., "Synposis: Application of Management Principles to Athletic Administration," *Proceedings of the National Federation's Fifth National Conference of High School Directors of Athletics*, Hershey, PA, December 8-11, 1974, pp. 45-49.

Canfield, Bertrand R., *Public Relations*, Richard D. Irwin, Inc., Homewood, IL, 1956.

Cutlip, Scott M., and Allen H. Center, *Effective Public Relations*, Fourth Edition, Prentice-Hall, Inc., Englewood Cliffs, NJ, 1971.

Dennis, James M., "Administrative Behavior of Successful and Unsuccessful Athletic Directors in Small Colleges and Universities," Unpublished doctoral dissertation, University of Southern California, 1971.

Gerber, Ellen W., Jan Felshin, Pearl Berlin and Waneen Wyrick, *The American Women in Sport*, Addison-Wesley Publishing Co., Reading, MA, 1974.

Griffiths, Daniel E., *Human Relations In School Administration*, Appleton-Century-Crofts, Inc., New York, 1958.

Henry, Charles D., "Communication—Needed to Save Sports," *The Physical Educator*, Bloomington, Ind, **32**:171-172 (December, 1975).

Hunsicker, Paul (ed.), "Administrative Theory and Practice in Athletics and Physical Education," *Proceedings of CIC Administrative Theory in Athletics and Physical Education*, The Athletic Institute, Chicago, p. 154, 1973.

Kozloff, Edward, "The Public Relations Gap—Can We Close It?," *The Physical Educator*, Bloomington, Ind, **26**:124 (October, 1969).

Leaf, Carol Ann, "Public Information Toteboard," *Journal of Health, Physical Education and Recreation*, Washington, D.C. **45**:15 (April, 1974).

Lepke, Phyllis, "Public Relations for Physical Education," *Journal of Health, Physical Education and Recreation*, Washington, D.C., **44**:10-11 (May, 1973).

Marshall, Stanley J., "The Organizational Relationship Between Physical Education and Intercollegiate Athletics in American Colleges and Universities," Unpublished doctoral dissertation, Springfield College, MA, 1969, 236 pages.

Massie, Joseph L., *Essentials of Management*, Prentice-Hall, Inc., Englewood Cliffs, NJ, 1971.

McCoy, Ernie, "Professional Status of Athletic Directors," *Report of the Third National Conference of the National Association of Collegiate Director of Athletics*, Washington, D.C., 1965, pp. 13-15.

McIntosh, Peter C., "Mass Media: Friends or Foes in Sport," *Quest*, Betty Spears (ed.), Monograph XXII:33-34, NAPECW and NCPEAM, University of Massachusetts, Amherst, (May, 1974).

McIntosh, Peter C. *Sport in Society*, C. A. Watts and Co., Ltd., London, 1971.

Melby, Ernest O., *Administering Community Education*, Prentice-Hall, Inc., Englewood Cliffs, NJ, 1965.

Orr, Richard E., "A Study of Selected Administrative Behaviors of Secondary School Athletic Directors." Unpublished doctoral dissertation, University of Southern California, 1975.

PEPI-PROJECT, *Journal of Health, Physical Education and Recreation*, **43**:12 (February, 1972).

Sage, George, H., *Sport and American Society: Selected Readings*, Addison-Wesley Publishing Co., Reading MA, 1970.

Shea, Edward J., and Elton E. Wieman, *Administrative Policies For Intercollegiate Athletics*, Charles C. Thomas, Springfield, IL, 1967.

Sisley, Becky, "Challenges Facing the Woman Athletic Director," *The Physical Educator*, Bloomington, Ind, **32**:121-123, (October, 1975).

Vanderzwagg, Harold J., "Sport Administration: Careers in Physical Education," *Briefings*, NCPEAM and NAPECW, United States, 1975, pp. 17-27.

Wells, Alan (ed.), *Mass Media and Society*, National Press Books, Palo Alto, CA, 1972.

Wilson, Clifford, "Excellence and Sports," *The Physical Educator*, Bloomington, Ind., **32**:171-172, (December, 1975).

chapter 11

the program in sports administration

ORGANIZATIONAL CONSIDERATIONS

Because of the relative newness of programs in sports administration, there are some differences of opinion regarding where it should be placed in an organizational structure. Colleges, schools, and departments of physical education often encompass programs in health, safety, dance, recreation, and physical training. Sports also represents, in the opinion of many, a significant aspect of the so-called "physical education" entity.[1] There appear to be four possibilities for the location of a program in sports administration:[2]

1. Department of sports in a school or college of physical education.
2. Department of sport studies in a school or college of physical education.
3. Department of sports in a college of arts and sciences or a school of education.

[1] Harold Vanderzwaag, Sport Administration, *Briefings, Careers in Physical Education*, NCPEAM and NAPECW, United States, 1975, p. 20.

[2] Ibid, pp. 20-22.

4. Department of sports in a school or college of business administration.

The advantages and disadvantages of placing a sports department in each of the above categories are somewhat obvious. It is unfortunate that vested interests often dictate where this program is placed with a resultant diminition of program quality. The important consideration should be implementation of the program that will always be dependent upon the personnel and the dynamics of that particular institution. The quality of the program will be determined largely by the qualifications and interests of the faculty assigned to it.

QUALIFICATIONS AND PREPARATION

The qualifications necessary for persons contemplating careers in sports administration are not unlike those required for any person in an administrative role. One qualification often overlooked is experience. A sports administrator, without some exposure to sport as a participant or in some type of active role, would encounter severe problems in the performance or his or her job. Some experience in subadministrative positions is also necessary in the training process. Note, however, that service is not the only requirement for athletic directors to be moved to more prestigious positions. Some formal education is required in the general area of administration.

The athletic director in a school is an example of one type of sports administrator. Because of the relative newness of specialization in sports administration, there is presently no established pattern of graduate work in the administration of athletics per se for either the secondary or collegiate level. However, a joint committee of representatives of AAHPER, NCAA, and NCPEAM have developed a list of competencies needed for professional preparation at the graduate level.[3] These competencies include an understanding of:

1. The role of athletics in education and our society and the rules, regulations, policies, and procedures of the various governing bodies.
2. Sound business procedures as related to athletic administration.

[3] AAHPER, Professional Preparation of the Administrator of Athletics, *Journal of Health, Physical Education and Recreation*, **41**:20-22 (September, 1970).

3. Administrative problems as related to equipment and supplies.
4. Problems related to facilities (indoor and outdoor).
5. School law and liability.
6. The factors involved in the conduct of athletic events.
7. Good public relations techniques.
8. Staff relationships.
9. The health aspects of athletics.
10. The psychological and sociological aspects of sports.

The reader will note the striking similarity between the competencies listed above and those discussed in Chapter 10 under the heading of Working Relationships.

Richardson recommends that the candidate for admission to a graduate program in athletic administration should have been a player, coach, or an administrator in athletics.[4]

An interesting approach to the search for competencies needed by athletic directors is advanced by Owen B. Kiernan, a former executive secretary of the National Association of Secondary School Principals.[5] He says that athletic directors should be assigned Q ratings. These quotients would include I.Q.—intelligence and integrity, A.Q. adaptability, G.Q.—gumption or guts, and a non-Q quotient called C.T. or common touch. These quotients are applicable not only to athletic directors but to everyone in sports administration positions.

CURRICULA

It has been previously noted that curricula are in the developing stages, and no patterns have been established that are peculiar to specific institutions.

Two institutions having programs in operation are the University of Massachusetts (undergraduate) and Western Illinois University (graduate).

[4] Deane E. Richardson, Preparation for A Career in Public School Administration, *Journal of Health, Physical Education and Recreation*, Washington, D.C., **42**:17-19 (February, 1971).

[5] Owen B. Kiernan, The A.D.—A Professional All the Way, *Proceedings of the National Federation's Fifth Annual Conference of High School Directors of Athletics*, Hershey, Pa., Dec. 8-11, 1974, pp. 24-26.

Massachusetts requires 120 semester hours of work, which can be completed in four years:[6]

COURSES	CREDIT
University Core Requirements (Distribution of course work in four areas: (1) rhetoric, (2) humanities and fine arts, (3) social and behavioral sciences, and (4) natural sciences and mathematics).	36
Basic Sports Studies Courses (Lecture Type) (Four courses—one each in history, philosophy, psychology, and sociology of sport).	12
Sport Studies Seminars (Four basic courses to be followed by seminars covering special topics in sport studies with a focus on student research).	12
Sports Administration Seminar ("Integrating" type course to be taken by the student during the semester immediately prior to the internship; primary purpose is to prepare the student for the internship).	3
Business Administration Courses (Distribution of course work in accounting, finance, marketing, and management).	30
Electives In Economics	12
Internship (One entire semester).	15
Total	120

Western Illinois University offers a master of science degree in physical education with emphasis in athletic administration. Forty-five quarter hours of work is required for completion of the degree.[7]

[6] Harold J. Vanderzwaag, "Sport Administration," *Briefings, Careers in Physical Education,* NCPEAM and NAPECW, United States, 1975, pp. 22-25.

[7] William Lakie, "Athletic Administration," *Graduate Bulletin,* Western Illinois University, Macomb, IL, June, 1976.

COURSES	CREDIT
Degree Program Core (Four courses—administration of athletics, the use and maintenance of facilities, organization and administration, and financial accounting).	14
Physical Education Electives	9-12
Cognate Courses (From the fields of business, education, sociology, communications, and psychology).	12-15
Practicum (Conducted under the supervision of a director of athletics in a secondary school or university or a professional sports organization).	6

Both programs described above illustrate the heavy concentration of courses from areas outside physical education and athletics. The physical education profession must accept the premise that it can no longer survive in isolation from the university community. A sports administrator with competencies in a broad range of subject-matter fields is the one most likely to succeed on the job.

INTERNSHIP

Both graduate and undergraduate programs should include a heavy concentration on the internship experience. This is undoubtedly the most practical and relevant phase of the total curricular offering. It serves as a valuable learning experience in much the same manner as student teaching for the teacher education major. The experience should be broad in nature in order to expose the intern to the multifarious operations of a sports organization. For example, an intern in a college athletic department would assist with such items as publicity, scheduling, ticket sales, facilities planning, and personnel management. Other opportunities for internships exist in high-school athletic programs, professional sports teams, ski resorts, commissioner's office in amateur or professional sports, or private sports clubs. A distinct advantage is offered in terms of career opportunities for interns because of the many personal contacts made during the course of the program. Educators conducting programs in sports administration should place a high priority on the internship phase because much of the knowledge and skill in administration is learned on the job. There should be no substitute for this part of the program.

CAREER OPPORTUNITIES

The decline in teaching positions at all educational levels has resulted in a major shift of program emphases in many colleges and universities. Fewer students are pursuing teaching as a career with a resulting increase in students selecting alternative careers. Sports administration can be placed in such a category and, because much of the work in the conduct of sports programs is of this nature, opportunities for employment have increased.

It is difficult to include all the available careers under the category of sports administration but the following represents some administrative positions that cut across several facets of the sports world.[8]

1. Athletic director.
2. Associate or assistant athletic director.
3. Financial manager or business manager.
4. Publicity director.
5. Ticket manager.
6. General manager.
7. Intramural sport director.
8. Associate or assistant director for intramural sports.
9. Head coach.
10. Head trainer.
11. Director of a sport instructional program.
12. Sport club manager.
13. Director of sport marketing.
14. Supervisor of sport facilities and equipment.

Opportunities for careers in sports administration are particularly bright for women. Recent federal legislation (Title IX) and the rapid expansion of intercollegiate and interscholastic sports for women are mainly responsible for this situation. This area represents one of the greatest potential markets for employment anywhere in the United States today.

[8] Harold J. Vanderzwaag, Sport Administration, *Briefings, Careers in Physical Education,* NCPEAM and NAPECW, United States, 1975, p. 26.

Students contemplating a career in athletic administration should be aware of the need for an apprenticeship before moving into a sports administrator position. It is uncommon for students to move into such positions directly upon completion of the undergraduate degree. These apprenticeships may take the form of assistant coach, head coach, teacher, intramural director, or any one of the many other functions that are usually associated with sports programs.

SELECTED REFERENCES

AAHPER, "Professional Preparation of the Administrator of Athletics," *Journal of Health, Physical Education and Recreation*, Washington, D.C., 41:20-22 (September, 1970).

Bischoff, David C., "Administrator," *Quest*, Pearl Berlin (ed.), Monograph VII:14-17, NAPECW and NCPEAM, Wayne State University, Detroit, (December, 1966).

Burelle, Jacques V., "Qualifications of Athletic Directors of Members Institutions of the Canadian Intercollegiate Athletic Union," Unpublished doctoral dissertation, University of Indiana, 1975.

Gerber, Ellen, Jan Felshin, Pearl Berlin, and Waneen Wyrick, *The American Women In Sport*, Addison-Wesley Publishing Co., Reading, MA, 1974, p. 562.

Hixson, Chalmer G., *The Administration of Interscholastic Athletics*, J. Lowell Pratt and Co., New York, 1967, p. 192.

Hunsicker, Paul (ed.), "Administrative Theory and Practice in Physical Education and Athletics," *Proceedings of C.I.C. Symposium on Administrative Theory in Athletics and Physical Education*, Chicago, 1973, p. 154.

Isaacs, Stan, *Careers and Opportunities in Sports*, E.P. Dultan and Co., Inc., New York, 1964, p. 192.

Kinder, Thomas M., "Criteria for a Graduate Program in Athletic Administration Based on a Job Analysis of Athletic Administrators in Selected Southern States," Unpublished doctoral dissertation, George Peabody College for Teachers, 1975.

McIntosh, Peter C., *Sport in Society*, C.A. Watts and Co., Ltd., London, 1971.

National Association of College Directors of Athletics, *Report of the Third National Conference*, Washington, D.C., AAHPER, 1965, p. 48.

National Association of Secondary School Directors of Athletics, *Proceedings of the National Conference,* Hershey, PA, December 8-11, 1974, p. 56.

Resick, Matthew C., Beverly L. Seidel, and James G. Mason, *Modern Administrative Practices in Physical Education and Athletics,* Addison-Wesley Publishing Co., Menlo Park, CA, 1970.

Richardson, Deane E. "Preparation for a Career in Public School Athletic Administration," *Journal of Health, Physical Education and Recreation,* Washington, D.C., 42:17-19 (February, 1971).

Sultan, Robert G., "Functions and Professional Preparation of Men Intercollegiate Athletic Directors," Unpublished doctoral dissertation, University of Utah, 1975.

Youngberg, Richard S., "A Comparative Analysis of Qualifications Suggested for Intercollegiate Athletic Directors," Unpublished doctoral dissertation, Indiana University, 1972.

Welsh, Raymond, "Employment Prospects for the Physical Educator," *Proceedings of the Seventy Eighth Annual Meeting of the National College Physical Education Association for Men,* Leo L. Gedvilas (ed.), 175-182, University of Illinois, Chicago Circle, Chicago, 1975.

Vanderzwaag, Harold J., "Sport Administration," *Briefings, Careers in Physical Education,* NCPEAM and NAPECW, United States, 1975, pp. 17-27.

chapter 12

learning experiences in coaching and sports administration

SPORTS ADMINISTRATION

Do you want to be a sports administrator? What are some of the qualities expected of a person in such a role? How can I be a successful and effective administrator? The learning experiences presented below may be of some assistance in providing answers to these questions.

1. Define in your own words:
   a. Sport.
   b. Athletics.
   c. Physical education.
   d. Recreation.
2. Assume that you have been appointed the athletic director of a "medium" sized high school (2000 students). Identify the various segments of the public you will be using in your new administrative role to promote the program. Identify at least 15 persons from these segments who can assist you.

3. Melby proposed several attributes in Chapter 10 that are needed to establish good working relationships between management and employees.[1] Select five persons whom you have known and worked with during your high school and college athletic career and rate them from one to five (five being highest) on a sheet similar to the one appearing below:

Attributes	High School Coach	High School Principal	College Coach	College Athletic Director
1. Humility				
2. Respect for personality				
3. Sympathetic listener				
4. Accessibility				
5. Integrity				
6. Creativity				
7. Elimination of annoyances				
8. Ability to get acquainted				
9. Recognition of achievement in others				
10. Use of staff resources				
11. Understand associates				
12. Allow for mistakes				

4. Owen B. Kiernan, considers the athletic director to be a true professional in every respect.[2] He believes a sports administrator can be evaluated by what he calls "Q" ratings. These ratings include: (1) intelligence and integrity, (2) adaptability, (3) gumption and, (4) common touch. Read Kiernan's article and then rate the athletic administrators you have known using these classifications.
5. Communication is considered to be the lifeblood of most organizations. It is a two-way process that includes consistency, commitment, content, and credibility. Define these terms in

[1] Ernest O. Melby, *Administering Community Education*, Prentice-Hall, Inc., Englewood Cliffs, NJ, 1965.

[2] Owen B. Kiernan, "The A.D.—A Professional All the Way," *Proceedings of the National Federation's Fifth Annual National Conference of High School Directors of Athletics*, Hershey, PA, December 8-11, 1974, pp. 24-26.

your own words and prepare a sample press release that includes implementation of these items.
6. The PEPI project described in Chapters 1 and 10 is making an impact on the profession because educators are now telling the story of the value of physical activity to individuals at all levels. Relate the PEPI concepts in your own words.
7. Identify the PEPI project coordinator in your school district and volunteer to assist him or her in explaining to the many sectors of the public the values of physical education and sports and the goals and objectives of our programs.
8. Select some of your classmates to work with you and prepare a paper on the subject, "How can we as sports administrators convince the public of the need for exercise?" Present the results of your finding to the local PTA in the neighborhood where you live.
9. Griffiths divides an administrator's behavior into seven categories.[3] These categories are initiator, improver, recognizer, helper, effective speaker, coordinator, and social man. After you have determined the meaning of these behavioral terms, rate yourself on each of them.
10. Read four recent contemporary books written by professional athletes (baseball, football, basketball, and golf). Discuss these books with your friends who are contemplating careers in professional sports.

SELECTED REFERENCES

AAHPER, "The Whole Thing," *Journal of Health, Physical Education, and Recreation*, Washington, D.C., 44:21-36 (May, 1973).

Gallemore, Sandra L., "The Teacher: Key to an Effective Public Relations Program," *The Physical Educator*, Bloomington, Ind., 30:66-68 (May, 1973).

Hunsicker, Paul (ed.), "Administrative Theory and Practice in Athletics and Physical Education," *Proceedings of C.I.C. Symposium on Administrative Theory and Practice in Athletics and Physical Education*, Athletic Institute, Chicago, 1973, p. 154.

Leaf, Carol Ann, "Public Information Toteboard," *Journal of Health, Physical Education and Recreation*, Washington, D.C., 45:59 (January, 1974).

[3] Daniel E. Griffiths, *Human Relations in School Administration*, Appleton-Century-Crofts, Inc., New York, 1956, pp. 244, 246, 248, 250-252.

Leaf, Carol Ann, "Public Information Toteboard," *Journal of Health, Physical Education and Recreation*, Washington, D.C., **45**: 15 (April, 1974).

Loy, Jr., John W., and Alan G. Ingham, "The Social System of Sport: A Humanistic Perspective," *Quest*, Lawrence F. Locke (ed.), Monograph XIX:3-23, NAPECW and NCPEAM, University of Massachusetts, Amherst, (January, 1973).

Resick, Matthews C., Beverly L. Seidel, and James G. Mason, *Modern Administrative Practices in Physical Education and Athletics*, Addison-Wesley Publishing Co., Reading, MA., 1970, p. 264.

Sisley, Becky, "Challenges Facing the Women Athletic Director," *The Physical Educator*, Bloomington, Ind., **32**:121-123 (October, 1975).

Slusher, Howard S., *Man, Sport and Existence: A Critical Analysis*, Lea & Febiger, Philadelphia, 1967, p. 243.

section 4
athletic training

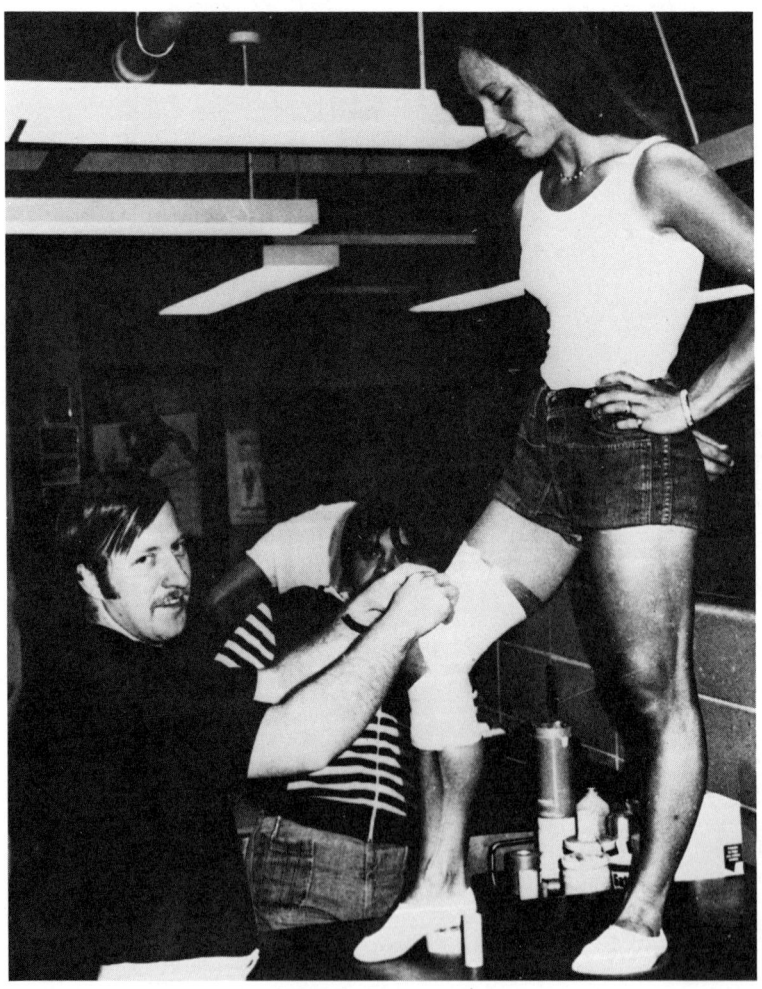

Reprinted by permission of the University of Illinois at Chicago Circle, Chicago.

13
athletic training
14
care and prevention of sports injury
15
the athletic trainer
16
learning experiences in athletic training

chapter 13
athletic training

> The emergence of the professionally qualified athletic trainer has accompanied the reorientation of sports in our society.[1]
> American Medical Association

NEED FOR ATHLETIC TRAINERS

The statistics regarding the number of sports-related injuries has reached epidemic proportions. The Department of Health, Education and Welfare estimates that there are 17 to 20 million sports injuries occurring in this country each year with 40,000 to 50,000 being traumatized knees that required surgical intervention. Further data indicate that football produces about one million injuries per year, basketball about 800,000, baseball one-half million, and other ball games about 700,000. If one adds to these figures the injuries resulting from all sports activities, it can readily be seen that steps must be taken to reduce the hazards associated with sports. Athletic trainers can play an important role in this task. They can provide leadership that will aid in preventing athletic injuries, control and reduce the injury inherent in athletic competition, and minimize the severity of injuries incurred in athletics.

A recent article in the *Chicago Tribune* presented further grim statistics regarding a nationwide inadequacy of health care services and a faculty of qualified

[1] American Medical Association, *Fundamentals of Athletic Training*, Chicago, 1971, p. viii.

coaches and certified athletic trainers. Dr. John Marshall, Chief Orthopedic Consultant to New York City's Public School Athletic League, estimates that only about 10 percent of the nation's 22,000 high schools have adequate athletic care.

An assistant professor in biomechanics at Michigan State University reported in a recent study that the prevailing situation in 216 Michigan high schools is that many of them have no health care at all. In the first in-depth study of its kind, the medical journal *The Physician and Sports Medicine* polled 47 schools in 17 states. These data revealed that only 4 of the 47 schools provided medical supervision or care during practice sessions, a time when more than half of all injuries occur. Nearly a third had no doctor in attendance during games. In the training rooms at many of the schools surveyed, elastic wraps and band-aids were the only first-aid devices found in a medical cabinet in the coach's office.[2]

One sports medicine journal reports that of the nation's 50 states, only 9 require coaches to be certified in sports injury prevention and treatment.

In California, less than half of the state's 25,000 high school coaches have physical education degrees. The reality far too often is that the mathematics, English, or science teacher coaches a sport because he or she played it in college.

Since the middle 1960s, the American Alliance for Health, Physcial Education and Recreation has been campaigning for every state to certify each coach in a wide but necessary variety of health-care subjects.

In 1974 New York state ruled that by 1977 all teacher-coaches must be certified "in the physiology of exercise" before they can coach athletic teams.

These statistics all confirm the fact that when highly trained paramedics are present on the athletic field, there is a definite decrease in sports injuries and an increase in sports safety. Yet, especially in high schools, a certified athletic trainer is the last person hired.

The need for qualified and certified athletic trainers is not confined to programs for boys and men nor to any specific level of competition. The expansion of competitive sports for women at all educational levels necessitates the provision of competent personnel

[2]Lou Gomalak, and Charlotte Gomalak, "High School Medical Facilities 'National Scandal'," *Chicago Daily Tribune,* October 10, 1975, pp. 1, 3.

responsible for the prevention and care of athletic injuries.[3] It is estimated that high school participation alone has increased 175 percent over the last two years. Athletic injuries transcend all sex lines. Qualified trainers, whether men or women, can provide the necessary measures for the prevention and care of athletic injuries, whether the athlete is male or female. At the present time, men are performing most of the athletic training work for women's programs. This is due to the shortage of women in this area. All educators and coaches should understand and respond to this need.

At a time when concern for the health and safety of interschool athletics is so great, the National Athletic Trainers Association is setting standards for the education and professional preparation of personnel to work in the areas of athletic-injury prevention, emergency care, and rehabilitation. Since 1969, the NATA has provided standards and criteria for the development of undergraduate and graduate level educational programs in athletic training.[4] To date, a total of 30 undergraduate curricula and 2 masters' level curricula in colleges and universities throughout the United States are receiving NATA approval. The number of approved athletic training curricula is increasing steadily as more and more colleges are implementing areas of specialization in athletic training. As a further step toward insuring the professional qualifications of athletic trainers, the NATA reinstituted certification procedures in 1970. An individual who meets the educational and clinical experience requirements set forth by the NATA is now recognized as a certified athletic trainer upon successful completion of a national certification examination.

HISTORY OF ATHLETIC TRAINING

The organization that has served an important leadership role in the athletic training profession is the National Athletic Trainers Association. It was founded for the express purposes of establishing professional standards and exchanging and disseminating information.

[3] Gary Delforge, "Educational Programs In Athletic Training," *Proceedings of the 78th Annual Meeting of the National College Physical Education Association for Men*, Leo L. Gedvilas (ed.), 194, University of Illinois at Chicago Circle, Chicago, 1975.

[4] Ruth Koenigsberg, and Margarite Arrighi, "Women Athletic Trainers," *Journal of Physical Education and Recreation*, Vol. 46:51 (January 1975).

The American College of Sports Medicine was founded in 1954. This organization composed of medical doctors, physical educators, physiologists, and others interested in the sports field, is dedicated to the promotion of research in medical problems encountered in physical exercise and sports. It has made numerous contributions to the area of training and has increased the understanding and knowledge of coaches and trainers with respect to more adequate training and caring for their athletes.

Efforts to establish adequate athletic injury controls in every school and college that sponsors athletic programs extends to many other organizations and individuals. An ABC television documentary program in 1974 provided important information regarding the nature of athletic injuries and the need for competent athletic coaches and trainers in our various schools. A resolution urging the individual states to establish an adequate athletic medical unit (licensed physician and athletic trainer) in every school supporting an athletic program was recently passed by the House of Delegates of the American Medical Association. Legislation has been enacted in Florida and Texas requiring that state licensed athletic trainers be associated with interscholastic athletic programs.

Federal legislation introduced to the United States House of Representatives in 1972 by the Honorable Ronald W. Dellums of California in the form of the Athletic Safety Act (H.R. 7795) is an effort to establish standards designed to reduce athletic injuries by applying stringent safety standards for intramural and varsity athletic programs. This legislation, if enacted, would require all intramural and varsity athletic programs at the high school levels to have a certified athletic trainer available at all practice sessions and games within eight years from the date of enactment. The enactment of this legislation could result in a great financial burden to high schools and, as a result, the National Federation of State High School Associations has urged its state executive officers not to support this legislation. Despite this lack of support, all states should give immediate attention to the athletic training implications related to interscholastic, intercollegiate, intramural and varsity athletics. Douglas and Spiker list four implications.[5]

> 1. *The Occupational Safety and Health Act is going to be rigidly enforced. Athletic injuries will be included as part of this act.*

---

[5] J. William Douglas and John C. Spiker, Athletic Training, *Careers In Physical Education, Briefings, 3,* National Association of Physical Education for College Women and National College Physical Education Association for Men, United States, 1975, p. 39.

2. Injuries are a problem in interscholastic, intercollegiate, intramural and varsity athletics.
3. As a general rule schools and colleges do not have qualified athletic training personnel associated with their athletic programs.
4. There is not a sufficient number of certified athletic trainers to fill the anticipated number of athletic training positions in our schools and colleges. At the annual meeting of the National Athletic Trainers Association in 1973, it was estimated that by 1977 there will be a need for an additional 22,000 certified athletic trainers. In the past four years the number of colleges and universities offering an undergraduate curriculum in athletic training has increased from eight to thirty. It is readily apparent that additional institutions of higher education must offer a professional preparation curriculum in athletic training.

Dr. Theodore Fox, who has written extensively about the sports injury epidemic, believes that prophylaxis or prevention has become as important in the health care of the athlete as the diagnosis and treatment of the injuries.[6] Prevention is how epidemics are ended, whether it be poliomyelitis, scarlet fever, or athletic injuries. The athletic trainer is an important member of the "health team," which includes the physician and the head coach.

Dr. James A. Nicholas, Founder of the Institute of Sports Medicine, was asked by a *U.S. News and World Report* editor to comment on how we can make sports safer. He believes that medicine and physical education are beginning to integrate with schools, parents, the government, and others. The result is that we are starting to learn more about sports, about related injuries, and effects on the body. In the future he says that we are going to have different types of sports with less interest in violent, aggressive team sports and more in individual sports. There is going to be more federal regulation of school athletic programs and more organized screening of participants. Protection against defective athletic equipment will be tightened. What we are going to see is increased sports activity early in life. Combine this with better equipment, and we'll have more and better sports for everyone.[7]

[6]Theodore A. Fox, "Athletic Injuries: A New Epidemic In America," *Chicago Tribune*, September 16, 1974, Chicago, pp. 2-3.

[7]James A. Nicholas, "How To Enjoy Sports and Avoid Injury," *U.S. News and World Report*, December, 29, 1975, pp. 37-39.

SELECTED REFERENCES

American Medical Association, *Fundamentals of Athletic Training*, Chicago, 1971, p. 128.

American Medical Association, *Proceedings of the Eighth National Conference On The Medical Aspects of Sports*, Las Vegas, November 27, 1968, p. 99.

American Medical Association, *Proceedings of the Seventh National Conference On The Medical Aspects of Sports*, Chicago, November 28, 1965, p. 81.

American Medical Association, *Standard Nomenclature of Athletic Injuries*, Chicago, 1968, p. 157.

Christensen, Carl S., "Relative Strength in Males and Females," *Journal of the National Athletic Trainers Association*, LaFayette, Ind., **10**:189-192 (December 1975).

Dayton, O. William, *Athletic Training and Conditioning*, The Ronald Press Co., New York, 1965.

Douglas, J. William, and John C. Spiker, Athletic Training, *Briefing 3, Careers In Physical Education*, NCPEAM and NAPECW, United States, 1975, p. 61.

Hutton, Linda I., "Needed: Women Athletic Trainers," *Journal of Health, Physical Education and Recreation*, **43**:77-78 (January 1972).

Klafs, Carl E., and Daniel D. Arnheim, *Modern Principles of Athletic Training*, C.V. Mosby Co., St. Louis, 1973.

Klafs, Carl E., and M. Joan Lyon, *The Female Athlete*, St. Louis, C.V. Mosby Co., 1973.

Morehouse, Laurence E., and Philip J. Rasch, *Sports Medicine For Trainers*, W.B. Saunders Co., Philadelphia, 1964.

chapter 14

care and prevention of sports injury

> The most important service offered by a good trainer is better medical management and the prevention of injuries.[3]
> National Athletic Trainers Association

PREVENTION OF SPORTS INJURY

Many physicians consider the prophylaxis or prevention phase of sports injuries to be as important as the diagnosis and treatment of the injuries. Dr. Allan J. Ryan, athletic team physician for the University of Wisconsin-Madison, has written extensively on the prevention aspect.[2] He states that the prevention of sports injuries may be thought of in terms of the many types of problems presented by the universitality of sports. He considers sports to be a specialized form of play as a part of life and not a phenomenon of any time or place.[3] As a part of the lives of many, we perform thousands of unsafe acts in recreational pursuits that involve physical activity. The very character of sports and games, since they are intensified and

---

[1] National Athletic Trainers Association, *Athletic Training Careers*, Greenville, NC, September, 1975, p. 6.

[2] Allan J. Ryan, "Prevention of Sport Injury: A Problem Solving Approach," *Journal of Health, Physical Education and Recreation*, 42:24-28 (April, 1971).

[3] Ibid, p. 24.

often competitive physical activities, gives assurance that the risk of accident is greater than in the usual activities of daily living. A great proportion of these accidents occur in games and sports, since they are a major preoccupation of young people in this age-group.

Professionals involved in sports or physical education activities should be aware of how the range of these activities has broadened during the last few decades. Participation figures compiled by the Athletic Institute in 1967 revealed that there were over 2.7 million baseball, 1.1 million basketball, 1.2 million football and 200,000 soccer players, in addition to 250,000 wrestlers and 725,000 participating in track and field sports. The National Federation of State High School Athletic Associations stated in 1969 that almost 3.5 million participants took part in 28 sports, which were sponsored by its member schools. The growth of women's sports at both the high school and collegiate levels has considerably increased those figures listed above. Dr. Ryan lists five steps in accident control/prevention: (1) gathering information about the occurrence of accidents in the activity and identification of the causes of these accidents, (2) the athlete himself, (3) the nature of the sport itself, including the regulations that govern it, (4) the use of protective equipment in sports, and (5) the atmosphere in which competitive sports operate today.[4]

The first consideration of the problems posed by accident prevention in sports generally might be directed toward those who supervise sports. This might include a high school principal, an athletic director, a community recreation supervisor, or even the president of a professional team. His or her direct approach toward the problem of injury control is to hire coaches, trainers, and physicians who understand the reasons for the occurrence of sports injuries and how they may be prevented as well as treated. The identification of these individuals is a secondary problem, but a vital one in order to ensure that the administrator of a team provides the needed information. This information includes such items as conference regulations, lack of adequate financing, proliferation of sports, and adequate facilities. High school football programs encounter such problems as inadequate time for proper conditioning of players from the opening of school until the first scheduled game; state and conference rules forbidding early starts and participation in summer camps where the school's coaches participate; the beginning of winter sports overlapping the latter part of the football season; overcrowded practice fields; and a continuing crisis in the athletic

[4]Ibid, pp. 25-28.

department budget caused by failure of attendance at games to match increases in expenditures. Those persons most directly connected with the sports program (i.e, athletic director, coach, trainer, team physician) should function as a team and provide the highest level of expertise possible in preventing injury.

The coaches should always remember that the price of winning should never be the health or welfare of an athlete which is the second consideration. Trainers and the coaches should share the responsibility for the training and conditioning of the individual or the team. Trainers must coordinate their efforts closely with those of the team physician and coach to bring about cooperation. This is essential to the success of an injury-control program. Their knowledge of the use of protective equipment, including the use of taping and bandaging, should be superior. Ideally, the sports physician should be aware of the whole range of information relating to injury control. They are: (1) a more complete knowledge of what training regimens are best for each sport, (2) more properly prepared persons to supervise these training programs, (3) more time to carry them out, and (4) better facilities in which to work.

The third major consideration in injury control is the nature of the sport itself, including the regulations that govern it. Every sport presents some hazard of injury. In contact sports, the acceleration of the player determines to some extent the number and seriousness of injuries. In motor-driven sports, the greater the speed, the greater the likelihood of injury and the greater the chance that injury might be fatal. In noncontact sports where the individual is self-propelled, the occurrence of injury may be related to speed if gravity is allowed to act with minimal friction encountered, as in snow skiing. Important in each sport is the environment in which it is practiced: on land, on the water, or in the air. To recommend proper precautions, equipment, and other safeguards, the sports physician must be familiar with all of the risks that people may be exposed to in these extremes of earthly environment. The objects used in games and sports each present particular hazards to the sportsman in both their correct and incorrect use; all sports have rules to allow for fair contests in addition to protecting the safety of the player. Since the rules are enforced and interpreted by officials, the actions of the officials cannot be ignored as factors in injury control.

The use of protective equipment in sports is the fourth consideration in injury control. Protective equipment must satisfy certain requirements in order to be effective:

1. Its specifications must approach maximum protective requirements for the part to be protected as closely as possible.
2. It must be sufficiently durable to withstand repeated use without significant decrease in the protective factors.
3. It must be properly fitted so that it covers adequately and stays in place under usual conditions of use.
4. It must not be so bulky or heavy that it impairs the normal and necessary free movement of the athlete.
5. It must not create a hazard to other contestants.
6. It must be replaced when it is so worn that it has not lost a significant amount of its protective factors.

A distinction must be made between equipment used for protection and that used for treatment. Casts and rigid splints are treatment devices and should not be used in contact sports. Prosthetic devices fall in the same category except under very special circumstances.

The atmosphere in which competitive sports operate today is a fifth aspect of injury control. Here the most important factor is the question of the necessarily different approach to amateur and professional sports. Professionals may have a small fortune at stake; they must appear regularly and perform to the best of their ability. It is inevitable that amateur sports be corrupted by improper practices used in professional sports because many amateurs and their coaches wish to emulate the success of the professional, and therefore fall easily into an acceptance of these practices. The professionalization of baseball, football, basketball, soccer, and ice hickey has brought a violence into these games that is exciting to the spectator but is a potent factor in bringing about serious injury. Since it seems unlikely that there will be a reversal of this trend in the near future, we must accommodate ourselves to it. For the sake of the younger generation of athletes, we must continue to endeavor to keep amateur sports free of this type of spirit.

The prevention of injury is closely allied to training. Most coaches and trainers believe that a lack of physical fitness is one of the prime causes of athletic injury. Such conditions as muscular imbalance, lack of flexibility, poor neuromuscular coordination, inadequate muscular bulk, and lack of strength in the ligaments and tendons are among the causes of injury directly attributed to insufficient or improper physical conditioning.

It is believed that the most serious athletic injuries are those to the head and neck. Proper and thorough physical conditioning can do much to obviate these injuries. The building up of muscle bulk and strength protects the muscles, and the strengthening and toughening of tendons and ligaments fortify the joints and permit full and effective range of movement and stability. Proper warm-up tends to prevent muscle tears or strains and to raise muscle and deep body temperatures to their most effective levels. The prevention of tendon and ligament pulls occurs when flexibility and range of joint motion is increased. Most physicians, coaches, and trainers believe that the awkward, slow, or tired athlete is the one most prone to injury.

Klafs and Arnheim list 10 cardinal principles of athletic conditioning that every trainer should know and identify.[5]

1. *Warming up.* See that proper and adequate warm up procedures precede all activities.
2. *Gradualness.* Add small daily increments to work. It takes from 6-8 weeks for a person to get into top-level condition.
3. *Timing.* Prevent over-doing. Relate all work to the athlete's general condition at the time. Practice periods should extend from 1 hour to 1 hours and 45 minutes, depending upon the sport. The tired athlete is prone to injury.
4. *Intensity.* Stress the intensity of the work rather than the quantity. Usually coaches and trainers fail to work their men hard enough in terms of intensity. They make the mistake of prolonging the work-out rather than increasing the tempo or the work load. As the degree of training increases, the intensity of training must also increase.
5. *Capacity level.* The athlete's performance is expected to be as close to his physiological limits as health and safety factors will allow. Only in working to capacity will the desired results be achieved.
6. *Strength.* Develop strength as a means of producing greater endurance and speed.
7. *Motivation.* Motivation is a prime factor. Use circuit training and isometric exercises as means for further motivating the athlete.

[5] Carl E. Klafs, and Donald D. Arnheim, *Modern Principles of Athletic Training,* C.V. Mosby Co., St. Louis, 1973, p. 75.

8. *Specialization.* Exercise programs should include exercises for strength, relaxation, and flexibility. In addition, special exercises geared to the demands made upon the body in specific activities should be used to develop specialization.
9. *Relaxation.* Specific relaxation exercises, which aid in recovery from fatigue and tension, should be taught.
10. *Routine.* A daily routine of exercise, both in-season and off-season should be established.

Specific warm-up activities for several sports are shown in Figure 14.1.

CARE OF SPORTS INJURIES

The trainer's job is injury care and prevention, not coaching, playing, or cheerleading. The trainer's time during the game should be spent watching for injuries and caring for those injuries that happen.

The American Medical Association has established a set of procedures and practices that the athletic trainer should use as a guide in the performance of his or her duties.[6] These practices, which pertain to the care of athletic injuries are:

1. Physical therapy—primary purpose is to aid the normal progression of the healing process. It picks up where first aid or emergency care leaves off and is considered treatment. Trainers should know the physiological principles involved in wound healing plus a knowledge of the physical agents that can be applied for therapeutic purposes (i.e., moist heat packs, infrared, whirlpool bath, massage, cryotherapy, massage, etc.).
2. Protective athletic equipment—the athlete must be protected by the best equipment available. Head protection includes the eyes, face, and mouth protectors. Body protection should consider shoulders, hips, legs, ankles, and knee. Special protection should be provided for girls and women who are now competing in sports in large numbers.
3. Protective taping—prevent undesired mobility of a body part to compress soft tissue and to secure a bandage or equipment piece in place. A competent trainer matches taping techniques that relate to the complete function of his attention to athletic injuries: injury prevention, first aid, treatment, rehabilitation, and protection from injury.

[6] American Medical Association, *Fundamentals of Athletic Training,* Chicago, 1971, pp. 55, 62, 68, 89, 110.

Sport	Trunk Stretch	Back Stretch	Shoulder Stretch	Hams. Stretch	Lateral Stretch	Gastroc. Stretch	Side Strad. Hop	Lateral Dip	Trunk Circling	Squat Thrust	Abdom. Curl	Arm Fling	Ankle Suppl.	Arm Circling
Baseball						X	X	X	X			X		X
Basketball						X	X	X	X			X	X	X
Football			X			X	X	X	X					
Gymnastics					X			X	X					
Skiing						X		X	X					X
Soccer						X	X	X	X					
Swimming						X	X	X	X					
Tennis						X	X		X				X	
Water polo		X	X			X	X		X				X	
Wrestling			X			X		X	X				X	
Track and field														
Sprinters				X		X	X	X	X			X	X	
High hurdlers				X		X	X	X	X				X	
Low hurdlers				X		X	X	X	X				X	
440 yd/400 m				X		X	X	X	X					
880 yd/800 m				X		X	X	X	X					
Mile run (1500 m)						X	X		X				X	
Two mile run (3000 m)						X	X		X				X	
Long distances (5000–10000 m)						X	X		X				X	
Cross country						X	X		X				X	
Weight events			X			X	X	X	X			X	X	X
Javelin			X	X		X	X		X			X		X
Volleyball			X		X		X		X			X	X	X
Water polo			X			X			X			X	X	X
Wrestling	X	X	X	X			X		X	X	X			X

FIGURE 14.1 Warm-Up activities.

Half Squat	High Kick	Hurdle Seat	Pect. Stretch	Push-Up	Shoulder Roll	Ski Stretch	Ant. Shoulder Stretch	Wrest. Br. and Pivot	Warm-Ups Specific to the Sport
						X			Warm-up throws with partner. Easy at first, then gradually increasing force of throw.
						X			Warm-up throws. One and 2-hand passing drills, relaxed and easy. Dribbling warm-up drills, pregame basket shooting practice.
X					X	X		X	1. Offensive-defensive warm-up. 2. Body contact simulated charge and block. Dip swings on parallel bars; splits. Run through complete routine several times.
X	X		X		X				Passing and heading drills.
	X		X			X	X		Warm up on board with approaches and preliminary bounces, gradually working into dives.
	X		X						Depending upon the event, swim 10 to 20 laps at moderate rate of speed.
			X			X	X		Following initial warm-ups, warm up on practice board, then move on court for practice serves and volleys.
	X					X			1. Alternate running at ½ speed and jogging, each for a distance of 50 yards, for a total of 400 yards. 2. Take 6 to 8 starts, running at ½ speed, finally working up to ¾ speed.

(FIGURE 14.1 continued)

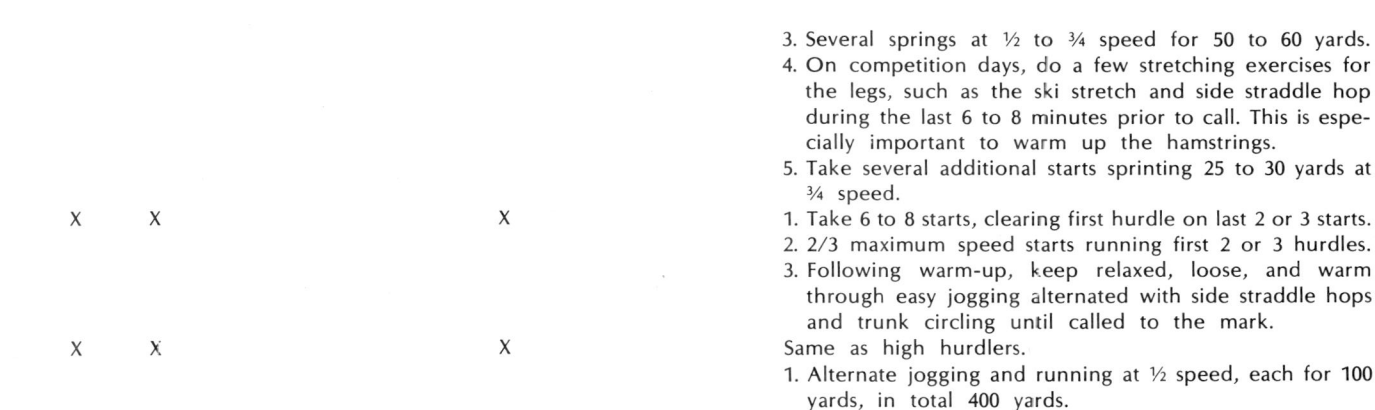

3. Several springs at ½ to ¾ speed for 50 to 60 yards.
4. On competition days, do a few stretching exercises for the legs, such as the ski stretch and side straddle hop during the last 6 to 8 minutes prior to call. This is especially important to warm up the hamstrings.
5. Take several additional starts sprinting 25 to 30 yards at ¾ speed.

1. Take 6 to 8 starts, clearing first hurdle on last 2 or 3 starts.
2. 2/3 maximum speed starts running first 2 or 3 hurdles.
3. Following warm-up, keep relaxed, loose, and warm through easy jogging alternated with side straddle hops and trunk circling until called to the mark.

Same as high hurdlers.

1. Alternate jogging and running at ½ speed, each for 100 yards, in total 400 yards.
2. Walk 2 to 3 minutes.
3. Run 200 yards at ½ speed.
4. Walk at least 3 minutes.

1. Alternately walk and jog 440 yards.
2. Walk 4 to 5 minutes.
3. Run ½ mile at intended 2-mile pace.
4. Walk 6 to 8 minutes.
5. Jog 440 yards finishing the last 150 yards in a sprint.
6. Finish with some light stretching exercises.

(FIGURE 4.1 continued)

4. Physical conditioning—can be implemented with widely differing methods and still be effective. The components of these physical conditioning programs are purpose, emphasis, level of athletic skill, environment, organization, and method.
5. First aid: recognition, care, and referral—a first aid master plan, coordinated by the athletic trainer and understood by all involved in the athletic program, insures a readiness for rendering prompt and proper care for athletes. All athletic personnel should be familiar with and knowledgeable of the First Aid chart for Athletic Injuries published by the American Medical Association, (See Figure 14-2).
6. Evaluation and records—components of these practices are decisions made by the trainer, keeping statistics, athlete's health record, knowledge of proper athletic injury terminology, preseason and referral examinations, forms, reports, interpretation, equivalent exposure, disability, and interpretation of cause and effect.

The ability to recognize basic physiological signs of injury is essential to proper handling of critical injuries. When making the evaluation of the seriously ill or injured athlete, the trainer or coach must be aware of nine response areas: heart rate, breathing rate, blood pressure, temperature, skin color, pupils of the eye, movement, the presence of pain, and unconsciousness.[7]

For athletic trainers to communicate effectively with other members of the "health team" (i.e., physician, coach, and athlete) concerning athletic injuries, he or she must use a mutually understood uniform terminology. Kenneth S. Clarke, acting on behalf of an American Medical Association subcommittee, in 1965 conducted a national survey of 900 trainers and physicians to learn the extent to which the prevalent use of vernacular in depicting athletic injuries contributes to ambiguity in communication.[8]

The significant outcomes of this study were revealed as follows:

1. A confusion stemming from the use of the vernacular was substantiated and documented. Terms are used that are thought to be accurate but, in fact, may be vague, misleading, incorrect, or unknown to others.

[7]Klafs and Arnheim, p. 208.

[8]Kenneth S. Clarke, "The Use of Vernacular For Sports Injuries," *Proceedings of the Eighth National Conference on the Medical Aspects of Sports*, AMA, Chicago, 1967, pp. 67-72.

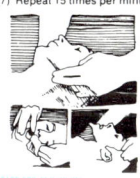

FIGURE 14.2 First aid chart. Reprinted by permission of the American Medical Association, Chicago.

2. Personal spontaneous expressions frequently found in the returned questionnaires were uniform in their desire and encouragement to rid the athletic medicine nomenclature of ambiguous and misleading terms.
3. Some groupings of vernacular reflected gaps existing in the formal medical terminology with respect to pathologies encountered in the athletic setting. One such illustration was the use of terms such as buzz, bell ring, lick, and knock to denote a type of concussion in which the athlete was not rendered distinctly unconscious.
4. The decision for inclusion or exclusion of a given vernacular term in a standard nomenclature of athletic injuries could now be based on more than singular opinion.

In order to determine what term was to be included in the nomenclature, it was necessary to review the jargon terms, reject the slang and colloquialism, and then determine the appropriate terminology. The final disposition of terms in the survey were divided into the categories of preferred, additional, glossary, and unacceptable (See Figure 14.3). Clarke says that health supervision of athletes must rely on terms to record observations, to exchange clinical observations, to accumulate information, to evaluate the statistical treatment of information, and thus to improve the bases for decision.[9] To the extent that imprecise vernacular continues to interfere with confidence in the meaning of shared terms—as being identical in input and retrieval from the substrate—confusion instead of insight is being perpetuated.

Training Room

The training room for the athletic trainer is analogous to a medical doctor's office. It is a special room isolated from the locker rooms but immediately adjacent to the dressing quarters of all athletes—both men and women. Its design should be multipurpose in nature to accomodate the many functions of the trainer. Areas should be provided for first aid, physical examinations, pregame and prepractice bandaging and strapping, treatment, and record keeping. Its use should be confined only to athletic training functions. The room should be well-lighted and ventilated and painted with a light color. The floor should be tile or other material of a type that is easily cleaned. The trainer's office should be incorporated into the training

[9] Ibid, p. 70.

Preferred Terms

Athlete's foot
Baseball finger
Brachial plexus
 stretch
Cauliflower ear
Charleyhorse
Concussion
Cuff strain
Hip pointer
Osgood-Schlatter's
 disease
Plantar wart
Spinal concussion
Sprain
Strain

Additional Terms

Black eye
Bone bruise
Boxer's fracture
Catarrhal fever
Chafing
Cinderburn
Clotheslined
Crabs
Dhobie itch
Dislocated shoulder
Fallen arches
Fat pad pinch
Floor burn
Gaulded
Grass burn
Groin strain
Hammer finger
Heel spur
Housemaid's knee
Jammed finger
Jammed neck
Jock itch
Joint mice
Low back pain
Little League elbow

Mallet finger
Matburn
Mouse
Piles
Prizefighter's ear
Pull
Punch drunk
Shiner
Shoulder separation
Skid burn
Slide burn
Solar plexus injury
Spur
Stone bruise
Stoved finger
Strawberry
Swimmer's ear
Trigger finger
Wrestler's ear

Glossary Terms

Athlete's heart
Blocker's disease
Calcium deposit
Cotton mouth
Drying out
Funny bone
Hot spot
Lace bite
Pinched nerve
Shin splints
Stale
Stitch in side
Tape burn
Triad

Unacceptable Terms

Baseball elbow
Baseball shoulder
Basketball knee
Bell rung
Burner

Buzz
Catch
Cold sore
Chinchopper
Coldcocked
Contact lens pain
Cracked ribs
Crick
Crud
Dazed
Dead arm
Dizzy
Fat lip
Fire nose
Fever blister
Foot crud
Football knee
Football shoulder
Football thumb
Frog
Frozen shoulder
Game back
Glass arm
Glass jaw
Goldbricker
Golfer's big toe
Golfer's elbow
Golfer's leg
Golfer's shoulder
Grandpa back
Gym itch
Hot flash
Inside sprain
Javelin elbow
Kink
Kissing disease
Knock
Knocked down
 shoulder
Knocked out
Lick
Locked knee
Muscle jam
Muscle poop
Outside sprain

Punched hip
Pitchers elbow
Pounded heel
Pump knot
Punch fracture
Punk knot
Rib out
Rider's bone
Scorch
Separation
Shoulder drop
Shoulder pointer
Slipped shoulder
Slunk knee
Slunk shoulder
Snap
Split nail
Sore hose
Spiked
Sprained elbow
Sprained knee
Spread
Sprinter's pull
Stabbed
Sternal punch
Stinger
Stretched elbow
Stunned
Tackle shoulder
Tennis elbow
Tennis heel
Tennis leg
Thrown away arm
Torn cartilage
Trick knee
Trick shoulder
Trigger knee
Tuned
Twist
Water on elbow
Water on knee
Weeping bursae
Wry neck

FIGURE 14.3 Standard nomenclature of athletic injuries. Reprinted by permission of American Medical Association, *Fundamentals of Athletic Training*, Chicago, 1971.

quarters with adequate storage and filing space for proper record keeping, a desk, chair, and telephone. A space 8 feet by 10 feet is considered adequate size for this office with glass partitions providing visibility to the training-room activities. A well designed training room should include areas for physical therapy, electrotherapy and hydrotherapy. A training room 1000 to 1200 square feet in size is considered satisfactory for most school situations but may not always be possible. Whatever the size, however, the existing facilities should be meticulously clean and uncluttered. This should be everyone's responsibility: coach, trainer, player, student manager, and team physician (See Figure 14.4).

Many training quarters lack adequate storage space, which is necessary for bulky equipment, medical supplies, adhesive tape, bandages, and protective devices.

Equipment and Supplies

The athletic trainer has an important role to play in the purchase, fitting, and checking of protective athletic equipment. The committee on the Medical Aspects of Sports of the American Medical Association has proposed some basic principles for optimal protection of any group.[10]

1. The best available equipment should be purchased.
2. Equipment should be carefully fitted to the individual.
3. Equipment should be maintained conscientiously and checked periodically as to continued proper fit and absence of acquired defects.
4. Equipment should be worn at all times, whether in practice or in games.

The amount of equipment needed in an athletic training room is a function of the school budget. They also specify equipment needed to serve from 100 to 600 participants per year (Figure 14.5).

The kind, number, and placement of supplies in the training room itself varies with the background of the athletic trainer as well as the budget and preference of the program's medical supervisor.

---

[10] American Medical Association, "Protective Athletic Equipment," *Tips on Athletic Training VI*, Chicago, 1964, pp. 4-5.

FIGURE 14.4 College athletic training room. Reprinted by permission of the University of Illinois at Chicago Circle, Chicago.

Standard Nomenclature

Every individual connected in any way with athletic activities should be familiar with the terms associated with athletic injuries. The American Medical Association has published a Standard Nomenclature of Athletic Injuries, which should be in the professional library of every coach and athletic trainer. A few of the more commonly used terms and their definitions appear below.

1. Abduction—the act of drawing a body segment away from the median line of a proximally conjoined segment.
2. Adduction—the act of drawing a body segment toward the median line of a proximally conjoined segment.
3. Athlete's heart—normal, healthy, efficient heart in well-conditioned athlete; apparent enlargement in silhouette may be from ventricular hypertrophy or increased distensibility; returns to prior size after cessation of training.

	Quantities for Number of Participants Per Year		
Item	Up to 200	200 to 400	400 to 600
Anatomy charts (set)	1	1	1
Ankle wrap roller	1	2	2
Blankets	3	5	5
Bulletin board	1	1	1
Callus file	6	12	18
Crutches	2 pairs	4 pairs	6 pairs
Diathermy (microwave or shortwave)*	1	1	1
Drinking dispenser	1	1	1
Electric clock	1	1	1
Electric muscle stimulator	1	1	1
Examining table (physician)	1	1	1
Exercise equipment (assorted)	*	*	*
Medicine dropper	3	6	9
Eyecup	1	2	3
Flashlight (pencil type)	1	2	3
Forceps (tweezers)	3	3	3
Hair clippers	2	2	2
Hammer	1	1	1
Heat lamp (infrared)	1	2	3
Hot pack (hydrocallator)	1	1	2
Ice maker	1	1	1
Mirror (hand)	3	5	7
Nail clippers	1	2	2
Oral screw	(Available for each first-aid kit)		
Oral thermometer	1	2	3
Paraffin bath	1	1	1
Plastic pillows	2	4	6
Pliers	1	1	1
Powder and benzoin box	1	1	1
Razor (safety, with blades)	1	1	1
Reconditioning equipment			
Barbells	†	†	†
Chinning bar	†	†	†
Dumbbells	†	†	†
Mats	†	†	†
Pulley weights	†	†	†
Shoe weights	†	†	†
Refrigerator	1	1	1
Resuscitator	1	1	1
Safety pins	200	400	600
Scales and weight chart	1		2
Scalpel	2	2	2
Scissors			
All-purpose	1	2	2
Bandage	3	5	7
Surgical	2	2	2

Screwdriver	1	1	1
Shoehorn	3	5	7
Sink and washbasin	1	1	1
Sitz bath	1	1	1
Slings (triangular bandages)	5	10	15
Splints (set of assorted pneumatic)	1	1	2
Steam cabinet (individual)	1	1	2
Sterilizer	1	1	1
Storage cupboards	‡	‡	‡
Stretcher (folding)	1	1	1
Surgical lamp	1	1	1
Tape cutters	5	8	10
Taping tables	2	3	4
Trainer's office			
Bookshelf	1	1	1
Desk	1	1	1
Filing cabinet	1	1	1
Telephone	1	1	1
Training kits	(Available for each sport)		
Training tables (massage)	1	2	3
Ultrasound	1	1	1
Waste container	2	3	4
Wheelchair	(Should be available)		
Whirlpool	1	2	3

*Assorted pieces of equipment sufficient for the given number of particpants.
†Should be on hand for each participant or funds be available for purchase when need arises.
‡Dry, cool storage areas should be provided to house the bulk of the training supplies.

FIGURE 14.5 Suggested basic equipment for individual programs

4. Calcium deposit—abnormal calcification of soft tissue from traumatic insult, usually repeated episodes.
5. Convulsion—seizure with or without unconsciousness, which may or may not be associated with various sensory or motor components described under epilepsy.
6. Drying out—practice of purposeful dehydration for artificial weight control.
7. Dyspepsia (indigestion)—symptom-complex including nausea, heart burn, flatulence, eructations; emotional tension or food incompatibility may produce symptoms, but underlying organic disease sometimes present.
8. Extension—the act of drawing a body segment toward a straight line position with its proximally conjoined body segment.
9. Flexion—the act of drawing a body segment away from a straight line with its proximally conjoined body segment or toward that joint's smallest acute angle.

10. Fracture—breaking of continuity of bone or cartilage (there are at least 23 different kinds of fractures).
11. Funny bone—contusion of ulnar nerve at the ulnar groove of the humeral-medial epicondyle producing a transiently disabling burning sensation and numbness along ulnar side of forearm and hand.
12. Heart burn—burning sensation over heart area but coming from esophagus or stomach; related to reflex of gastric contents; frequently of functional origin but organic cause may be present; nervousness, faulty digestion contributory.
13. Heart murmur—a typical heart sound(s); may be functional and of no clinical significance; or, may be indicative of pathological valvular lesions requiring clinical attention.
14. Heat fatigue—transient deterioration in performance from exposure to heat, humidity, and resulting in relative state of dehydration and salt depletion.
15. Hemotoma—pooling of extravasated blood within tissues or organs.
16. Inversion—the act of rotating the supinated foot medially on the ankle.
17. Muscle atrophy—wasting away of muscle tissue as the result of immobilization cast, inactivity, loss of innervation, or nutritional disorder.
18. Muscle cramp—painful involuntary contraction of skeletal muscle group; causes include salt depletion (heat cramp), fatigue, and reflex reaction to trauma.
19. Myopia (nearsightedness)—defective eyesight because of refractive error in the eye causing rays from distant objects to focus on the retina.
20. Nausea—sensation of distension or discomfort in region of stomach often followed by vomiting; numerous causes: psychogenic, overeating, food intolerance, local disease, reaction to systemic disease or condition, manifestation of drug toxicity.
21. Pronation—the act of rotating a hand or foot internally on its long axis.
22. Shin splints—pain and discomfort in leg from repetitive running on hard surface or forcible excessive use of foot flexors; diagnosis should be limited to musculotendinous inflammations, excluding fatigue fracture or ischemic disorder.

23. Shock—a clinical condition characterized by variable signs and symptoms that arise when the cardiac output is insufficient to fill the arterial tree with blood under sufficient pressure to provide organs and tissues with adequate blood flow; often present with severe trauma and hemorrhage.
24. Spearing—act of butting head into midsection or chest of opponent; hazardous to spearer (cervical spine injury) as well as to opponent (direct trauma).
25. State (slump)—a psychological or physiological state of overtraining that manifests as deteriorated athletic readiness.
26. Supination - the act of rotating a hand or foot externally on its long axis.
27. Tendon dislocation—displacement of tendon from its normal position in a groove over bony fulcrum or neighboring soft tissue.
28. Unconsciousness—loss of wakefulness and responsiveness to one's environment.
29. Whiplash—popular term for hyperextension—hyperflexion injury to cervical spine; does not imply any specific resultant pathology.

SELECTED REFERENCES

American Medical Association, *Fundamentals of Athletic Training*, Chicago, 1971, p. 128.

American Medical Association, *Standard Nomenclature of Athletic Injuries*, Chicago, 1968, p. 157.

American Medical Association, "Tips On Athletic Training II," *Conditioning For the Athlete*, Chicago, 1960, p. 1.

American Medical Association, "Tips On Athletic Training III," *Athletics and Fitness*, Chicago, 1961, p. 3.

American Medical Association, "Tips On Athletic Training V," *Heads and Helmets*, Chicago, 1963, p. 3.

American Medical Association, "Tips On Athletic Training VI," *Conditioning and Contact Sports*, Chicago, 1964, pp. 2-3.

American Medical Association, "Tips On Athletic Training VI," *Protective Athletic Equipment*, Chicago, 1964, p. 5.

American Medical Association, "Tips On Athletic Training VI," *Quackery In Sports*, Chicago, 1964, p. 1.

American Medical Association, "Tips On Athletic Training VII,"

Athletics For Girls, Chicago, 1965, pp. 3-4.

American Medical Association, "Tips On Athletic Training VIII," *Safeguarding the Health of the Athlete,* Chciago, 1966, p. 22.

American Medical Association, "Tips On Athletic Training VIII," *Safety In Track and Field,* Chicago, 1966, pp. 19-20.

American Medical Association, "Tips On Athletic Training IX," *Health Education Through Sports,* Chicago, 1967, pp. 3-5.

Appel, James Z., "Sports Medicine In Perspective," *Proceedings of the Seventh National Conference On the Medical Aspects of Sports,* Philadelphia, 1965, pp. 23-26.

Appenzeller, Herb, *Athletics and the Law,* The Michie Company, Charlottesville, VA, 1975.

Balzina, Martin E., "Protective Equipment In the Prevention of Head and Neck Injuries In Football," *Proceedings of the Seventh National Conference On the Medical Aspects of Sports,* Philadelphia, 1965, pp. 20-22.

Dayton, O. William, *Athletic Training and Conditioning,* The Ronald Press, New York, 1965.

Dixon, Dwayne, *The Dixonary of Athletic Training,* 119 No. Jefferson St., Bloomington, Ind, 1965.

Fagan, Clifford B., "What Every Parent Should Know About Competitive Athletics," *Journal of the National Athletic Training Association,* Greenville, N.C., **10**:30 (March 1975).

Gillette, J., "When and Where Women Are Injured In Sports," *The Physician and Sports Medicine,* Chicago, IL, **3**:663 (May 1975).

Grieve, A., "Legal Implications For the Trainer", *Scholastic Coach,* **45**:46 (October 1975).

Hein, Fred V., "The American Medical Association Committee On the Medical Aspects of Sports: The First Ten Years," *Proceedings of the Eighth National Conference On the Medical Aspects of Sports,* AMA, Chicago, 1966, pp. 1-4.

Klafs, Carl E., and Daniel D. Arnheim, *Modern Principles of Athletic Training,* C.V. Mosby Co., St. Louis, MO, 1973.

Klafs, Carl, and M. Joan Lyon, *The Female Athlete,* C.V. Mosby Co., St. Louis, MO, 1973.

Knox, G., "Sports Injuries: What's The Prognosis," *Better Homes and Gardens,* **53**:2 (June 1975).

Rode, Clifford, A., and Boyd B. Baker, "Legal Implications Covering the Use of Physical Therapy Modalities by Athletic Trainers," *Journal of the National Athletic Trainers Association,* **10**:208-211 (December 1975).

Ryan, Allan J., "Prevention of Injury: A Problem Solving Approach," *Journal of Health, Physical Education and Recreation,* **40**:24-29 (April 1971).

Trickett, Paul C., *Prevention and Treatment of Athletic Injuries,* Appleton-Century-Crofts, New York, 1965.

chapter 15
the athletic trainer

> The key to employment for athletic trainers in the future rests largely with the extent to which federal law mandates the employment of athletic trainers in schools, colleges and universities.
>
> J. William Douglas[1]
> John C. Spiker

DUTIES AND RESPONSIBILITIES

Many individuals and organizations have been responsible for the changing role of the athletic trainer from a "water boy" or the "handy man" to a professional in the athletic department. Today's trainer is a well-qualified individual who frequently possesses an advanced academic degree and has an extensive understanding of the principles of conditioning, the mechanisms of athletic injuries, and rehabilitation following such injuries.[2] His or her primary responsibility is the prevention and care of athletic injuries. The athletic trainer is an integral part of the health team. Other members of this team are the physician, the coach, and the student trainer. The following is a partial list of duties and responsibilities of the athletic trainer at the college level:

[1] J. William Douglas and John C. Spiker, "Athletic Training," *Briefings 3, Careers In Physical Education*, National College Physical Education Association For Men and National Association of Physical Education for College Women, United States, 1975, p. 45.

[2] Carl E. Klafs, and M. Joan Lyon, "*The Female Athlete*," C.V. Mosby Co., St. Louis, 1973, p. 93.

1. Responsible for care and prevention of athletic injuries for the total athletic program.
2. Serve as the liaison between the physician and the injured athlete.
3. Make available a conditioning program for all sports, with cooperation and assistance of the coach.
4. Responsible for safety of athletic equipment and facilities.
5. Initiate and administer a student trainer program.
6. Initiate and process all injury reports.
7. Conduct in-service programs for the coaching staff in the care and prevention of athletic injuries.
8. Review physical exams of all athletes.
9. Advise the coach as to when an athlete may participate in practice or game following injury or illness.
10. Administer first aid to injured athletes on the field, in the gymnasium, or in the training room.
11. Apply protective or injury-preventing devices, such as strapping, bandaging, or braces.
12. Work under direction of physician with respect to: reconditioning procedures, operation of therapeutic devices and equipment, fitting of braces and guards, referrals to the physician, health services and hospital.
13. Work with coach and physician in selecting protective athletic equipment and gear.
14. Supervise training room, which includes the requisitioning and storage of supplies and equipment, keeping records, maintaining a standing and running inventory, and maintaining an annual budget.
15. Teach a limited load of classes to allow ample time to give daily treatments and carry out above assignments.

It is paramount that the athletic trainer should at no time try to be a physician. On all matters pertaining to the athlete's health and medical care, he or she works under the direct supervision of a medical doctor, who is actively engaged in sports on the college, university and high school levels.[3]

[3]Robert Rumph, "The Training Room Staff," *Journal of Health, Physical Education and Recreation,* **45**:30 (October 1974).

THE HEALTH TEAM

The "head" of the health team referred to above is the team physician. Dr. Theodore A. Fox, orthopedic surgeon for the Chicago Bears professional football team, has developed the "Team or Sports Physician Ten Commandments," which specify the role of this most important person.[4]

1. He should be, as previously stated, trained in all modalities of prevention, recognition, diagnosis, and treatment; first aid as well as definitive, of soft tissue and skeletal injuries and their mechanisms.
2. He must personally examine and evaluate all candidates for the sport or team, *prior* to their participation to determine the individuals fitness for same.

    This should include a history of all the previous illnesses, accidents, and surgical procedures as well as a psychological evaluation, and a thorough physical examination.

    The physical evaluation should include observations of any physical characteristics and defects predisposing him to injury, especially in the collision sports.

    This physical examination should include determination of the individual's maturity, balance, coordination, agility, stamina, and strength.
3. The physician should know the basic fundamentals of the particular sport that he is involved with, to better understand the mechanism of the injuries occurring, as well as the injured participant and his problem.
4. He should observe and evaluate the emotional well-being of the athlete, especially the young. Is the candidate being pushed by a frustrated parent to be a super-star or made apprehensive by one of his parents because "he might get hurt?"
5. The physician should *fit* and select all protective gear and equipment and check same as to type and quality, especially in the collision sports.
6. He should also supervise the trainer, or the coach in the proper use of physio-therapeutic modalities used in the

---

[4]Theodore A. Fox, "Team or Sports Physician Ten Commandments," *Speech at Northwestern University,* September 14, 1970, p. 3.

training room which includes the local applications of cold and heat. He should prescribe conditioning and rehabilitative exercises including a supervised weight-lifting program necessary for the continuing well-being of the participant.

The physician is to be responsible for the total rehabilitation, physical as well as mental of the injured athlete and he is to be sure that the participant is fully recovered by performing a careful examination before allowing him to return to participate.

7. The physician should also advise the coach not to teach dangerous blocking and checking practices and to avoid injudicious match of players, especially in the young.

   The doctor should also advise the coach or trainer about hot and humid weather precautions, especially as to light-loose clothing, frequent water breaks and rest periods, and adequate salt intake; to prevent heat stress syndromes (heat exhaustion and heat stroke).

   He should also urge the coach and the trainer to watch for fatigued and injured players and to remove them from the game or practice sessions before injury, or re-aggravation of an injury occurs. He should also encourage the coach to make frequent substitutions before fatigue becomes a problem.

8. The physician should be available at all times to examine the injured player *as soon as possible* after the injury is sustained, preferably on the field or on the side-lines. This is especially true in collision sports.

   Youngsters anxious to continue to play frequently mask injuries and the physician is the only one able to determine that the player is fit to continue to play.

   The coach and/or trainer is not equipped to make decisions concerning injuries of the head or neck that might prove fatal or even in less serious injuries, where returning the player to the game could lead to aggravation of the injury into something more damaging.

9. The team physician is to prevent the injured player from returning to a game if there is a reasonable doubt as to his condition and to prevent a physically unqualified individual from participating. The physician is to resist all pressures from the coach, parents, alumni, and the individual himself to return to the game.

10. The physician is to obtain roentgenograms (x-rays) of all injuries and personally review them before passing on the condition of the injured part.

The coach, as a member of the health team, should be well acquainted with the art and science of the sport involved. The ability to teach proper blocking and checking techniques in collision sports such as football is of vital importance in the prevention of injuries. The coach should be aware that such techniques as knee-level, blindside crack blocking and head butting are dangerous and represent the major causes for serious head and neck injuries and calamitous knee trauma. He should be a leader who can instill into his players the spirit of fair play and sportsmanship and above all be an individual who places the welfare of the players above "winning at all costs."

The student trainer, the fourth member of the health team, is often forgotten as a contributing member to the success of an athletic program. This person is often one who is interested in and enjoys athletic participation but chooses not to compete because of size, skill requirements, or injury that prevents participation. A partial list of duties of the student trainer follows:[5]

1. Responsible for keeping the training room clean and stacked with supplies.
2. Aid the coach in treatments and taping.
3. Pack and check field kits and have them on the field or on the court.
4. Keep the coach and trainer informed about any new injuries.
5. Prepare electrolyte drink and have it ready for breaks in practice or game situations.
6. Complete any special course in athletic training and attend any study sessions presented by coach, trainer, or physician.
7. Will not dispense drugs or medications without specific instructions.
8. Keep all student trainer duties separate from student manager responsibilities.
9. Provide tape and bandages for practicing various tapings.
10. Has special consideration on class assignment to allow time in training room.
11. Keeps and updates records on all player injuries and treatment.

[5]Ibid, p. 4.

Once the health team is constituted, the following prophylactic measures should be taken in all athletic programs to prevent athletic injuries:

1. Careful and thorough precompetition examinations, including psychological evaluation so that unfit candidates are eliminated.
2. All participants are to be in top physical condition before allowing them to participate.
3. Properly fitted and adequately designed new protective equipment should be provided to each player.
4. Taping and splinting of vulnerable areas to protect them from injury.
5. Coaching the player in proper and safe techniques for playing the game. A coach who sets the example of good sportsmanship, and who is a leader respected by the players places their welfare above winning the game.
6. Rule enforcement and closer officiating by emotionally and technically qualified officials is necessary in the prevention of injuries in all athletic contests, especially in collision sports.

QUALIFICATIONS

The qualifications necessary for an athletic trainer can be categorized into two areas—personal and professional. In many respects, the personal qualities are most important because he or she will work with many different and complex personalities. Experts in athletic training list the following personal qualities needed by the athletic trainer: calmness, cleanliness, compassion, competence, responsibility, ethics, fairness, good appearance, good health, industriousness, intelligence, judgment, kindness, leadership, maturity and emotional stability, philosophy, sense of fair play, and understanding. No attempt was made to prioritize the above list but all are essential if one is to be a good trainer.

PROFESSIONAL PREPARATION

Athletic training is not a teaching field. It is, instead, a professional service field, and generally, is not included as a part of accredited teacher education programs except as an endorsement (or specialization).[6] The National Athletic Trainers Association, which establishes

[6] O. William Dayton, *Athletic Training and Conditioning*, The Ronald Press Company, New York, 1965, pp. 10-13.

the standards for certification, requires that all individuals seeking certification have completed a baccalaureate degree. They also must be certified to teach. This certification need not be in the areas of health or physical education, but the NATA recommends that a minor be completed in one or the other of these fields. Douglas and Spiker believe that an athletic training curriculum should be under the sponsorship and in concert with departments, schools, or colleges of health, physical education, and recreation for the following reasons:[7]

1. A vast majority of the competencies necessary for NATA certification can be met through courses generally offered as an integral part of the professional preparation of physical educators and, to a limited degree, health (and safety) educators.
2. Institutions offering an NATA approved athletic training curriculum will have one or more NATA certified trainers on the teaching faculty who will be directly responsible for coordinating the curriculum, teaching the basic and advanced athletic training courses, and supervising the laboratory practice. In most cases these individuals will be affiliated with an academic unit which generally will be HPER.
3. Due to the inclusion of athletics (at least conceptually) within the parameters of the professional preparation of physical educators and the corresponding student understanding and appreciation of athletics, it is felt that the HPER unit is more appropriate than other academic units.
4. Athletic training is a recognized entity within the American Alliance for Health, Physical Education and Recreation and, like other HPER related areas, athletic trainers are encouraged to become members and be involved in AAHPER. It is felt that the NATA and its membership can function in concert with the AAHPER.
5. The facilities and equipment necessary to offer an athletic training curriculum are generally necessary to support a professional preparation curriculum in HPER or as part of athletics. In most colleges and universities a working relationship exists between HPER and athletics; in some, athletics is a part of the total unit, e.g., Division of Health, Physical Education, and Athletics. Because of this relationship and at a time when finances in higher education are critical, it is not necessary to duplicate the devel-

[7] J. William Douglas, and John C. Spiker, "Athletic Training," Briefings 3, Careers in Physical Education, NCPEAM and NAPECW, United States, 1975, p. 40.

opment and/or operation of athletic training related facilities and equipment.
6. Faculty who are certified as athletic trainers generally possess expertise in areas complimentary to athletic training per se, but not mutually exclusive e.g., biomechanics. Thus, they will be able to assume teaching responsibilities, if needed, in courses offered by an HPER unit. This will eliminate or reduce the need for additional faculty in specialty areas. Operationally, this results in a most efficient employment of faculty.

Correspondingly, due to the need for athletic trainers for intercollegiate varsity athletic programs, the dual appointment (HPER and athletics) permits athletic departments to have one or more athletic trainers at a minimal cost.
7. Faculty in HPER are generally known by secondary school coaches, physical educators, athletic directors, and principals throughout the respective states. These individuals will be responsible for employing graduates of approved athletic training curricula. It is imperative that communication channels be developed and maintained to further the need for and employment of graduates certified as athletic trainers.

Correspondingly, similar relationships generally exist with state secondary school athletic association personnel. It is critical that the state recognize the need for and the availability of athletic trainers to be associated with intramural and interscholastic athletic programs. HPER units can best facilitate this.

Although it is recognized that other units on college or university campuses could sponsor an athletic training curriculum, perhaps effectively, it is felt the logical sponsoring unit is HPER for reasons cited. It is suggested, however, that other potential sponsoring units, that is, biology, sociology, or psychology, physical therapy or athletics, be involved in planning for the implementation of the curriculum. It is particularly recommended that those institutions having a medical school develop a working relationship with the department of anatomy and physical therapy. If a department of sports medicine is available, it is recommended that athletic training be included. The administration of the professional preparation curriculum in athletic training should, however, be retained in HPER.

At the 1974 Professional Preparation Conference it was recommended that approval of the NATA basic minimal requirements for the athletic training curriculum be as follows:[8]

I. *A Major Study (including teaching license in physical education, health and/or a secondary education field, variable by states)*
   A. Total of 24 semester hours in biological and social sciences.
      1. Biology—Zoology (anatomy and physiology)—8 hours
      2. Social sciences (at least 6 hours in psychology)—10 hours
      3. Electives strongly advised, minimum of—6 hours
         a. additional biological and social sciences
         b. physical education (group activities, dancing, etc.)
         c. hygiene
         d. speech
         e. physics
         f. chemistry

II. *Specific Required Courses (if not included in I, then must be added).*
   A. Anatomy—one or more courses which include human anatomy.
   B. Physiology—circulation, digestion, excretion, nerve, brain, and sense organs.
      Note: one course will not meet the two requirements listed above.
   C. Physiology of Exercise.
   D. Applied Anatomy and Kinesiology—the muscles, with emphasis on their function and development in specific activities.
   E. Psychology—one advanced course beyond the basic general psychology course (e.g. Sports Psychology).
   F. First Aid and Safety—minimum of Advanced Red Cross First Aid Certification.
   G. Nutrition and Foods.

[8] AAHPER, "Professional Preparation in Dance, Physical Education, Recreation Education, Safety Education, and School Health Education," *Athletic Trainer Specialization*, Washington, D.C., 1974, pp. 59-60.

1. Basic principles of nutrition
2. Basic diet and special diet
H. Remedial Exercise, Therapeutic Exercise, Adapted Exercise or Corrective Exercise—exercise for atypical persons and/or for temporarily and permanently handicapped persons.
I. Personal, Community and School Health.
J. Techniques of Athletic Training—basic courses (acceptable for all coaches).
K. Advanced Techniques of Athletic Training.
1. Special course(s) for athletic training candidates with full academic background.
2. Laboratory practices (6 semester hours credit or two years equivalent work of 600 clock hours).

III. Recommended Courses
A. Laboratory Physical Science—six semester hours in physics and/or chemistry (should be required of students planning to study physical therapy).
B. Pharmacology—specific side effects of drugs.
C. Histology—tissues and methods of studying them.
D. Pathology—laboratory study of tissues in pathological condition.
E. Organization and Administration of Health and Physical Education Programs.
F. Psychology of Coaching.
G. Coaching Techniques.
1. Highly recommended—football, basketball & track.
2. Also recommended—soccer, wrestling and preferred sports by geographic areas.

NATA CERTIFICATION

In addition to the curricular requirements referred to in the previous chapter all individuals wishing to become NATA certified athletic trainers must pass the NATA certification examination and present proof of at least one year of continuous active or student membership in the NATA. Ways in which individuals can become eligible for certification include:

1. Completing a NATA approved athletic training curriculum. Students graduating from an NATA approved curriculum are eligible to take the NATA Certification Examination during the last semester of the senior year, or anytime thereafter. A list of institutions

that have NATA approved curricula can be obtained by writing to Otho Davis, Executive Director of the NATA, Philadelphia Eagles, Veterans Stadium, Philadelphia, Pennsylvania 19145.

2. Serving an apprenticeship. For individuals interested in athletic training but enrolled at a college or university that does not have a NATA approved curriculum, it is possible to become a certified trainer by completing 1800 hours of laboratory experience under the supervision of an NATA certified trainer; by showing proof of graduation from an accredited college or university; and by submitting letters of recommendation from the team physician and athletic trainer. These individuals are then eligible to take the NATA certification examination.

3. Actively engaging in the profession but not certified. By showing proof of five year's experience as an athletic trainer, by showing proof of graduation from an accredited college or university, and by submitting letters of recommendation from a team physician and a NATA certified trainer, these individuals are eligible to take the NATA Certification Examination.

4. Completing a physical therapy curriculum. Graduates of a physical therapy curriculum are eligible to take the NATA Certification Examination if they have worked a minimum of two (2) years, beyond that as a student athletic trainer at the secondary school level, under direct supervision of a NATA certified trainer.

The NATA Certification Examination, including written and practical aspects of athletic training, is administered by the NATA's Professional Examination Service.

LEGAL IMPLICATIONS

Since it appears that injuries and illnesses often occur as a result of athletic participation, it is of paramount importance that coaches and trainers follow proper procedures in treating these maladies, being very aware of statutory provisions that may govern the extent of such treatment. Special attention should be paid to existing statutory provisions, which, in several states, prohibit persons from practicing acts that could be construed as physical therapy, physiotherapy, hydrotherapy, chiropody, or nursing, without first obtaining the proper license to do so.

There are many legal implications concerning the use of physical-therapy modalities by athletic trainers. Baker and Rode have placed all of the states into categories in which a comparison is made of the various states' statutes governing the practice of physical therapy.[9] Texas is the only state that has thus far defined the role of the athletic trainer, and it is the only state that presently requires licensure of athletic trainers. Every aspiring, and indeed every practicing athletic trainer should become familiar with the state statutes and comply with the regulations applicable to the use of physical therapy modalities (i.e., exercise, massage, heat, cold, water-radiant energy, electricity, or sound).

Grieve points out some areas that might pose legal questions for the athletic trainer.[10] He should never overstep the legal boundaries in prescribing "treatment" for athletic injuries. Treatment is not the domain of the trainer; it is strictly a medical responsibility. Three legal concepts applicable to athletic training should be understood by every athletic trainer—malfeasance, misfeasance and nonfeasance. Malfeasance implies that the individual performed an act that was definitely illegal and one that he or she should not have performed. Misfeasance indicates that an individual had the right to perform the function but performed it incorreclty. Nonfeasance involves the failure to perform an act that should have been performed. The use of internal medication is another procedure that could result in a negligence suit. Many trainers do administer various internal medications with no adverse reaction, but it could lead to legal action. The administration of such medication is clearly malfeasance. Adhesive strapping or taping is another area of concern. Preventive taping is performed with the sole purpose of preventing injuries and can be done by the trainer. Therapeutic taping, however, should never be performed by anyone but medical personnel.

Athletic trainers should avail themselves at every opportunity to read and be conversant with the legal aspects of their profession. In *Modern Principles of Athletic Training* Klafs and Arnheim provide an excellent summary of legal implications to safeguard the athlete and the trainer.

[9]Boyd Baker, "Coaches Should Know Their Legal Responsibilities," *The First Aider*, Gardner, Kans, **45**:2 (March 1976).

[10]Andrew Grieve, "Legal Implications for the Athletic Trainer," *Scholastic Coach*, **45**: 46-48, 79 (October 1975).

CAREER OPPORTUNITIES

Probably no other area in the broad spectrum of athletics and physical education offers better employment opportunities than athletic training. If federal law is enacted that mandates the employment of athletic trainers in schools and colleges, the demand will exceed the supply for some time. In a previous chapter the authors have alluded to the need for trainers and of the federal law still awaiting passage (i.e., Dellums Bill). The employment of trainers in many high schools has been stalled because of budgetary problems and a lack of professional trainers.[11] Another problem arises in some areas because of a muddled image of athletic training and athletic trainers despite great efforts by the medical profession and the National Athletic Trainers Association.

Many students select an academic area in which to specialize and combine this with an athletic training specialization thus enhancing their potential for employment in the secondary schools.

The athletic trainer/physical therapy combination has many advantages in the area of employment. Some of the employment possibilities are:

1. Full-time athletic training responsibilities at a college or university. A physical therapy background and experience in the paramedical area is much in demand.
2. Teach adapted sports in a high school or college.
3. Teach physical education in a high school or college and serve as athletic trainer. Most work in athletic training is confined to the late afternoon and evenings.
4. Many physical therapists maintain a private practice in the evenings and weekends.

Many athletic and physical education departments in colleges and universities employ athletic trainers who have a dual role of teaching and athletic training. The rapid growth in women's sports at all levels has resulted in a larger number of women entering athletic training programs.

[11] NATA, *Athletic Training Careers*, NATA, Lafayette, Ind, p. 3, 1974.

The rapid increase in the number of professional sports teams who employ full-time athletic trainers opens up another potential job market for athletic trainers.

For additional information related to careers in athletic training, interested individuals should consult the NATA publication entitled, *Athletic Training Careers*.[12] The December, 1975 issue of the Journal of the NATA lists those educational programs leading to professional certification in athletic training in the United States.[13]

SELECTED REFERENCES

AAHPER, *Professional Preparation in Dance, Physical Education, Recreation Education, Safety Education, and School Health Education*, Washington, D.C., 1974, p. 192.

American Medical Association, *Fundamentals of Athletic Training*, Chicago, 1971, p. 128.

American Medical Association, *Standard Nomenclature of Athletic Injuries*, Chicago, 1968, p. 157.

Appenzeller, Herb, *Athletics and the Law*, The Michie Company, Charlotteville, VA, 1975.

Baker, Boyd B., and Clifford A. Rode, "Legal Implications Concerning the Use of Physical Therapy Modalities by Athletic Trainers," *Journal of the National Athletic Trainers Association*, **10**:208-211 (December 1975).

Carey, Richard, Gary D. Reinholtz, John W. Schrader, and Mark J. Smaha, *Athletic Training: A Programmed Instructional Text*, Beta Publishing Co., Glenview, IL, 1975.

Delforge, Gary, and Richard Klein, "High School Athletic Trainers' Internship," *Journal of Health, Physical Education and Recreation*, **44**:42-43 (March 1973).

Delforge, Gary, "Educational Programs In Athletic Training," *Proceedings of the 78th Annual Meeting of the National College Physical Education Association for Men*, Leo L. Gedivalas, (ed.), 193-196, University of Illinois, Chicago Circle, Chicago, 1975.

Douglas, J. William, and John C. Spiker, *Athletic Training, Briefings 3, Careers in Physical Education*, NCPEAM and NAPECW, U.S.A., 1975.

[12] Ibid. p. 4.

[13] NATA, "Announcements," *Educational Programs Leading to Professional Certification in Athletic Training*, Lafayette, Ind., **10**:224-225 (December 1975).

Douglas, J. William, "Professional Preparation in Athletic Training," *Journal of Physical Education and Recreation*, **47**:40-41 (May 1976).

Dixon, Dwayne, *The Dixonary of Athletic Training*, Bloomington, Ind., 1965.

Gallon, Arthur J., *Coaching: Ideas and Ideals*, Houghton Mifflen Co., Boston, 1974.

Grieve, Andrew, "Legal Implications for the Athletic Trainer," *Scholastic Coach*, **45**:46 (October 1975).

Hinckley, Penelope, and Doris A. Wickal, "A Coach Looks at the Trainer," *Scholastic Coach*, **45**:46-48 (August 1975).

Hirata, Isao, *The Doctor and the Athlete*, J.B. Lippencott Co., Philadelphia, 1974.

Klafs, Carl E., and Daniel D. Arnheim, *Modern Principles of Athletic Training*, C.V. Mosby Company, St. Louis, 1973.

Klafs, Carl E., and M. Joan Lyon *The Female Athlete*, C.V. Mosby Co., St. Louis, 1973.

Kuenlgsbert, Ruth, and Margarite Arrighi, "Women Athletic Trainers," *Journal of Physical Education and Recreation*, **46**:51-52 (January 1975).

Lowman, C.L., "Some Thoughts by an Orthopedist," *The Physical Educator Magazine*, **28**:34-35 (March 1971).

McLean, Lindsy, "Does the National Athletic Trainers Association Need a Certification Examination," *The Journal of the National Athletic Trainers Association*, **4**:31, (Spring 1969).

Miller, Sayers J., "Educating Trainers—Neophyte and Veteran," *Journal of the National Athletic Trainers Association*, **1**:33, (Summer 1966).

Miller, Sayers J., "The Role of the Athletic Trainer as an Educator in The NATA's Educational Program," *Journal of the National Athletic Trainers Association*, **6**:68-71, (Summer 1971).

Miller, Sayers J., and Walter C. Schwank, "New Dimensions for the Athletic Training Profession," *Journal of Health, Physical Education and Recreation*, **42**:41-43 (September 1971).

Morehouse, Laurence E., and Philip J. Rasch, *Sports Medicine For Trainers*, W.B. Saunders Co., Philadelphia, 1964.

Nixon, John E., and Ann E. Jewett, *An Introduction to Physical Education*, W.B. Saunders Co., Philadelphia, 1974.

Rockwell, J., "National Notes," *The Journal of the Athletic Trainers Association*, **5**:29, (Fall 1970).

Rumph, Robert, "The Training Room Staff," *Journal of Health, Physical Education and Recreation,* **45**:30-31 (October 1974).

Savastano, A.A., "Rhode Island Shows the Way: In Service Training For the Prevention and Treatment of Athletic Injuries," *Journal of Health, Physical Education and Recreation,* **41**:54-57 (April 1970).

Sheehan, G.A., "The Doctor and Sports," *Medical Times,* **101**:97-98 (June 1973).

Treadway, Linda, "Not For Men Only," *The Journal of the National Athletic Trainers Association,* **9**:62 (June 1974).

Trickett, Paul C., *The Prevention and Treatment of Athletic Injuries,* Appleton-Century-Crofts, New York, 1965.

Weldon, Gail, "Not For Men Only," *The Journal of the National Athletic Trainers Association,* **9**:62-63 (June 1974).

Wilson, Holly, "Not For Men Only," *The Journal of the National Athletic Trainers Association,* **10**:206-207 (December 1975).

chapter 16

learning experiences in athletic training

Anyone interested in the field of athletic training should take full advantage of all the possible experience one encounters.[1]

Marge Albohm

The urgent need for athletic trainers of both sexes as well as the job market for certified athletic trainers has been discussed previously but a comment made by the team physician for the Chicago Bulls professional basketball team is relevant to the present-day situation in competitive sports. "A high school would never have a swimming pool in use without a trained lifeguard, but team practice sessions and games are often conducted without a physician or certified athletic trainer in attendance."[2]

Most athletic trainers support an early and continuous exposure for undergraduate students to many types of learning experiences. This chapter is devoted to increasing competencies among students pursuing a

---

[1] Marge Albohm, "Not For Men Only," *The Journal of the National Athletic Trainers Association*, **9**:61 (June 1974).

[2] Dave Van Dyck, "Medical Course Will Aid Trainers," *Daily Tribune* Chicago, March 29, 1976.

career in athletic training. We have divided these learning experiences into preparing, planning and performing categories.

PREPARING ACTIVITIES

1. Prepare a list of the anatomical and physiological differences between men and women athletes and describe how these differences affect participation in sports.
2. Describe the role of the student trainer in various emergencies.
3. Prepare a lecture for the P.T.A. on the topic, "What Should Athletes Eat?"
4. Develop a list of controversial exercises and submit this list to the head trainer for his or her review and comments.
5. Talk with the wrestling coach about weight control and wrestling.
6. Visit and observe the training rooms of high schools, colleges, and professional sport teams in the city where you live or attend school.
7. Prepare a list of athletic training clinics and workshops for women.
8. Serve as a student trainer in the athletic program; in the intramural program.
9. Conduct a seminar on the topic, "Preventive treatment and taping techniques used on female athletes."
10. Develop a conditioning program for a high school football team (preseason) and submit it to the athletic trainer for his or her review and comments.
11. Serve as a student trainer (volunteer) for the local or international Special Olympics.
12. Prepare a lecture for a student trainer seminar on the topic, "Do drugs improve athletic performance?"
13. Contact the Rainbow Sports Medicine Center in Cleveland, Ohio and request materials regarding the center.
14. Prepare an extensive bibliography on the subject of sports injuries and athletic training. Include books and periodicals with publication dates no earlier than 1966.
15. Investigate the procedure to be followed in obtaining approval for an athletic training curricula in a college or university.
16. Discuss with the team physician the guidelines he or she uses for deciding when athletes may return to competition.

17. Design an athletic training room for a high school or a college. The facility should be for both men and women.
18. Assist the head trainer in developing a system for record keeping of athletic injuries.
19. Prepare a complete job description of the student trainer for the head trainer in a high school or college.
20. Attend as many athletic events as possible in addition to those assigned to you as a student trainer.
21. Talk with the head trainer and the team physician regarding their techniques for identifying injured players.
22. Prepare a seminar topic on the subject, "Prevention of athletic injuries through education."
23. Attend workshops and clinics in athletic training.
24. Assist in the preparation of weight and weekly weight-training charts.
25. Discuss the topic, "Physical fitness and the athletic trainer" with the head trainer and ask for his or her comments.
26. Investigate the National Electronic Injury Surveillance System of the U.S. Consumer Product Safety Commission and determine its role and importance in your future profession of athletic training.
27. Prepare a list of "do's" and "don't's" for your interview in seeking a job as an athletic trainer and discuss this list with the head trainer.
28. Discuss with the team physician the topic, "Do women have certain structural and physiological characteristics that predispose them to certain injuries?"
29. Define the following terms in your own words and compare your definitions with the head trainer and team physician:
    a. Heat stroke.
    b. Heat exhaustion.
    c. Warm-up.
    d. Dellums bill.
    e. Cryotherapy.
    f. Dislocation.
    g. Separation.
    h. Second wind.
    i. Weight training.
    j. Weight lifting.

30. Discuss with the school's legal counsel the legal responsibilities of an athletic trainer and student trainer.

PLANNING ACTIVITIES

1. There are approximately 30 undergraduate training curricula in the United States. Secure the location of these programs from the athletic trainer in your school.
2. Michael L. Pollock, former director of the Physical Fitness Research Laboratory at Wake Forest University, stated that both professinal undergraduate and graduate students should have an early and continuous involvement with a research laboratory. He diagrams in Fig. 16.1 the multipurposeness of such a facility.[3] See Fig. 16.1.

```
                    Research laboratory
                   /      |      |      \
              Professor  Graduate  Undergraduate  Graduate and
                         training   training      undergraduate
                                                  exposure
```

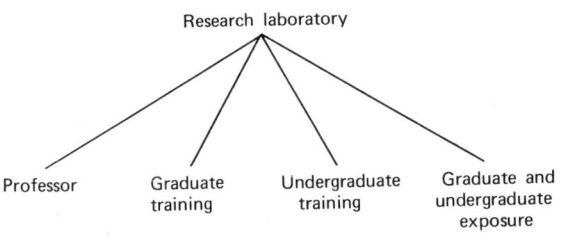

FIGURE 16.1 The multipurposeness of a physical fitness research laboratory. Reprinted by permission of Michael Pollock, Dallas, Texas, 1977.

Assume your are an undergraduate student enrolled in an athletic training program. Substitute the athletic training room for the research laboratory and describe the types of experiences (exposure) emanating from this laboratory that would be useful to you as a prospective athletic trainer.

3. Dan Lowe, Head Trainer at Syracuse University, has developed an evaluation program for student trainers.[4] See Fig. 16.2. Submit this evaluation form to the head trainer and ask him to complete and return it to you at the end of the school year. Prior to receipt of his or her evaluation, make your own assessment of your competencies and compare the two responses.
4. Fred Allman, an authority in sports medicine, served as the keynote speaker at the 1969 convention of the National Athletic

---

[3]Michael L. Pollock, "Expose Undergraduate Students to Research Early," *Journal of Health, Physcial Education and Recreation*, **41**:25 (May 1970).

[4]Dan Lowe, "Evaluating Student Trainers Leads to Efficiency," *The First Aider*, Gardner, Kans., **45**:5 (January 1976).

Athletic Training Department
Student Trainer Evaluation

Name _____ Date _____

SKILLS AND ABILITIES	EXCELLENT	ABOVE AVERAGE	AVERAGE	BELOW AVERAGE
1. Taping techniques	_____	_____	_____	_____
2. Treatment techniques	_____	_____	_____	_____
3. Recognition of injuries	_____	_____	_____	_____
4. Strength, conditioning, and rehabilitation routines	_____	_____	_____	_____
5. Use of therapy modalities	_____	_____	_____	_____
6. Knowledge and use of training room supplies	_____	_____	_____	_____
7. Works with speed and efficiency	_____	_____	_____	_____
8. Training room procedures	_____	_____	_____	_____
9. Training room attitude and discipline	_____	_____	_____	_____
10. Maintains neat and clean training room	_____	_____	_____	_____
11. Maintains accurate, legible records of injuries and treatments	_____	_____	_____	_____
12. Can see work without being told	_____	_____	_____	_____
13. Gets along well with athletes	_____	_____	_____	_____
14. Gets along well with coaches, administrators, and team physicians	_____	_____	_____	_____
15. Appearance and dress	_____	_____	_____	_____

Comments:

FIGURE 16.2

Source: Dan Lowe, "Evaluating Student Trainers Leads to Efficiency," *The First Aider.* Kramer Products Co., Gardiner, Kans., 45:5 (January 1976)

Trainers Association. He presented an extensive listing of what a trainer ought to be.[5] See Fig. 16.3. As a prospective athletic trainer, evaluate yourself on a scale of 1-5 on the following characteristics that he has listed. Define, in your own words, what these terms mean.

[5]Fred L. Allman "What a Trainer Ought to Be," *Journal of the National Athletic Trainers Association,* 5:3-7 (Fall 1970).

LEARNING EXPERIENCES IN ATHLETIC TRAINING 253

	YOUR RATING (1=high; 5=low)				
TRAIT	1	2	3	4	5
Compassion					
Understanding					
Sincerity					
Perfection and excellence					
Leadership					
Determination					
Perseverance					
Thirst for knowledge					
Enthusiasm					
Self-reliance					
Courage					
Self discipline and self control					
Versatility					
Judgment					
Responsible					
Responsible citizen					
Health					
Love					
Greatness					

FIGURE 16.3
Source. Fred L. Allman, "What a Trainer Ought to Be," *Journal of the National Athletic Trainers Association*, **5**:3-7 (Fall 1970).

PERFORMING ACTIVITIES

The following case studies represent performing activities for student trainers:

Communication

John Powers, a senior student at Hillsdale College, was preparing for a career in athletic training. He was married and the father of a six-year-old son. John's wife, an active member of the local P.T.A., was elected program chairman and thus responsible for planning the coming year's events. It was suggested that because of John's interest in athletics and his desire to become an athletic trainer that he could be the speaker for one of the monthly meetings. He was given the topic, "What every parent should know about competitive athletics?" If you were in John Power's situation, how would you handle this speaking engagement?

Equipment

Alan Neuman served as head trainer for Ravenswood College, a private institution in Massachusetts. The athletic director planned to purchase new equipment for the football team at that school and asked Alan to assist him in selecting the proper equipment. Alan sought the advice of the senior student trainer, John Williams, in preparing the list of equipment to be ordered. If you were John Williams, what are the items that must be considered in responding to Alan's request?

Budget

Bill Anderson was a third-year student in Gettysburg College, majoring in physical education and athletic training. He was a student trainer in the football and basketball programs and looked forward to a career as a teacher and athletic trainer. The head trainer, Jim Edwards, was responsible for the athletic training budget and sought Bill's help in preparing it prior to submission to the athletic director. What resources should Bill use to answer this request from Mr. Anderson?

Student Trainers

Heather Hall was a sophomore preparing for a career in athletic training at the University of McIntyre. She served as a student trainer in the athletic program working with the gymnastics and volleyball programs. The head trainer told her during the Spring prior to her junior year that she would not be needed for football and track for the coming year because the athletic training staff was complete. She was very disappointed at this turn of events but was determined to continue to learn as much about her profession prior to graduation as possible. She wondered if the university intramural program had need of a student trainer and decided to talk with the Intramural Director, Harriet Phillips. Ms. Phillips was delighted to learn of Heather's interest and willingness to assist with the program and felt that the intramural program needed someone with expertise in athletic training. She suggested that Heather prepare a brief outline for her dealing with several items for their discussion. The major topics included selection of participants, coaching and teaching of skills, training and conditioning, protective equipment, safe play areas, supervision and officiating, accident reporting, and first aid and medical treatment. Heather pondered how she would respond to this request.

Women In Sports

One of the local service clubs in the city where Linn Stewart attended Appalacian State College was planning its schedule of meetings for the coming year. The program committee chairman was interested in women's sports but disagreed that there should be equitable funding for competitive athletic programs for men and women. He believed there were great physiological and anatomical differences between men and women. Linn was asked to serve on a panel to dispute this premise. What should she say to support her side of the argument?

SELECTED REFERENCES

Allman, Fred L., Jr., "What a Trainer Ought to Be," *Journal of the National Athletic Trainers Association,* LaFayette, Ind., **5**:3-7 (Fall 1970).

Arrighi, Margarite, and Ruth Koenigsberg, "Women Athletic Trainers," *Journal of Physical Education and Recreation,* Washington, D.C., **46**:51-52 (January 1975).

Blazina, Martin E., "Medical Guidelines for Return to Participation," *Journal of National Athletic Trainers Association,* LaFayette, Ind., 5:7-9 (Summer 1970).

Clarke, Kenneth S., "Research Design and the Athletic Trainer," *Journal of National Athletic Trainers Association,* LaFayette, Ind., 7:139-143 (October 1972).

Encyclopedia of Sport Sciences and Medicine, MacMillan Company, New York, p. 1703, 1971.

Gieck, Joe, "Investigating a New Position in Athletic Training," *Journal of National Athletic Trainers Association,* LaFayette, Ind., **9**:36.

Harres, Bea, "Attitudes of Students Toward Women's Athletic Competition," *Research Quarterly,* Washington, D.C., **39**:278-284 (May 1968).

Jernigan, Sara Staff, "Research Needs in Girls and Women's Sports," *The Fourteenth International Congress of the International Council on Health, Physical Education and Recreation,* Washington, D.C., 1972, pp. 93-95.

Klafs, Carl E., and Daniel D. Arnheim, *Modern Principles of Athletic Training,* C.V. Mosby Co., St. Louis, 1973.

Klafs, Carl E., and M. Joan Lyon, *The Female Athlete,* St. Louis, C.V. Mosby Co., 1973.

Klein, Richard, and Gary Deltorge, "High School Athletic Trainers, Internship," *Journal of Health, Physical Education and Recreation,* Washington, D.C., **44**:42-43 (March 1973).

Morgan, William P., "Research Studies on the Female Athlete," *Journal of Physical Education and Recreation,* Washington, D.C., **46**:32-44 (January 1975).

Pollock, Michael L., "Expose Undergraduate Students to Research Early," *Journal of Health, Physical Education and Recreation,* Washington, D.C., **41**:25 (May 1970).

Powers, Hallis W., "The Organization and Administration of an Athletic Training Program," *Journal of the National Athletic Trainers Association,* LaFayette, Ind., **11**:14-16 (Spring 1976).

Rumph, Robert, "The Training Room Staff," *Journal of Health, Physical Education and Recreation,* Washington, D.C., **45**:30-31 (October 1974).

Trickett, Paul C., *Prevention and Treatment of Athletic Injuries,* Appleton-Century-Crofts, New York, 1965.

section 5
corrective therapy

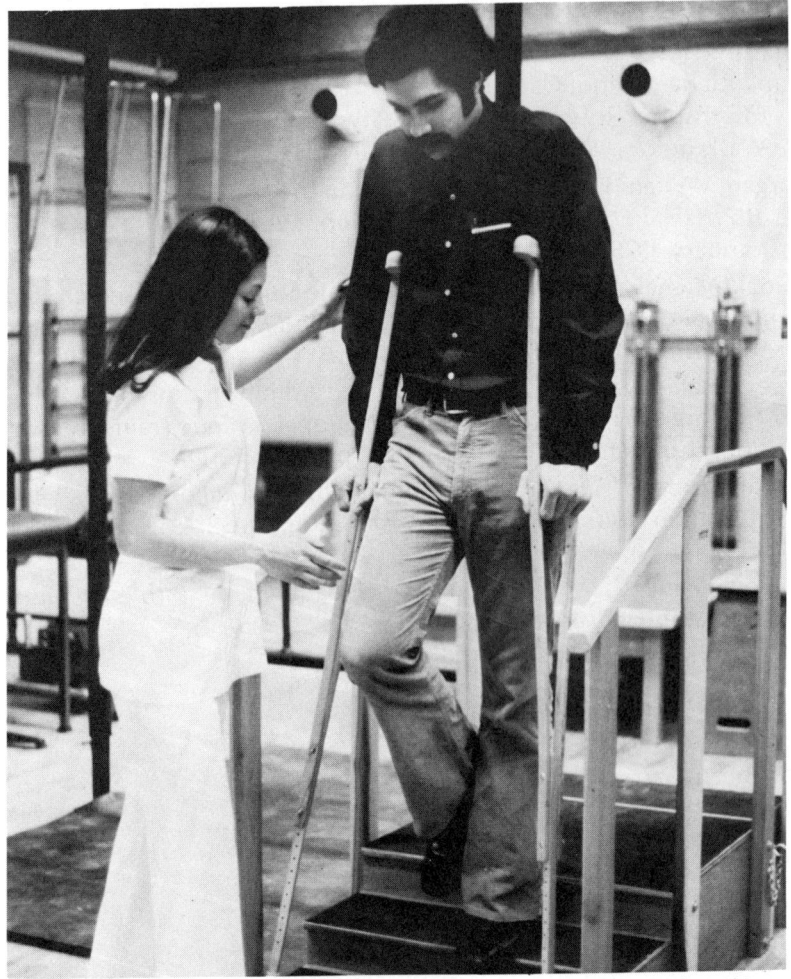

Reprinted by permission of University of Illinois at Chicago Circle, Chicago.

**17
the profession
18
professional preparation in corrective therapy
19
role of the corrective therapist
20
learning experiences in corrective therapy**

chapter 17

the profession

The wise, for cure, on exercise depend.[1]
John Dryden

HISTORY

Corrective therapy is a relatively new profession whose origins date back to prehistoric man where cave drawings indicate the use of exercise for therapeutic and corrective puposes. Throughout history, exercise as medical rehabilitation had its peaks and valleys. In 3000 B.C., the Chinese implemented medical gymnastics as a method of healing disease. The Greeks, around 480 B.C., performed similar practices by conducting ritual ceremonies at health temples.

Therapeutic exercises continued to be practiced by Greek physicians as medical treatment for the Romans during 124 B.C. to 200 A.D. However, during the age of Christianity, when emphasis was on the life hereafter and the soul, interest and practice of corrective exercises declined. Not until the modern period was the interest and practice of remedial and corrective exercises renewed. Then, bodily exercises were developed for the athlete, the military, and the cure of disease.

In the 1800s, attention was directed to a reaffiliation of exercise and medicine, a reintroduction of medical gymnastics, and establishing a scientific basis for gymnastics. The formal system of gymnastics developed

[1] *A Brief Introduction to Corrective Therapy,* American Corrective Therapy Association, prepared by Kermit Rhea, p. 1.

by Per Henrik Ling in Sweden greatly influenced the use of exercise for corrective and remedial purposes, thus forming the foundation for the profession known today as corrective therapy.

During World War II, physical reconditioning programs were established for the U.S. armed forces, and this stimulated the development of corrective therapy and adapted physical education. Two men largely responsible for inaugerating these programs were Major General Norman T. Kirk, the U.S. Surgeon General, and Howard Rusk, M.D.

In 1943, Major General Kirk was inspired by the work of a British physical reconditioning battalion and envisioned a similar program for American servicemen. He realized that a program of this nature would provide a quick return of American convalescents to active duty. At this same time, physicians became acutely aware that *Rest* as a therapeutic measure was not only undesirable but hazardous for physical conditions such as rheumatic fever, cardiac disorders, tuberculosis, vascular accidents, certain orthopedic disabilities, and even brain surgery.

Soon, physical reconditioning programs were established in military hospitals. Training schools were started to obtain qualified physical reconditioning instructors. By the end of 1946, over 8000 persons, primarily physical educators, had received extensive training in medically prescribing exercises to various patient types. Dr. Howard Rusk, who was concerned with the undesirable and harmful effects of bed rest, demonstrated the value of the physical reconditioning program by results of a shortened hospitalization period, reduced hospital readmissions, and improved morale for various patient types.

In 1946, military physical medicine and rehabilitation programs were incorporated into the veteran's administration and became known as corrective physical rehabilitation. This new member of the rehabilitative team, together with enlarged physical therapy departments and added occupational therapy clinics, and other ancillary services provided care and treatment to the vast number of returning disabled servicemen.

On the recommendation of Dr. Howard Rusk, the Veterans' Administration hired 400 personnel. These instructors, who were former physical educators, were concerned with using medically prescribed exercises to treat the hospitalized handicapped. However, because they encountered a variety of disabilities, many returned to school for review and advanced courses in anatomy, physiology, kinesiology, and other basic sciences. The knowledge gained in these areas stimulated the development of new techniques and exercises that could be prescribed for a specific disability. This expertise and the teaching methods derived from physical education contributed to the excellent progress made by their patients.

Corrective physical rehabilitation, as a newcomer to the rehabilitation team, suffered severe criticism from the older, more firmly established professions. This caused physical rehabilitation instructors to seriously examine the philosphy, purpose, and scope of their profession.

In October 1946, a group of professionals met at the Veterans Administration Hospital at Topeka, Kansas and formally organized the Association for Physical and Mental Rehabilitation (APMR), the first professional association. Three aims of the newly organized APMR were: (1) to promote the use of medically prescribed exercise therapy and adapted physical education, (2) to advance the professional standards of education and training in the profession, and (3) to encourage and promote research. A medical advisory board was selected to assist the APMR in matters of professional concern. This advisory board was composed of leading physicians and physical educators. Specifically, they were: Rusk, Covalt, Menninger, Greenwood, Davis, Stafford, Clarke, and Rathbone.

By 1947, the professional name was changed from physical rehabilitation to corrective therapy. Research was conducted and exercises were developed that encompassed the rehabilitation of persons in hospitals and adapted physical education. The APMR established a constitution and bylaws, communicated scientific information through a bimonthly publication, sponsored an annual scientific and clinical conference, conferred awards, and presented scholarships.

In 1953, the American Board for Certification of Corrective Therapists was organized by the APMR. The purpose of establishing certification was to approve the qualifications of therapists and to form a national register of certified professionals. Certification in corrective therapy consisted of completing a bachelor's degree in an approved four-year curriculum with courses in designated areas, serving a clinical internship of at least 250 hours, and passing a three-part examination (written, practical, and oral) administered by the APMR.

The clinical internship mentioned was approved in 1956 by the Office of Education and the Physical Medicine and Rehabilitation Service, now known as the Veteran's Administration Central Office. Clinical training was conducted in Veterans' Administration hospitals that met the basic criteria established by the APMR. The inclusion of certification for corrective therapists substantiated the profession as having qualified practitioners in the profession and offered the public a means of protection and a guarantee of competent service. In 1967, the Association for Physical and Mental Rehabilitation became the American Corrective Therapy Association, Incorporated (ACTA), hereinafter referred to as the Association.

PHILOSOPHY AND PURPOSES

Corrective therapy as defined by the Association is "the application of the principles, tools, techniques and psychology of medically oriented physical education to assist the physician in the accomplishment of prescribed objectives."[2] Together, corrective therapy and adapted physical education have been identified as unique and important disciplines in prevention, development, habilitation and rehabilitation, of the handicapped.

Both function similarly in the process and procedures used in treating disabled persons and, under medical referral, are performed in public and private facilities. Corrective therapy functions primarily in hospitals and centers for physical and mental restoration, habilitation, or both. Adapted physical education functions as an integral part of the total education process in a regular school or exceptional childrens' program at various age and educational levels.

As a paramedical discipline, corrective therapy is not mutually exclusive of physical therapy, occupational therapy, and recreational therapy. However, although similarity exists in subject matter, there are differences in the training programs. In physical and occupational therapy, undergraduate training occurs in a hospital situation. However, recreational and corrective therapy, and adapted physical education require the completion of a four-year curriculum in their major subject that is followed by didactic instruction and clinical training in their respective professions.

The adapted physical educator, who is a certified corrective therapist, follows similar procedures in treating the handicapped individual as a total person. In the "total person" concept, it is not only treatment of a person's physical disability, but the psychological problems that accompany that adjustment. While the corrective therapist is trained to effectively work in a hospital setting, he or she

[2]*American Corrective Therapy Association Brochure,* American Corrective Therapy Association, Chairman, Public Relations Committee: Evangelo M. Gerontinos, 1781 Begen Avenue, Mountain View, California, 94040, Revised, June, 1974, p. 1.

is also most highly qualified to fill an adapted physical education position in a school.

The essence of the profession is the ability to understand and appreciate the patient's total needs and attitudes while treating their disability. The corrective therapist is able to work with the total individual in the rehabilitation process by acquiring the proper educational background, clinical training, and knowledge for administering prescribed exercises.

The uniqueness of the corrective therapy profession that distinguishes it from other paramedical disciplines is manifest in its contributions, functions, and skills. The corrective therapist is first of all an educator. This accounts for a knowledgeable, understanding, and intelligent approach to working for and with the individual as a total person. As an educator, the corrective therapist is able to bring about cohesive participation while promoting therapy principles. The disabled individual becomes inspired and motivated to achieve greater heights in his or her own level of ability when guided in individual and group activities.

In corrective therapy programs, the therapist receives a physician's prescription for the appropriate care and treatment of disabled individuals. As a member of the rehabilitation team, the corrective therapist reports patient progress to the attending physician and yet is prepared to initiate the proper action when the physician is not readily available. The corrective therapist cooperates with the physician in meeting treatment objectives on a prescribed basis for the rehabilitation and habilitation of patients.

All corrective therapy is administered under medical guidance with patients being treated through the prescription of a qualified physician known as a physiatrist. Physical education modalities are adapted to treat specific disabilities. Localized and general exercises are used to develop muscular strength, range of motion, muscular endurance, cardiovascular endurance, and gross motor skills with resulting physiological and psychological improvement. Psychiatric patients are treated by games, sports, rhythms, and activities that are specifically oriented toward the accomplishment of psychiatric objectives.

One of the greatest contributions is in the area of kinesiotherapy, which is concerned with human movement and action. It is based on the principle of rehabilitation through exercising. These principles are related not only to handicapping conditions but also to prevention, development, rehabilitation, and habilitation.

The corrective therapist is skilled at recognizing, correcting, and improving postural deviations, neuromuscular reeducation, promotion of circulation, general conditioning of unaffected areas, proprioceptive orientation, and visual training of people. In corrective therapy, the utilization of progressive-relaxation techniques is most helpful in the psychological adjustment encountered by many disabled individuals.

As a part of the inspirational process of adjustment and habilitation, the corrective therapist uses definitive means of measuring results that visually show the patient's progress. In working with neuropsychiatric, mentally retarded and emotionally disturbed persons, the corrective therapist provides challenging experiences in sports and related activities. Areas of rehabilitation and habilitation most often associated with corrective therapy are the use of the crutch, cane, and prosthetic, driver education for the handicapped, gait training, and wheelchair operation. The corrective therapist is dedicated to assist disabled individuals to live a more independent and abundant life.

The growth and development of the corrective therapy profession originates from the leadership afforded by members of the American Corrective Therapy Association. Among these outstanding professionals are: Carl Haven Young, John E. Davis, Charles H. McCloy, Josephine Rathbone, H. Harrison Clarke, George Stafford, and Karl K. Klein.

Fundamental to the Association's philosophy are the following objectives:[3]

1. To encourage the use of medically prescribed therapeutic activities including exercise techniques and psychology of medically oriented physical education.
2. To advance the professional standards of education and training in the fields of these medically prescribed activities.
3. To develop and sponsor programs of the highest scientific and professional character in these areas of medically prescribed activities related to development, prevention, habilitation, and rehabilitation through corrective and therapeutic treatment.
4. To encourage research and publication of scientific articles dealing with the advancement of physical and mental rehabilitation.
5. To engage in and encourage ethical activities related to growth and development of this profession and Association.

[3]*By-Laws of the American Corrective Therapy Association, Inc., Administrative Year 1975-76,* American Corrective Therapy Association, Inc., Donald R. Howell, By-Laws Chairman, p. 3.

The Association is incorporated by the State of New York, and 12 chapters have been chartered by the various states involved. The Association operates under its constitution, bylaws and code of ethics.

There are seven kinds of memberships in the Association: active, past active, associate, life, student, member emeritus, and honorary. This memberhsip is composed of corrective therapists and adapted physical educators located throughout the country in schools, hospitals, and rehabilitation centers for the handicapped. Membership to the Association is a professional responsibility and, once a member, work is conducted in accordance with the code of ethics for maintaining standards within the Association and the people served.

Association membership offers numerous benefits and activities, some of which are certification, public relations, recruitment and placement, scholarships and grants, legislation, conventions and workshops, The American Corrective Therapy Journal, and medical liaisons. The Association is an affiliate of the American Alliance for Health, Physical Education, and Recreation.

ACCREDITATION

The Association has established certification requirements and minimum standards for accreditation of educational and clinical affiliations offering courses and requirements for programs in corrective therapy and adapted physical education. Institutions applying to the Association for accreditation must be a four-year accredited educational institution and offer a recognized major curriculum in physical education that leads to the baccalaureate degree.

Completion of a specialization in corrective therapy and adapted physical education necessitates a fifth year of study. The didactic (instructional) curriculum and academic categories needed for accreditation includes courses in the applied sciences, psychology, health, physical education, corrective therapy, and adapted physical education. Specific courses and credit hours describing certification standards are listed in Chapter 10.

Accredited educational institutions offering corrective therapy must also receive Association approval of a hospital affiliate for conducting clinical internships. The majority of approved clinical affiliations are Veterans' Administration hospitals, while others include state, university, and private hospitals. The Association encourages educational institutions to organize and establish a student corrective therapy association.

By 1975, the accreditation council of the Association was formed to approve educational institutions and Veterans' Administration affiliations. A framework of accredited educational institutions and their affiliations have been approved throughout the nation. The accreditation process continues to rapidly expand and to grow in stature, thus raising the status and recognition of the professions. Every five years, each accredited educational institution is subject to an evaluation by the Association for retention of accredited status. Application for accreditation is made by the educational institution to:

>Carl Haven Young, Ed.D., D.O.S., Director
>Accreditation Council
>American Corrective Therapy Association, Inc.
>3231 Coolidge Avenue
>Los Angeles, California 90066

SELECTED REFERENCES

American Corrective Therapy Association Brochure, American Corrective Therapy Association, Chairman, Public Relations Committee: Evangelo M. Gerontinos, 1781 Begen Avenue, Mountain View, California, 94040, Revised, June, 1974.

Clein, Marvin I., "The Early Historical Roots of Therapeutic Exercises," *Journal of Health, Physical Education and Recreation,* **41**:89-91 (April 1970).

Freeman, Richard V., "The Unique Value of Physical Education for Corrective Therapists," *Department of Medicine and Surgery, Physical Medicine and Rehabilitation Service, IB* **10-58**, pp. 12-16, June 1954.

Hodges, Alton, "Directional Considerations and Proactive Planning," *American Corrective Therapy Journal,* **29**:35-38 (March-April 1975).

Hodges, Alton, "Licensure: An Issue Analysis," *American Corrective Therapy Journal,* **30**:3-6 (January-February 1976).

Mason, Earl W., and Harry B. Dando, *Corrective Therapy and Adapted Physical Education,* The Association for Physical and Mental Rehabilitation, Inc., 105 St. Lawrence Street, Rehoboth Beach, Delaware, 1965.

Piscopo, John, and Bert Jacobsen, "Flexibility, Options and Early Specialization," *Journal of Physical Education and Recreation,* **46**:39-40 (March 1975).

Ser, David, and Kirk Hodges, "Challenges and Response: 1975 Conference Keynote Address," *American Corrective Therapy Journal,* **29**:206-212 (November-December 1975).

Smith, Warren C., "Corrective Therapy Certification Policies and Procedures," *American Corrective Therapy Journal,* **25**:91-93 (May-June 1971).

Stende, David A., "The Scope of Corrective Therapy," *American Corrective Therapy Journal,* **29**:76-80 (May-June 1975).

Thomas, John, "Message From the President," *American Corrective Therapy Journal,* **28**:30 (January-February 1974).

Wertz, Stanley H., "Corrective Therapy in the Rehabilitation of the Quadraplegia Patient," *American Corrective Therapy Journal,* **28**:120-125 (July-August 1974).

Young, Carl Haven, "Accreditation of Institutions Preparing Corrective Therapists," *Journal of the Association for Physical and Mental Rehabilitation,* **15**:148-149 (September-October 1961).

Young, Carl Haven, "An Extending Orbit of Physical Education: Challenges in the Corrective Therapy Profession," *Journal of Health, Physical Education and Recreation,* **30**:43-44 (October 1959).

Young, Carl Haven, "Reflections on the Changing Tides of Developmental Physical Education," *American Corrective Therapy Journal,* **28**:190-198 (November-December 1974).

Young, Carl Haven, "The Contributions, Functions, and Skills Unique to the Corrective Therapy Profession," *American Corrective Therapy Journal,* **26**:27-29 (January-February 1972).

chapter 18
professional preparation in corrective therapy

Once certified always certified is a fallacy.[1]
Alton Hodges

CURRICULUM

Professional preparation in corrective therapy requires a bachelor's degree in physical education and at least 400 hours of clinical internship. Specializing in corrective therapy necessitates a fifth year of studies and experiences. As mentioned in the "Physical Education" section, courses are required in anatomy, physiology, kinesiology, analysis of movement, tests and measurements, and teaching methods. In corrective therapy, there are courses required in the applied sciences, psychology, health and physical education, and corrective therapy and adapted physical education. A specific listing of educational eligibility requirements established by the American Corrective Therapy Association, Inc. is given in Figure 18.1. Notice that candidates for certification in corrective therapy must also complete a clinical internship of 400 hours, and be an active member in the Association.

[1] Alton Hodges, "Directional Considerations and Proactive Planning," *American Corrective Therapy Journal,* 29:37 (March-April 1975).

In the didactic curriculum and field work experiences, emphasis is on content, methods, and practical experiences needed to develop breadth of experiences and competencies for certification. The corrective therapy student must be competent in knowing how the body is built (structure) and how it works (function). Knowledge about human growth, development, and movement must be accompanied with an understanding of muscle origin, insertion, and function. The student should be able to assess and analyze motor functions and movement patterns in the normal person, if he or she is to meet the needs of impaired, disabled, and handicapped individuals of all ages.

In methods and practical experiences, competencies must be developed in applying prescribed exercise techniques, demonstrating human relations skills with patients and medical personnel, and adjusting to a variety of work settings. The corrective therapy curriculum at the University of Illinois-Chicago Circle serves to illustrate required and elective courses in general education, education certification, major in physical education and corrective therapy (see Figure 18.2). Compare the association's educational eligibility requirements to this corrective therapy curriculum. Attention is directed to required and elective courses.

CLINICAL INTERNSHIP

At the University of Illinois-Chicago Circle, the clinical internship consists of 440 hours at local Veterans' Administration hospitals, 80 to 100 hours in adapted physical education at schools, and 10 to 20 hours at agencies for rehabilitating the blind. Prior to clinical internship in corrective therapy, the student has experienced microteaching and student teaching in physical education. These experiences may have been at the elementary, middle, or secondary levels of education. At some institutions, these experiences may have been in mainstreamed or adapted physical education classes, as well as in a regular class. Yet, at other institutions, the student gains practical experience by serving as a volunteer in a community agency that offers programs for exceptional persons.

Fieldwork experiences are the single most important aspect of professional preparation. This breadth and depth of experiences contributes to the student's competence in meeting the needs, interests, and abilities of persons who are mentally retarded, emotionally disturbed, and physically and multiply handicapped.

The American Corrective Therapy Association, Inc. recommends minimum standards for approved clinical training affiliations. Clinical internships are directed and supervised by certified corrective therapists, chiefs of various therapies, the director of ancillary services, physicians, physiatrists, and surgeons. The objectives of clinical internship are for the student to develop an understanding of pathological and neurological conditions, an insight into patient disabilities, concepts for treating patients, and the ability to plan a program to fulfill treatment objectives. These objectives are met through various teaching methods and field experiences in hospitals, schools, and related facilities. The purpose, types of training, and minimal training requirements for specific areas are illustrated in Figure 18.3.

During clinical internship the student is oriented to the medical environment. Part of this training includes knowledge about hospital services in nursing, social work, dietetics, vocational counseling, and special services. In visits to psychiatric, muscular dystrophy, scoliosis, tuberculosis, and orthopedic clinics, the student experiences the nature of habilitation and rehabilitation.

As a participant in lectures, observations, and discussions with physicians, physiatrists, surgeons, and physical, occupational, educational, and recreational therapists, the student learns how to relate to the physical and mental phases of individual's potentials at all age levels. Knowledge in administering the appropriate rehabilitation techniques is gained from experiences in domiciliary care, cardiac intensive care, gerontology, blind rehabilitation, surgery, autopsies, and brace facilities.

The rehabilitation team is composed of a physician, physiatrist, corrective therapist, and medical staff from ancillary services. During internship, the student observes and later demonstrates his or her ability as a practitioner. The concept underlying a rehabilitation team is the efficiency and economy with which the objectives of preventional treatment are met.

For the corrective therapy student, knowledge must be acquired regarding the techniques administered for rehabilitation in ambulation, muscular strengthening and endurance, analysis of movement, range of motion, therapeutic exercise, and pool therapy. Observe the techniques being administered in Figure 18.4. In all instances, the corrective therapist must be concerned with the patient's mental, social, and emotional adjustment to the disability. This is particularly important when the patient's treatment necessitates a prosthesis, wheelchair operation, or gait training.

Clinical internship prepares the student to perform effectively as a corrective therapist on a rehabilitation team. In the medical

American Corrective Therapy Association, Inc.
Professional Preparation for Careers in Corrective Therapy

Candidates desiring to prepare for specialization in corrective therapy and adapted physical education should select a four-year accredited educational institution that offers a recognized major curriculum in physical education leading to the baccalaureate degree. It is impossible to complete the four-year major curriculum plus specialization in the time available, since the requirements for the major in physical education, educational and institutional requisites demand so many courses for graduation.

Therefore, following the undergraduate program, it is imperative that the candidate enroll for a fifth year of graduate study, either at the same school or where specialization in corrective therapy is available. During this period the student is able to complete the specified didactic courses and clinical or field experiences of 400 hours, where the institution has an acceptable hospital affiliation that is approved by the American Corrective Therapy Association, Inc.

Didactic curriculum and academic categories, with asterisks indicating required courses.

Applied Sciences

*Anatomy	12-18
*Kinesiology	Semester
*Physiology	units or
*Physiology of Exercise	
Growth & Development	18-27
Neuroanatomy	Quarter
*Neurology	credits
*Pathology	

Psychology

*General Psychology	6-12
*Abnormal Psychology	Semester
*Physiological Psychology	units or
Developmental Psychology	
Mental Health	9-18
Psychotherapy	Quarter credits
Social Psychology	credits

Health & Phsyical Education

*Analysis of Human Movement	16-24
*Health Education and Problems	Semester
*Principles of Health and Physical Education	units or
*Physical and Mental Habilitation	24-36
*Tests and Measurements	Quarter
Evaluation of Health and Physical Education	credits
Research in Health and Physical Education	
*Skills and Applied Techniques	

Corrective Therapy and Adapted Physical Education

*Physical Education for Atypical	8-14

*Organizational and Administrational Corrective Therapy *Kinesiotherapy Recreation in Rehabilitation Intertherapy Relations Evaluation and Research Applied to *Corrective and Adapted Programs	Semester units or 12-21 Quarter credits

All candidates for certification in corrective therapy must show evidence of completing a minimum of 400 hours of clinical internship. Such experience must be upon referral of a physician, under the supervision of a certified corrective therapist. Candidates must be active members of American Corrective Therapy Association, Inc. to apply for the certification examination.

FIGURE 18.1 Reprinted by permission of the American Corrective Therapy Association, Inc.

Physical Education Major—B.S. in Teaching
   Option I. (K-12) or Option II. (6-12)
Kinesiotherapy Program—Requirement for eligibility for
   Certification in Corrective Therapy

	Based on Quarter Hours
I. General Education Required for Options I. and II. American History (4), Biology (10), English (8), Health (4), Humanities (4), Philosophy (4), Political Science (4), Psychology (4), Sociology (4), Speech (5).	51 credits
Electives for Option II.	34 credits
II. Education Certification Required for Options I. and II. Education Foundations (8), Curriculum and Instruction (20).	28 credits

III. Major in Physical Education
Core: Required for Options I. and II.
Introduction (2), History and Philosophy (4), Evaluation (4), Kinesiology (5), Physiology of Exercise (4), Physiology of Exercise Practicum (2), Application of Kinesiological Principles:
  Dance (2),
  Aquatics (2), Gymnastics (2).
	27 credits

Activity Courses: Required for Options I. and II. Individual and Dual (10), Team (8), Option I. Electives	18 credits
Physical Education Physical Education or another field Option II. Electives	14 credits 8 credits
Physical Education or another field Foundations: Required for Options I. and II.	6 credits 18 credits

FIGURE 18.2 (Continued)

First Aid and Athletic Training (4), Instructional Techniques (4), Organization and Curriculum (4), Supervised Teaching (2).
Option I. Required   4 credits
Leadership Practicum (2), Adapted (2).
Option II. Required   4 credits
Student Coaching (4).

IV. Corrective Therapy—Option III.
Applied Sciences: Required   6 credits
Neurobiology (4), Introduction to   (Balance in major)
Pathology (2).
Electives: Structure and Development of Vertebrates (5),
Neuroanatomy (5), Drugs in our Society (3).
Psychology: Required   16 credits
Introduction to Research in Psychology (4),   (Balance in major)
Psychology of Personality (4), Physiological Psychology (4), Abnormal Psychology (4).
Electives: Developmental Psychology (4), Mental Deficiency (4), Social Psychology (4).
Health and Physical Education: Required   14 credits
Perceptual-Motor Development (4), Therapeutic Activities (4), Organization of School Health Programs (4), Instructional Techniques in Swimming (2).
Electives: Problems in Physical Education (2), Research in Health and Physical Education (2-4), Motor Learning (4), Movement in Early Childhood Education (4).
Corrective Therapy and Adapted Physical Education: Required   14 credits
Principles and Practice of Exercise Therapy (4), Adapted Physical Education (2), Adapted Physical Education Programs (8).
Electives: Special Population Programs in Recreation (3), Research applied to Corrective Therapy and Adapted Physical Education (2-4), Introduction to Special Education (4).
Clinical Internship: Required   15 credits
Hospitals—440 hours, Schools, adapted physical education—80 to 100 hours, Rehabilitation Centers for the blind— 10 to 20 hours.

FIGURE 18.2 Corrective therapy curriculum offered by the University of Illinois— Chicago Circle.

RECOMMENDED MINIMUM STANDARDS FOR APPROVED CLINICAL TRAINING AFFILIATIONS

Purpose:

To provide hospital and school affiliated experiences for the trainee in corrective therapy or adapted physical education that are adequate to supplement his prior or concurrent didactic instruction within the educational institution.

Types of Training:

Lectures—theory, ethics, orientation, disability discussion.
Medical prescriptions and terminology.
Treatment demonstration—techniques, modalities, equipment.
Professional meetings and consultation.
Observation of treatment and its organization.
Supervised clinical practice—corrective, developmental, habilitative.
Administration—treatment planning, recording, progression, reporting, clinic management.
Laboratory and research experience.

Minimal Training Requirements in Specific Areas: (at least 400 hours total)

Introduction—(20 hours).
Orientation—hospital or school, nursing service, medical guidance, vocational and social services, special application to the physically handicapped or retarded child.
Function of each phys. med. and rehab. or health dept. service.
History, philosophy, and scope of corrective therapy and adapted physical education.
Mission of corrective program concerned—areas and disabilities served, coordination with other health services, immediate and longer-range goals.
Administrative procedures, ethics, and professional advancement.

Orthopedics—(60 hours)
Diagnoses and disabilities (applicable to all areas).
Evaluation of strength, endurance, contraindications, range of motion.
Exercise routines—active, selected muscle setting, progressive resistance, postural, isotonic and isometric, practice in affected activities of daily living.
Ambulation techniques—nonweight-bearing, partial to full weight-bearing, use of prostheses, crutches, canes and walkers.
Proper body mechanics—safe, effective lifting and handling of patients or other loads
Bracing—corrective, supportive, functional.

Neurological—(60 hours)
Evaluation of paralysis, spasticity, ROM, coordination, ADL skills, work, and pain tolerance.
Exercise- passive, assistive, active, reciprocal, stretching, relaxing, toning, and PRE.
Bracing—body jackets and supports, full-length leg braces, below-knee bracing.
Ambulation or other locomotion—use of wheelchair, balance and weight bearing, walking aids.
ADL training, with adaptive devices if needed—mobility, dressing, feeding, hygiene, transfer activities.

FIGURE 18.3 (Continued)

NeuroPsychiatric—(60 hours)
  Diagnosis and symptoms—psychosis, psychoneurosis, psychomatic and personality disorders.
  Evaluation of behavior patterns, individual or group, and attitude toward self, instructor, and activity.
  Treatment objectives—acceptable expression of aggressions, relief of guilt feelings, narcissistic gratification, arousal of interest, resocialization and physical conditioning.
  Treatment activities—individual and group prescription, purposeful exercise, rhythms, games and sports, drama, arts and other socially acceptable action.
  Role of therapist in observing symptoms and results—levels of achievement, motivation, adaptability to readjustment, socialization progress, and physical well-being.

General Rehabilitation—(60 hours)
  Paraplegia and quadriplegia—passive to active exercise, stretching, PRE, mat program, ROM, relaxing spasticity, bracing, ADL training.
  Amputees—stump shaping and conditioning, prosthesis fitting, ambulation and gait training for lower-extremity amputation, muscle control and ADL function for lower-extremity amputation, care and adjustment of prosthesis.
  Cardiac and general medical—disability and prognosis evaluation, graduated exercise routines, checking of vital signs.

Special Categories—(60 hours)
  Blind—orientation to situation and surroundings, ambulation with cane or dog, ADL and occupational training.
  Mentally retarded and emotionally disturbed—disability and prognosis evaluation, ADL and educational training, conditioning exercise and adapted sports.
  The multiply handicapped—diagnosis and evaluation of disabilities, muscle-toning and re-education, balance and locomotion training, functional self-care, individual and group activities.

Developmental and Adapted Physical Education—(80 hours)
  Diagnosis and evaluation of the atypical child—medical guidance, comparison normal, tests and measurements.
  Prevention of poor health habits—hygiene, nourishment, rest, elimination.
  Functional development—physiological and psychological.
  Recovery from disability—remedial, compensatory, assistive.
  Adapted growth activities—corrective exercise, socialization, adapted games and sports.
  Habilitation with handicaps—utilizing personal resources, whether physically handicapped or retarded child.
  Maintenance of vital capacities—respiration, circulation, strength, coordination, stamina.
  Rehabilitation to fitness for living—maximum possible return, substitution for residual disability, mechanical and emotional aids.

FIGURE 18.3 Recommended minimum standards for approved clinical training affiliations. Reprinted by permission of the American Corrective Therapy Association, Inc.

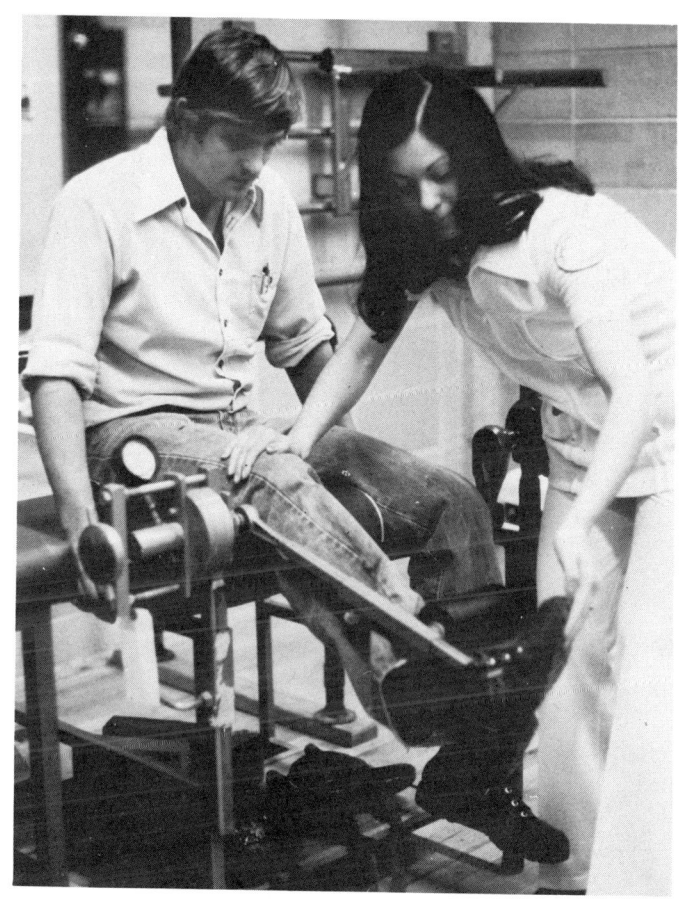

FIGURE 18.4 Corrective therapy apparatus. Reprinted by permission of the University of Illinois at Chicago Circle, Chicago.

environment, the student is confronted with obeying orders explicitly, accepting criticism, and practicing punctuality. An understanding of the professional philosophy, theory, and scientific foundations of corrective therapy must include a mastery of therapy functions and medical terminology. A glossary of corrective therapy and medical terms appears at the end of this chapter.

In the didactic curriculum and clinical internship the student is prepared with professional skills needed to work with physicians in relating to the patient's problem and determining the best method for treatment. Those persons who enter corrective therapy should exhibit great potential and have a sincere desire to achieve a high degree of quality professionally. The uniqueness of this profession

PROFESSIONAL PREPARATION IN CORRECTIVE THERAPY 279

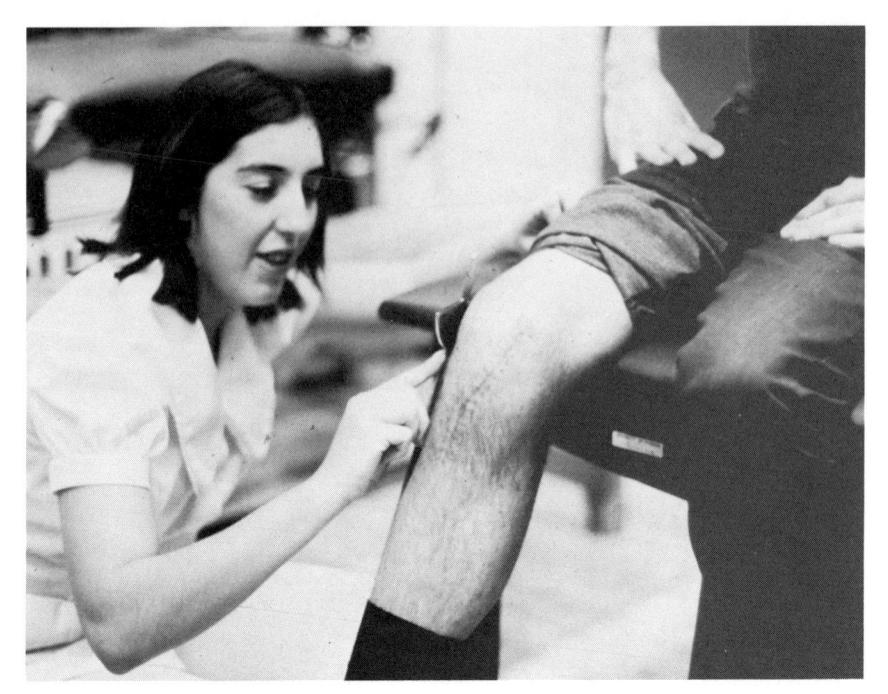

FIGURE 18.4 Corrective therapy student. Reprinted by Permission of the University of Illinois at Chicago Circle, Chicago.

dictates that one must be dedicated to service for the good of humankind.

CERTIFICATION

There are several procedures that must be completed prior to becoming a candidate for certification in corrective therapy. The student must hold a bachelor's degree with a major in physical education, complete the didactic curriculum and clinical intership in corrective therapy, and be an active member of the Association. Referrals from a physician and the supervising certified corrective therapist are necessary to verify completion of the clinical internship.

Application for certification is the candidate's responsibility. The candidate must secure and submit a formal application for the certification examination to the Secretary to the Certification Board of the Association. This is to be accompanied by a nominal application fee and a complete college transcript. These documents are evaluated by the Association and the candidate is notified about eligibility to take the examination.

The certification examination has two parts, oral and written. Each part has a numerical value of 100 points. The candidate must score a minimum of 70 points on each part to pass the examination. A physician and two certified corrective therapists administer the examination. Annually, examinations are given in eight geographical locations in the United States. One person is designated as the area examiner. A physiatrist, physician, corrective therapist, or other members of the rehabilitative team conduct the examination. Examinations are also administered at the Annual National Conference of the Association.

All examinations are evaluated by the Association and the Secretary to the Certification Board notifies candidates of the results. Failure to pass either or both parts of the examination requires repeating those respective parts at a later date. Upon passing the examination, the candidate receives a certificate in corrective therapy. Printed on this certificate is the candidates name, date, register number, signatures of the secretary and president, and the official ACTA Seal. See Fig. 18.5 illustrating the emblem worn by certified corrective therapists. Certification as a corrective therapist is retained by maintaining active membership in the Association and following the continuing education recommended program.

FIGURE 18.5 Corrective therapy insignia. Reprinted by permission of the American Corrective Therapy Association, Inc.

PLACEMENT

The certified corrective therapist has several advantages for placement compared to the noncertified therapist. In many private hospitals there are separate pay scales for each. Also, only the certified corrective therapist is eligible to treat the medicare patient. Another advantage of certification is the placement services the Association provides to active members.

Employment opportunities for a certified corrective therapist are available in private, state, and federal hospitals, rehabilitation centers, nursing homes, schools and camps for the handicapped, and private and church-sponsored retirement homes. In a nationwide placement survey, conducted by the Association in 1973, certified corrective therapists were employed in the following settings.[2]

73.6%—Veterans Administration facilities.

26.4%—Full-time positions outside VA.

11.0%—Professors and teachers in colleges and universities.

5.7%—Public school teachers of physically and multiply handicapped adapted physical education classes.

5.0%—Public and private hospitals and institutions.

2.1%—Private schools and mental retardation institutions.

.7%—Private clinics and sanitariums, and other facilities.

.7%—State mental health and mental retardation insititutions.

.7%—Athletic trainers.

1.2%—Differential not defined.

In 1976, the Association estimated the starting pay for a certified corrective therapist to be between $8,900 and $12,000. Persons who were in supervisory and administrative positions were estimated to earn from $12,000 to $18,000 annually.[3]

Future trends for placement in corrective therapy include blind rehabilitation facilities, alcohol and drug treatment centers, public health centers and clubs, private practice on referral of physicians, geriatric centers, hospital-affiliated mobilized medical teams, and industrial safety settings. The opportunities within the scope of the

---

[2]Carl Haven Young, "Significance of the Curriculum and Prerequisites for the Certification of Corrective Therapists," *American Corrective Therapy Journal,* **27**:133-134 (September-October 1973).

[3]Joyce Lain Kennedy, "Opportunities in Corrective Therapy," *Chicago Sun-Times,* Monday, January 5, 1976, p. 72.

profession are unlimited and offer a real challenge to the ambitious candidate with proper credentials and competencies. Being certified is not only advantageous, but a matter of personal pride in the profession.

GLOSSARY OF TERMS

1. **A.D.L.**—activities of daily living.
2. **Abduct**—move away from the midline of the body.
3. **Adduct**—move toward the midline of the body.
4. **Ambulate**—to walk.
5. **Anomaly**—deviation from the common rule; irregularity.
6. **Articulation**—a joint or juncture between bones or cartilage.
7. **Axis**—a line about which movement takes place.
8. **Bilateral**—pertaining to both sides.
9. **Calcification**—a hardening by the deposition of salts in the muscular tissue.
10. **Cartilage**—a transluscent elastic tissue that composes most of the joints of the skeleton.
11. **Circumduction**—movement in which the part describes a cone with the apex at the joint.
12. **Cryotherapy**—treatment of cold substances, such as ice, ethyl chloride, carbon dioxide, and snow.
13. **Distal**—farthest end of a structure or part; opposite of proximal.
14. **Etiology**—the source or origin of a symptom or disease.
15. **Exceptional person**—someone impaired, disabled, or handicapped.
16. **Eversion**—turning outward; opposite of inversion.
17. **Extension**—the straightening of a flexed limb; opposite is flexion.
18. **Flexion**—act of bending or being bent; decreasing the angle between two bones.
19. **Geriatrics**—a medical speciality dealing with the problems of the aging and old age.
20. **Gerontology**—the study of the aging process.
21. **Habilitation**—term sometimes used for the training of a skill an individual never had before, as contrasted with rehabilitation.
22. **Impairment**—medical condition resulting in a diminution of function as evaluated by a physician.
23. **Inversion**—turning inward; opposite is eversion.
24. **Kinesiology**—the study of muscular movement.

25. **Kinesiotherapy**—the treatment of the effects of disease and injury through active movements or exercise.
26. **Lateral**—directed toward or movement toward the side.
27. **Ligament**—a tough band of tissue serving to connect the articular extremities of bones or to support an organ in place.
28. **Mainstreaming**—the integration of handicapped and nonhandicapped students into one class, exception is severely handicapped.
29. **Mechanotherapy**—therapeutic exercises with the help of apparatus.
30. **Metrotherapy**—therapeutic use of repeated measurements, showing the patient the relationship between treatment and result.
31. **Motor**—a muscle, nerve, or center that affects movement.
32. **Neuromuscular**—pertaining to the relationship between nerve and muscle.
33. **Ontological**—pertaining to the development of the organism throughout its lifetime.
34. **Pathology**—the study of changes in function and structure caused by disease.
35. **Plane**—the surface that lies at right angles to the axis and in which the movement takes place.
36. **Prognosis**—prediction of the probable outcome of a disease or injury.
37. **Pronation**—the turning of the palm downward; rotation of a limb toward the midline.
38. **Proximal**—nearest the trunk, center, or median line; opposite is distal.
39. **Rehabilitation**—the reablement of a patient to the maximum of his or her potentialities in every respect.
40. **Rotation**—turning about an axis in an angular motion.
41. **Supination**—the turning of the palm of the hand upward; rotation of the arm away from the midline of the body; turning the palm outward.
42. **Tendon**—a tough cord or band of dense, white fibrous connective tissue, uniting a muscle with a bone and transmitting the force exerted by the muscle.
43. **Therapeutic**—curative; pertaining to the treatment of a disease.
44. **Traction**—act of pulling or being pulled.
45. **Trauma**—an injury, wound, or shock.
46. **Vertical axis**—lies parallel to the line of gravity and movement about it is in a horizontal plane.
47. **Vertigo**—dizziness.

SELECTED REFERENCES

Adams, Ronald C., *Games, Sports and Exercises for the Physically Handicapped*, Lea & Febiger, Philadelphia, 1970.

American Association for Health, Physical Education and Recreation, *Guidelines for Professional Preparation Programs for Personnel Involved in Physical Education and Recreation for the Handicapped*, AAHPER, Washington, D.C., 1973.

American Association for Health, Physical Education and Recreation, *Professional Preparation in Dance, Physical Education, Recreation Education, Safety Education and School Health Education*, AAHPER, Washington, D.C., 1974.

Arnheim, Daniel D., David Auxter, and Walter C. Crowe, *Principles and Methods of Adapted Physical Education*, Second Edition, C.V. Mosby Co., St. Louis, 1973.

Bennett, Carl, "Physical Education and the Exceptional: The Coming of Mainstreaming," *Briefings: Careers in Physical Education*, National Association for Physical Education of College Women and National College Physical Education Association for Men, Printed in United States, 1975, pp. 28-37.

Bosco, James S., "The Role of Physical Education in Preventive Medicine," *American Corrective Therapy Journal*, 25:97-98 (July-August 1971).

Broer, Marion, *Efficiency of Human Movement*, W.B. Saunders, Philadelphia, 1973.

Brunnstrom, Signe, *Clinical Kinesiology*, F.A. Davis Co., Philadelphia, 1971.

Clarke, H. Harrison, and David H. Clarke, *Developmental and Adapted Physical Education*, Prentice-Hall, Inc., Englewood Cliffs, NJ, 1963.

Crist, Robert W., "Clinical Training in the Practice of Corrective Therapy," *American Corrective Therapy Journal*, 24:6-10 (January-February 1970).

Dando, Harry B., "Corrective Therapy," *Journal of Health, Physical Education and Recreation*, 32:35-37 (November 1961).

Daniels, Arthur S., and Evelyn Davies, *Adapted Physical Education*, Third Edition, Harper & Row, New York, 1975.

Daniels, Lucille, and Catherine Worthingham, *Muscle Testing: Techniques of Manual Examination*, W.B. Saunders, Philadelphia, 1972.

Dorland's Illustrated Medical Dictionary, Twenty-Fourth Edition, W.B. Saunders, Philadelphia, 1965.

Ersing, Walter F., and Ruth Wheeler, "The Status of Professional Preparation in Adapted Physical Education," American Corrective Therapy Journal, 25:111-118 (July-August 1971).

Fait, Hollis F., Special Physical Education: Adapted, Corrective, Developmental, Third Edition, W.B. Saunders, Philadelphia, 1972.

Geddes, Dolores, Physical Activities for Individuals with Handicapping Conditions, C.V. Mosby Co., St. Louis, 1974.

Hodges, Alton, "Directional Considerations and Proactive Planning," American Corrective Therapy Journal, 29:35-38 (March-April 1975).

Kelly, Ellen D., Adapted and Corrective Physical Education, Fourth Edition, Ronald Press Co., New York, 1965.

Kurasik, Steve, "The Role of Corrective Therapy in the Hospital Based Home Care Program," American Corrective Therapy Journal, 24:59-60 (March-April 1970).

Rhea, Kermit, "A Perspective for Corrective Therapy and Adapted Physical Education," American Corrective Therapy Journal, 22:89-91 (May-June 1968).

Rogers, Ruth M., "Practical Experience in the Community—A Necessary Part of a Course in Adapted Physical Education," American Corrective Therapy Journal, 27:176-178 (November-December 1973).

Rowlett, John D., "A University Examines its Resources with Implications for Rehabilitation Medicine Today," American Corrective Therapy Journal, 22:112-114 (July-August 1968).

Ser, David, and Kirk Hodges, "Challenges and Response: 1975 Conference Keynote Address," American Corrective Therapy Journal, 29:206-212 (November-December 1975).

Scott, Leonard L., "Clinical Training in Corrective Therapy as Preparation for a Professional Career," American Corrective Therapy Journal, 29:165-168 (September-October 1975).

Smith, Warren C., "Corrective Therapy Certification Policies and Procedures," American Corrective Therapy Journal, 25:91-93 (May-June 1971).

Stende, David A., "The Scope of Corrective Therapy," American Corrective Therapy Journal, 29:76-80 (May-June 1975).

Wells, Katharine, Kinesiology, W.B. Saunders, Philadelphia, 1971.

Willhite, Charles E., "The Corrective Therapist in the Industrial Safety Setting," *American Corrective Therapy Journal,* **27**:24-27 (January-February 1973).

Young, Carl Haven, *Directional Goals for Clinical Therapy Experiences,* Association for Physical and Mental Rehabilitation, Inc., 1472 Broadway, New York, 1958.

Young, Carl Haven, "Give Them the Keys to Service," *Journal of the Association for Physical and Mental Rehabilitation,* **15**:19-20 (January-February 1961).

Young, Carl Haven, "Integrative Field Work Experiences for Pre-Therapists," *Journal of the Association for Physical and Mental Rehabilitation,* **11**:11-16 (January-February 1957).

Young, Carl Haven, "Significance of the Curriculum and Prerequisites for the Certification of Corrective Therapists," *American Corrective Therapy Journal,* **27**:131-135 (September-October 1973).

chapter 19

role of the corrective therapist

We must work WITH not on or for, the person being treated.[1]

John E. Davis

The need for qualified professionals in corrective therapy is evident when one realizes "that approximately one out of every seven persons in the United States has a severe, permanent physical disability."[2] See the "Glossary of Terms" at the end of this chapter. This disability may have occurred at birth, in the aging process, or as a result of an injury or illness. Nonetheless, the person is faced with the problem of adjusting to the disability. In making this adjustment, a qualified physician provides medical guidance and prescribes the treatment for the corrective therapist to administer. Procedures and techniques applied by the therapist are those that contribute to the patient's total

---

[1] Earl W. Mason and Harry B Dando, *Corrective Therapy and Adapted Physical Education*, Association for Physical and Mental Rehabilitation, Inc., 105 St. Lawrence St., Rehoboth Beach, Delaware, p. 1, 1965.

[2] Stan Labanowich, "The Leisure Outlook for the Physically Disabled in the 1970s," Leo L. Gedvilas (ed.), p. 78, *Proceedings: National College Physical Education Association for Men*, University of Illinois—Chicago Circle, Office of Publications, 1974.

adjustment: social, emotional, and mental as well as physical. It is the corrective therapist's objective to enable the patient to adjust and become as physically independent as possible. This is known as habilitation, learning to live with the disability incurred.

In medicine, there are three phases in which the corrective therapist functions: (1) prevention, (2) diagnosis, prognosis and treatment, and (3) rehabilitation. In phase one, treatment activities are administered to bedridden or inactive patients to prevent atrophy and mental deterioration. Among the treatment activities are exercises in ambulation, lying, sitting, and standing; relaxation techniques, preoperative and postoperative psychological preparation; activities for daily living (A.D.L.), and others.

Phase number two—diagnosis, prognosis, and treatment—requires the corrective therapist to collect and record data from tests and measurements of the patient's ability to perform designated activities related to specific rehabilitation objectives. The patient is tested on motor ability, neuromuscular efficiency, range of motion (R.O.M.), and needs and abilities as related to A.D.L. This objective data, together with subjective data gathered from observing the patient, are reported and discussed with the physician and rehabilitation team. An evaluation is made of the patient's condition, and treatment is planned with the physician prescribing both treatment and dosage.

The objective of the third phase, rehabilitation, is to restore the patient to the maximum status of capability and return him or her to an environment outside the hospital. This is not feasible for all patients, especially those with severe disabilities. However, patients who can be discharged are provided with training in self-care activities that contribute to their independence and adjustment. In each phase of medicine, the corrective therapist plays a unique role, which is to work *With* the patient in therapeutic exercises that are fun and beneficial and to communicate a positive, can-do, will-do attitude for accomplishment.

CARE AND TREATMENT

Patient care and treatment in corrective therapy are determined by a medical doctor who, by prescription, sets the goals and limits of therapy. The corrective therapist is obligated to follow this prescription when employing procedures and techniques of treatment. There is a broad range of patient types for which the corrective therapist provides care and treatment. Therefore, objectives in corrective therapy are both general and specific. The general objectives pertain to all patients, while the specific objectives relate to the treatment of an individual patient.

The corrective therapist needs to be knowledgeable about the general objectives in treating patients. Conditioning and reconditioning exercises are administered for disabled patients to develop improved respiratory conditions, strength, neuromuscular coordination, flexibility, cardiovascular endurance, agility, and balance. According to the prescription, determinations are made for administering these fitness components.

In making this selection, the corrective therapist refers to the specific objectives. The corrective therapist is concerned about the physical and psychological improvement for all patients and adheres to this general objective. Emphasis is on socialization and resocialization activities for the mentally atypical. This is congruous to psychiatric objectives. The corrective therapist provides instruction in postural alignment, adapted sports, games, rhythms, and basic motor learning activities. Fundamentals of transfer activities in A.D.L. are taught to patients. And, the corrective therapist utilizes all types of orthotic and prosthetic devices, including manually controlled motor vehicles.

The procedures and techniques administered by the corrective therapist adhere to the prescribed treatment and dosage specified by the physician. As a professional, the corrective therapist must know what best affects human movement on muscle and, conversely, what affects muscle on human movement. A selection is made from activities that range from mild to strenuous, simple to complex, individual to group, and low to high organizational levels. Determinations are made about the time duration of the activity, number of repetitions, and number of treatments per day or week.

The role of the corrective therapist is to guide the patient toward improved performance (strength development) and improved appearance (hypertrophy), the results of therapeutic exercise. In corrective therapy, patient progress is approached in a manner that obtains maximum results and the speediest recovery.

Patients

In treatment, the corrective therapist must be knowledgeable about the many and varied forms of injury and illness. There are patients who are arthritics, alcoholics, drug addicts, geriatrics, blind, deaf, palsy, cancer, or stroke patients. The corrective therapist must be able to work With all patients, and not neglect the mentally retarded, amputee, paraplegic, cardiac, and psychiatric patients.

The condition of mental retardation is classified into four categories: educable (IQ 50-75), trainable (IQ 35-50), severe (IQ 20-35), and profound (IQ below 20). Although procedures vary for individuals in different categories, they also vary within the same category. Treatment of the mentally retarded patient should be consistent to the individual's stage of development upon entering the program, then progress should occur at his own rate. This kind of treatment is referred to as "guided discovery," and success is ensured with goals that are challenging and yet attainable.

When employing procedures and techniques for the mentally retarded patient, the corrective therapist must remember to avoid overestimating the patient's ability and making the activity or exercise too difficult for him to perform. Similarly, the therapist needs to avoid underestimating the patient and making the activity or exercise too easy.

A program for the mentally retarded patient utilizes modified and adapted individual and team sports, physical fitness, balance, gross motor coordination, and reflex based postural adjustment activities. Relaxation training, perceptual-motor developmental activities, prosthetic training for congenital anomalies, mobility, ambulation, and gait (manner of walking, i.e,, cane, crutches) training, and self-care activities are also included. Application of the KISS-MIF theory is useful in working with the mentally retarded. KISS-MIF means Keep It Simple System and Make It Fun.[3]

Treatment objectives for an amputee patient concern both physical and psychological progress. The loss of a limb involves an irrevocable anatomical and physiological impairment. Before surgery, the corrective therapist prepares the patient psychologically and physically for the amputation. An amputation for the upper extremity could involve a finger or thumb (phalanges), hand (metacarpals), lower arm (ulna and radius), or upper arm (humerus). In the lower extremity, the toes (phalanges), foot (metatarsals), lower leg (tibia and fibula), or upper leg (femur).

Therapy for amputation is prescribed before and after surgery to maintain a range of motion (R.O.M.) in the joints and prevent contracture, a shortening of soft tissue that cannot be returned to its normal length. The corrective therapist provides exercises to strengthen the proximal muscles that will be used and needed for a

---

[3]Julian U. Stein, "Movement and Physical Activity: The Foundation for the Most Important 'R'," *American Corrective Therapy Journal,* **29**:193 (November-December 1975).

future fitting of the prosthesis, an artificial part of the body. The patient is also instructed in balancing exercises needed for standing and walking when the amputation involves the lower extremity.

Individuals who are paralyzed because of disease or spinal cord injury (S.C.I.) may be classified as diplegia (paralysis of any two extremities), hemiplegia (paralysis of one symmetric half of the body or part of it), paraplegia (paralysis of the lower limbs), and quadriplegia (paralysis of all four limbs) patients. Treatment and rehabilitation for amputee and paralyzed patients could include ambulation, gait training, or wheelchair operation. Observe the therapeutic exercises performed in Figure 19.1.

Driving an automobile is a kind of mobility appealing to most patients. In 1975, driver training programs were mandated for the handicapped in all Veterans' Administration hospitals that had spinal-cord injury programs. To a handicapped person, driving an automobile is a psychosocial substitute for bodily mobility and part of America's culture. In most hospitals and for many years, the driver training program has been conducted by the corrective therapist.

Instruction is provided according to the medical, kinesiological, mechanical, and psychological capabilities of the patient. Protection of the handicapped person and the general public has been ensured by the development of "Tentative Standards and Specifications for Adaptive Automotive Driving Aids" by Charles C. Freeman.[4] Aviation is another form of mobility available to the licensed handicapped driver. The Federal Aviation Administration has approved adaptive aircraft controls and flying lessons for wheelchair pilots.

Treatment for the cardiac patient is composed of four stages in the corrective therapy cardiovascular rehabilitation program: cardiac intensive care unit, cardiac laboratory, corrective therapy clinic, and the exercise program to be followed after discharge.[5] The cardiac patient is provided with exercises that yield maximum oxygen uptake to benefit heart circulation, increase cardiovascular endurance and respiratory functions, and prevent general physical deconditioning.

The physician carefully screens and selects the cardiac patients who enter this program. During treatment, heart rate and blood pressure are continually monitored in relation to the exercise dosage. The

[4]Charles C. Freeman, "The Corrective Therapist and the Handicapped Driver," *American Corrective Therapy Journal*, 29:138-142 (July-August 1975).

[5]Ralph Hooker, "The Corrective Therapy Cardiovascular Rehabilitation Program," *American Corrective Therapy Journal*, 29:126 (July-August 1975).

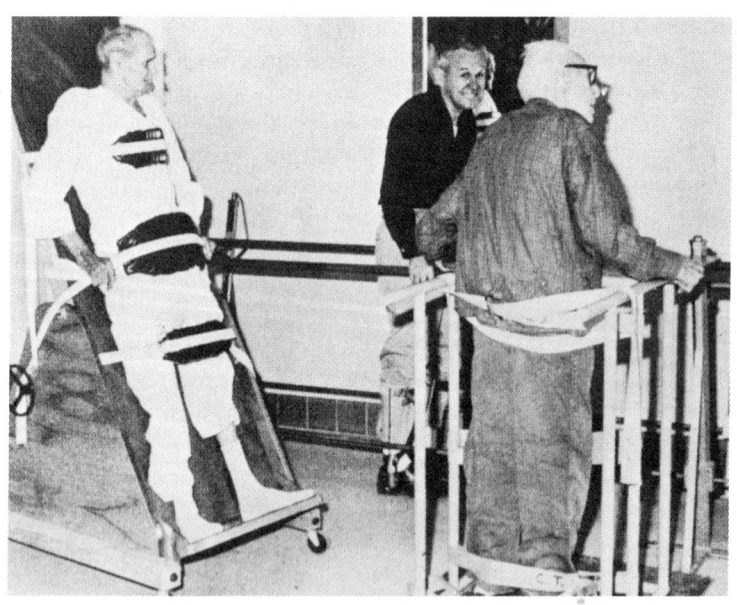

FIGURE 19.1 (a) Physical maintenance in geriatrics through exercise apparatus. (b) Three stages of elevated activity progressing toward independent ambulation. Reprinted by permission of the American Corrective Therapy Association, Inc.

patient is also observed for external symptoms of fatigue. Usually, the exercise dosage is gradually increased while the rest periods are decreased, until eventually the activity becomes sustained.

Psychiatric patients, as with all other individuals, need to be recognized for worth and dignity. Treatment through games, rhythms, swimming, and sports is designed to channel socially unacceptable behavior into socially acceptable expressions. The corrective therapist makes these experiences meaningful, interesting, and purposeful for the patient. One such activity is therapeutic hydrogymnastics or exercises performed in a swimming pool.

In a study conducted by Conte, DeWolfe, Klein, and Barrell, three methods of therapeutic hydrogymnastics for psychiatric patients were tested. A comparison was made between free swimming experience, nongroup-oriented instruction, and group-oriented instruction. The latter was evidenced to have greater gains in group cohesion among chronic psychiatric patients. This was measured by the amount of social participation of patients when away from the swimming pool environment.[6]

In terms of all patients and treatments, the corrective therapist is most concerned with the person and not solely about his or her deficiency, deformity, or deviation.

Exercises

A therapeutic exercise program consists of activities, rhythms, games, sports, and exercises. The disabled patient is tested, evaluated, and discussed by the physician and members of the rehabilitation team. The physician then prescribes treatment and dosage.

In a therapeutic exercise program, the corrective therapist must know people and therapeutic exercises. By knowing the people, or patient, the corrective therapist is able to assess the patient's attitude and establish a rapport conducive for accomplishing the treatment objectives. Knowledge about therapeutic exercise enables the corrective therapist to apply procedures and techniques with regard to *What* exercises to utilize, *Why* to use a particular exercise, and *How* to administer the exercise.

The corrective therapist realizes that the body functions as a whole unit and that muscle groups overlap. Therefore, exercises cannot be

[6]Paul Conte, Alan S. DeWolfe, Jack Klein, and Robert P. Barrell, "The Effects of Group-Centered and Nongroup-Centered Instruction on Group Cohesion of Psychiatric Patients," *American Corrective Therapy Journal*, 25:129-131 (September-October 1971).

restricted to only one area of the body. In administering the exercise, the corrective therapist knows that benefits are derived from exercises that overload the patient, are gradual and continuous. Exercise and activities may be administered in bed or at the bedside, in a chair or wheelchair, in the shower or bathroom, in the swimming pool or gymnasium, on a litter or on the floor and, for that matter, anywhere available and acceptable for treatment. In Figure 19.2, a patient exercises with an overhead pulley from a wheelchair.

The corrective therapist ensures the patient's cooperation in therapeutic exercise by presenting clear instructions and performance expectations. In this presentation, the exercise is briefly explained and may be accompanied by a demonstration. The patient is positioned for the exercise, performs it, and the corrective therapist makes corrections in a positive manner and gives praise.

In therapeutic exercise, there are two types: active and passive. Active exercises are performed by the patient without assistance. Passive exercises are movements by the patient but executed by the therapist, another individual, another body part of the patient, or a mechanical device. Active exercise is most important with effective modalities (method of application) in clinical administration of exercise. Passive exercise promotes and maintains normal joint motion. Active exercises are classified as voluntary movements in free exercise, assisted exercise, assisted-resisted exercise, and resisted exercise; as involuntary movements in reflex movement. Passive exercises are classified as relaxed passive movement and forced (manipulative) passive movement.

The corrective therapist is cautious about exercise. Although many values can be derived from exercise, it is not a panacea for all human injuries and illnesses. Precautions are taken to prevent the patient from experiencing excessive pain, swelling, inflamation, and accidental injury. There are even some exercises considered to be controversial in their effect. Among these are the full squat, straight leg sit-up, leg lift from floor, toe-touching from a standing position, heel raises, bent-over rowing motion, and back hyperextension from a prone position on the floor.[7]

TREATMENT FACILITIES AND EQUIPMENT

Basically, there are four types of recognized units in treatment facilities for corrective therapy: the bed program, the therapeutic

[7]Philip J. Rasch and Fred L. Allman, Jr., "Controversial Exercises," *American Corrective Therapy Journal*, **26**:95-98 (July-August 1972).

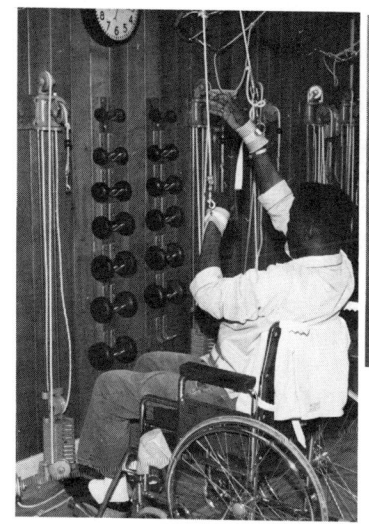

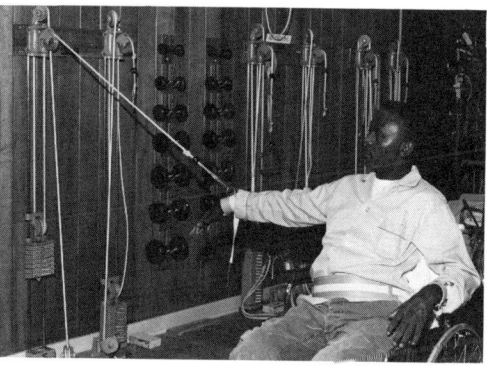

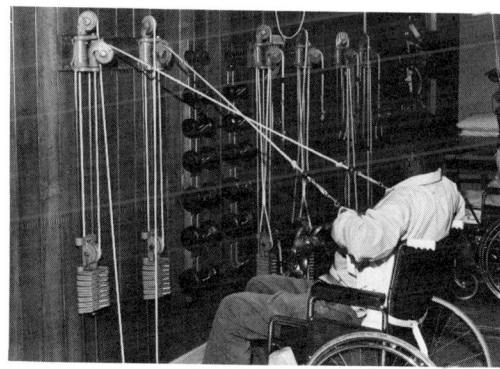

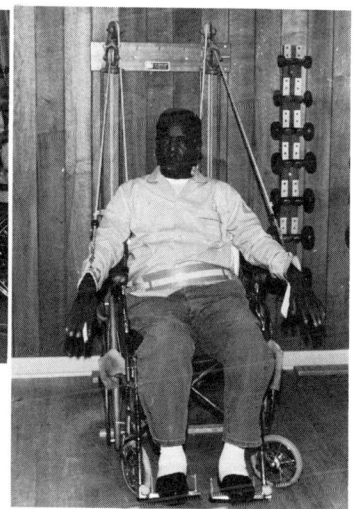

FIGURE 19.2 Therapeutic exercise examples in paraplegia. Reprinted by permission of the American Corrective Therapy Association, Inc. (a) Overhead pulley exercise. (b) Shoulder retraction exercise. (c) Arm adduction exercise. (d) Forearm extension exercise.

exercise clinic program, the relaxation techniques clinic program, and the therapeutic swimming pool program. Additional treatment facilities, common to many, are psychiatric units, poststroke units, geriatrics units, cancer rehabilitation units, cardiopulmonary rehabilitation centers, alcohol and drug centers, halfway houses, and arthritic units. These treatment facilities may be housed in hospitals, schools, community or church-affiliated rehabilitation centers, or nursing homes.

In these treatment facilities, there are standard pieces of equipment and equipment to serve specialized functions. Some of the equipment used in corrective therapy for geriatrics were illustrated in Figure 19.1 on page 294. Notice the stationary bicycle, exercycles, parallel bars, and incline board. Equipment not pictured, but included in a treatment facility, are stall bars, mats, wall pulleys, dumbbells, scales, weights, elastic exercisers, and a horizontal ladder.

During treatment, the corrective therapist employs other equipment. The dynamometer is an instrument used to measure the power of a muscle or muscle group. A different but more common type dynamometer is used to measure the strength of one's grip. A goniometer is used to measure angles or the R.O.M. of a joint. Some treatment facilities are equipped with an Elgin Table, the proprietary name of a table equipped with pulleys, weights, and other devices for exercising in a sitting or recumbent position. The posture mirror is a standing mirror, sometimes with two or three glasses, and it is used to teach patients correction of posture. A shoulder wheel, a wheel usually mounted to the wall with the axle about shoulder high, is turned at the handle for developing R.O.M. at the shoulder joint. A tilt-table, NK table, staircase, ramp, crutches, and canes are usually standard equipment.

GLOSSARY OF TERMS

1. **Ankylosis**—state of a joint that cannot be moved actively or passively.
2. **Anoxia**—lack of oxygen.
3. **Apraxia**—the inability to perform purposeful or skilled movements because of a cerebral lesion, without weakness, sensory loss, or incoordination.
4. **Ataxia**—failure of muscular coordination.
5. **Atrophy**—reduction in tissue mass, a wasting of tissues. Muscular atrophy is usually the result of tissue, as in infantile paralysis.
6. **Brace**—a device applied to a part of the body serving as a supportive, assistive, adaptive, preventive, or corrective function. Three types: dropfoot brace, knee brace, and long, left-leg (LLL) brace.
7. **Chronic**—continuing over a long period of time.

8. **Compression**—a forcible pushing together, for example, when the vertebrae suffers in a head-on collision.
9. **Convulsion**—an involuntary contraction of muscles of a variable degree with or without loss of consciousness.
10. **Disability**—status of diminished function, dependent upon the impairment of an individual and his or her adjustment to it.
11. **Hypokinesia**—lack of motion.
12. **Isometric contraction**—activity of a muscle while its length does not change, its extremities being fixed.
13. **Isotonic contraction**—both shortening and lengthening of the muscle takes place.
14. **Kyphosis**—humpback or exaggerated dorsal curve.
15. **Lordosis**—swayback or exaggerated lumbar curve.
16. **Orthopedics**—branch of surgery dealing with the treatment, amelioration, or correction of diseases and anomalies of the muscles and of the joints, spine, and other parts of the skeletal system.
17. **Overload**—a load that requires exertion beyond previous requirements.
18. **Scoliosis**—abnormal lateral curvature of the spinal column.
19. **Socket**—the part of a prosthesis that contains the amputation stump.
20. **Splint**—a device, usually lighter than a brace, but for comparable purposes of support.
21. **Suction socket**—prosthetic socket, usually for the thigh, which is held in place by negative pressure, when limb is suspended.

SELECTED REFERENCES

"A Clarification of Terms," *Journal of Health, Physical Education and Recreation,* **42**:63-66, 68 (September 1971).

American Alliance for Health, Physical Education and Recreation, *State Provisions and Regulations for Physical Education for the Handicapped,* AAHPER, Washington, D.C., June, 1974.

American College of Sports Medicine, *Guidelines for Graded Exercise Testing and Exercise Prescription,* Lea & Febiger, Philadelphia, 1975.

Arnheim, Daniel D., and William A. Sinclair, *The Clumsy Child,* C.V. Mosby Co., St. Louis, 1975.

Association of Rehabilitation Centers, Inc., *Manual of Standards for Rehabilitation Centers and Facilities,* Association of Rehabilitation Centers, Inc., Evanston, IL, June, 1965.

Auxter, David, "Basic Movement Experiences for the Mentally Retarded," p. 60, *The Best Challenge,* AAHPER, Washington, D.C., 1971.

Berner, Leo, "Driver Training for the Severely Handicapped," *American Corrective Therapy Journal,* 22:18-20 (January-February 1968).

Bobath, Berta, *Adult Hemiplegia: Evaluation and Treatment,* William Heinemann Medical Books, Ltd., London, 1970.

Brunnstrom, Signe, *Movement Therapy in Hemiplegia,* Harper & Row Publishers, New York, 1970.

Chasey, William C. (ed.), "Bibliography on Therapeutic Hydrogymnastics," *Journal of American Corrective Therapy Association,* American Corrective Therapy Association, Inc.

Chasey, William C. (ed.), "Bibliography on Vocational Rehabilitation," *Journal of the American Corrective Therapy Association,* American Corrective Therapy Association, Inc.

Colson, John, *Progressive Exercise Therapy: In Rehabilitation and Physical Education,* Second Edition, The William and Wilkins Company, Baltimore, 1969.

Cureton, Thomas K., *Physiological Effects of Exercise Programs on Adults,* Charles C. Thomas Publisher, Springfield, IL, 1969.

Frazier, Jr., L.M., "A Non-Medical Hospital Director Looks at C.T.," *American Corrective Therapy Journal,* 29:99-104 (July-August 1972).

Gardiner, M. Dena, *The Principles of Exercise Therapy,* Third Edition, G. Bell and Sons Ltd., London, 1966.

Handy, Imena A., Anna Chernicoff, and Margaret Mindish, "Patients in Nursing Homes and Their Future," *American Corrective Therapy Journal,* 25:166-172 (November-December 1971).

Hirschberg, Gerold G., Leon Lewis, and Dorothy Thomas, *Rehabilitation: A Manual for the Care of the Disabled and Elderly,* J.B. Lippincott Company, Philadelphia, 1964.

Hodges, Alton, "Corrective Therapy Adaptations to the Mentally Retarded: A Program of Passive Reflex Therapy," pp. 151-153, *The Best of Challenge,* AAHPER, Washington, D.C., 1971.

Kraus, Hans, *Therapeutic Exercise,* Second Edition, Charles C. Thomas Publisher, Springfield, IL, 1963.

Krusen, Frank, Frederic Kotthe, and Paul Ellwood, Jr., *Handbook of Physical Medicine and Rehabilitation*, W.B. Saunders, Philadelphia, 1971.

Licht, Sidney (ed.), *Therapeutic Exercise*, Elizabeth Licht Publisher, New Haven, Conn, 1961.

Logan, Gene A., *Adapted Physical Education*, William C. Brown Company, Dubuque, IA, 1972.

Lowman, Charles Le Roy, and Carl Haven Young, *Postural Fitness: Significance and Variances*, Lea & Febiger, Philadelphia, 1960.

McCloy, Charles H., "Physical Reconditioning of the Ill," 694-702, Warren R. Johnson (ed.), *Science and Medicine of Exercise and Sports*, Harper and Brothers, 1960.

Nixon, John E., and Ann E. Jewett, *An Introduction to Physical Education*, Eighth Edition, W.B. Saunders, Philadelphia, 1974.

Oermann, Karl C.H., Carl Haven Young, and Mitchell J. Gary, *Conditioning Exercises, Games, Tests*, Third Edition, Naval Institute, Annapolis, Maryland, 1960.

Olson, DonaeBill G., "Role of Corrective Therapy in Mental Retardation," p. 156, *The Best of Challenge*, AAHPER, Washington, D.C., 1971.

Rasch, Philip J., "Some Aspects of Muscular Movement: A Review," *American Corrective Therapy Journal*, 23:151-153 (September-October 1969).

Rathbone, Josephine, and Valerie V. Hunt, *Corrective Physical Education*, Seventh Edition, W.B. Saunders, Philadelphia, 1965.

Rhea, Kermit, "A Perspective for Corrective Therapy and Adapted Physical Education," *American Corrective Therapy Journal*, 22:89-91 (May-June 1968).

Rudd, J.L., and Reuben J. Margolin, "Physical Fitness and the Emotionally Disturbed Adult," *American Corrective Therapy Journal*, 23:154-157 (September-October 1969).

Rusk, Howard A., and Eugene J. Taylor, *Living With a Disability*, Blakiston Co., Garden City, NY, 1953.

Rusk, Howard A., *Rehabilitation Medicine*, Third Edition, C.V. Mosby Co., St. Louis, 1971.

Satler, Robert, *Textbook of Disorders and Injuries of the Musculoskeletal System*, William and Wilkins, Baltimore, 1970.

Shatin, Leo, "The Situational Attitudes Schedule: A Morale Scale for the Chronic Medical Patient," *American Corrective Therapy Journal*, 23:137-140 (September-October 1970).

Smith, Warren C., "Corrective Therapy Involvement in the Veterans Administration," *American Corrective Therapy Journal,* **29**:94-96 (May-June 1975).

Smith, Warren C., "Corrective Therapy Survey," *American Corrective Therapy Journal,* **23**:167-170 (November-December 1969).

Smith, Warren C., "Message From the President—The Doors of Progress," *American Corrective Therapy Journal,* **27**:90-91 (May-June 1973).

Stafford, George T., Harry B. DeCook, and Joseph L. Picard, *Individual Exercises: Selected Exercises for Individual Conditions,* A.S. Barnes and Co., New York, 1935.

Stafford, George T., *Preventive and Corrective Physical Education,* A.S. Barnes and Co., New York, 1928.

Stage, Thomas B., "Corrective Therapy," *American Corrective Therapy Journal,* **25**:4-6 (January-February 1971).

Strickland, Donald A., and Louis J. Souza, "Corrective Therapy Guidelines in a Neuropsychiatric Hospital," *American Corrective Therapy Journal,* **23**:139-143 (September-October 1969).

Wertz, Stanley H., "Corrective Therapy in the Rehabilitation of the Quadriplegia Patient," *American Corrective Therapy Journal,* **28**:120-125 (July-August 1974).

Wessel, Janet, and Wayne Van Huss, "Therapeutic Aspects of Exercise in Medicine," 665-693, Warren R. Johnson (ed.), *Science and Medicine of Exercise and Sports,* Harper and Brothers, New York, 1960.

Wheeler, Ruth H., and Agnes M. Hooley, *Physical Education for the Handicapped,* Lea & Febiger, Philadelphia, 1969.

chapter 20

learning experiences in corrective therapy

Corrective therapy has been discussed from the perspectives of profession, professional preparation, and role of the corrective therapist. Investigation and consideration must be given to all aspects of corrective therapy before deciding to pursue it as a profession. Therefore, some serious questions are presented for introspection that solicit honest, candid answers. Can I emotionally handle working with physically and mentally disabled people? Am I patient enough to be satisfied with the progress made by handicapped individuals? Do I have the ability to comprehend the science courses included in the didactic curriculum?

In terms of time, energy, and money, can I afford to remain in college for an additional year? Am I "people-oriented"—do I relate to people of all ages, races, religions, disabilities, and both sexes? Have I demonstrated to others promptness in keeping appointments and completing assignments? Do I accept suggestions and criticisms in a positive manner? Am I able to follow directives from other people, as would be needed in adhering to a physician's prescription for treatment and dosage. Planning, preparing, and performing learning experiences are provided to assist in answering these questions.

PLANNING

Planning starts by identifying the nearest educational institution that offers a corrective therapy program approved by the American Corrective Therapy Association. Identification can be made from this alphabetized listing.[1]

ALABAMA
Alabama State University—Montgomery
Auburn University—Auburn
Talladega College—Talledega
Tuskegee Institute—Tuskegee
University of South Alabama—Mobile
ARKANSAS
Harding College—Searcy
CALIFORNIA
California State University at Fullerton
California State University at Long Beach
California State University at San Jose
CONNECTICUT
University of Bridgeport—Bridgeport
FLORIDA
Bethune-Cookman College—Daytona Beach
Florida A & M University—Tallahassee
University of Miami—Coral Gables
IDAHO
Northwest Nazarene College—Nampa
ILLINOIS
DePaul University—Chicago
University of Illinois—Urbana Champaign
University of Illinois—Chicago Circle
INDIANA
Indiana University—Bloomington
Taylor University—Upland

[1]American Corrective Therapy Association, Inc., *Educational Institutions and Veterans Administration Affiliations in Corrective Therapy,* Accreditation Council, American Corrective Therapy Association, Inc., 1975.

KENTUCKY
Eastern Kentucky University—Richmond
Kentucky State College—Frankfort
University of Louisville—Louisville
LOUISIANA
Dillard University—New Orleans
Southern A & M University—Baton Rouge
Xavier University—New Orleans
MAINE
University of Maine at Orono
University of Maine at Presque Isle
MASSACHUSETTS
Boston University—Boston
Northeastern University—Boston
MINNESOTA
Augsburg College—Minneapolis
Mankato State College—Mankato
MISSISSIPPI
Alcorn A & M College—Lorman
Jackson State College—Jackson
University of Southern Mississippi—Hattiesburg
NEW MEXICO
University of New Mexico- Albuquerque
NEW YORK
Adelphi University—Garden City
Herbert H. Lehman College—Bronx
Hunter College—New York
Long Island University—Brooklyn
New York University—New York
State University of New York at Buffalo
OHIO
Bluffton College—Bluffton
Central State University—Xenia
Kent State University—Kent
Ohio State University—Columbus
Ohio University—Athens
OKLAHOMA
Oklahoma State University—Stillwater
SOUTH CAROLINA
University of South Carolina—Columbia

TENNESSEE
East Tennessee State University—Johnson City
Middle Tennessee State University—Murfreesboro
Tennessee A & I State University—Nashville
TEXAS
Huston-Tillotson College—Austin
Texas A & M University—College Station
Texas Southern University—Houston
Texas Women's University—Denton
University of Texas—Austin
VIRGINIA
College of William & Mary—Williamsburg
Hampton Institute—Hampton
Norfolk State College—Norfolk
Old Dominion University—Norfolk
WASHINGTON
Eastern Washington State College—Cheney
Pacific Lutheran University—Tacoma
WEST VIRGINIA
Shepherd College—Sheperdstown

Once the educational institution has been identified, a letter of inquiry can be sent to the corrective therapy department.

In this letter of inquiry, information can be requested about residence, tuition, and hospital affiliates. There may also be information available on the corrective therapy program, course offerings, and part-time and summer employment.

PREPARING

Learning experiences in terminology, anatomy, therapeutic exercises, patient disabilities, and review of the literature are provided in preparing for corrective therapy. Recalling the "Glossary of Terms" in Chapters 18 and 19, determine the term opposite from these given. For example, given the term "abduct," its antonym is "adduct." What are the antonyms for distal, pronation, extension, and eversion. Define A.D.L., mainstreaming, etiology, R.O.M., atrophy, motor, disability, impairment, orthopedics, and overload.

Anatomy is fundamental in preparing for corrective therapy. In the text, bones were identified for the upper and lower extremities of the body. Identify the body parts for: phalanges, femur, ulna, tibia, fibula, humerus, metatarsals, and radius. By referring to Figure 22.1, identify the "muscles" of the chest, shoulders, humerus, upper back and femur.

Knowledge in anatomy, physiology, and kinesiology is necessary in the application of therapeutic exercises. There are various therapeutic exercises that may be classified as active, passive, or both. Listed below in Column A are some of the commonly used exercises in corrective therapy. Find the description in Column B that best matches the therapeutic exercise given in Column A.

COLUMN A	COLUMN B
1. Digital exercises	(a) Uses adjustable weight plates added to a shoelike frame
2. Extremity exercises	(b) Movements of the fingers and toes
3. Isometric exercises	(c) The R.O.M. of a joint is decreased as the muscle shortens during contraction
4. Isotonic exercises	(d) Involves a number of muscles or muscle groups
5. Reciprocal exercises	(e) Movements of the arms and legs
6. Mass-movement exercises	(f) The muscle is contracted without change in length
7. Apparatus exercises	(g) Movements either with or without resistance
8. Boot weight exercises	(h) Therapeutic exercises involving machines and devices

ANSWERS:

1.-b., 2.-e., 3.-f., 4.-c., 5.-g., 6.-d., 7.-h., and 8.-a.

Two of the many types of patient disabilities are orthopedic and neurological. Orthopedics is a branch of surgery concerned with the treatment of bone and joint injury, and disease. Neurological disabilities are a group of disabilities primarily affecting the nervous system. Using the lists of orthopedic and neurological disabilities and the numerical clues, complete the crossword puzzle illustrated in Figure 20.1. Compare your answers to the solution given in Figure 20.2.

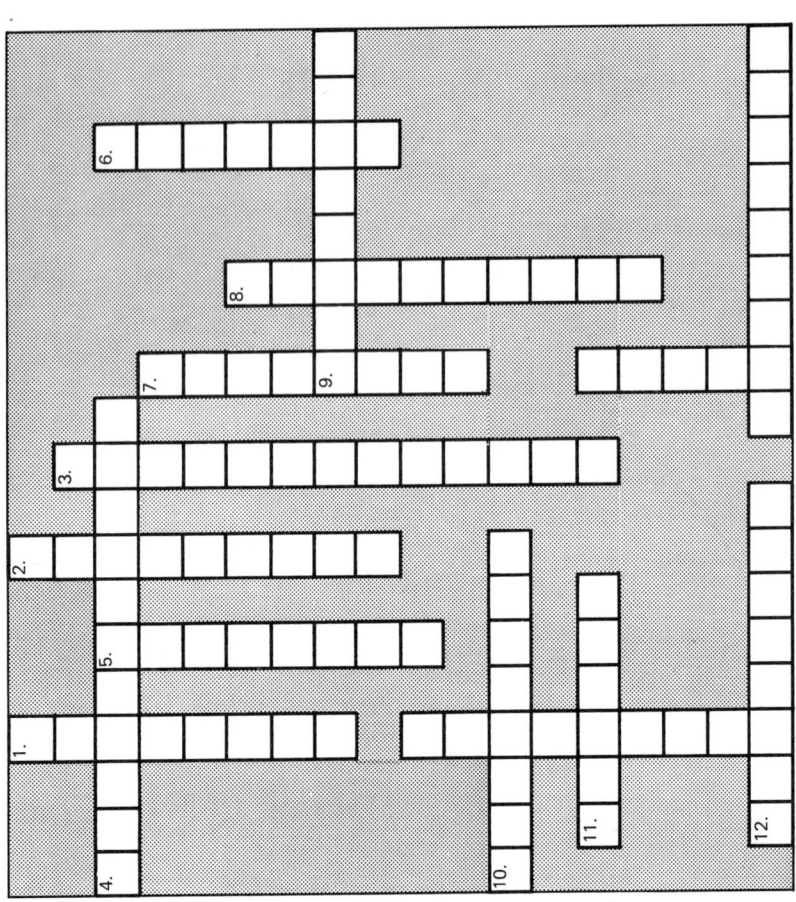

FIGURE 20.1 Corrective therapy crossword.

Across

4. Results in a complete tearing of some portion of the joint capsule. The head of the bone is displaced from its normal position.
9. Common to the joints and caused by irritation of bony protuberances from outward pressure on internal friction.
10. A syndrome, rather than disease that can precipitate a seizure and loss of consciousness.
11. Incomplete tearing of one or more ligaments and concentration of excess fluid and hemorrhage into and about the joint.
12. Two words. Chronic, noncontagious, progressive disease characterized by weakness and muscle atrophy.

Down

1. Two words. A progressively crippling disease common to persons between 20 and 40 years of age.
2. Synonymous with inflammation of a joint.
3. Epidemic forms reduced with the advent of the Salk vaccine.
5. A congenital deformity of the foot.
6. A nutritional disease of infancy that affects the strength and growth of bones.
7. Two words. Results from damage to the motor area of the brain before or at birth, or during infancy and childhood causing a neuromuscular condition.
8. Paralysis of the legs and lower portion of the body.

308 CORRECTIVE THERAPY

ORTHOPEDIC DISABILITIES	NEUROLOGICAL DISABILITIES
sprain	paraplegia
dislocation	epilepsy
arthritis	poliomyelitis
bursitis	multiple sclerosis
clubfoot	muscular dystrophy
rickets	cerebral palsy

A review of the literature is necessary to locate information about a specific subject or person. The "Selected References" can serve as a source for information about leaders, history, scientific research, organizations, and programs in corrective therapy. Among the professional publications pertinent to corrective therapy are:

American Corrective Therapy Journal
Journal of the Association for Physical and Mental Rehabilitation
Journal of Physical Education and Recreation
Research Quarterly

Use these and other publications, and books to complete the following learning experiences that are concerned with developing an efficient and effective system for reviewing the literature.

Refer to the "Selected References" and choose a publication for further investigation. On a separate sheet of paper, write the author, title, and other information needed to locate the original source. Visit the library and record the sequential steps followed to obtain this selected reference. How much time was spent in locating the original source? Using the same procedures, locate references about one of these subjects: swimming therapy, ambulation, gait training, wheelchair basketball, or treatment programs for geriatrics. Record the reference index(es) used to locate the sources pertaining to the subject selected.

PERFORMING

In the performing stage, learning experiences are provided for viewing films, visiting a treatment facility, and meeting with a certified corrective therapist. The library, audiovisual department, or educational media center of an institution has a listing and description of various films. Films have been produced on adapted physical education, corrective therapy, alcohol, drugs, geriatrics, activities for blind or deaf, and other disabilities. Consult with the

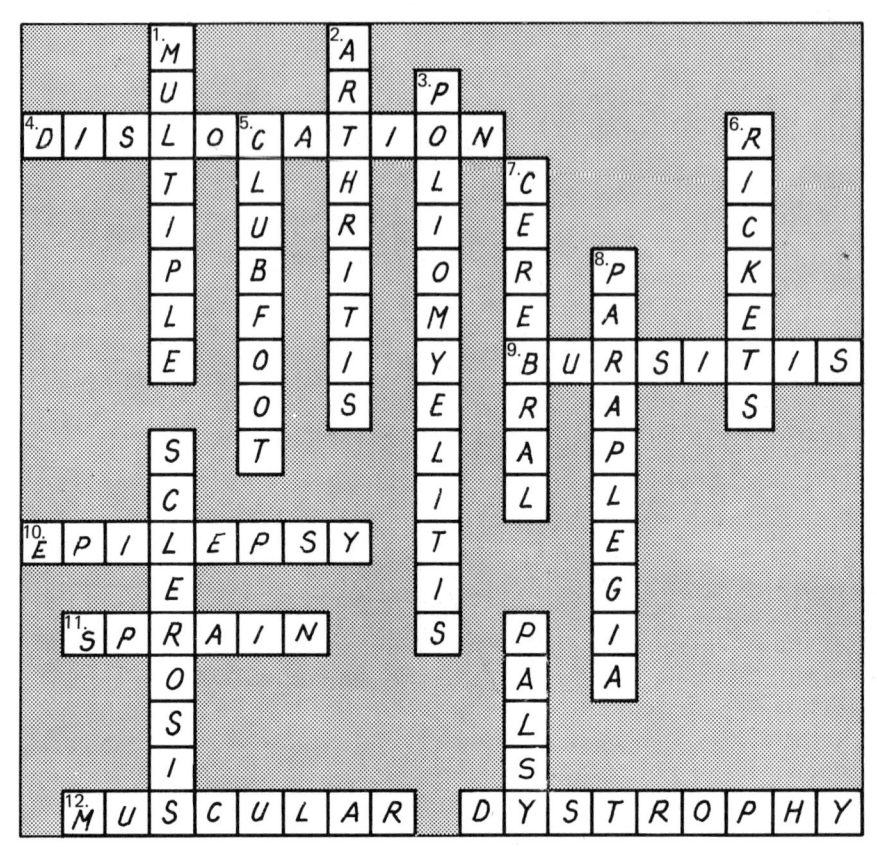

FIGURE 20.2 Corrective therapy crossword puzzle solution.

classroom instructor about using this film list and viewing a film individually or as a class. Accompany this with a brief written report summarizing and critiquing the film.

Confer with the classroom instructor about the possibility of arranging an individual or class visit to a nearby treatment facility for corrective therapy. A visit to a treatment facility may be arranged with a hospital, community rehabilitation center, an adapted physical education class, or a halfway house for drug addicts or alcoholics. This kind of learning experience provides valuable information for deciding to become a certified corrective therapist.

During this visitation or at another time scheduled by the classroom instructor, a meeting with a certified corrective therapist could be arranged. Either as a personal interview or guest speaker to a class, the certified corrective therapist can provide valuable information about the profession. Prior to this meeting, questions should be formulated that will solicit the advantages and disadvantages of becoming a certified corrective therapist.

SELECTED REFERENCES

Clarke, H. Harrison, and David H. Clarke, *Developmental and Adapted Physical Education,* Prentice-Hall, Inc. Englewood Cliffs, NJ, 1963.

Gardiner, M. Dena, *The Principles of Exercise Therapy,* Third Edition, G. Bell and Sons Ltd., London, 1966.

Mason, Earl W., and Harry B. Dando, *Corrective Therapy and Adapted Physical Education,* Association for Physical and Mental Rehabilitation, Inc., 105 St. Lawrence St., Rehoboth Beach, Delaware, 1965.

Wells, Katharine, *Kinesiology,* W.B. Saunders, Philadelphia, 1971.

section 6
health clubs

Reprinted by permission of the Health and Tennis Corporation of America, Chicago Health Clubs, 1976.

21
health club industry and consumer
22
adult physical fitness
23
health club instructor
24
learning experiences for health club instructors

chapter 21

health club industry and consumer

> Everyone is looking for the magic formula to control body weight and maintain a pleasing, body contour or physique.[1]
>
> Bud Getchell

The terms health club and health spa are often used interchangeably. Actually, health spas can be traced back to the ancient Egyptians and Roman Empire. The word "spa" is derived from the Latin—spatium, a mineral spring or locality of such springs. As Romans conquered various lands, mineral springs were discovered and spas erected. These mineral waters were used in the Roman baths and believed to have had a healing effect on the body.

In the 1700s, spas were constructed around the mineral springs located in Europe. Then, as today, a health spa included lodging and dining facilities. It is this residential feature of a health spa that distinguishes it from a health club. Since the 1700s, health spas have been built in Europe, England, Canada, and the United States. Facilities have been modernized in health spas such as those founded in the 1850s at Hot Springs, Arkansas. Now, as independent or corporate enter-

---

[1] Bud Getchell, *Physical Fitness: A Way of Life*, John Wiley & Sons, Inc., New York, 1976, p. 105.

prises, health spas offer lodging, dining, and indoor and outdoor areas for bathing, recreation, and sunning. Some even include beauty salons and barbershops on the premises.

Unique to citizens in Germany, France, and Italy is that health spa treatment is covered by their government's health insurance program. In fact, this treatment is directed and supervised by medical doctors. Visits to a health spa in the United States are paid for by the consumer. These costs vary for daily, weekend, and weekly programs. This can become considerably expensive when there are additional charges for membership and special services.

HEALTH CLUB INDUSTRY

In the United States, there are approximately 800 health clubs. These are independent businesses and corporate empires. Health clubs provide facilities for exercising, swimming, sunning, and bathing on a daily basis. Business is usually conducted seven days a week from 7:00 A.M. to 10:00 P.M. This is especially true of health club corporations. Another characteristic is the use of the term "spa" as part of their name. This is a misnomer according to the previous description of a "spa."

It has been estimated by the President's Council on Physical Fitness and Sports that only 3 percent of the 109 million adult Americans participate in exercise programs conducted at health clubs, YMCAs, and community agencies.[2] Nonetheless, the 1972 earnings of one health club corporation had increased at a rate of 40 percent annually.

The majority of health clubs are located in large cities and surrounding suburbs. A health club is no different than any other business—the ledger must show a profit. This is the reasoning behind radio, television, and newspaper advertisements. Profit is based upon the sale of memberships or classes. Health club employees: director, manager, and instructors receive commission on their sales. All employees are expected to perform two functions, sales and service. The latter concerns instructing members in an exercise program.

Frequently, health clubs are luxuriously decorated to provide an attractive, pleasant environment for exercising. This is quite innovative when one considers that exercising is an unpleasant, gruelling, and painful task for most people. But, health clubs appeal to housewives, business executives, and professional people. A key

[2]President's Council on Physical Fitness and Sports, Newsletter, Washington, D.C., Special Edition: 8 (May 1973).

factor in joining a health club is vanity. Most people want to lose weight or inches to maintain a trim, youthful appearance. And, the quickest and easiest method for reducing is of prime importance. This kind of attitude has been reflected in the two types of health clubs that have evolved. One is a program using machines and chemical treatment instead of physical activity. The other provides classes in a planned exercise program.

Facilities and Equipment

Many health clubs have facilities that are aesthetically appealing. There are oil paintings hanging from papered walls and pieces of sculpture decorating the lobby and office areas. Some of these health clubs have been referred to as elegant palaces. Is there any wonder when deep-pile carpeting and soft, stereo music envelop the exercise rooms. This environment of comfort and relaxation also contains chrome machinery used for exercising. The fully equipped exercise room has weight machines, flexion-extension tables, stationary bicycles, treadmills, incline boards, and padded benches. Wall pulleys, stall bars, chromium-plated barbells, a multiple station gym machine, and vibrator belts are also standard equipment.

A health club provides more than exercise rooms. There are whirlpools, saunas, sun and steam rooms, inhalation chambers, and a swimming pool. The facilities of some health clubs even include handball and racquetball courts, tennis courts, and a jogging track. And, of course the posh locker rooms have showers, hair-dryers, and ... a scale.

Governmental Regulatory Agencies

The health club industry is subject to governmental regulation for consumer protection. Among these agencies are the Federal Trade Commission, Food and Drug Administration, U.S. Postal Service, American Medical Association's Committee on Exercise and Physical Fitness, and Better Business Bureaus. According to the Federal Trade Commission regulations, health clubs are prohibited from using "bait and switch" advertising. This is the advertisement of a program at a reduced rate or sale price that serves as the "bait." Once the potential customer is informed about this program, he or she is encouraged to "switch" to a better but more expensive program.

Specifically, the Federal Trade Commission prohibits health clubs from making:[3]

[3]"The Facts About Those Health Clubs," Good Housekeeping, 177:195 (October 1973).

1. Statements that limited memberships are available when, in fact, no limit has been set.
2. Exorbitant claims of weight or inch loss by members following the program recommended by the institution.
3. Statements that results shown in "before and after" photographs are possible for all when they are not.
4. Claims that health club programs would eliminate or alleviate constipation, arthritis, high blood pressure or back problems.

Membership and Participation

As a profit-making industry, health clubs offer two types of price rates for services—membership or classes. At many health clubs, membership is based on "future service contracts." This means that a person who wants to participate in an exercise program or use the facilities must agree to the contract terms. In a "future service contract," one must sign on the dotted line prior to engaging in the program. This signed contract is binding, and the member is liable to a lawsuit if he or she drops out or refuses to pay. The health club is also legally bound to this contract and subject to a lawsuit for deceptive advertising, high-pressure sales tactics, and negligent supervision.

Membership contracts vary in duration, rates, and privileges. The duration of membership may be six months, one year, two years, three years, or life. At some health clubs there is a limit on the number of members allowed to join. Probably, the individual membership to a health club is the most expensive, even though there are different rates for men and women. In the health club industry, price rates vary for corporate, associate, junior, and family memberships. A corporate membership offers a reduced rate for three people from the same firm and lower rates for any additional corporate employees. An associate membership is available upon the recommendation of a member, however, this is usually limited to using the facilites. Membership prices are substantially lower for the categories of junior (under 30 years of age), husband and wife, and family. The price rates for membership to a health club range from $150 per year to $700 for life. Renewals are much lower.

The privileges accompanying membership may include "carte blanche" to use other health clubs within the corporation. Some members receive discount rates on yachting or ski trips and other vacation tours. There are even reduced prices on sports apparel and equipment. It is usually standard to include limited guest privileges to members. The health clubs having tennis, handball, and racquetball courts often impose an additional charge for use of these facilities by members or guests.

Health clubs that charge for classes usually offer a selection of programs and price rates. These rates are based on classes for one-half hour, one hour, or number (block) of classes. Frequently, the block of classes must be completed within a designated time period. This could be 30, 60, or 90 days. In many instances, it is necessary to make an appointment for each class. Another stipulation is to cancel the appointment within 24 hours or be charged for the services regardless. This business procedure not only insures profit, but encourages the consumer to attend class. The price range for classes is from $2.50 per one-half hour to $125 for five sessions.

CONSUMER

Advertisements by the health club industry emphasize diet and exercise. But, by any other name, the commodity being marketed in "future services contracts" is physical fitness. Yet, the average consumer who has dedicated a lifetime to putting on fat believes it can be shed in a relatively short time. Everyone is looking for the easy way out, the magic formula to develop a "body beautiful." Certainly vanity and the desire to *appear* young and healthy are strong motivating forces.

Health clubs offer an appealing place to accomplish these objectives, no matter what the price. In the social atmosphere provided, people *like* to exercise because they are doing it together. There is also a certain joy in being free from telephone calls and other interruptions.

Health Status

Regretably, too few people actively participate in an exercise program for health reasons. This is astounding when annually 1.2 million Americans die or are permanently disabled from coronary heart disease (CHD). It has been estimated that heart attacks cost American business 132 million workdays a year. And, half of these heart attacks are premature. This waste of human resources is a deficit of $2.5 billion a year to American business.

These kinds of statistics have prompted more and more business firms to invest in their employees' health. While some businesses purchase memberships to health clubs for their employees, others construct exercise rooms at their plant. As more and more people become knowledgeable and active participants in physical fitness programs, there could be a pronounced affect on life expectancy. In 1975, the at-birth life expectancies for Americans were: 74.9 years for a white women, 67.5 years for a white man, 67.5 years for a nonwhite woman, and 60.1 years for a nonwhite man.[4]

Although health and increased longevity are often topics of discussion for Americans, seldom are these the motivating factors for becoming and staying physically fit. Generally, the consumer is uninformed about the values derived from physical fitness. It is not surprising for people to believe that one's outward appearance signifies his or her health status. The consumer needs to know that one's health is dependent upon the efficiency with which the heart, lungs, and muscles function.

Deplorable as it may seem, in 1975, 60 million Americans were estimated to be grossly overweight. Results from scientific research indicate that the average American man has a middle-aged body by the time he is 26 years old. Obviously this is due to chronic obesity, more spectating and less participating, and using more energy-saving devices.

Health Club Selection

The consumer needs to be informed about physical fitness and about the criteria used for selecting a health club. Before joining a health club, the consumer should have a thorough medical examination. This will indicate whether or not the individual is physically able to participate in an exercise program.

Among the criteria used to select a health club are facility, cleanliness, and space. A reputable health club will have a highly trained, qualified staff of instructors, manager, and director. The exercise program should emphasize cardio (heart)—pulmonary (lungs) fitness on an individual prescription basis. It is paramount that instructors evidence knowledge in this area. Programs of this caliber have been offered by YMCAs and YWCAs for a number of years. The consumer should also know who the health authorities are that regulate a health club. Another factor to consider is the schedule for

---

[4]Lawrence E. Lamb, "Stay Youthful and Fit," *Testimony on Physical Fitness for Older Persons*, p. 36, Selected Hearings before the Sub-committee on Aging of the Committee on Labor and Public Welfare, U.S. Senate, Ninety-Fourth Congress, National Association for Human Development, Department of HEW, Washington, D.C., April 23, 1975.

using the facilities and, last but not least, to fully understand the terms of the future service contract for membership.

Health clubs vary in scheduling members for classes or use of the facilities. In a two-week block, men and women members may be scheduled on alternate days. Or, the women may be scheduled for late morning, early afternoon and the men for early morning, late afternoon, and evening. Some health clubs have facilities for both men and women. Therefore, each can participate on a daily basis. There are even a few health clubs with coed or mixed classes. Regardless of the group composition, each person's exercise program must be individually planned. Exercising can be done with other people, since this provides psychological as well as physical benefits.

Exercise Program

The consumer needs to realize that his or her present physical condition is a determinant in how long it will take to become physically fit, and that it takes as much exercise to stay physically fit as it does to attain it. This, of course, means the health and cosmetic desires to be physically fit are an ongoing process. And, the often costly, usually ineffective, and sometime dangerous fitness fads are *not* the answer.

Unfortunately, many consumers have the misconception that passive devices and equipment can make them physically fit. On the contrary, one becomes physically fit by regularly following an individually prescribed exercise program and adhering to a nutritionally balanced diet.

The public's desire to use machines for weight reduction is reflected in the equipment found in any health club. It is essential for the consumer to know that some of this equipment is virtually ineffective for reducing and may even be physiologically harmful. There needs to be a better understanding about vibrator belts, herbal wrappings, inflatable belts or clothing, rubber suits, steam baths, saunas, and spot reducing. Some of these passive devices may help to stimulate circulation and bring minor relief from nervous tension. However, there is little, if any, affect on one's cardiopulmonary physical fitness.

In the literature, vibrator belts are reported to shake a person to the extent that damage may be caused to the skin and tissue from bruises incurred. Physiologists Arthur H Steinhaus and Vernon Hernlund completed research on vibrator belts. It was shown in the results of this research that it would take 15 minutes a day, everday for one year on the vibrator belt, to lose one pound. Furthermore, there was no indication that a vibrator belt shifted fat deposits from one place to another.[5] There is only minimal weight reduction after using the vibrator belt for one year because caloric expenditure is low when little, if any, muscle contraction occurs.

Herbal wrappings, inflatable belts and clothing, and rubber suits bind the body. This form of weight reduction is actually dehydration (loss of water) and atrophy. Wraparound devices limit movement and prohibit the body from allowing perspiration to evaporate. The consumer should be aware that a severe rise in body temperature is caused by these devices. This could eventually lead to heat stroke and death.[6]

Steam baths and saunas stimulate perspiration or sweating. By applying this kind of heat to the body, there may be a rise in body temperature, blood pressure, and pulse rate. Sweating when in a steam bath or sauna occurs because the body functions to maintain its heat balance. The weight lost by this method is attributable again to dehydration. By using this method, the body's water balance and chemical balance is upset. This places unusual stress on the human body and yields only a temporary weight loss. As soon as water is made available, either in food or drink, the body retains the water it needs to compensate for what had been previously lost. The consumer should know that excess body weight is only lost by burning calories, not by losing water.

Since the innovation of saunas in Finland, the heap of stones heated by a wood fire has been replaced by electrically heating the wooden bath lodge. Both U.S. manufacturers and experts on saunas caution the consumer to follow these rules when using a sauna.[7]

☐ Don't go to a sauna after a heavy meal. Wait an hour or two.
☐ Don't take any alcoholic drinks immediately before, during or after a sauna.
☐ Don't go to a sauna if you are tired.

[5] Vernon Hernlund and Arthur H Steinhaus, "Do Mechanical Vibrators Take-Off or Redistribute Fat?," *Journal of the Association for Physical and Mental Rehabilitation*, **11**:3 (1957).

[6] Bud Getchell, *Physical Fitness: A Way of Life*, John Wiley & Sons, Inc., New York, 1976, p. 216.

[7] John Ferris, "The Sauna Scene—Where a Hot Time is Had by All," *Today's Health*, **52**:51 (November 1974).

- ☐ Never wear a bathing suit.
- ☐ Don't wear jewelry—watches, bracelets, earrings, necklaces will get too hot.
- ☐ No smoking and no toweling.

The American Medical Association's Committee on Exercise and Physical Fitness further warns the consumer that sauna baths do not contribute to physical fitness and there is the danger of being burned.

There is evidence from scientific research that one can *not* reduce weight or inches—spot reduce—in a particular area of the body. When a person exercises one part of the body, the entire body is affected. The consumer also needs to be cautioned against using liquid diets, drugs, and starvation methods for controlling or losing weight.

In any exercise program, the health and safety of the participant has the highest priority. The participant should be encouraged to maintain an accurate record of height, weight, body measurements, caloric intake and expenditure, pulse rate and exercises.

By maintaining an accurate record, the consumer will notice progress and revisions in the exercise program can be made at the proper time. One's weight should be taken at least twice weekly and at a standardized time. Tape measurements should be made at the chest, waist, hips, and legs with the person standing erect and in the proper posture. The area being measured should be free from clothing or other objects that could contribute to a false measurement. The tape must be wrapped around the area firmly, but not so tightly as to be an inaccurate measurement.

Since the burning, or expenditure of calories is necessary for weight reduction, a continuous record should be made of both caloric expenditure and intake. A calorie is defined as the amount of heat required to raise the temperature of one kilogram of water one degree Centigrade. Caloric intake is the number of calories in food consumed per unit of time. Caloric expenditure is the number of calories used in body metabolism per unit of time.

The safety principles of persons participating in an exercise program concern age, physical condition, general health, and type of activity. It is essential that a health club instructor have a degree in physical education and a thorough knowledge about biology, anatomy of the human body, and the physiological effects of exercise. The opinion of many authorities on adult physical fitness is that his knowledge should be supplemented with further study.

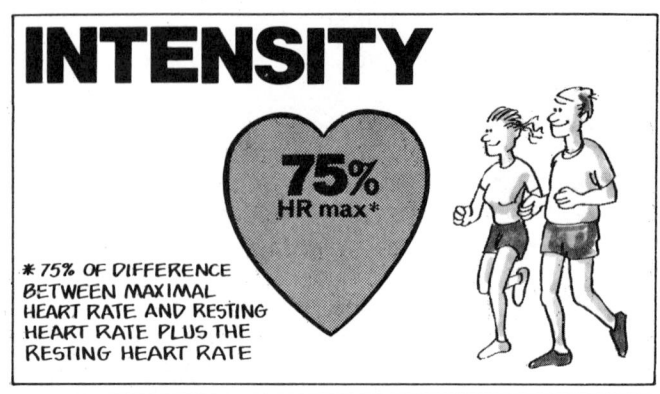

FIGURE 21.1 Three phases of exercise. Reprinted by permission of Bud Getchell, *Physical Fitness: A Way of Life*, John Wiley & Sons, New York, 1976.

There is more to an adult physical fitness exercise program than leading people in the exercises. Cardiovascular, heart and lungs, stress testing of the participant is strongly recommended prior to prescribing an exercise program. The prescribed exercise program should include the intensity, frequency, duration of exercise, and type of exercise (see Figure 21.1). When the exercise program is established, the participant should know *why*, as well as *how* each exercise is performed. A qualified health club instructor takes and records the participant's resting heart rate before exercise and heart rate recovery after exercise.

SELECTED REFERENCES

Beasley, Bob L., "Physical Fitness Quackery," *Journal of Physical Education and Recreation,* **46**:35 (June 1975).

Bricklin, Mark, "Will the Spa Be Tomorrow's True Health Center?," *Prevention,* **27**:35-36, 38, 40, 42, 44, and 46 (May 1975).

Cogan, Max, "The Heart Makes No Aesthetic Judgments," *School and Community,* **61**:31, 37 (April 1975).

Dowd, Maureen, "Corporate Thinkers Now Want Employees to Get into Shape," *The Washington Star,* Section E-6, Sunday, June 20, 1976, Washington, D.C.

Epstein, Helen, "Suburban Health Spas: Boons or Booby Traps?", *McCall's,* **101**:40 (October 1973).

Flythe, Jr., Starkey, "New Life in the Old Spas," *Saturday Evening Post,* **224**:88-89, 129 (Summer 1972).

"Gadgets that Promise to Slim You Quick," *Changing Times,* **28**:19-20 (January 1974).

Galbreath, Beth, "Are you Looking for a Summer of Fun in the Sun? Then Shape Up," *Chicago-Tribune,* Section 3, p. 1, Friday, April 23, 1976.

Garrison, Linda, Phyllis Leslie, and Deborah Blackmore, *Fitness and Figure Control: The Creation of You,* Mayfield Publishing Company, Palo Alto, CA, 1974.

"How to Succeed in Fitness Without Really Trying," *Nation's Business,* **63**:45-47 (January 1975).

Johnson, Perry, and Donald Stolberg, *Conditioning,* Prentice-Hall, Inc., Englewood Cliffs, NJ, 1971.

Joseph, Richard, "Six of the Healthiest Vacation Spots in the U.S.A.," *Today's Health,* **49**:24-27, 65-66, 68-69 (June 1971).

Kasch, Fred W., "Fitness and Cardiovascular Health," George H. McGlynn (ed.), pp. 63-72, *Issues in Physical Education and Sports,* National Press Books, Palo Alto, CA, 1974.

Kelley, Kitty, "Fat Farms for Lean Budgets," *McCall's* **102**:37 (August 1975).

Koch, Joanne, and Susan Petrillo, "What You'd Better Know Before Joining a Health Club," *Today's Health*, **50**:16-18, 67-68 (February 1972).

Kotulak, Ronald, "Eat, Drink—and Die Young," *Chicago-Tribune*, Section 1, pp. 1, 12. Sunday, April 25, 1976.

McLean, Keitha, "The Truth About Health Spas," *American Home*, **79**:10, 70 (June 1976).

"Maine Chance Report from a Recent Visitor to this Health Oasis in the Arizona Desert," *Vogue*, **157**:12, 125 (February 15, 1971).

Maness, Bill, "What Do You Really Know About Exercise?," *Today's Health*, **53**:15-17, 53 (November 1975).

Mano, D. Keith, "The Health Clubs," *National Review*, **24**:1302-1303 (November 24, 1972).

Messinesi, Despina, "Uni-Spas: Resorts Here and Near Make Men and Women Feel and Look Great," *Vogue*, **159**:74, 76 (April 1, 1972).

Myers, Clayton, *The Official YMCA Physical Fitness Handbook*, National Board, Young Men's Christian Association, 1975.

Pleasants, Jr., Frank, "Fitness Education," *The Physical Educator*, **25**:77-78 (May 1968).

"Shake and Bake," *Newsweek*, **73**:104 (May 19, 1969).

Sherrill, Robert, "Before You Believe Those Exercise and Diet Ads Read the Following Report," *Today's Health*, **49**:34-36, 63-70 (August 1971).

"Spa Check," *Vogue*, **158**:16 (September 15, 1971).

"Staying Trim, Productive ... and Alive," *Nation's Business*, **62**:26-28 (December 1974).

"The Body Oases," *Harper's Bazaar*, **3109**:134-135 (December 1970).

"What It Takes to Acquire Physical Fitness," *Consumer Bulletin*, **54**:27-28 (January 1971).

chapter 22

adult physical fitness

Unfit persons age more quickly because they suffer from a deficiency of sufficient exercises and all the benefits exercise means to the body.[1]

Hans Kraus

OVERVIEW

During 1972, the President's Council on Physical Fitness and Sports conducted a national research survey of adult Americans who engaged in physical activity for the purpose of exercise. Personal interviews were completed with 3875 adult men and women aged twenty-two and older. This sampling was taken from a population of 109 million adult men and women. The results were that 55 percent or 60 million adults engage in physical activity for the purpose of exercise. There appeared to be an overlapping of adults participating in a variety of activities. In the survey results, 44 million adults walk, 18 million ride bicycles, 14 million swim, 14 million do calisthenics, and 6.5 million jog. Another finding was that 39 percent of Americans aged 60 and over engage in systematic exercise.[2]

[1] Lynn Miller Rinehart, "Exercise: The Key to a Healthy Old Age," *Fitness For Living*, **7**:22 (July-August 1973).

[2] *Newsletter*, President's Council on Physical Fitness and Sports, Washington, D.C., Special Edition:1 (May 1973).

Since there are 45 percent of the adult American population who do not participate in physical activity, reasons for this behavior need to be explored. Many people do not exercise because it takes too much time, is too painful, or just too much trouble. The problem of motivation to exercise is twofold. These adults need to overcome the habits of sedentary living that they have formed over a period of years. They also need to be willing to substitute habits of regular physical activity into their life-style. The latter proposes a number of obstacles. Although the adult may be willing to exercise, there is the obstacle of finding the place, time, program, and money to participate. Some people may start a program and then drop out. Adults are easily discouraged from exercising, either by themselves or by others. This is in the form of making excuses to avoid exercise or a fear that death will result.

Some adults approach fitness in a "bits and pieces" fashion. They are the ones who take the stairs to the third floor, rather than the elevator. This avoidance of energy-saving devices produces only minimal results in muscular strength and endurance and contributes practically nothing to cardiopulmonary conditioning.

Therefore, adults need to establish a regular routine for exercise such as participation in groups, knowing and understanding the results of fitness programs, and learning to count their pulse rate for comparing past and present performances. Progress testing is a positive approach to adult physical fitness, since progress toward a given goal can be evidenced. The attainment of this goal requires adjustment to the exercise program. This may be as long as two to six months for many middle-aged men and women. Obese people have more difficulty, both with commitment and ability.

Adult physical fitness has been an area of study and research for many years by physicians (cardiologists), exercise physiologists, and physical educators. There has been an accumulation of knowledge that evidences the values of exercise, especially cardiopulmonary fitness. Cardiopulmonary fitness refers to both the heart and lungs; cardiovascular refers to the heart and blood vessels. In the circulatory system, the *veins* are the vessels that carry blood *to* the heart, and *arteries* are vessels that carry blood *away* from the heart. During respiration—breathing—there is an exchange of oxygen and carbon dioxide. This exchange of the inhaled oxygen and expelled carbon dioxide occurs in the air sacs of the lungs, known as alveoli. An objective of adult physical fitness is to increase circulorespiratory capacity. This is the ability of the body to perform strenuous total body tasks for long periods of time, otherwise referred to as work capacity.

At this time, it is necessary to distinguish between physical fitness and motor fitness. The definitions given are those of Thomas Kirk Cureton, Jr., a well-known practitioner and authority on physical fitness. Motor fitness is the ability to perform specific physical aspects of fitness, such as the capacity to run, jump, dodge, fall, climb, swim, ride and lift. This includes balance, flexibility, agility, strength, power, and endurance. Dr. Cureton concludes that motor fitness has to do with the physical abilities dominated by kinesthetic sense. Physical fitness is generally described as the condition of one's circulatory system, resistance to fatigue, and the ability to withstand disease.[3] Therefore, to increase muscular strength, such as in the biceps, is not physical fitness. Instead, physical fitness is the efficiency of the heart, lungs, and muscles.

Adult physical fitness programs should promote the principles and practice of cardiovascular health, especially with respect to smoking, obesity, diet, alcohol, hypertension, and anxiety. Fred W. Kasch and John L. Boyer, experts in adult physical fitness, suggest the following principles as guidelines for adult physical fitness:[4]

1. Medical examination.
2. No alcohol prior to exercising.
3. Warm up.
4. Lateral trunk flexion prior to forward trunk flexion.
5. Proper sequence of exercises.
6. Exhale on each exercise repetition.
7. Avoid arm support exercises.
8. Tilt table effect.
9. Slow and rhythmic.
10. Time is in your favor.
11. Interval training.
12. Specific warm-up.
13. Concentrate on cardiovascular endurance.

[3]Thomas K. Cureton, Jr., *Physical Fitness & Dynamic Health*, The Dial Press, New York, 1973, pp. 30-35

[4]Fred W. Kasch and John L. Boyer, *Adult Fitness: Principles and Practice*, National Press Books, Palo Alto, CA, 1968, pp. 41-42.

14. Individualize programs and gradually increase dosage.
15. Follow trunk hyperextension with trunk flexion.
16. Good leadership.
17. Avoid isometrics.
18. Regularity.
19. Taper-off and relax.
20. Avoid over-fatigue.

Physical fitness is more than the ability to do a day's work without becoming fatigued to participate in physical activity afterwards. There is an exhilarating, "come-back" feeling after exercise that contributes to the quality of life. Some of the other values derived from physical fitness are confidence, poise, posture, physical ability, improved circulation, better sleep, and diminished stress.

SCIENTIFIC FOUNDATIONS

The human body is a complex and intricate organism. It is essential that adult physical fitness programs be conducted by competent, knowledgeable professionals. This requires a thorough understanding of disciplines specific to the scientific foundations. Physical, biological, and social sciences are the stepping-stones for these disciplines. In studying the human body, heart and circulation, and nutrition for adult physical fitness, each is related to the scientific foundations.

Human Body

W.H. Sheldon, a medical doctor and educator, classified the human body (males) into 343 body types. This method of classification of individuals according to body types is known as somatotyping. Generally there are three somatotypes: endomorph, mesomorph, and ectomorph. However, everyone has some of the physique characteristics of each. An endomorph is characterized by a "pear-shaped," fat build. The mesomorph is muscular and well-developed. A thin, slight build characterizes an ectomorph.

In the human body there are 208 bones and 639 muscles. Muscles are responsible for movement of the joints, maintenance of posture, support of body weight, circulation, respiration, and elimination. It is the muscles that enable the body to perform various movements through flexion, extension, adduction, abduction, and rotation. All skeletal muscles work in pairs, one in opposition to the other. In the pair, as one muscle contracts, the other relaxes to permit movement. Refer to Figure 22.1 to examine the function of selected muscles and muscle groups. Both the anterior (front) and posterior (back) views are given.

In total fitness, there must be the right portion of muscle to fat. This is not necessarily determined by the charted weight for a specific height and body structure. Muscle strength and tone is usually improved by a program of weight training, a method utilizing weights as resistance to muscular movements. This method does not cause muscle bulkiness, which is due to the level of testosterone, a hormone, in the body.

In advancing years, there is a loss of muscle mass with some muscle groups being affected more than others. For every three days a person is immobile, about one-fifth of the maximal muscle strength is lost. When muscles are used they stay firm, strong, supple, and shapely. The maintenance of muscular strength is essential to the functions of the circulatory, respiratory, digestive, and nervous systems of the body. The human body functions as a unit and is a totally integrated organism.

Study of the human body is concerned with body composition, body density, and body fat. Body composition is the relative proportions of lean body weight and body fat tissue. The ratio of body mass (weight) to body volume is body density. Body fat is the fat storage in the human body.

The lack of physical fitness of a person can also be determined by the extreme external conditions of the body. Dr. Cureton identifies these conditions to be an excessively soft and protruding abdomen, body weight that is one-third greater than charted average weight, and a measured abdominal girth larger than the measured fully expanded chest girth.[5]

Anthropometry is the measurement of the body and body parts, such as height and weight. Girth measurements are taken of the chest, abdomen, hips, arms, and legs. Calipers are used to take skinfold measurements for determining the amount of body fat.

Whether standing still or moving, on earth the human body is subject to the pull of gravity. Every object has a center of gravity. In the human body the center of gravity is the theoretical point at which the entire weight of the body can be considered to be acting.

---

[5] Thomas K. Cureton, Jr., *Physical Fitness & Dynamic Health*, The Dial Press, New York, 1973, p. 28.

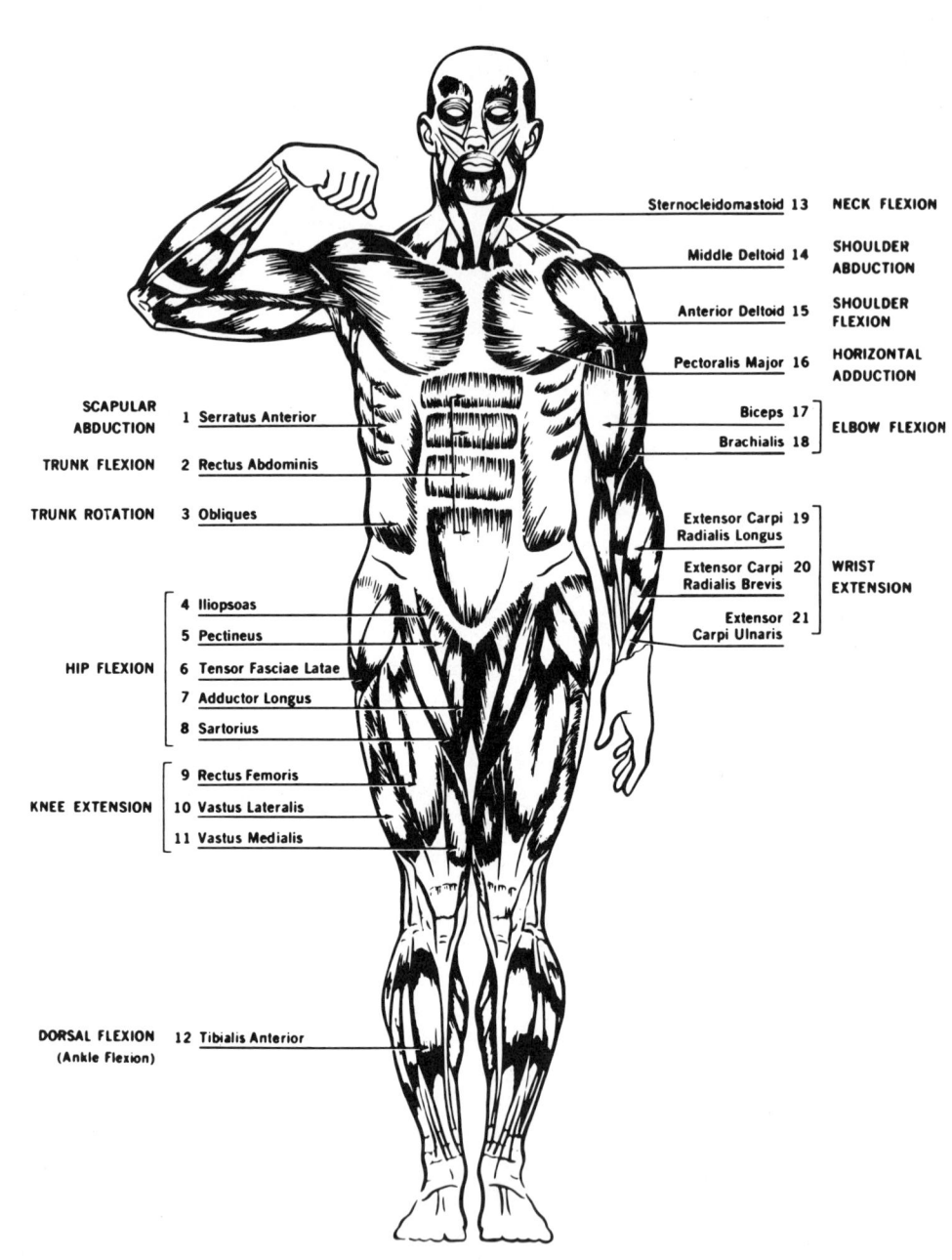

FIGURE 22.1 Total body—muscles and functions. Reprinted by permission of Wayne D. Van Huss, Roy K. Niemeyer, Herbert W. Olson, and John A. Friedrich, *Physical Activity in Modern Living*, Second Edition, Prentice-Hall, Inc., Englewood Cliffs, NJ, 1969.

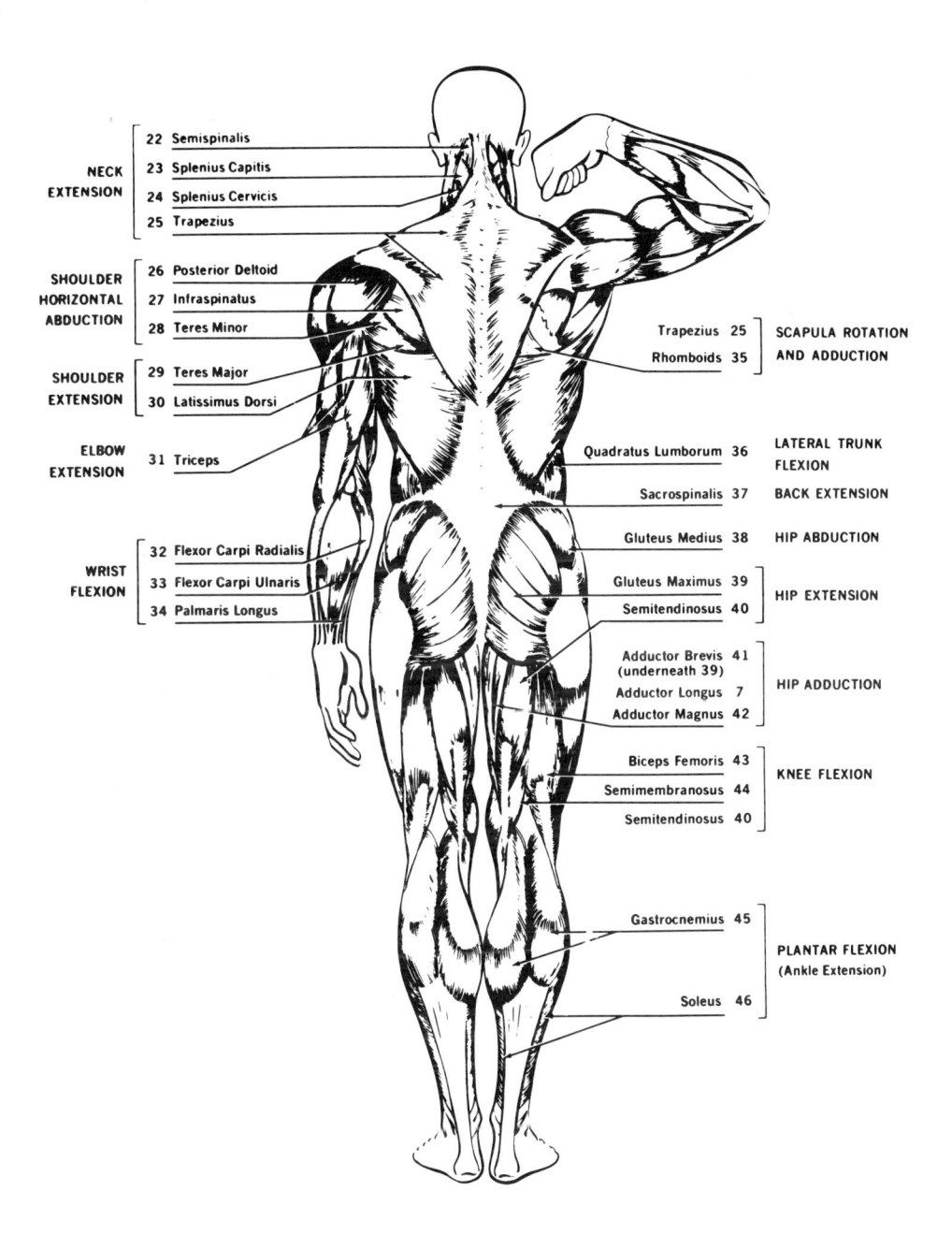

NECK EXTENSION	22 Semispinalis 23 Splenius Capitis 24 Splenius Cervicis 25 Trapezius		
SHOULDER HORIZONTAL ABDUCTION	26 Posterior Deltoid 27 Infraspinatus 28 Teres Minor	Trapezius 25 Rhomboids 35	**SCAPULA ROTATION AND ADDUCTION**
SHOULDER EXTENSION	29 Teres Major 30 Latissimus Dorsi		
ELBOW EXTENSION	31 Triceps	Quadratus Lumborum 36	**LATERAL TRUNK FLEXION**
		Sacrospinalis 37	**BACK EXTENSION**
		Gluteus Medius 38	**HIP ABDUCTION**
WRIST FLEXION	32 Flexor Carpi Radialis 33 Flexor Carpi Ulnaris 34 Palmaris Longus	Gluteus Maximus 39 Semitendinosus 40	**HIP EXTENSION**
		Adductor Brevis 41 (underneath 39) Adductor Longus 7 Adductor Magnus 42	**HIP ADDUCTION**
		Biceps Femoris 43 Semimembranosus 44 Semitendinosus 40	**KNEE FLEXION**
		Gastrocnemius 45 Soleus 46	**PLANTAR FLEXION** (Ankle Extension)

Each body part also has a center of gravity. This center of gravity changes with movement, different body positions, and the shifting of body weight.

The human body encounters a number of medical problems because of incorrect posture or improper exercise techniques. For example, a common adult complaint is that of lower back pain. This may be attributable to standing, sitting, or lying in poor posture. During exercise, people frequently experience problems with feet, ankles, legs, and knees. This could be caused from running on hard surfaces, such as pavement, or running in-place.

Circulation

The majority of Americans who exercise for their health frequently respond, "it's good for my heart" or "I can breathe better." An Italian by the name of Angelo Mosso was one of the first physiologists to hypothesize the values of cardiovascular efficiency. In 1884, Mosso hypothesized that muscular efficiency was dependent upon circulatory factors. This has been substantiated through advances made in science and medicine. Data from a study, conducted by Dr. Kenneth H. Cooper in 1971 to 1974 on 3000 men, supported the hypothesis that protection from coronary heart disease appears to be associated with a higher level of fitness.[6]

Primarily, physical fitness depends on the condition of the circulatory and respiratory systems of the body. These systems are comprised of the heart and lungs, the vessels supplying blood to all parts of the body, the oxygen-carrying capacity of the blood, and the capillary system receiving the blood. The condition of the circulatory system determines the ability of the bloodstream to pick up oxygen from the alveoli of the lungs and to transport it to the working cells of the muscles. Respiration involves the exchange of gases, that is, the amount of oxygen to be delivered to the bloodstream and the amount of carbon dioxide to be taken from the bloodstream. One's vital capacity is an important factor in this process. Vital capacity is the volume of air that can be forcibly exhaled from the lungs, after maximal inhalation.

The human body is dependent on oxygen for life. Oxygen intake or consumption is the amount of oxygen used per minute. These amounts vary according to the kind of activity a person performs.

[6]Ronald Kotulak, "Exercise Cuts Heart Attack Risk: Study," *Chicago-Tribune*, Section B-4, Tuesday, July 13, 1976.

During stress testing, this is measured and referred to as oxygen uptake. Stress testing is a physiological record and analysis of a person starting at rest and progressing to a heavy work-load tolerance. This is usually conducted on a motorized treadmill by an exercise physiologist or medical doctor. The person's oxygen requirement, amount of oxygen needed per minute for a given activity, is determined. Then oxygen deficit and oxygen debt are calculated. Oxygen deficit is the difference between oxygen consumption and oxygen requirement. The amount of oxygen used during exercise recovery that is in excess of the amount needed when the body is at rest is oxygen debt. A steady state is attained when oxygen consumption equals the oxygen requirement.

Cardiovascular fitness is the ability to sustain a high level of oxygen transport to the muscle cells for the duration of at least 15 minutes. Often this is referred to as cardiovascular endurance and is developed by periods of continuous and rhythmic exercises such as swimming, jogging, or cycling. Dr. Cooper developed the aerobics exercise program for the U.S. Air Force, which emphasizes cardiovascular endurance. Aerobic means to function in the presence of oxygen. The antonym, anaerobic, is to function in the absence of oxygen. Aerobic power is the ability to take oxygen and circulate it to various parts of the body.

A person's cardiovascular efficiency can be inhibited by the presence of arteriosclerosis. This is a condition in which the lining of the blood vessel contains masses of fatlike tissue. These clogged vessels prevent an adequate supply of blood from reaching the heart. Because these passageways or vessels are narrower than normal, an increase in blood pressure can result. Blood pressure is measured with a sphygmomanometer (pumping device) that indicates the systolic and diastolic blood pressure. Systolic blood pressure is that pressure attained during the peak of the contraction phase of the cardiac cycle. Diastolic blood pressure is the lowest pressure attained during the relaxation phase of the cardiac cycle. When blood pressure is extremely high, there is an indication that not enough blood is being supplied to the heart and brain. This can result in a heart attack or stroke. The term hypertension is frequently used to mean high blood pressure.

Oxygen uptake, blood pressure, and heart rate must be considered in conducting adult physical fitness programs. Heart rate is the number of contractions or beats of the heart per minute. This can be measured by a heartometer or more commonly by an electrocardiograph, (ECG). The latter provides sound impulses and a recording of the action potential or electrical activity of the heart muscle. This is similar to the electroencephalograph (EEG) that is used to record the electrical activity of the brain and an electromyograph (EMG) used to record action potentials from contracting muscles. Recordings are made by placing electrodes at the appropriate external areas of the body. During stress testing, the electrocardiograph is frequently used to monitor the action of the heart as the person progresses from a state of rest to a heavy work load.

Normal resting heart rates range from 40 to 90 beats per minute. One's heart rate can be counted by taking the pulse rate at the radial (wrist) artery or carotid (neck) artery. Resting heart rate is taken with the person sitting quietly and not moving. To take the pulse rate at the carotid artery, place the first three fingers of either hand at the concave part of the neck, just below the jawbone. Press firmly with the fingers to feel the blood pulsating through the artery. Pulse rate is counted by watching the sweep hand of a clock for 15 seconds, counting each beat felt. Multiply this number by four to get the number of beats per minute (b.p.m.).

Heart rate increases as a person engages in progressively heavier work loads. For example, in a sitting position, the resting heart rate is 70 b.p.m., walking it is 110 b.p.m., and jogging it is 150 b.p.m. Maximum heart rate is the fastest heart beat that can be attained during exercise and, to exceed it, can be dangerous. Therefore, an exercise or work load should be no more than 75 percent of the maximal heart rate. The maximal heart rate needs to be attained during exercise in order to get a cardiovascular overload, which builds up the body's reserve capacity.

Pulse rate decreases after exercise because the cardiac output decreases. Cardiac output is the amount of blood pumped by the heart per unit of time. Stroke volume is the amount of blood that is pumped by the heart during each contraction. The greater the amount of blood pumped per stroke, the greater the amount of oxygen transported through the bloodstream. Heart rate recovery is determined immediately after exercise. This is the amount of time necessary for the heart to return to rest. The person assumes a sitting position, and the pulse rate is taken as the minutes and seconds are counted. The less time it takes for the heart to return to the resting state, the quicker is heart rate recovery. This indicates that the stroke volume of the heart is strong and sustained.

Nutrition

An adequate amount of rest, sufficient exercise, and a nutritional diet are necessary for health maintenance. A balanced diet consists of milk, fruit and vegetables, meat, and bread and cereal. The body needs proteins, carbohydrates, and fats as part of its caloric intake. Caloric expenditure is the number of calories used in body metabolism per unit of time. Metabolism is a function of the body that chemically changes food to produce energy or new tissue to all bodily processes. Basal metabolism is the minimum energy expenditure required to maintain the vital processes of life while the body is at rest.

Food provides fuel for calories to be expended during work. The term work is often used in relation to exercise. Work may be defined as the energy required to move a given weight through a given distance. By this definition, weight and distance are constant. Therefore, to walk or jog one mile requires the same amount of caloric expenditure. The number of calories expended for walking or jogging one mile can be calculated by multiplying one's body weight by 0.73. Notice that the more a person weighs, the higher the caloric expenditure.

PROGRAMS

Physical fitness programs for adults should be based on exercise prescription. This is the physical activity recommended for an individual's specific needs. The needs of an individual can be met after evaluating his or her physical condition through selected tests. Once this is established, exercises are prescribed and the physical fitness program in planned.

Tests

Adult physical fitness tests may differ slightly from the physical fitness tests for youth. In 1955, Drs. Hans Kraus and Sonja Weber developed and administered one of the first youth fitness tests given to American children. Since that time, there has been an explosion of knowledge concerning physical fitness tests. Today, a number of adult physical fitness tests exist that are valid and reliable. The validity of a test asks if the test actually tests what it purports to test. The reliability asks if the same results can be obtained when the same test is administered by another person.

Physical fitness tests are designed to measure components of physical fitness. Among these components are agility, balance, coordination, endurance, flexibility, reaction time, strength, speed, and power. These may be defined as:[7]

1. Agility—the ability to change direction quickly, while moving.
2. Balance—maintenance of equilibrium.
3. Coordination—summation of several movements into one smooth motion.
4. Endurance—ability to persist in a task.
5. Flexibility—range of possible movement in the body joints.
6. Reaction time—length of time required to initiate a response to a specific stimulus.
7. Strength—ability to exert force.
8. Speed—velocity of movement.
9. Power—force exerted over a designated period of time.

There are tests designed to measure the movement at various joints of the body. Specifically, these measure trunk flexion, trunk extension, shoulder extension, knee extension, and plantar flexion. Power is commonly measured by a vertical jump test. There are also graded exercise tests performed on a stationary bicycle, or treadmill, breath holding, progressive pulse-ratio, and step tests.

Exercise

In any physical fitness program it is necessary to have qualified, competent instructors. The stronger and more dedicated the leadership, the more likely are participants to be motivated. It is imperative that the instructor know each person and give the proper help when needed. The instructor should know people and know physical fitness.

Adults who intend to participate in a physical fitness program should be urged to visit their family physician for a complete medical examination. Verification of this examination provides the instructor with knowledge about the individual's readiness to participate in

[7]Dale Hanson, *Health Related Fitness,* Wadsworth Publishing Company, Inc., Belmont, CA, 1970, pp. 113-129.

exercise. Adults must be provided with the proper exercises, especially those adults with previously existing medical problems. Most authorities recommend adults receive a stress test prior to engaging in an exercise program. This test should be supervised by a physical educator with expertise in exercise physiology.

The instructor should lead adults in exercises for warm-up, flexibility, general muscle tone, and body contour. All of the muscles should be involved during exercise. The purpose of a warm-up is to loosen, stretch, and strengthen the major muscle groups. Adults who suffer from hypokinetic disease, human deterioration caused by sedentary living, should proceed with caution the first two months of exercising. Many physical fitness experts recommend exercising three nonconsecutive days a week for a minimum of 20 minutes each day. Then, conditioning should be gradual, from mild to more strenuous exercises.

There are four aspects to consider when exercising: (1) the type of exercise, (2) intensity, (3) duration, and (4) frequency. There is a training effect when certain exercises are performed in certain quantities, at certain speeds, and with certain regularity. The ability to exercise is affected by age, climatology, and time of day. Many authorities suggest that exercises be done either at 5:00 P.M. or noon. When adults finish exercising, breathing should return to normal within 10 minutes.

If true benefits are to be derived from exercise, the principle of overload needs to be applied. Overload is any resistance that is greater than what is normally encountered. By exercising with an overload, the participant is likely to reach a maximal heart rate. It is important for the instructor to know the participant's physical, work, and respiratory capacity. Physical capacity is the capacity of an organism for doing work. One's maximal ability to continue work, as represented by oxygen consumption, is work capacity. Respiratory capacity is the capacity of the respiratory system to exchange oxygen and carbon dioxide.

Physical Fitness

The objective of all physical fitness programs should be improved speed, skill, strength, stamina, circulation, and range of motion. Cardiovascular fitness is the most important dimension of physical fitness. The human body requires continuous stimulation of the heart in order to function efficiently. It has been evidenced in research that physical activity enhances physiological and emotional functioning. In a study conducted by Keith A. James and others, differences were found in the personality characteristics of physically active and inactive mature males, the former demonstrating aggressiveness and confidence in their self-image.[8]

Physical fitness programs for the elderly are supported in Sweden and the United States. In Sweden, physical fitness programs are highly regarded not only because of the health benefits derived, but because they reduce governmental health care costs.[9] Also, the cost for physical fitness programs is less than the cost for health care. In the United States, the National Association for Human Development has joined with the President's Council on Physical Fitness and Sports to start physical fitness programs for the elderly (over 60).[10]

Among the physical fitness programs developed are Dr. Cureton's low-gear, middle-gear, and high-gear exercise program. This consists of 22 lessons and must be completed in six to nine months. Interval training is an endurance training program emphasizing repetition, pace, distance, and rest. The interval training program provides a system of conditioning that consists of a series of repeated bouts of exercise alternated with periods of relief. The relief period usually is composed of light or mild exercises.

Circuit training is a program of conditioning developed in England during the end of World War II. R.E. Morgan and G.T. Adamson devised the circuit training program to motivate students at the University of Leeds to engage in conditioning. Circuit training is a systematic and progressive conditioning program. The circuit is comprised of a specific number of exercise stations arranged consecutively. A person's maximum work capacity is calculated, a target time is established, and the overload principle is applied. Weight training pertains directly to the development of muscular strength. Two factors in this program are the amount of weight and number of repetitions.

[8] Keith A. James, John H. Spurgeon, Steven N. Blair, and L. Wayne Carter, "Motivational Differentials Among Physically Active and Inactive Mature Males as Measured by the Motivational Analysis Test," *Research Quarterly*, **45**:217-223 (October 1974).

[9] Beritt Brattnas Stanton, "Fitness Over Sixty: Swedish Style," *Aging*, **258**:17-19 (April 1976).

[10] "Workshops Spark Fitness Programs," *Aging*, **258**:14 (April 1976).

There are a number of adult physical fitness programs, and only the most well-recognized have been mentioned here. A unique challenge is provided to adults throught the Presidential Sports Award program of the President's Council on Physical Fitness and Sports. Adults who participate in selected sports, such as swimming, jogging, and skiing, can log this activity and meet other standards for receiving an award. Additional information may be obtained free by writing to: Presidential Sports Award, P.O. Box 129, Radio City Station, New York, N.Y. 10019. See Figure 22.2 for a rating of fourteen sports and exercises.

SELECTED REFERENCES

Astrand, Per-Olof, and Kaare Rodahl, *Textbook of Work Physiology,* McGraw-Hill Book Company, New York, 1970.

Blievernicht, David L., "Let's Emphasize the Positive Way to Fitness," *The Physical Educator,* 31:34 (March 1974).

Clarke, David H., *Exercise Physiology,* Prentice-Hall, Inc., Englewood Cliffs, NJ, 1975.

Conrad, C. Carson, "When You're Young at Heart," *Aging* 258:11-13 (April 1976).

Cooper, Kenneth H., *The New Aerobics,* Bantom Book, M. Evans Company, Inc., New York, 1970.

Cureton, Jr., Thomas K., *Physical Fitness & Dynamic Health,* The Dial Press, New York, 1973.

Cureton, Jr., Thomas Kirk, *Physical Fitness Workbook for Adults,* Stipes Publishing Company, Champaign, IL, 1970.

DiGennaro, Joseph, "The Exercise Risk Factor in Coronary Heart Disease," *The Physical Educator,* 30:192-194 (December 1973).

Duffy, Janice Day, "Fitness Program of the Experts," *Fitness For Living,* 7:29-31 (May-June 1973).

"Fitness Movement Seen Curbing High Cost of Illness to U.S. Industry," *Commerce Today,* 5:11-14 (February 3, 1975).

Fox, Edward L., and Donald K. Mathews, *Interval Training: Conditioning for Sports and General Fitness,* W.B. Saunders Company, Philadelphia, 1974.

Frankel, Lawrence, "How Physical Fitness Became My Career," *Fitness for Living,* 7:43-47 (January-February 1973).

Franks, B. Don, (ed.), *Exercise and Fitness—1969,* The Athletic Institute, Chicago, 1969.

	Jogging	Bicycling	Swimming	Skating (Ice or Roller)	Handball/Squash	Skiing-Nordic	Skiing-Alpine	Basketball	Tennis	Calisthenics	Walking	Golf*	Softball	Bowling
Physical Fitness														
Cardiorespiratory endurance (stamina)	21	19	21	18	19	16	16	19	16	10	13	8	6	5
Muscular endurance	20	18	20	17	19	18	18	17	16	13	14	8	8	5
Muscular strength	17	16	14	15	15	15	15	15	14	16	11	9	7	5
Flexibility	9	9	15	13	16	14	14	13	14	19	7	8	9	7
Balance	17	18	12	20	17	21	16	16	16	15	8	8	7	6
General Well-Being														
Weight control	21	20	15	17	19	15	15	19	16	12	13	6	7	5
Muscle definition	14	15	14	14	11	14	14	13	13	18	11	6	5	5
Digestion	13	12	13	11	13	9	9	10	12	11	11	7	8	7
Sleep	16	15	16	15	12	12	12	12	11	12	14	6	7	6
Total	148	142	140	140	140	139	134	134	128	126	102	66*	64	51

FIGURE 22.2 A quick scorecard on 14 sports. Here's a summary of how seven experts rated various sports and exercises. Ratings are on a scale of 0 to 3, thus a rating of 21 indicates maximum benefit. Ratings were made on the basis of regular (minimum of 4 times per week), vigorous (duration of 30 minutes to one hour per session) participation in each activity. Courtesy of the President's Council on Physical Fitness and Sports.

Gallbreath, Beth, "Let Your Heart Set Pace in Fitness Program," *Chicago-Tribune*, Section 3-1, Friday, April 23, 1976.

Getchell, Bud, *Physical Fitness: A Way of Life*, John Wiley & Sons, New York, 1976.

Haberern, John, "New Evidence Shows How Exercise Helps Prevent Heart Disease," *Fitness for Living*, 7:27-31 (July-August 1973).

Johnson, Perry, and Donald Stolberg, *Conditioning*, Prentice-Hall, Inc., Englewood Cliffs, NJ, 1971.

Johnson, Perry B., Wynn F. Updyke, Donald C. Stolberg, and Maryellen Schaeffer, *Physical Education: A Problem-Solving Approach to Health and Fitness*, Holt, Rinehart and Winston, Chicago, 1966.

Karpovich, Peter V., *Physiology of Muscular Activity*, W.B. Saunders Company, Philadelphia, 1966.

Kasch, Fred W., and John L. Boyer, *Adult Fitness: Principles and Practice*, National Press Books, Palo Alto, CA, 1968.

Keelor, Richard, "Physical Fitness and Health—Highlights of the Senate Subcommittee on Aging Hearing," *Aging* 258:6-10 (April 1976).

Knerr, Bud, "One Doctor's Views on Exercise," *Fitness For Living*, 7:43-47 (January-February 1973).

Kugler, Hans J., "The Kugler Experiments: A Model for Longer, More Active Life," *Prevention*, 27:60-67 (December 1975).

Kuntzleman, Charles T., "Exercise: How Much is Enough?" *Fitness For Living*, 5:18-22 (May-June 1971).

Liu, Nora Yan-Shu, and Thomas Kirk Cureton, Jr., "Effects of Training on Maximal Oxygen Intake of Middle-Aged Women," *American Corrective Therapy Journal*, 29:56-61 (March-April 1975).

Maxa, Kathleen, "Go Take a Stress Test If You Have Any Doubts," *The Washington Star*, Section E-6, Sunday, June 20, 1976, Washington, D.C.

Mott, Jane A., *Conditioning and Basic Movement Concepts*, Wm. C. Brown Company Publishers, Dubuque, IA, 1968.

Myers, Clayton R., "Legal Aspects of Physical Fitness Testing," *Journal of Physical Education*, 72:107-109 (March-April 1975).

Nelson, Dale O., "Dynamic Fitness," *The Physical Educator*, 32:59-60 (May 1975).

Newman, Joseph (ed.), *Physical Fitness*, U.S. News and World Report Inc., Washington, D.C., 1970.

Peebler, J.R., *Controlled Exercise for Physical Fitness,* Charles C. Thomas Publisher, Springfield, IL, 1962.

Physical Fitness Research Digest, President's Council on Physical Fitness and Sports, Washington, D.C., Series 3, July, 1974.

Physical Fitness Research Digest, President's Council on Physical Fitness and Sports, Washington, D.C., Series 4, October, 1974.

Physical Fitness Research Digest, President's Council on Physical Fitness and Sports, Washington, D.C., Series 5, October, 1975.

Ricci, Benjamin, *Physical and Physiological Conditioning for Men,* Second Edition, Wm. C. Brown Company Publishers, Dubuque, IA, 1972.

Shephard, Roy J., *Endurance Fitness,* University of Toronto Press, Canada, 1969.

Siedentop, Daryl, *Physical Education: Introductory Analysis,* Wm. C. Brown Company Publishers, Dubuque, IA, 1972.

Smith, Hope (ed.), *Introduction to Human Movement,* Addison-Wesley Publishing Company, Reading, MA, 1968.

Smyser, Steven, "The Last Word—The President's Council at the Crossroads: Will Success Spoil Fitness in Industry Programs?," *Fitness For Living,* **8**:91-95 (March-April 1974).

Steinhaus, Arthur H, *How to Keep Fit and Like It,* Dartnell Corporation, Chicago, 1963.

Testimony on Physical Fitness for Older Persons, National Association for Human Development, Department of HEW, Washington, D.C., April 23, 1975.

Van Huss, Wayne D., Roy K. Niemeyer, Herbert W. Olson, and John A. Friedrich, *Physical Activity in Modern Living,* Second Edition, Prentice-Hall, Inc., Englewood Cliffs, NJ, 1969.

Wilkinson, Bud, *Modern Physical Fitness,* The Viking Press, New York, 1967.

Williams, Jill, "Over Sixties Keep Fit at Waxter Center," *Aging,* **258**:15-16 (April 1976).

chapter 23

health club instructor

The role of a health club instructor is presented from the standpoints of curriculum, certification, and profession. The area of curriculum is discussed with respect to professional preparation. Certification is related according to three different aspects. The profession concerns the health club instructor's responsibilities and commitment to the program.

CURRICULUM

Professional preparation of a health club instructor is a very new concept in educational institutions. The relevance of this curriculum is apparent with the declining job market in teacher education. Another reason is the need to provide health clubs with knowledgeable and competent adult physical fitness instructors. Two educational institutions are recognized for pioneering professional preparation in health club instruction that leads to a bachelor's degree in physical education. The comprehensive and flexible programs offered by the University of Utah (Salt Lake City) and Oregon State University (Corvallis) are planned in conjunction with the knowledge needed in the health club industry.

At Oregon State University, there are course requirements in physical education, humanities and science, and university requirements. Courses in the physical education core concern the scientific foundations of human movement and total 24 quarter hours. The humanities and science requirements total 56 to 59 quarter hours. University requirements total 5 to 6 quarter hours. Together, required courses consist of 85 to 89 quarter hours. A total of 192 quarter hours are needed to complete the requirements for a bachelor's degree at Oregon State University.

The remaining quarter hours are decided by student and advisor, who jointly plan the curriculum needed to become a health club instructor. Within this planned program, there must be at least 12 quarter hours of physical education, and 24 of the total physical education quarter hours must be upper division.

It is the student's responsibility to submit this program to the department chairperson for review and approval by university administrators. The student is encouraged to begin this process in the sophomore year in order to avoid graduation delays that could occur with a late application. Although this is a flexible program, departmental policy requires that this program be filed and approved at least one year prior to graduation.[1] See the following figures for programs with a degree in physical education from Oregon State University, and human movement careers having a physical education foundation.

Four premises underlie the individualized curriculum offered at the University of Utah. First, the student has a large degree of latitude in course selection, second, the physical education curriculum is composed of various tracks that are of an interdisciplinary nature; third, field experiences begin in the sophomore year; and fourth, introduction to physical education, a required course, is used as a selection and retention course. During this class, various tests are given to acquire a psychological, physiological, and proficiency competencies profile of each student. This is a meaningful guide in advising students toward the areas of physical education for which they are best suited.

At the University of Utah, 183 quarter hours credit are needed for graduation. General requirements consist of 9 quarter hours in English and history, and the selection of three approved courses each for four of five areas in liberal education. Foundation courses required in physical education total 25 quarter hours. These courses

---

[1]Charlotte Lambert, Department Chairperson of Physical Education, *Physical Education: Major Program*, Oregon State University, Corvallis, Oreg., 97331.

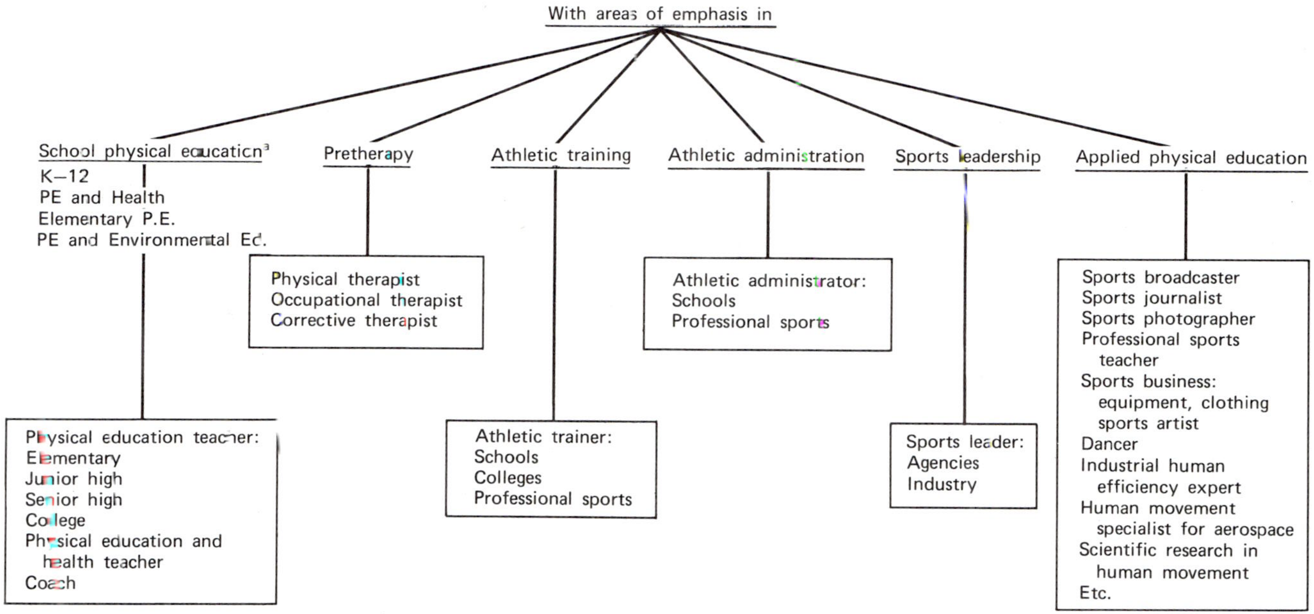

With areas of emphasis in

School physical education[3]
K—12
PE and Health
Elementary P.E.
PE and Environmental Ed.

Physical education teacher:
Elementary
Junior high
Senior high
College
Physical education and health teacher
Coach

Pretherapy

Physical therapist
Occupational therapist
Corrective therapist

Athletic training

Athletic trainer:
Schools
Colleges
Professional sports

Athletic administration

Athletic administrator:
Schools
Professional sports

Sports leadership

Sports leader:
Agencies
Industry

Applied physical education

Sports broadcaster
Sports journalist
Sports photographer
Professional sports teacher
Sports business: equipment, clothing
Sports artist
Dancer
Industrial human efficiency expert
Human movement specialist for aerospace
Scientific research in human movement
Etc.

[a] A Coaching minor is available for students obtaining certification in a teaching area other than physical education.

347

Human movement careers.

PUBLIC SCHOOLS

Teaching physical education
Coaching
Perceptual-Motor
Athletic training
Adapted physical education
Administration
Mentally, physically handicapped

COLLEGES/UNIVERSITIES

All of the above plus:
Kinesiology
Exercise physiology
Sports history
Sports sociology
Sports literature
Coaching psychology
Sports information
Athletic administration
Athletic nutrition
Intramural director
Child development
Motor learning
Research
Safety in sports equipment

PROFESSIONAL ATHLETICS

Many of the above plus:
Player
Facilities manager
Sports journalism
Sports broadcasting
Sports photography
Sports art

PROFESSIONAL DANCE/THEATRE

Dancing
Dance production
Teaching
Photography/Art
Body coaching (stage movement)

PUBLIC FITNESS

Fitness consulting
Health clubs/spas
Weight control centers
Athletic clubs
Tension control
Human form engineering
Infant development
Retirement center
(Deterioration delay)
Physical education extension agents
Living skills analysis

PUBLIC SPORTS AND RECREATION

Sports leadership
Private clubs
Agencies, Y's, boys/girls' clubs
Urban community recreation (inner city)
Churches
Penitentiaries
Veterans hospitals
Camps
Commercial recreation

BUSINESS/INDUSTRY

Commercial teaching—tennis, golf, swimming, etc.
Sports camps—above plus team sports
Sports design—equipment, facilities, toys
Sports safety consultant—equipment, surfaces, protective devices (invent, test, research)
Sporting goods, clothing—sales
Protective services—physical training for police, firemen
Industrial recreation; work skills analysis
Executive fitness; work efficiency analysis
Injury prevention; dance studies

MILITARY

Fitness training
Sports leadership
Coaching
Movement efficiency

MEDICINE

Physical therapy
Occupational therapy
Corrective therapy
Preventive medicine
Sports medicine assistant
Rehabilitation therapy assistant

Recreational therapy
Play therapy
Movement therapy
Coordination therapy
Emergency medical technician
Emergency or disaster specialist
Prosthesis testing (work, play, living)
Rehabilitation equipment and design
Movement rehabilitation
Movement adaptation
Antigravity movement therapy
Handicapped career education agent

Handicapped aide
C-V Technician
C-V rehabilitation technician
Electromyography technician

Developmental physical education
Visual-Motor training

PRIVATE EDUCATION

Mobility laboratory for brain damaged
Movement therapy for emotionally disturbed
Child care centers (child development)

OTHER ENVIRONMENTS

Fitness In space;   Underwater efficiency
Play in space;   Underwater play
Movement efficiency in space

Human movement careers. Reprinted by permission of Oregon State University, Department of Physical Education, 1976.

meet general education requirements. The physical education core is comprised of theory and field experience courses amounting to 15 quarter hours. In the track curriculum, all physical education majors are required to complete a minimum of 48 hours and select two tracks to meet graduation requirements.

In the physical education curriculum at the University of Utah there are 12 tracks from which the student may select. Among these are elementary physical education, secondary teaching, and commercial physical education. The last track is designed to provide the courses necessary for prospective health club instructors. Therefore, it is quite possible to receive a degree in physical education that includes teacher certification and commercial physical education. Within the commercial physical education track courses can be selected from business, health, and physical education.[2] A specific listing of University of Utah, commercial physical education track is given in Figure 23.1.

Professional preparation for a health club instructor consists of curriculum with a physical education core of courses. In the broadest terms, emphasis is on human movement, which includes courses in biology, anatomy, kinesiology, physiology, exercise physiology, psychology, physical education activities, and adult physical fitness programs. By blending a physical education background with courses in business, human relations, foods and nutrition, and physical therapy, prospective health club instructors should be well-qualified.

[2]Keith P. Henschen, "A New Deal in Professional Preparation," *Journal of Health, Physical Education and Recreation*, 45:65-66 (May 1974).

Select 30 hours from the following business courses: Credit Hours

Accounting 121, 122	Elementary Accounting	4-4
Accounting 127	Automated Business Information Systems	4
Computer Science 101	Programming	3
Finance 321	Business Finance	4
Finance 324	Risk and Insurance	4
Management 150	Introduction to Business	2
Management 350	Principles of Management	4
Management 356	Small Business Management	4 Select
Management 357	Office Systems Management	4 30
Management 541	Business Law	4 hrs
Management 580	Business Society and the Individual	4
Marketing 141	Principles of Marketing	4
Marketing 350	Introduction to Advertising	4
Marketing 570	Sales Management Decisions	4
Marketing 575	Sales Management Problems	4

Select 19 hours from the following:

Ed. Psych. 561	Human Relations & Group Development	3
Health Science 101	Personal Health Problems	3
Health Science 310	Health Care in U.S.	3 Select
Home Economics 144	Fundamentals of Nutrition	3 17
Physical Therapy 300	Preventive Exercise Procedure	2 hrs
Speech	Fundamentals of Speaking	3

Select 6 hours from the following:

Leisure Studies 544	Commercial Recreation	3
Leisure Studies 546	Commerical Recreation Concepts & Dynamics	Select 3 6

Leisure Studies 549	Seminar in Commerical Recreation Problems	hrs 3

Select 19 hours from the following:

Course	Title	Hours	
Physical Education 101	Basic Physical Fitness	1	
Physical Education 111	Weight Training	1	
Physical Education 116	Posture and Conditioning	1	
Physical Education 120	Exercise for Fitness	1	
Physical Education 212	Movement Fundamentals	2	
Physical Education 301	Teaching Exercise and Body Mechanics	2	
Physical Education 305	Water Safety, Swimming Activities and Pool Management	3	
Physical Education 312	Adult Fitness	2	
Physical Education 330	Training Room Procedures	2	
Physical Education 346	Supervised Laboratory Experience	2	Select
Physical Education 382	Physical Education for the Handicapped	3	19 hrs
Physical Education 383	Tests and Measurements	3	
Physical Education 392	Individual Study	1-5	
Physical Education 501	Scientific Surveys of Athletic Injuries	3	
Physical Education 509	Adult Fitness Workshop	1	
Physical Education 524	Psychology of Motor Learning	3	

Total .... 72 Hours

FIGURE 23.1 University of Utah. Commercial physical education track (physical education major with business emphasis). Reprinted by permission of the University of Utah, Salt Lake City.

Some health clubs today have personnel with limited knowledge in adult physical fitness. Frequently, the program director of a health club has only a minimal educational background. And few instructors hold a college degree. Training is usually conducted at the health club, and often this is a quick briefing on the exercise program.

Between 1959 and 1968, Drs. Fred W. Kasch and John L. Boyer conducted extensive research in the area of adult physical fitness. An outcome of their research was the development of guidelines for initiating an adult physical fitness program. These guidelines are presented because of the kinds of relationships that can be drawn for fitness programs in health clubs.

Some of the guidelines for initiating an adult physical fitness program include:[3]

1. Selection of a director. This person should be knowledgeable and serve as an example of a physically fit adult. Two "musts" are for the director to be dedicated to physical fitness and participate with classes.
2. Responsibilities of a director. Lead the exercise phase and oversee all aspects of the program. This includes medical, legal, financial, testing, publicity, and directing the physical fitness laboratory.
3. Selection of instructors. Review the educational background and experience of applicants with expertise in adult physical fitness.
4. Personal characteristics of a director. A warm, friendly personality that is reflected in the program. Continued participation within the classes.
5. Limit exercise groups to 20 per instructor.
6. One or more physicians should be actively engaged in the leadership exercise phase of the program.
7. Require participants to verify a recent medical examination.
8. Administer the Kasch Pulse Rate Recovery Step Test.

These experts in adult physical fitness further suggest that instructors need to have an understanding of adults in terms of pathology, objectives, methods, and testing.

A curriculum with sophomore through senior year field experiences can be beneficial to the student, educational institution, and health club. This opportunity for the student to observe and assist

---

[3]Fred W. Kasch and John L. Boyer, *Adult Fitness: Principles and Practice*, National Press Books, Palo Alto, CA, 1968, pp. 10-16.

helps the student decide on a firm commitment to the profession. There are several advantages for health clubs to provide these kinds of experiences. Through a closer, working relationship with faculty in educational institutions, knowledge about current research in adult physical fitness can be shared. Also, the commitment to work with an educational institution can lend credibility to a health club.

The business demands for health club instructors to provide service and increase sales could be better performed by professionally prepared personnel. In business, sales are essential to keep the profits high. But, this is no more important than providing proper instruction to people in an adult physical fitness program.

CERTIFICATION

Certification for health club instructors is in a state of flux. Therefore, it will be discussed from three different aspects: (1) proposed legislation for state certification, (2) certification at an institution of higher education and (3) certification by a health club.

Across the country, a number of professional leaders concerned about improving the status of health clubs through competent leadership and creditable programs are seeking legislative approval of certification standards. The purposes for proposing legislation for certification of health club instructors are many and varied. It is believed that certification will lead to professionally planned and valid exercise programs. This is a necessity because instructors are involved in leadership roles that affect another person's health.

Certification could also insure the safety of participants with the administration of standardized testing procedures. Since the health club industry is a rapidly growing field establishing a permanent place in society, certification could provide quality control of personnel and services. Certification of health club instructors by institutions of higher education could provide a real service to the health club industry. The communication of recent research findings in the areas of equipment, programming, and even business principles could contribute to a creditable and profitable health club industry.

There are two factors necessary in proposing legislation for certification of health club instructors. The criteria for certification and support from professional organizations. Within the criteria are: definition of a health club instructor; the competencies required; the stipulation of receiving a college degree; and the requirements that professional preparation programs be offered at institutions of higher education. Among the professional organizations supporting certification are those representative of physical education, health, medicine, recreation, nutrition, and physical therapy.

The second aspect concerns certification at an institution of higher education. This is currently a part of the program in the College of Health at the University of Utah. Certification may be awarded by a program of study or by examination. In the program of study there are two phases, a correspondence course and a workshop. This program of study was designed to serve people in the health industry who are beyond college age.

The correspondence course consists of 10 lessons. Course content includes anatomy, exercise physiology, kinesiology, cardiovascular disease, posture, diet, nutrition, therapeutic exercise, first aid, and fitness testing and programming. In the workshop phase, students are introduced to the latest in equipment, theory, and research associated with adult physical fitness. Both the correspondence course and workshop must be completed prior to becoming certified. An examination for certification is available to applicants who are physical education graduates, corrective therapists, and physical therapists.[4]

Certification by a health club represents the third aspect. At the Health and Tennis Corporation of America (Chicago Health Clubs), employees become certified after successfully completing a five-week, in-service training program. This program is conducted by Paul Ward, P.E.D., Director of Education, Research and Development. Dr. Ward instructs all classes in the five-week program and periodically conducts seminars for certified employees. Both instructional areas are provided to employees at the company's expense.

The five-week training program involves 30 to 40 hours of instruction covering the following topics:[5]

1. Cardiopulmonary resuscitation (CPR)	3-4 hours
2. Equipment	3-4 hours
3. Basic anatomy	3-4 hours
4. Basic exercise—physiology	3-4 hours
5. Circuit training	3-4 hours

[4] Keith P. Henschen, "Commercial Physical Education," *Proceedings: National College Physical Education Association for Men*, 189-190, Leo L. Gedvilas, (ed.), NCPEAM, University of Illinois at Chicago Circle, Office of Publications Services, 1975.

[5] Paul Ward, "Interview: Health Clubs," Friday, July 9, 1976 at Chicago Health Club, 626 Talcott, Road, Park Ridge, IL.

6. Body composition, weight control	3-4 hours
7. Diet and nutrition	3-4 hours
8. Physical fitness	3-4 hours
9. Weight training programs and exercises, other exercise programs	3-4 hours
10. Evaluation	3-4 hours
	30-40 hours

The instruction involves a lecture and laboratory procedure.

Students are required to participate in all practical applications. Reference is made to the professional literature, and students are provided a recommended bibliography. At the conclusion of instruction, each student is given a comprehensive examination. All students who perform 70 percent competency on the final written examination are then certified as instructor by Dr. Ward and the Health and Tennis Corporation of America. This is illustrated in Figure 23.2.

PROFESSION

The professional competencies of a health club instructor depend on the standards established by the health club and the leadership of the program director. Health clubs with an advisory board composed of physicians, physical educators, exercise physiologists, nutritionists, and equipment experts can lend professional guidance to any program. The program director's primary objective is to develop educational programs for employees and members.

Through consultation with an advisory board, an effective, scientifically based exercise program can be implemented. Futhermore, active participation in research on adult physical fitness and the club's exercise program can contribute credibility to the club and knowledge to instructors and members.

A health club instructor is responsible for meeting on-the-job requirements and servicing members. On-the-job requirements may include personal initiative for adding to members' knowledge about adult physical fitness. This may be accomplished by postings on a bulletin board such as the function of specific muscle groups or the record of an outstanding member (see Figure 23.3). The health club instructor is also responsible for generating new members and club maintenance.

HEALTH AND TENNIS CORPORATION OF AMERICA

CERTIFIED INSTRUCTOR

This certificate is awarded to

I. M. CERTIFIED

In recognition of attendence, participation and successful completion of course requirements in the training school of the Health And Tennis Corporation of America, and is duly recognized as a certified instructor.

Director of Education, Research and Program Development

President
Health And Tennis Corporation of America

FIGURE 23.2 Certified instructor certificate. Reprinted by permission of the Health and Tennis Corporation of America, Chicago Health Clubs, 1976.

Attire, appearance, promptness in keeping appointments, and behavior all serve as criteria for temporary or permanent dismissal of an instructor. The instructor must frequently check equipment to insure safety, cleanliness, and operation. Maintenance of the gym, such as vacuuming the carpet also comes with the job.

Salaries for health club instructors are often very low. They may range from the minimum hourly wage to a base salary of $10,000. A health club instructor's earnings are derived from both salary and commission from sales. A full-time employee differs from a part-time employee by working at least 30 hours a week. The full-time employee receives more benefits in medical care, insurance, and vacations than the part-time employee.

The health club is obligated to meet the needs of its members. Therefore, in servicing members, instructors must enforce club

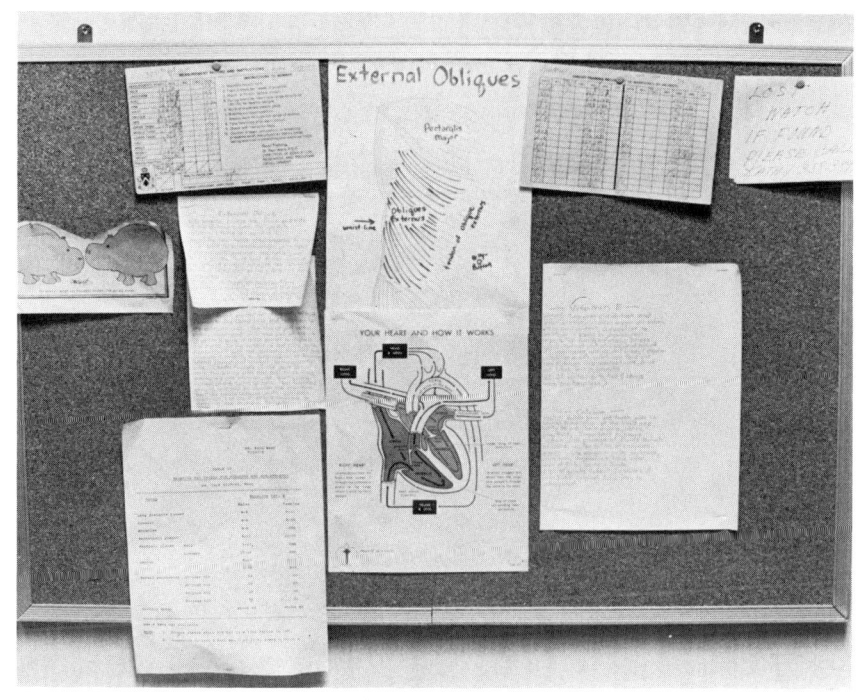

FIGURE 23.3 Health clubs bulletin board. Reprinted by permission of the Health and Tennis Corporation of America, Chicago, Health Clubs, 1976.

regulations and knowledgeably conduct exercise programs. Some of the regulations governing members are specified exercise attire, safety precautions, and care with equipment. Instructors are required to conduct the exercise program used in the health club and not to deviate from this with different exercises. An instructor must refrain from offering medical advice and seek consultation from supervisors when in doubt about certain exercises.

There are a variety of exercise programs within the health club industry. However, a sample program is provided to illustrate the role of a health club instructor. This sample program is representative of the Health and Tennis Corporation of America, Chicago Health Clubs. In their program, it is standard operating procedure to instruct members in taking their own pulse rates. Before starting the exercise program, the health club instructor administers to the member the Kasch Pulse Rate Recovery Step Test (Figure 23.4).

A one-to-one relationship is established between the instructor and member throughout the program. Each member is provided with a measurement record that both member and instructor use to record

FIGURE 23.4 Physical fitness step test. Reprinted by permission of the Health and Tennis Corporation of America, Chicago Health Clubs, 1976.

progress. This card also illustrates the exercises contained within the program. See Figure 23.5 showing the typical recordings made by a member.

At the Chicago Health Clubs, members are instructed in a circuit weight training program. The men's program is slightly different from the women's. A point of emphasis for both men and women is when circuit weight training, running on the treadmill, or riding the bicycle ergometer, the intensity or effort should bring the heart rate into the range of 130 to 150 beats per minute. Pulse rates are taken by the member or instructor.

Standard in the circuit weight training program for both men and women are: 10 stations, 3 laps, 15-second rest periods, and measurement of heart rate recovery. A lap refers to going through all 10 stations one time.

There are four parts to the men's exercise program:

1. Five to fifteen minutes warm-up jog, treadmill, or bicycle ergometer.
2. Thirty minutes of circuit weight training or a specialized program.
3. Fifteen minutes or longer on the bicycle ergometer or treadmill.
4. Cool down.

The men's circuit is comprised of these stations: (1) leg press, (2) pullover machine, (3) Roman chair, (4) leg curls, (5) shoulder machine, (6) pull-downs, (7) bench press, (8) triceps extension, (9) E-Z curl, and (10) sit-up. One minute is spent at each station.

In the four areas composing the women's program are:

1. Fifteen minutes of calisthenics (trimnastics).
2. Fifteen minutes of circuit weight training.
3. Fifteen minutes or longer on the bicycle ergometer or treadmill.
4. Cool down.

Among the 10 stations in the women's circuit weight training program are: (1) leg press, (2) bench press, (3) sit-up, (4) seated shoulder press, (5) upright rowing, (6) pull-down, (7) high chair, (8) back arch, (9) incline board, and (10) squat. Thirty seconds are spent at each station. The women's circuit weight training program and measurement of heart rate recovery are shown in Figure 23.6.

In 1975, research on a variation of this women's circuit weight training program was directed by Jack H. Wilmore, Ph.D. at the National Athletic Health Institute in Inglewood, California. Research was completed and written by Dr. Jack H. Wilmore and others. The results were that circuit weight training for women can bring about increases in strength, local muscle endurance, and cardiovascular endurance while simultaneously reducing body fat and improving body contour.[6]

---

[6] Paul Ward, "Research Report: Circuit Weight Training," Chicago Health Clubs, Health and Tennis Corporation of America, Fall 1975.

HEALTH & TENNIS CORPORATION OF AMERICA

NAME_____ DATE_____

ADDRESS_____ CITY_____ STATE____ ZIP____

AGE____ PHONE_____ CARD #_____ CLUB_____

MUSCLE GROUPS	CIRCUIT 1	LOAD	LEVEL A|B|C	CIRCUIT 2	LOAD	LEVEL A|B|C	CIRCUIT 3	LOAD	LEVEL A|B|C
1. ANT. THIGH Quadriceps & Gluteal Mus.									
2. POST. THIGH Hamstrings & Gluteal Mus.									
3. LOW BACK Trunk Extensors (Lumbar Region)									
4. SHOULDERS Deltoids									
5. UP. BACK Lats/Trapezius									
6. CHEST Pectoralis Major									
7. ANT. ARM. Biceps/Forearm Flexors									
8. POST. ARM. Triceps									
9. ABDOMINALS									
10. MISC.									
DATE TAKEN									
INSTRUCTOR									

CIRCUIT TRAINING RECORD (TO BE MAINTAINED BY MEMBER)

DATE	WT	TRIM	HR1	HR2	HR3	LEV	DATE	W/U	TRIM	HR1	HR2	HR3	LEV	MIN
3/30	131	140	?	120	120	160/100	4-21	128	7.	35	36	36	41/28	40
3/31	131	160	130	136	140	173/120	4-22	25 min. #2		+ INTERVAL				W-UP 20 COOL-10
4/1	131	140	140	140	140	160/108	4-23	128	37	34	35	34	40/28	42
4/3	129	36	37	38	38	35/28	4-26	131	41	37	36	35	41	42
4-5	128	40	38	35	32	41/25	4-27	130	7.	37	36	36	41	40
4-6	129	NA	34	37	38	38/25	4-28	129.5	38	30	33	37	41/23	42
4-7	131	35	36	36	35		4-29	130	38	34	32	32	41/28	42
4-8	131	35	32	32	34	35/25	4-30	131	30	30	33	34	41/26	40
4-11	129	40	38	32	37	38/27	5-1	131	45 MIN. BIKE					
4-12	131	34	31	31	33		5-2	131	45 min BIKE					
4-13	129.2	40	34	34	35	41/26	5-4	129	38	34	34	32	42/26	45
4-14	130	?	34	34	36	38/29	5-5	129	30	32	32	36	41/23	45
4-16	130	42	35	36	36	42/29	5-6	128	7	30	32	34	41/25	45
4-17	130	37	36	34	35	38/26	5-7	129	34	32	34	37	41/25	45
4-19	131	39	34	38	38	39/26	5-10	129	36	36	37	34	41/25	45
4-20	130	38	37	36	37	38/26	5-11	129	38	36	33	34	41/25	45

FIGURE 23.5 Health club record card. Reprinted by permission of the Health and Tennis Corporation of America, Chicago Health Clubs, 1976.

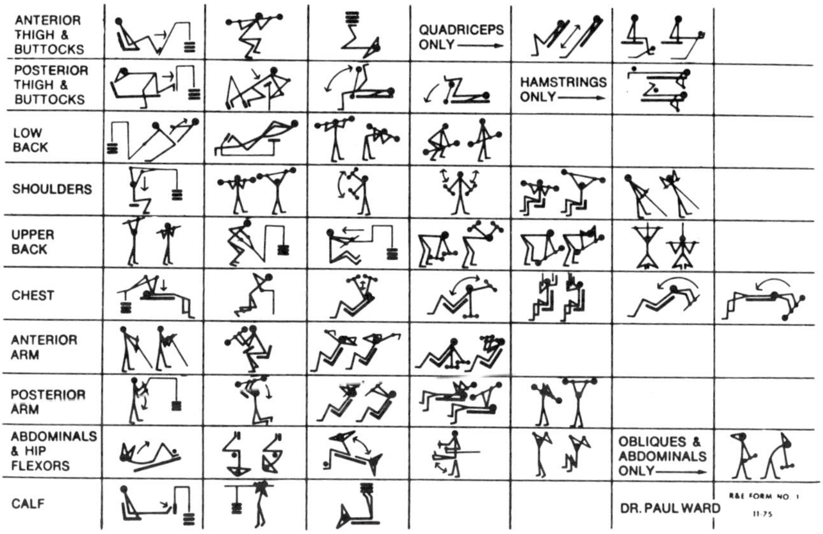

ANTERIOR THIGH & BUTTOCKS
QUADRICEPS ONLY
POSTERIOR THIGH & BUTTOCKS
HAMSTRINGS ONLY
LOW BACK
SHOULDERS
UPPER BACK
CHEST
ANTERIOR ARM
POSTERIOR ARM
ABDOMINALS & HIP FLEXORS
OBLIQUES & ABDOMINALS ONLY
CALF
DR. PAUL WARD
R&E FORM NO. 1
11-75

18% fat

MEASUREMENT RECORD AND INSTRUCTIONS

MEASUREMENTS WOMEN		BEG.	1 MO.	2 MO.	GOAL
NECK	12½	12	12¼		12
UNDERARM	33	32¾	33½		32
BUST	32½	32¾	33½		33
ARM	10¾	10¾	11		10¾
WAIST	25¾	25¾	26½		24½
OBLIQUE	33½	34	33½		32
HIPS	36½	37	37¼		34
UPPER THIGH	21½	21¾	22		20
MIDDLE THIGH	19¼	19¼	19		18½
LOWER THIGH	16	15	15¾		15
CALF	12¾	12¾	13		12¾
ANKLE	7¾	7¾	8		7¾
HEIGHT		—	—		
WEIGHT	128	130	131		123
Resting Heart Rate		60			
DATE TAKEN / INSTRUCTOR	2-12	4-16	6-16		
DATE / INSTRUCTOR					

HEALTH PROBLEMS:

FITNESS CATEGORY: VERY POOR ☐ POOR ☐ FAIR ☐ GOOD ☒ EXCELLENT ☐

INSTRUCTIONS TO MEMBER

1. Maintain record card.
2. Train 3 times per/week, if possible.
3. Warm up 15 min. before circuit.
4. During exercise, heart rate range should be 130-150, for healthy people.
5. Work at moderate steady pace.
6. Breathe out upon exertion.
7. Always work through full range of motion.
8. Take heart rate after each circuit.
9. Check with instructor daily.
10. *Caution:* If heart, circulatory, or breathing problems exist, see physician before undertaking exercise or extending your exercise limits.

Good Training,

Dr. Paul Ward, P.E.D.
DIRECTOR OF EDUCATION, RESEARCH, AND PROGRAM DEVELOPMENT

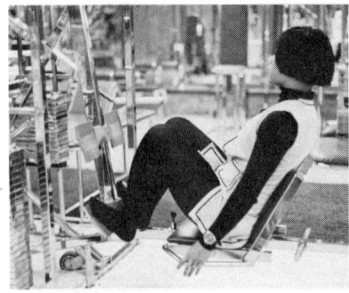

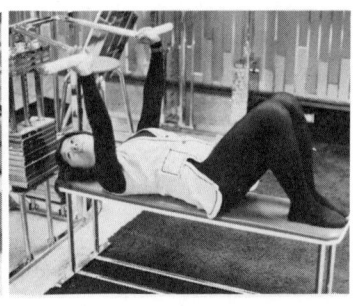

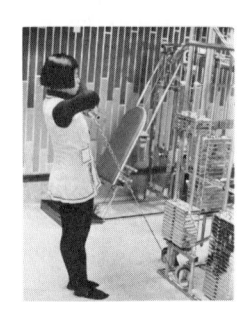

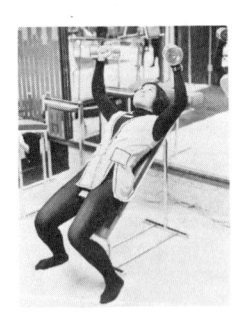

FIGURE 23.6 Circuit weight training program for women. Reprinted by permission of the Health and Tennis Corporation of America, Chicago Health Clubs, 1976.

SELECTED REFERENCES

Bulletin of the University of Utah, General Catalog 1975-1976, University of Utah, Salt Lake City, Utah, 84112.

"Healthier Health Spas," *University of Utah Review,* **9**:7 (November 1975), University of Utah, Salt Lake City, Utah.

Henschen, Keith P., Correspondence: Pending Legislation on Certification of Health Spa Operators, Friday, February 13, 1976, College of Health, University of Utah, Salt Lake City, Utah.

Henschen, Keith, "Health Spa Certification," *Briefings: Careers in Physical Education,* National Association for Physical Education of College Women—National Physical Education Association for College Men, 1975, pp. 47-55.

Kasch, Fred W., and John L. Boyer, *Adult Fitness: Principles and Practices,* National Press Books, Palo Alto, CA, 1968.

Keelor, Richard, "Physical Fitness and Health—Highlights of the Senate Subcommittee on Aging Hearing," *Aging,* **258**:8 (April 1976).

Leslie, David K., "The Preparation of Physical Education for Expanded Leadership and Service Roles," *Journal of Health, Physical Education and Recreation,* **41**:71-73 (November-December 1972).

"The University of Utah," *Up Date,* American Alliance for Health, Physical Education and Recreation, Washington, D.C., January, 1976, p. 10.

chapter 24

learning experiences for health club instructors

The learning experiences provided for a prospective health club instructor also have implications for professional preparation in other human movement professions. Both practical and theoretical problems are given. The solutions to these problems depends on the individual's knowledge, physical characteristics, physiological functions, and opinions.

Problems are posed concerning the identification of muscles and muscle groups, pulse rates, and the Kasch Pulse Rate Recovery Step Test. Some of the other challenges include anthropometry and the metric system. Comprehension and analytical abilities can be examined by the case studies described.

PRACTICAL

Identify the muscles having the closest proximity to bones listed. The number appearing after the bone(s) is a clue to the number of muscles that must be located. Consult Figure 22.1 on pages 332-333 if necessary.

1. Neck—anterior (1).
2. Ulna and radius—posterior (3).
3. Fibula and tibia—anterior and posterior (3).
4. Humerus—anterior and posterior (5).

Determine the function for each of the following muscles and muscle groups. Perform this movement.

1. Tibialis anterior.
2. Sternocleidomastoid.
3. Triceps.
4. Gastrocnemius

The ability to count pulse rates is necessary for performing the next learning experience. Find a watch or clock with a sweep hand to observe while taking the resting heart rate (R.H.R.). Assume a sitting position and, for one minute, count the pulse rate at the carotid artery. Use the method described in the text. Record the number of beats per minute (b.p.m.).

Maximal heart rate (M.H.R.) for men and women can be calculated to approximation by subtracting the age in years from 220 b.p.m. Record the M.H.R. The intensity of exercise can be established by subtracting the R.H.R. from the M.H.R. Record this difference. Multiply the difference by 75 percent then add the R.H.R. This represents the intensity of exercise needed for an overload.[1] Record this figure. More data on the human body can be collected in this next learning experience.

Dr. Fred W. Kasch developed a three-minute step test but, before participating in this test, refrain from eating and smoking for at least two hours. The performance of this test must be professionally supervised. A bench 12 inches high and a sweep-hand clock are needed. Practice the stepping sequence in the following way making certain to fully extend the legs when stepping up. The term "STEP" refers to the summation of these four movements.

1. Step up with the right foot.
2. Bring up the left foot.
3. Step down with the right foot.
4. Step down with the left foot.

[1]Clayton Myers, *The Official YMCA Physical Fitness Handbook*, National Board, Young Men's Christian Association, 1975, p. 100.

The timing of this stepping sequence is four counts per "STEP" or 96 counts per minute. This is the same as stepping up and down with both feet 24 times a minute.

At the completion of three minutes, sit down on the bench. Relax *but* do not talk. Within five (5) seconds take and record the pulse rate for one minute. Continue this procedure for each minute until the pulse rate returns to normal R.H.R. Record the amount of time in minutes and seconds needed for heart rate recovery.

The results of the Kasch Pulse Rate Recovery Step Test is a valuable measurement used in assessing physical fitness. After the initial test and participation in an exercise program, repeat the test. More significant results can be obtained when cardiovascular endurance is emphasized in an exercise program with frequency and duration. Maintenance of an accurate record is necessary. By repeating the Kasch Pulse Rate Recovery Step Test at the end of the exercise program, a comparison can be made between the pre-test and post-test results. At this time, heart rate recovery should be reduced.

The task of taking and recording measurements accurately is an important function performed by the health club instructor. This is especially true when converting from the U.S. Standard Measurement System to the metric system. Competency can be developed in converting U.S. Standard Measures to the metric system by reviewing these prefixes of metric measurements.

MICRO = one millionth.
MILLI = one thousandth.
CENTI = one hundredth.
DECI = one tenth.
DECA = ten.
HECTO = one hundred.
KILO = one thousand.
MEGA = one million.

Study the following standard abbreviations of the Metric System.

LENGTH	WEIGHT
millimeter (mm)	milligram (mg)
centimeter (cm)	gram (g)
meter (m)	kilogram (kg)
kilometer (km)	metric ton (t)

CAPACITY
milliliter (ml)
liter (l)

Look at the values comprising the metric system and the U.S. Standard Measures equivalents.

10 mm = 1 cm	1000 mg = 1 g
100 cm = 1 m	1000 g = 1 kg
1000 m = 1 km	1000 kg = 1 t
	1000 ml—1 l

1 cm = 0.3937 inches	1 inch = 1.54 cm
1 m = 3.2808 feet	1 foot = 0.3048 m
1 m = 1.0936 yards	1 yard = 0.9144 m
1 km = 0.6214 mile	1 mile = 1.6093 km

1 ml = 0.0338 fluid ounce	1 fluid ounce = 29.5729 ml
1 l = 1.0567 liquid quarts	1 liquid quart = 0.9463 l
1 l = 0.2642 liquid gallon	1 liquid gallon = 3.7853 l

1 g = 0.0353 ounces	1 ounce = 28.3495 g
1 kg = 2.2046 pounds	1 pound = 0.4536 kg

Calculate the metric system equivalents for your height and weight.

A thorough understanding of the metric system is meaningful when performing skinfold measurements. Since metal calipers are not readily available refer to the illustrated "Fitness Finder" in Figure 24.1. Follow these directions to make a Fitness Finder.

1. Trace the Fitness Finder.
2. Use the tracing as a pattern for making a copy on a piece of cardboard.
3. Cut each piece and place arm A on top of part B. Make sure that the points of both pieces touch and that the holes are aligned.
4. Thread a rubber band through the holes. Tie a knot close to the outside areas of arm A and part B allowing the arm to swivel.
5. Practice using the arrow on arm A to read the measurements on part B.

YOUR FITNESS FINDER

PART Ⓑ

ARM Ⓐ

SKINFOLD—millimeters 0 5 10 15 20 25 30 35 40 45 50

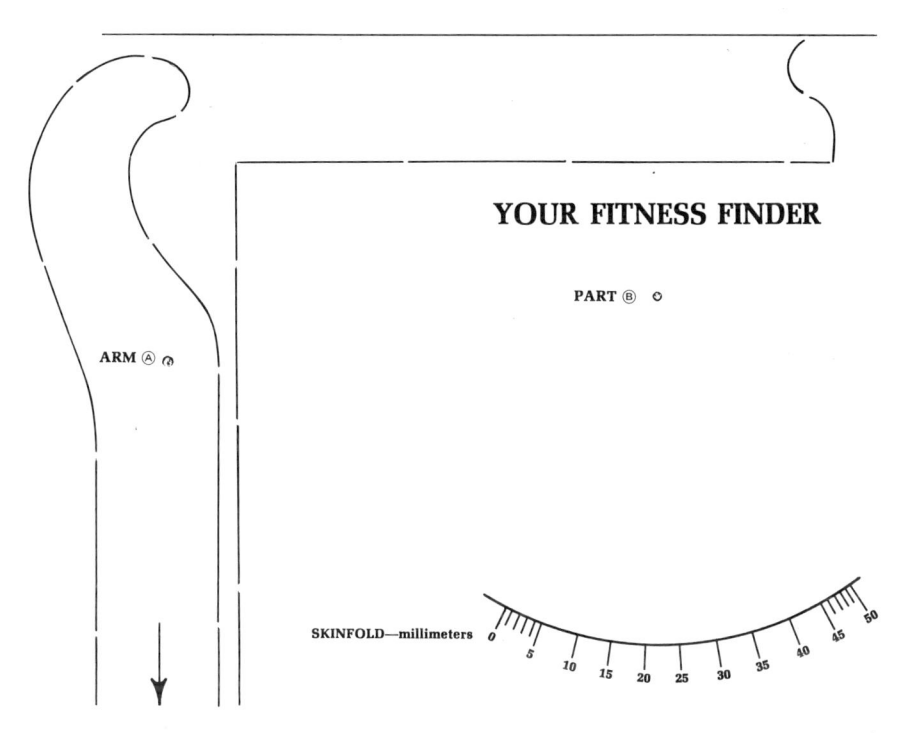

FIGURE 24.1 Fitness finder. Reprinted by permission of Charles T. Kuntzleman, *Activetics and Women Sports*, Peter H. Wyden, Publisher, New York, 1975.

Skinfold measurements are used in determining the percentage of total body fat. These measurements require a partner and are taken on the right side of the body. The skinfold measurements are taken at the back of the arm (triceps) and hip (suprailiac). These are taken for both men and women. However, two additional skinfold measurements need to be made for men. All measurements require the subject to sit on a chair letting both arms hang at the sides:[2]

Women. Partner measures the arm by firmly grasping the skin at the triceps, midway between shoulder and elbow. The skin is pulled slightly away from the underlying tissues. Measure this skinfold vertically by gently "pinching" it between the two ends of the Fitness Finder. A more accurate reading is obtained by pressing the calipers together and creating an indentation in the

[2] Charles T. Kuntzleman, *Activetics*, Peter H. Wyden, Publisher, New York, 1975, pp. 53-57.

skin. Read and record to the nearest millimeter. The suprailiac skinfold measurement is taken by grasping the skin midway between the lower rib and hip bone. This is about one inch above the hip. As the subject leans toward the right, the partner takes the measurement parallel to the belt line. Read and record the measurement. Partners exchange places and repeat procedures.

Men. Repeat the procedures for skinfold measurements made on women. Partner takes the third measurement on the front of the arm (biceps). Arms hanging at sides. The skinfold is vertically taken midway between the shoulder and elbow. Read and record. The fourth measurement is made at the upper back (subscapular). This is taken just below the lower part of the shoulder blade at about a 45-degree angle to the vertical. Read and record. Partners exchange places and repeat procedures.

Total these skinfold measurements. Two for women and four for men. This becomes the total skinfold score. Refer to the Table on "Fat as Percent Body Weight" shown in Figure 24.2. Locate the appropriate total skinfold score and find the corresponding percentage of total body fat.

"Activetics" is a word coined by Dr. Charles T. Kuntzleman, National Program Director of the YMCA Fitness Finders Program. Activetics is used to describe a "program of diet-free weight loss through activity."[3] This is a self-directed exercise program based on utilizing body measurements as an evaluative instrument and method for selecting activities.

The Activetic ideal weight can be located for both men and women by referring to the tables shown in Figure 24.3. Read by locating present body weight (at top) and total percentage of body fat (at side). The ideal Activetics weight appears where the two columns intersect. Read and record for future comparisons.

THEORETICAL

This phase of learning experiences tests one's abilities to absorb realistic situations and analytically explore possible solutions. Perhaps one of these case studies will reflect a similar, personal incident.

1. At Bridgeview College, Ann Rose was a junior majoring in physical education. She planned to teach and coach at the secondary level upon graduating the following year. Late in her

[3] Ibid., p. 5.

Men Total Skinfold Score (mm)	% Fat	Women Total Skinfold Score (mm)	% Fat
15	5	8	13
20	9	12	14
25	11	14	15
30	13	18	16
35	15	20	17
40	17	24	18
45	18	26	19
50	20	30	20
55	21	32	21
60	22	34	22
65	23	38	23
70	24	40	24
75	25	42	25
80	26	44	26
90	27	48	27
100	28	50	28
110	29	52	29
120	30	56	30
130	31	58	31
140	32	62	32
150	33	64	33
160	34	68	34
175	35	70	35
190	36	72	36
205	37	76	37
220	38	80	38
235	39	82	39
255	40	86	40
275	41	88	41
295	42	90	42

FIGURE 24.2 Fat as percent body weight. Reprinted by permission of Charles T. Kuntzleman, *Activetics*, Peter H. Wyden, Publisher, New York, 1975.

junior year, Ann began to question her decision to go into teaching and coaching.

While at college Ann had visited a nearby health club on several occasions. These visits caused her to seriously think about changing her course of study. What should Ann do? Who could she talk to about preparing to become a health club instructor? Where would she be able to receive a degree in this specialized area? What were the written sources of information that she could find and use? What were the job opportunities in this area compared to teaching and coaching?

2. Richard Johnson was enrolled in the athletic training program

	% of Fat	\multicolumn{25}{c	}{Body Weight (lbs)}
		120	125	130	135	140	145	150	155	160	165	170	175	180	185	190	195	200	205	210	215	220	225	230	235	240
Ideal weight	19	120	125	130	135	140	145	150	155	160	165	170	175	180	185	190	195	200	205	210	215	220	225	230	235	240
Acceptable %	21	117	122	127	132	137	142	146	151	156	161	166	171	176	181	186	190	195	200	205	210	215	220	225	229	234
Fair range	23	114	119	124	129	133	138	143	148	152	157	162	167	171	176	181	186	190	195	200	205	210	214	219	224	229
	25	111	116	121	125	130	135	139	144	149	153	158	162	167	172	176	181	186	190	195	200	204	209	214	218	223
	27	109	113	118	122	127	131	136	140	145	149	154	158	163	167	172	176	181	186	190	195	199	204	208	213	217
	29	106	110	115	119	123	128	132	137	141	145	150	154	159	163	167	172	176	181	185	189	194	198	203	207	211
	31	103	107	111	116	120	124	129	133	137	141	146	150	154	159	163	167	171	176	180	184	189	193	197	201	206
Range of obesity	33	100	104	108	113	117	121	125	129	133	137	142	146	150	154	158	162	167	171	175	179	183	188	192	196	200
	35	97	101	105	109	113	117	121	125	130	134	138	142	146	150	154	158	162	166	170	174	178	182	186	190	194
	37	94	98	102	106	110	114	118	122	126	130	134	137	141	145	149	153	157	161	165	169	173	177	181	185	189
	39	91	95	99	103	107	110	114	118	122	126	130	133	137	141	145	149	152	156	160	164	168	171	175	179	183
	41	89	92	96	100	103	107	111	114	118	122	125	129	133	137	140	144	148	151	155	159	162	166	170	174	177
	43	86	89	93	96	100	104	107	111	114	118	121	125	129	132	136	139	143	146	150	154	157	161	164	163	171

A man who weighs 175 pounds and has a percentage of fat 27% would have an ideal activetic weight of 158 pounds.

FIGURE 24.3 (a) Activetic Ideal Weight Table. Ideal Weight for 19% Fat (men). Reprinted by permission of Charles T. Kuntzleman, *Activetics*, Peter H. Wyden, Publisher, New York, 1975.

	% of Fat	Body Weight (lb)																									
		90	95	100	105	110	115	120	125	130	135	140	145	150	155	160	165	170	175	180	185	190	195	200	205	210	215
Ideal weight	23	90	95	100	105	110	115	120	125	130	135	140	145	150	155	160	165	170	175	180	185	190	195	200	205	210	215
Acceptable %	25	88	93	98	102	107	112	117	122	127	132	137	141	146	151	156	161	170	171	176	180	185	190	195	200	205	210
Fair range	27	86	90	95	100	105	109	114	119	124	128	133	138	143	147	152	157	162	166	171	176	181	185	190	195	200	205
	29	83	88	93	97	102	107	111	116	120	125	130	134	139	144	148	153	157	162	167	171	176	181	185	190	194	198
	31	81	86	90	95	99	104	108	113	117	122	126	131	135	140	144	149	153	158	162	167	171	176	180	185	189	193
	33	79	83	88	92	96	101	105	110	114	118	123	127	132	136	140	145	149	153	158	162	167	171	175	180	184	188
	35	77	81	85	89	94	98	102	107	111	115	119	124	128	132	136	141	145	149	153	158	162	166	170	175	179	183
Range of obesity	37	74	79	83	87	91	95	99	103	108	112	116	120	124	128	132	137	141	145	149	153	157	161	165	170	174	178
	39	72	76	80	84	88	92	96	100	104	108	112	116	120	124	128	132	136	140	145	149	153	157	161	165	169	173
	41	70	74	78	82	86	89	93	97	101	105	109	113	117	121	124	128	132	136	140	144	148	152	156	159	163	167
	43	68	72	75	79	83	87	90	94	98	102	105	109	113	117	121	124	128	132	136	139	143	147	151	154	158	162

A woman who weighs 135 pounds and has a percentage of fat that is 25% would have an ideal Activetics weight of 132 pounds.

FIGURE 24.3 (b) Activetic Ideal Weight Table. Ideal Weight for 23% Fat (women). Reprinted by permission of Charles T. Kuntzleman, *Activetics*, Peter H. Wyden, Publisher, New York, 1975.

at Herringbone State University. He hoped to find a position as a certified athletic trainer at a college or university upon graduation. An assignment in one of his athletic training courses involved a visit to a local health club. Richard was very impressed with the adult physical fitness program conducted at this health club. In the past he had heard so many negative things about health clubs that he was quite surprised about this program. This made Richard wonder whether he had made the right decision in choosing athletic training for a profession.

Because of a need to find part-time employment, Richard decided to talk with the health club manager about employment. He was delighted to learn that they were seeking part-time student workers. During this inquiry, Richard was asked to appear for a personal interview. He had approximately one week to prepare for this interview. As Richard began to make an outline listing the points he should cover (in order to enhance his chances for obtaining the position) what would you suggest he include?

3. At LaMar College, Lee Marks was enrolled in the introductory course for physical education majors. One of her assignments was to visit a health club and prepare a written report to present to the class. Lee was directed to cover staffing, facilities, equipment, program, and funding during her visit. She really "freaked out" because she knew nothing about health clubs! After the shock wore off, Lee got down to work. She realized that she must prepare herself before going to the health club. She wanted to ask the right questions, but where did she start?

4. George Roberts had decided while he was in high school that he wanted to become a professional athlete. His total efforts were geared to this goal. But during his senior year at Hawkeye College, George severely injured his leg. He learned that if undue stress were placed on his leg he could be crippled for life. This prevented George from trying out for pro sports and completely shattered his dream. In fact, it also destroyed his chances for a coaching career. George was heartbroken at this turn of events. Nevertheless, he was determined to continue his education and graduate.

One day a friend of George's told him about the rapid growth of health clubs and their need for qualified instructors. Should George investigate this profession? How useful was his professional preparation in physical education for this new profession?

Did he have the personality required for such a position? Whose advice should George seek to find an answer to these puzzling questions?

SELECTED REFERENCES

Johnson, Perry B., Wynn F. Updyke, Donald C. Stolberg, and Maryellen Schaeffer, *Physical Education: A Problem-Solving Approach to Health and Fitness,* Holt, Rinehart and Winston, Chicago, 1966.

Kasch, Fred W., and John L. Boyer, *Adult Fitness: Principles and Practice,* National Press Books, Palo Alto, CA, 1968.

Kuntzleman, Charles T., *Activetics,* Peter H. Wyden, Publisher, New York, 1975.

Kuntzleman, Charles T., "Activetics: Exploding the Myth of the Scales," *WomenSports,* **3**:57-61 (August 1976).

Myers, Clayton, *The Official YMCA Physical Fitness Handbook,* National Board, Young Men's Christian Association, 1975.

name index

Adams, Robert F., 58
Adamson, G.T., 340
Albohm, Marge, 249
Allman, Fred L., 252
Amateur Athletic Union (AAU), 115
American Academy of Physical Education, 22
American Alliance for Health, Physical Education and Recreation, (AAHPER), 11-12, 21, 58, 69, 73, 184, 206, 239, 267
American Association for the Advancement of Physical Education, 69, 71
American Association for Health, Physical Education and Recreation (AAHPER), 72, 102, 156, 165, 190
American Association for Leisure and Recreation (AALR), 11
American Association of University Professors (AAUP), 21
American Association of University Women (AAUW), 21
American Basketball Association, 123
American Board for Certification of Corrective Therapists, 263
American College of Sports Medicine, 22, 208
American Corrective Therapy Association (ACTA), 264, 266-268, 271-272, 280 283, 304
American Federation of Teachers (AFT), 21
American Medical Association (AMA), 205, 208, 216, 220, 224-225, 317, 323
American Physical Education Association, 71
American School and Community Safety Association (ASCSA), 11
Arnheim, Donald D., 215, 244
Association for the Advancement of Health Education (AAHE), 11

Association of Intercollegiate Athletics for Women (AIAW), 116
Association for Physical and Mental Rehabilitation (APMR), 263-264
Association for Research, Administration, and Professional Councils and Societies (ARAPCS), 11
Athletics Institute, 212

Baker, Boyd, 243
Baker, Terry, 162
Barker, Roger G., 54
Barrell, Robert P., 295
Boyer, John L., 329, 352
Briggs, Paul W., 53
Bronson, Alice Oakes, 16
Brookings Institution, 124
Bucher, Charles A., 162
Butterworth, Julian A., 55

Canadian Association for Health, Physical Education and Recreation, 22
Center, Allen H., 182
Check, John F., 14
Chicago Bears, (Illus.), 123, 235
Chicago Bulls, 249
Chicago Health Clubs, 354, 357, 358
Clarke, H. Harrison, 266
Clarke, Kenneth S., 220, 222
Coleman, James, 113
Commission on Olympic Sports, 145
Conant, James B., 57
Conte, Paul, 295
Cooper, Kenneth H., 334, 335
Cureton, Thomas Klik, Jr., 329, 331, 340
Cutlip, Scott M., 182
Cutting, Richard A., 83

Davis, John E., 266, 289

Davis, Otho, 243
Dellums, Ronald W., 208, 245
Delta Psi Kappa, 10
Department of Health, Education and Welfare, 205
DeWolfe, Alan S., 295
Douglas, J. William, 208, 233, 239
Dryden, John, 261
Dworsky, Daniel L., 86

Educational Facilities Laboratory, 87

Federal Aviation Administration, 293
Federal Trade Commission, 317
Field, David, 52
Flath, Arnold W., 115
Food and Drug Administration, 317
Ford, President Gerald R., 116, 145
Fox, Theodore, 209, 235
Freeman, Charles C., 293
Frost, Reuben B., 156
Fuzak, John, 125

Gallon, Arthur J., 151, 157-158
Gans, Marvin, 84, 85
Getchell, Bud, 315
Graham, George M., 18
Grieve, Andrew, 158, 244
Griffiths, Daniel E., 199
Gump, Paul V., 54

Hallberg, Edmond C., 51
Harvard University, 41
Health and Physical Directors Association of YM-YWHA's and Jewish Community Center, 22
Health and Tennis Corporation of America, 345-355, 357
Hellison, Donald R., 17
Hernlund, Vernon, 321
Hetherington, Clark W., 161
Hodges, Alton, 271
Holbrook, Leona, 5, 136

Ingham, Alan, 176
Institute of Sports Medicine, 209
International Council of Health, Physical Education and Recreation (ICHPER), 22

Jamerson, Dick, 101
James, Keith A., 340

Jewett, Ann E., 29
Joliet Junior College, 38
Kasch, Fred W., 329, 352, 366
Kiernan, Owen B., 191, 198
Kirk, Norman, 262
Klafs, Carl E., 215, 244
Klein, Jack, 295
Klein, Karl K., 266
Kneer, Marian, 64
Knezevich, Stephen J., 33
Kraus, Hans, 327, 337
Kullman, N.W., Jr., 55
Kuntzleman, Charles T., 370

Lawther, John W., 162
Ling, Per Henrik, 262
Little League, 112
Loucks, H. Donald, 7, 66
Lowe, Dan, 252
Loy, John W., 176

Madden, John E., 54
Mandel, Arnold J., 144
Marshall, John, 206
Matthews, David O., 98, 151
McCloy, Charles H., 266
McIntosh, Peter, 184
Melby, Ernest, 177, 198
Michigan State University, 99
Moore, J.W., 151, 158, 164
Morgan, R.E., 340
Mosso, Angelo, 334
Mushier, Carol, 109

National Association for Girls and Women in Sport (NAGWS), 11
National Association for Human Development, 340
National Association of Intercollegiate Athletics (NAIA), 115-116
National Association for Physical Education of College Women (NAPECW), 22
National Association of Secondary School Principals, 191
National Association for Sport and Physical Education (NASPE), 11, 15
National Athletic Health Institute, 359
National Athletic Trainers Association (NATA), 207, 209, 211, 238-239, 241-243, 245-246, 252
National Basketball Association, 123, 125

National College Physical Education Association for Men (NCPEAM), 22, 190
National Collegiate Athletic Association (NCAA), 103, 115-116, 190
National Dance Association (NDA), 11
National Education Association, (NEA), 21, 113
National Federation of State High School Associations, 208
National Federation of State High School Athletic Associations, 113, 212
National Foundation for Health, Physical Education and Recreation (NFHPER), 22
National Intramural Association, 97
National Junior College Athletic Association, (NJCAA), 114
Neal, Patsy, 167
Neilson, N.P., 16
Nicholas, James A., 209

Office of Education and the Physical Medicine and Rehabilitation Service, 263
Ogilvie, Bruce, 137
Oregon State University, 345-346
Owens, R.C., 136

Parent Teachers Association (PTA), 15, 20, 199
Paterson, Ann, 51
Phi Epsilon Kappa, 10
Philadelphia Eagles, 243
Physical Education Public Information (PEPI), 15-16, 184-185, 199
Physical Education Society of the YMCA's of North America, 22
Poindexter, Hally B., 109
Pollock, Michael L., 252
President's Commission on Olympic Sports, 116
President's Council on Physical Fitness and Sports, 22, 145, 316, 327, 340, 341
Purdue University, 99

Rathbone, Josephine, 266
Reed, William R., 165
Richards, Jack W., 111, 113, 164
Richardson, Deane E., 191
Ridini, Leonard M., 54
Rode, Clifford A., 243
Rothstein, Hy, 58
Rusk, Howard, 262

Ryan, Allan J., 211-212

Schultz, Frederick, 163
Secondary Center, Greensboro, North Carolina, 38
Shea, Edward, 120
Sheldon, W.H., 330
Sigma Delta Psi, 11
Sims, Edward J., 63
Singer, Robert N., 109, 120
Society of State Directors of Health, Physical Education and Recreation, 22
Spiker, John C., 208, 233, 239
Stafford, George, 266
Staley, Seward C., 135
Steinhaus, Arthur H, 321
Stern, Barry E., 162
Student Action Council (SAC), 11
Sullivan, James V., 87
Syracuse University, 252

Theibert, P.R. (Dick), 83, 87
Tutko, Thomas A., 111, 113, 164

U.S. Postal Service, 317
Ulrich, Celeste, 13
University of Illinois, Chicago Circle, 272
University of Illinois, Urbana Champaign, 99
University of Leeds, 340
University of Massachusetts, 175, 191-192
University of Utah, 345-346, 349
University of Wisconsin, Madison, 211

Veteran's Administration, 262-263, 267-268, 272, 282, 293

Wake Forest University, 252
Ward, Paul, 354, 355
Weatherill, Robert A., 87
Weber, Sonja, 337
Western Illinois University, 191-192
Wieman, Elton F., 120
Wilmore, Jack H., 359
Woods, Sherwood M., 161

YMCA, 316, 320, 370
Young, Carl Haven, 266, 268
Young Women's Christian Association (YWCA), 22, 320

subject index

Adult physical fitness, aerobics exercise program, 335
  awards, 341
  cardiopulmonary fitness, 328
  cardiovascular fitness, 328, 335
  circulorespiratory capacity, 320-329
  description, 329
  national survey, 327-328
  program guidelines, 329-330
  starting a program, 352
  values, 330
  see also Adults; Aerobic; Exercising; Health clubs; Human body; and Physical fitness
Adults, exercising, 338-339
  hypokinetic disease, 339
  prescribed exercise program, 324-325, 337
Aerobic, aerobic power, 335
  anaerobic, 335
  definition, 335
Alternative careers, choices, 348-349
  curriculum, 347, 350-351
Amateur athletes, governing organizations, 115-119
  Olympics, 116
Anatomy classroom, (ill.), 8
Athlete, see Athletic trainer; Intercollegiate sports; Interscholastic sports; and Professional sports
Athletic director, competencies, 190-191. See also Sports administrator
Athletic injuries, care, 216, 220
  first aid chart, (ill.), 221
  physiological signs, 220
  prevention, 209, 213, 238
  protective equipment, 224
  standard nomenclature, (ill.), 223, 225, 227, 229
  terminology, 220, 222
  see also Athletics; Athletic trainer; and Sports injury
Athletic trainer, certification, 206-208, 242-243
  characteristics, (ill.), 254
  duties and responsibilities, 233-234
  health team, 213, 220, 233
  licensure, 244
  need, 205
  qualifications, 233, 238
  standard nomenclature, (ill.), 223, 225, 227-229
  student trainer, 237, (ill.), 253
  traits rating, 254
  see also Athletic injuries; Athletics; Injury control; and Training room
Athletics, Athletic Safety Act, 208
  definition, 175-176
  health care services, 205-206
  injuries, 208
  injury prevention, 209, 213, 238
  see also Injury control; Intercollegiate sports; Interscholastic sports; Professional sports; and Training room
  sports equipment, 209
Athletic training, (ill.), 202
  career opportunities, 245-246
  case studies, 255-256
  curriculum, 239-242
  Dellums Bill, 245
  history, 207-209
  legal implications, 243-244
  NATA standards, 207
  planning activities, 252-253
  preparing activities, 250-251
  sports, 208-209
  team physician, 235-237

see also Athletic trainer

Coach, attitude, 164
   career directions, (ill.), 160
   certification, 156-157, 206
   competencies profile, (ill.), 140
   personal experiences, 152-154
   personality characteristics, (ill.), 141
   profile chart, (ill.), 139
   qualifications, 154-156
   qualities, 164-165
   role, 160-163
   see also Athletics
Coaching, athletes, 166-167
   career opportunities, 158-160
   competencies profile, 136, 140
   learning experiences, 197-199
   legal aspects, 157-158
   nature of profession, 152-154
   philosophy, 164-165
   physical education, 165-166
   profession profile, 136, 139
   teaching, 151-152
   training rules, 163
   see also Title IX
Cointramural programs, 98-99
College and university, concept, 41
   organizational structure, (ill.), 41-42
   physical education, (ill.), 40, 43-44, (illustration), 91
   program, 42-43
   student, 42
   teaching rank, 44
Community, adaptation, 58-60
   adaptation chart, (ill.), 59
   study, 75-76
   overview, 51
Community college, concept, 38
   organizational structure, 39-40
   physical education, 39-41
   program, 38-39
   student, 39
Competitive sports, activities, 137-142
   case studies, 142-144
   facility, (ill.), 80
   non-school, 111-112
Consolidated school districts, 54-55
Corrective physical rehabilitation, 263. See also Corrective therapy
Corrective therapist, function, 290-296
   need, 289

placement, 282
rehabilitation team, 265, 273
salaries, 283
skills, 266, 273
see also Corrective therapy; Corrective therapy patients
Corrective therapy, (ill.), 258
   accreditation, 267-268
   adapted physical educator, 264
   certification, 280-282
   clinical training, 272-273, 277-279
   curriculum, 271-272, 274-277
   definition, 264
   driver training program, 293
   educational institutions, 304-306
   exercises, 294, 307
   facilities and equipment, 296-298
   history, 261-264
   insignia, (ill.), 283
   objectives, 266
   performing activities, 309-311
   philosophy and purposes, 264-267
   physical reconditioning, 262-263
   students, (ill.), 280-281
   terms, 283-285, 298-299, 306-310
Corrective therapy patients, injury and illness, 291-295
   paraplegic, (ill.), 297
   therapeutic exercise program, 295-296

Diet, balanced, 337
   caloric expenditure, 323, 337
   caloric intake, 323
   calorie, 323
   see also Health club consumer; Human body

Education, formula, 13
   magnet school, 36-37
   preschool, 33-34
   scheduling, 57-58
   visitations, 76
Electrocardiograph (ECG), 335-336
Electroencephalograph (EEG), 336
Electromyograph (EMG), 336
Elementary school, concept, 30
   organizational structure, (ill.), 31
   physical education, 30-31
   program, 30
   student, 32-33
Exercising, aspects, 339

medical examination, 338-339
overload, 339
physical capacity, 339
respiratory capacity, 339
work capacity, 339
see also Adult physical fitness
Extramural sports, 101

Facilities, design, 85-86
　indoor, 86-87
　management, 83
　outdoor, 89
　planning, 84-85
　surfaces, 87-89
　utilization, 89-91
　see also Title IX
First aid chart, (ill.), 221
Fitness finder, (ill.), 369

Goniometer, 298

Health club consumer, club selection, 317, 320-321
　exercise program, 321-325
　health status, 319-320
　herbal wrappings, 322
　membership, 318-319
　safety principles, 323
　saunas, 322-323
　see also Adult physical fitness; Diet; and Health clubs
Health club instructor, case studies, 370, 374-375
　certificate, (ill.), 356
　certification, 353-355
　competencies, 355
　curriculum, 345-351
　responsibilities, 356-357
　role, 357-362
　salaries, 356
　student field experience, 352-353
　see also Health clubs; Physical fitness
Health clubs, (ill.), 312
　background, 315-316
　circuit weight training, 358-361, (ill.), 362
　employees, 316
　facilities and equipment, 317
　governmental regulatory agencies, 317-318
　industry, 316-317
　program, 351-355, 357, 360-361

see also Health club instructor
Heart, cardiac output, 336
　maximum rate, 336, 366
　pulse rate measurement, 335-336
　recovery rate, 336
　resting rate, 336
　stroke volume, 336
Human body, basal metabolism, 337
　blood pressure, 335
　center of gravity, 331, 334
　circulation, 334-335
　composition, 331
　density, 331
　fat, 331, 370-371
　heart, 335-336
　measurements, 323, 331, 368-370
　medical problems, 334
　metabolism, 337
　muscles, 330-333, (ill.), 332-333, 365-366
　respiration, 334-335
　types, 330
　weight, 367-368, 370-373
　work, 337
Human movement, 7
Human movement careers, (ill.), 348-349
　curriculum, 345-351
Human organism, 16

Injury control, health team, 212-213, 220, 233
　prevention, 209, 213, 238
　program, 213-214
　protective equipment, 213-214
　training and conditioning, 213, 215-219
　see also Athletic injuries; Athletics; and Sports
Intercollegiate sports, (ill.), 117, 118, 148
　coaching, 115
　governing organizations, 114-119
　legal aspects, 157-158
　programs, 115-116
　see also Amateur athletes; Athletic training
Interscholastic sports, (ill.), 36
　coaching, 110-111, 113-114
　education, 113
　governing organizations, 113
　high school, 113-114
　injuries, 112
　legal aspects, 157-158
　middle school, 109-112

SUBJECT INDEX　383

see also Athletic training
Intramural sports, (ill.), 36
　college facility, (ill.), 100
　definition, 98
　organizational structure, (ill.), 102,
　　104-105
　see also Athletic training

Legal terms, 244

Metric system, 367-368
Middle school, concept, 34
　organizational structure, 31
　physical education, 35-36
　program, 34
　student, 37

Oxygen, debt, 335
　deficit, 335
　intake, 334
　requirement, 335
　steady state, 335
　uptake, 335

Physical education, (ill.), 2, 32, 33
　case studies, 76-78
　certification, 11-12
　curriculum, 5-6, 7-10, 68-70, 350-351
　definition, 5
　degrees, 42-43
　extracurricular, 10-11
　graduate education, 22-24
　PEPI, 15-16, 184-185, 199
　perceptual motor learning, 31
　professional leaders and organizations,
　　11, 20-22, 71-73
　research, (ill.), 23, 73-74, 252
　see also Athletic trainer; Coach;
　　Corrective therapist; Health club
　　instructor; Physical educator; Public
　　relations; Sports; Sports administrator;
　　and Title IX
Physical educator, characteristics, 66-68, 141
　communication, 74-75
　instruction, 10, 16-18, 30-31
　placement, 12-13
　role, 13-16, 18-20
　teaching behaviors, (ill.), 18
　values, 64-66
Physical fitness, exercise, (ill.), 324
　instructor, 338-339

programs, 331, 339-340
research laboratory, (ill.), 23, 73-74, 252
sports ratings, (ill.), 342
tests, 337-338, 357-358, 366-367
see also Adult physical fitness
Physical reconditioning, 262-263
Professional sports, associations, 123
　background, 119-120
　career, 126-127
　case studies, 144-146
　earnings and profits, 121-124
　governing organizations, 125
　interviews, 127-129, 130-131
　player reservation system, 122-125
　recruitment, 125
　see also Title IX
Public relations, characteristics, 182
　communication, 181-183
　management function, 182
　media, 183-184
　operating concept, 182
　PEPI, 15-16, 184-185, 199
　process, 183
　various publics, 183

Recreational sports, college survey, 103
　definition, 97
　facilities, 99
　history, 98
　organizational structure, 102, 104-105
　programs, 98-99
　see also Intramural sports
Rural community, description, 54
　economics, 56
　physical education, 55-56
　social, 55-56
　teacher salaries, 56

Secondary school, concept, 36
　organizational structure, 31
　physical education, 37-38
　programs, 36-37
　student, 37
Sports, accident control, 212
　activities, 212
　definition, 175-176
　human values, (ill.), 137
　participation rating, 136, 138
　personality characteristics, 137, 141
　physician's role, 235-237
　supervision, 212-213

warm-up activities, (ill.), 217-219
  see also Training room
Sports administration, apprenticeships, 195
  career opportunities, 194-195
  curriculum, 190-193
  definition, 175
  department, 189-190
  internship, 193-194
  profession, 176-177
  see also Title IX
Sports administrator, attributes, 177-179
  competencies, 190-191
  management concepts, 180-181
  need, 176
  see also Public relations
Sports clubs, activities, 101
  characteristics, 100
  definition, 100
Sports injury, see Athletic injuries
Suburban community, description, 56
  economics, 57-58
  physical education, 57
  social, 56-57
  teacher salaries, 58

Title IX, athletics, 166-167
  facilities, 83-84
  physical education, 34
  professional sports, 120
  sports administration, 194
Training room, (ill.), 225
  design, 222
  equipment and supplies, 226-227
  purpose, 222-223
  size, 224

Urban community, description, 52
  economics, 53
  physical education, 52-54
  social, 52
  teacher salaries, 53
U.S. standard measurements, 368

Vital capacity, 334

SUBJECT INDEX 385